Now you see it

There have been hundreds of films with homosexual characters in them, and hundreds of lesbians and gay men have worked before and behind the film camera, but there have been very few films made by lesbians and gay men with lesbian and gay subject matter. *Now You See It* is about some of them.

In part it provides a record of these films up to 1980, putting familiar titles such as *Girls in Uniform*, *Un Chant d'amour*, and *Word is Out* in their lesbian/gay context and bringing to light many other forgotten but remarkable films. Each film is examined in detail in relation to both film type and tradition and the sexual sub-culture within which it was made.

There is more at stake however than simply uncovering and re-evaluating what has been hidden from history – *Now You See It* is also a case study in the dynamics of lesbian/gay cultural production. These films were formed from the filmic and sub-cultural images, assumptions, styles, and feelings available to them, which both made the films possible and also defined and delimited the forms they could take and what they could say. Such processes of formation and deformation characterise all cultural production, but they carry a special charge for lesbians and gay men seeking both to break free from and be heard in the languages of a homophobic society.

Richard Dyer teaches film at the University of Warwick. He is the author of *Gays and Film*, *Stars* and *Heavenly Bodies: Film Stars and Society* and is currently working on a collection of essays on entertainment and a book on whiteness as a cultural construction.

Now you see it
Studies on lesbian and gay film

Richard Dyer

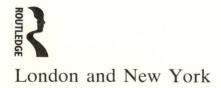

London and New York

First published 1990
Reprinted 1991
by Routledge
11 New Fetter Lane, London EC4P 4EE

Simultaneously published in the USA and Canada
by Routledge
a division of Routledge, Chapman and Hall, Inc.
29 West 35th Street, New York, NY 10001

Disc conversion by Columns of Reading
Printed in Great Britain by
TJ Press (Padstow) Ltd, Padstow, Cornwall

British Library Cataloguing in Publication Data
Dyer, Richard,
   Now you see it: studies on lesbian and gay film.
   1. Cinema films. Special subjects: Homosexuality
   I. Title
   791.43653

   ISBN 0–415–03555–4

Library of Congress Cataloging in Publication Data
Dyer, Richard.
   Now you see it: historical studies on lesbian and gay film /
   Richard Dyer.
     p. cm.
   Includes bibliographical references.
   ISBN 0–415–03555–4. — ISBN 0–415–03556–2 (pbk.)
   1. Homosexuality in motion pictures. I. Title.
PN1995.9.H55D94 1990
791.43′653—dc20 90–32996

to the memory of

DAVE SARGENT
1952–1985

Contents

List of illustrations

Introduction

There have been hundreds of films with homosexual characters in them[1] and hundreds of lesbians and gay men have worked before and behind the film camera,[2] but there have been very few films made by lesbians and gay men with lesbian and gay subject-matter. This book is about some of them.

These are films made, to some significant degree, by people who considered themselves to be, in whatever the parlance of their day, lesbian or gay and which openly embrace gay/lesbian subject-matter. Some were produced with a definite intention of promoting lesbian/gay rights and identities, while others were made out of the socially constructed but privately realised imperatives of self and sexual expression. They are not covert or disguised articulations of lesbian/gay feelings and perceptions, but examples of that rare, and perhaps rather extraordinary enterprise of the deliberate, overt and owned expression of such feelings and perceptions in film.

This does not mean that they are the untrammelled embodiment of an authentic homosexual experience stripped of social contamination. They are not, as it were, what lesbian/gay film would be if only we did not live in a hetero obsessed society. They are what could be done within actual social and historical reality. Like all cultural production, gay/lesbian films exist only in and through the confluence of ways of making sense, the terms of thought and feeling, available to them. These limit what can be said but also make saying possible; they both form and deform all expression. The studies that follow look at two of the sets of terms most salient to these particular films: lesbian and gay sub-cultures and filmic traditions.

Even each of these is itself enormously complex and although I have in part treated the films as a point of entry into an investigation of, especially, the sub-cultures, I do not pretend to provide a comprehensive guide to the total sub-cultural and filmic states of play at the time each set of films was made, but only to look at those particular aspects of both most evidently relevant to the films under investigation. Neither aspect is unaffected by the other. Lesbians and gay men working in film helped mould it, either covertly, in a history we still mainly have to guess at, or else sometimes openly, notably in relation to the shape of experimental and documentary film as discussed in chapters three, four and five. Equally, lesbian/gay film has used for its own ends many of the images and structures of non-lesbian/gay film, discussed here for instance in the practices of camp or the use of traditional romance and adventure narrative structures. Yet there is also always a tension, a divergence of interests, between the film traditions and the deviant position of the sub-cultures, a tension now smoothed over (as in many of the films of gay/lesbian 'affirmation'), now exploited or heightened (as in *Mädchen in Uniform*, *Un Chant d'amour*, *Flaming Creatures* or *Madame X*). It is this interaction, this within and against, of historically specific lesbian/gay sub-cultures and particular filmic traditions, as worked through in the texts of the films, that is the focus of this book.

*   *   *

I have confined myself rather arbitrarily to films made before 1980, though I do where appropriate point to films made later which either build on or radically depart from those discussed here. This is largely to do with manageability. Since 1980 there has been an enormous growth in the amount of lesbian/gay films, of which the clearest index are the gay/lesbian film festivals (notably in Amsterdam, Berlin, Brussels, Chicago, London, Los Angeles, New York, San Francisco, Sydney and Turin), all of which draw for the most part on recent product. I wanted this book to be some kind of record of overt gay/lesbian film making, but I also wanted to avoid writing a book of lists, which is what going beyond 1980 would have entailed. Drawing the line at 1980 has certain inevitable conse-quences, however. It means more films made by and about men than women, and next to no representation of non-white, non Northern/Western people. Film, more perhaps than any other art, requires money, time and confidence (to believe that it is even appropriate for one to 'say' something); existing gender and ethnic relations mean that white men are going to be among the first and most frequent to have access to the medium. Moreover, the specificity of the idea of 'being' lesbian or gay means that the very different way same-sex relations are constructed and experienced in Japan or Third World countries does not come into my purview.

Even so, I am aware of some gaps in coverage before 1980, notably in European experimental film. I am also aware of the fact that I am a gay man writing about lesbian film. Gay men – even 'out' gay men – have many of the privileges and attitudes of straight men; gay men are also the least qualified to speak from response about the representation of lesbian sexuality. Yet I decided from the outset that I would cover both gay and lesbian film, partly because I knew I was in a position to do so (with experience of research, the right connections and time), partly because I have always believed in the alliance of lesbians and gay men, partly because of the encouragement I received from many lesbian film-makers and writers on film. In writing the book, the ways in which lesbian and gay film overlap *and* diverge have seemed to me especially illuminating, enabling one to see both more clearly.

Some practical points. I have, to save space, used the dubious term 'gay/lesbian film' at various points, but this is not meant to imply that only films as deliberate and overt as these count as lesbian/gay films. I have stuck with the laborious 'lesbian/gay', 'gay/lesbian', even though there is some indication that 'gay' is becoming acceptable to some lesbian women – the book was conceived and largely written during a period when this was not so. Titles of non-English language films that are not discussed at length in the text are translated in an appendix.

*   *   *

I could not have written this book without the support and help of an enormous number of people. I'd like to thank especially Mark Finch, Karola Gramann, Heide Schlüpmann, Jackie Stacey and Tom Waugh for their unfailing help and encouragement as well as the constant inspiration and stimulation of their example. Many others, some of whom I had or have never met, helped me in a variety of ways, supplying films, drawing my attention to articles, reading drafts, lending material, discussing issues and much else besides: my thanks then to Yann Beauvais, Annette Förster, Barbara Hammer, Ron Magliozzi, Miles McKane, Paul Verstraeten and Andrea Weiss as well as Gunnar Almér, Sandro Avanzo, Rosemary Betterton, Pieter Van Bogaert, Noll Brinckmann, Charlotte Brunsdon, Elaine Burrows, Jane Caplan, Tom Chomont, Emmanuel Cooper, Honey Lee Cottrell, Jon Davies, Bernard Devlin, John Foot and Dave Belton, Sarah Franklin, Sue Friedrich,

Michka Gorkis, Donna Gray, Larry Gross, Linda Flint, Jane Harris and the women at Circles, Miriam Hansen, Sylvia Harvey, Judith Higginbottom, J Hoberman, Jim Hubbard, Gertrud Koch, Eric de Kuyper, Michael Kloss, Al LaValley, Jukka Lehtonen, Phil van der Linden, Teresa Caldas and the women at Cinemien, Michael Lumpkin, Robert Malengreau, Jonas Mekas, Giovanni Minerba, Margaret Moores, Jeff Nüts, Mark Padnos, Leigh Raymond, Tony Rayns, Ruby Rich, Thomas Robsahm, Vito Russo, Manfred Salzgeber, Akira Shimuzu, Charles Silver, Rose Marie Soto, Felicity Sparrow, Ginette Vincendeau, Maggie Warwick, Simon Watney, Brenda Webb, Claire Whitaker, Janice Winship, Karsten Witte, Debra Zimmerman and the women at Women Make Movies. Like all film scholars, I owe an incalculable debt to the British Film Institute library, not only for its unsurpassed holdings but for the help and kindness of its staff; likewise I should like to thank Richard Parker, Richard Perkins and above all the staff of the Inter-Library Loans desk at Warwick University library. Further thanks are due to the film archives in Amsterdam, Brussels, Koblenz, London, Washington DC and Wiesbaden, to the Canadian Filmmakers Distribution Centre and the New Zealand Film Commission, to Circles, Cinema of Women, BFI Distribution, Peter Darvill Associates, the London Film-makers' Co-op and Harris Films. Warwick University gave me grants to visit archives and much of the research presented here was undertaken while working as a visiting professor at the Annenberg School of Communications at the University of Pennsylvania. The encouragement of Paul Crane at an early stage in the writing and of Jane Armstrong, Bill Germano and Helena Reckitt at Routledge have been very important to me. Finally, I am grateful for the support given to me by my colleagues in the Film Studies department at Warwick University, especially Susan Dufft and Victor Perkins, and above all by the friends with whom I live, Malcolm Gibb and Jo Li.

During the writing of this book, Jack Babuscio, Arthur Bressan, Cal Culver, Guy Hocquenghem, Roger Jacoby, Curt McDowell and Jack Smith died of AIDS. They are all discussed in this book, and I honour them all. In 1985 Dave Sargent, a young American living in Sydney, also died of AIDS. He wrote and lectured on film, academically and otherwise, and administered the Sydney Film-makers' Co-op; he had also edited the Australian gay magazine *Campaign*, worked in a gay bookshop, written stories and political essays. All his work had the openness and flexibility that this range suggests. I first got to know him through his writings in *Gay Information* and we corresponded. I finally met him when I visited

Sydney in 1984. I was apprehensive of actually meeting him – would we get on as well in person as we did in letters? I need not have worried – he was one of the kindest, most interesting and thoughtful and fun to giggle with people I have ever known. I have felt few things so bitterly as his being taken away from me, and the loss to gay and film thought and politics of such a good person is incalculable.

1 Weimar

Less and more like the others

In Germany at more or less the beginning and end of the Weimar republic, the first gay and lesbian films appeared: *Anders als die Andern* (*Different from the Others*) 1919 and *Mädchen in Uniform* (*Girls in Uniform*) 1931. These are remarkably early dates. Not only are there no other lesbian/gay films before or during this period,[1] there are also very few images of homosexuality in film – except in Germany. Even Vito Russo (1981), in by far the most comprehensive survey of images of gays in films, has only a handful of examples, all of which only figure momentarily in the films and some of which you could easily not see as representing gays or lesbians at all. Yet in Germany, in 1919 and 1931, here are two films placing homosexuality centrally, unambiguously and positively.

In the German film context they do not stand quite so alone. Though often quite negative, there were other films depicting homosexuality. *Michael* 1924, the story of the tragic love of a painter for his model/protégé, was a rather less homosexually committed remake of the 1916 Swedish film *Vingarne* (Finch 1987). *Der Fall des Generalstabs-Oberst Redl* 1931 dealt directly with the Colonel Redl scandal later used by John Osborne in *A Patriot for Me* and István Szabó in *Colonel Redl*. At least one of the several films dealing with Frederick the Great (*Fridericus-Rex-Zyklus* 1922) pointed to his homosexuality, although all the films dealing with Ludwig II of Bavaria managed to keep quiet about his (Theis 1984b:104–6). A lesbian and a gay man are central to the plots of, respectively, *Die Büchse der Pandora* 1928 and *Geschlecht in Fesseln* 1928, the latter notable, despite the fact that it ends unhappily for all concerned, for the tender physicality shown between the two men in prison. Gays are part of the general ambience of decadence in two of the films about the master-criminal Dr Mabuse (*Dr Mabuse der Spieler* 1921/2 and *Das Testament des*

Dr Mabuse 1933) and in films, of which there were apparently many, like *Nächte der Weltstadt*, in which lesbians dancing together were shown as characteristic of cosmopolitan nightlife (Moreck 1926). Other films kept the gay references more ambiguous: *Aus eines Mannes Mädchenjahren* 1919 is about a gay? hermaphrodite; *La Garçonne* 1925, based on an explicitly lesbian book, toned down the sexuality of its career woman protagonist; *Das Bildnis des Dorian Gray* 1917 was, like Wilde's novel, open to gay interpretations.

In addition to these more or less explicit images, there were many films of lesbian/gay appeal. There was a string of 'Hosenrolle' films, in which the female star spent a great deal of her time disguised as a man and entangled with a woman – titles include *Exzellenz Unterrock* 1920, *Dona Juana* 1927, *Der Geiger von Florenz* 1927, and the original version of *Viktor und Viktoria* 1933. This extends back to *Jugend und Tollheit* in 1912 and well into the Nazi period with *Capriccio* in 1938 (Gramann and Schlüpmann 1981:80–8). *Acht Mädels im Boot* 1932 and *Ich für Dich, Du für Mich* 1934 both dealt with female groups (a sporting club and Nazi land girls), evoking the intensity and strength of female bonding. The male physique was celebrated in an all-male context in the first ten minutes of *Wege zu Kraft und Schönheit* 1925, the whole of which had numerous shots of half-naked athletes of both sexes. There are other films too that can be read as gay, notably those directed by F. W. Murnau and in particular *Der Knabe in Blau* 1919, based on Gainsborough's painting, then a favourite in gay circles (Theis 1984b:106–8, Waugh 1979). Beyond all this, there was a general openness about sexuality in German cinema. There were the Aufklärungsfilme (enlightenment films) dealing with social, mainly sexual, 'problems', of which *Anders* is an example. Two of the most famous films of the period, *Die Büchse der Pandora* and *Der blaue Engel* 1930, dealt with the power of heterosexual female sexuality, embodied in the incandescence of Louise Brooks and Marlene Dietrich. And there was a flourishing heterosexual pornography (Koch 1989, Stark 1982).

All this is of a piece with Weimar Germany's sexual reputation, crystallised for English-speaking people in Christopher Isherwood's Berlin novels and their adaptation as the musical *Cabaret*. Liza Minnelli belting her hopes out at the end of a Hollywood movie may not be historical authenticity, but general notions of the 'divine decadence' of pre-Nazi Germany are not pure myth either: Berlin, at any rate, probably deserved its reputation as the sex capital of the world.

Certainly that was how it was widely perceived at the time. Isherwood only moved to Berlin because, as he later put it, 'Berlin meant boys' (1977:10). Hostile foreign observers were no less convinced that Germany was characterised by sexual depravity. Ambroise Got, a French attaché in Berlin, saw Germany's demoralised post-war condition expressed in a febrile hedonism, of which homosexual pleasures were major specimens. He gives a vivid account of wandering out one Sunday morning in October 1923 for a cup of coffee and coming upon the Konditorei Karlsbad. It turns out the Karlsbad has a floorshow, a young man, eyes widened by morphine, with ripped shirt and bare legs, dancing wildly and indefatigably to a rhythm that is 'at once muted and savage'. To make matters worse, groups of young men, who have been partying all night, stream in and one of them 'meeting up with his friend, throws himself on him and frenziedly, without caring who sees – and why need he? – kisses him full on the mouth'. As he leaves in haste, Got muses 'Will the debauchery last the whole of Sunday right up to Monday morning?' (1923:674–5).

No doubt people like Isherwood and Got were responsible for making Berlin's sex life seem, according to view, more infernal or more glamorous, more wretched or more fun than it really was, but there does seem to have been a great deal of it, and I speak now only of lesbian/gay matters. Adèle Meyer's book *Lila Nächte* (1981) details the lesbian scene in Berlin in the period and in both quantity and variety it makes even New York in the 1970s look inadequate. You could buy gay guides, in some cases aimed at heterosexual tourists, detailing the extensive lesbian and gay nightlife of Berlin. There were gay and lesbian meeting places, magazines, novels, even a theatre (Theater des Eros 1921–4) (Theis and Sternweiler 1984, von Lengerke 1984) and there was a gay movement, large enough to have different organisations and overlapping in part with the women's movement (Adam 1987:17–25, Baumgardt 1984, Pieper 1984, Steakley 1975). The lesbian/gay organisations, like so much else in Weimar's sexual culture, had their roots in the late nineteenth century, and had links with other movements of the time, not only feminism but the 'life-style' movements (Lebensreformbewegungen) such as vegetarianism, nudism, pacifism, fitness, as well as more traditional politics, socialism especially but even at times Nazism.

To all of this one might add the general sense of experimentation – or crisis and instability – in Weimar Germany's political, economic and artistic culture,[2] conditions in which new ideas and styles of sexuality could also flourish. Yet the uncertainty and riskiness of the times may also account for the fact that, given the development of sexual culture in the period, there are *only* two lesbian/gay films. Both were made possible but also blocked and deformed by the conditions of Weimar culture.

ANDERS ALS DIE ANDERN

The version of *Anders als die Andern* that is most easily seen today lasts about twenty minutes. The print quality is poor and it has inter-titles in cyrillic script. Most histories of the German cinema mention or footnote the film only as a curiosity and yet it was not a 'little film', produced and shown on the margins of the cinema of the day. It was a full feature-length film with three rising stars in it, Conrad Veidt, Reinhold Schünzel and Anita Berber, as well as an appearance by Magnus Hirschfeld, the leader of the most prominent gay organisation of the time. It opened in one of the major Berlin cinemas, the Apollo-Theater, and was fully reviewed in the press, where it was recognised as another of the highly successful run of Aufklärungsfilme. It was also straightaway news. The police banned it in Vienna, Munich and Stuttgart; there was uproar at many screenings, with walk-outs in Berlin led, to the accompaniment of boos and hisses, by soldiers in uniform. (A fascinating detail this: the military still represented a major conservative force in Germany but all the major homosexual scandals of the past had centred on soldiers.) Such was the controversy that a public forum of doctors, scientists and writers was held at the Prinzeß-Theater in Berlin to defend the film against its vociferous detractors. As Wolfgang Theis observes, 'despite, or perhaps precisely because of, these expressions of displeasure, the film was an out-and-out box office success' (1984a:28). Why then are there now only fragments of a supposedly obscure film?

The critical reception of the film was for the most part favourable and it was a commercial sucess, yet in August 1920, just over a year after the premiere, it was banned (Steakley 1987:152–5). Though there had been a liberalisation of expression with the establishment of the republic, the constitution still allowed for film censorship. The Aufklärungsfilme, and the pornography confused with them (doubtless correctly in some cases), caused concern: *Anders* was not the only film whose screenings occasioned rioting in the cinemas and protests outside (Kracauer 1947:44–7, Monaco 1976:52–4). However, the censor board's main brief was less to rid cinemas of filth than to protect youth and ban films that gave a bad image of Germany. *Anders* was presumably guilty on both counts.

The ban was not total. The film could still be shown 'to doctors and those concerned with medicine, in places of learning and scientific institutions', which suggests that the court perceived it as an educational work rather than pornography (Lamprecht 1968:11), but the ruling had the effect of marginalising it. In 1927 it was re-released in a shortened version as part of Hirschfeld's wider ranging *Gesetze der Liebe*, which was also censored to ribbons (Theis 1984a:30). Some time in the late twenties or early thirties *Gesetze* was shown in the Soviet Union, where there had been a temporary liberalisation in the situation of homosexual people, and this accounts for the cyrillic inter-titles in the copy that survives. Perhaps its truncated state is due to its being shortened to fit into a film covering various aspects of sexuality; or perhaps it was cut in the USSR with the reintroduction of anti-gay legislation and repression in 1934; or perhaps just this bit was saved by a gay man who could not risk hiding more. Whatever the explanation, even this fragment is precious, for in May 1933 the Nazis stormed and destroyed the holdings of Hirschfeld's organisation. Since most screenings accompanied Hirschfeld's lectures, it is likely that all the German copies of the film were destroyed then or soon after.

Even in its present fragmented and murky form *Anders* is a film that audiences can still find moving and stirring. There are essentially two elements: a love story and a lecture. The account that follows is based on a detailed synopsis published in the year of its release by the *Jahrbuch für sexuelle Zwischenstufen*; the sections not in brackets are what remain in the extant prints.

Famous violinist Paul Körner (Veidt) reads in the paper of the apparently inexplicable suicides of three young men; he thinks he can guess the reason. (In his mind's eye he sees an unending line of women and men processing beneath a sword of Damocles with §175 marked on it. He takes on as his pupil, and falls in love with, a young man, Kurt Sivers (Fritz Schulz)). In a park, Paul and Kurt encounter Franz Bollek (Schünzel), a youth whom Paul had known fleetingly. (After some misgivings, Kurt's parents allow him to stay with Paul, and Paul's parents, who have tried to persuade him to marry, learn from a doctor that nothing can be done to change his proclivities. Paul and Kurt appear in a concert together during which) Franz breaks into Paul's flat. He is discovered by Kurt on his return who struggles with him until

Paul arrives, at which point Franz says to Kurt, 'Don't be so grand, you're only his paid boy'. Paul and Franz struggle, till the latter is sent packing. (Kurt is so distraught that he leaves Paul, goes to work in a bar, tells his sister Else (Berber) no-one is to look for him.) Paul thinks back over his life: (his love for a fellow pupil, Max, at school, leading to his dismissal; his visit when a student to a brothel, where he was overcome with revulsion); his visits to a sex researcher (Hirschfeld), who assured him he can serve humanity as a homosexual, and to a hypnotist who tried unsuccessfully to cure him; and meeting Franz at a gay dance, taking him home and finding he was a blackmailer. Roused from his memories, he tears up one of Franz's blackmail letters. (He goes with Else, who has fallen in love with him, to a lecture given by Hirschfeld and she realises and accepts the truth about him. Meanwhile, Franz has been to the police and) both he and Paul are sent to jail, the former for blackmail, the latter for homosexuality. When Paul comes out of jail, he has lost all former friends and cannot get work; he finally poisons himself. (Kurt hears the news and at Paul's death-bed [figure 1.1] threatens to kill himself, but a doctor persuades him he should put his energies into fighting for the repeal of §175. The film ends with a shot of the statute book and a hand magically wiping away §175.)

What often strikes audiences today about the film is what seems a discrepancy between the tragic, down-beat story part of the film – yet another gay film with an unhappy ending – and the unambiguously affirmative character of the lecture elements. This has partly to do with what is missing, notably the more up-beat ending of Kurt's vow to fight for homosexual freedom which could mobilise spectator identification for the film's cause. Yet the tone of the story part of the film is ambivalent, partly because it is much more fully rooted in the conventions of German cinema of the time and partly because it is founded on a disquieting tension between competing contemporary definitions of gay identity.

The film context

The story in *Anders* is more caught up in the norms of contemporary film conventions than the lecture, due in part to the director, Richard Oswald, who was not, so far as we know, gay. Hirschfeld was not only the 'medical advisor' but co-scriptwriter

1.1   Anders als die Andern: Kurt weeps over Paul's body – a tragic ending but also the event precipitating Kurt into gay activism. (National Film Archive)

with Oswald, and there is no reason to suppose he did not fully participate in the writing, but he may not have given much attention to the built-in implications of genre, cast and film style and it is in these that some of the film's ambiguities lie.

The Aufklärungsfilm was a genre with which Oswald was particularly associated, possibly even being its inventor. Among the 'problems' dealt with in his films were pacifism (*Das eiserne Kreuz* 1915), alcoholism (*Das Laster* 1915), venereal disease (*Es werde Licht!* 1916/17, with sequels in 1917 and 1918) and prostitution (*Das Tagebuch einer Verlorenen* 1918 and *Prostitution* 1921, in which Magnus Hirschfeld again participated as specialist advisor) (Kaul and Scheuer 1970). These and others were commercially successful and much discussed, so that audiences going to see *Anders* as the latest example would have certain expectations and read the film accordingly.

The genre's more salacious reputation may have made some scenes seem more titillating to contemporary audiences than to us. A conga line of androgynous-looking women and men at the ball where Paul picks up Franz; the way Paul stands behind Franz when he takes him home and momentarily caresses his (fully clothed) chest – such images may have carried more of a frisson because people expected to see something thrilling, as well as because they were genuinely taboo-breaking. The reaction of shocked titillation (all those soldiers walking out) may well have been responding to a prurience which did characterise many Aufklärungsfilme (though not Oswald's). On the other hand, their tendency to construct the issues covered as 'problems' also meant that audiences were used to seeing such subjects as matters that needed dealing with, curing, even eradicating. The plot of *Anders* makes it absolutely clear that the 'problem' is social attitudes towards homosexuality, as legitimated by §175 of the penal code (outlawing homosexual relations between men). These attitudes make blackmail possible, cause Paul to be thrown in prison, to be refused work, to kill himself – the downward trajectory of the narrative is at every point, bar one, set in motion by hostile social attitudes. That one exception is however significant: it is Paul's act of picking up Franz. Up to this point his life, especially his relationship with Kurt, has been basically happy; it is an act of lust, of gay desire, that brings about his downfall. Thus although the overall intention of the plot is to stress the problems caused by social attitudes and the law, an intention spelt out in Hirschfeld's lecture, it would be as easy to take the film as showing that it is gay lust itself that causes, or simply is, the problem.

Anders is, like other Aufklärungsfilme, basically realist in approach, yet there is another dimension to it, closer to the fantastic cinema of the period. Oswald was equally at home with this tradition, with credits including *Der Hund von Baskerville* 1914, *Hoffmanns Erzählungen* 1916, *Das Bildnis des Dorian Gray* 1917, *Peer Gynt* 1918 and *Unheimliche Geschichten* (based on Poe) 1919. Veidt appeared regularly in his films and casting him as Paul in *Anders* is a major factor in the 'negative' feeling in the story part.

He was not yet a major international star but already a distinctive screen presence. On the one hand, he was handsome, a heart-throb, a popular pin-up in the film magazines (figure 1.2), generally playing the hero and love interest. It is important to remember this when seeing *Anders* – whatever our own responses to Paul, he is being played by someone considered at the time attractive and seductive. Yet his looks, his tall, gaunt figure, drawn, pallid, even skeletal face and dark, brooding eyes, also gave him a tragic or sinister air, which his roles often expanded upon: Cesare in *Das Kabinett des Dr Caligari* 1919, the somnambulist who murders and rapes under hypnosis; Jekyll and Hyde in *Der Januskopf* 1920; *Der Student von*

1.2 Conrad Veidt – the star of *Anders* as pin-up. (National Film Archive)

Prag 1926 who sells his mirror image to the devil, only to find it taking on a life of its own, killing his beloved's father and hounding him to his own death. This duality – handsome but at once melancholic and sinister, the very embodiment of a dual nature – hangs over him as Paul, suggested especially in the way he steals up behind Franz when he first takes him home and caresses him with his long, white hand, in the strong contrast of his deathly white face against a black backdrop in his suicide scene, in the clash of his secret sex life (where he picks up Franz) with his life with Kurt, and in the fact, reinforced by the sequence in which Paul reads of friends' 'inexplicable' suicides, that what blackmail works on is the homosexual's terror of exposure, his dual life revealed.

Despite these overtones, *Anders* as an Aufklärungsfilm is essentially social in perspective, something achieved especially by the way the camera is used. This remains, as was still usual in German cinema, at ninety degrees to the action, but positioned anywhere from an extreme close-up to a long shot. Scenes start not with an establishing shot but with a close-up and only then is there a cut back to show where the particular character stands in relation to others. This is sometimes effected by the use of an iris: the face of the character is seen centre of the frame but everything else is blacked out around it; then the circle containing the face widens, the black recedes, to reveal the space around the character. This technique, and the rigour with which it is used in *Anders*, is very effective for the social treatment of issues that are lived as personal problems. It presents first the intensity of personal feeling and then shows how this makes sense in a wider, social setting.

Two examples are the scenes where Paul picks up Franz and where Kurt catches Franz in Paul's flat. The former begins on an iris close-up of Franz, with a malevolent expression on his face, followed by one of Paul, looking with an expression of troubled desire to his right, and then cutting back to Franz, still in iris close-up, turned to his left and making a clear sexual come-on. Only now does the film cut back to a mid shot without iris, showing them in relation to each other and standing in front of groups of lesbians and gay men dancing together, in couples and later in a conga line. The feelings of the two men – Franz's malignancy, Paul's troubled lust – are clearly shown to us, intensified by close-up, but that is then put into its social context, a gay dance. This is not just a particular encounter, but a typical one. Franz turns and walks in amongst the dancers; Paul gestures for a glass of champagne and then follows Franz. There is no return to close-up. Paul is drawn into the world represented by Franz and the dancers, drawn into the dangerous gay milieu that will bring about his downfall. This is not just a personal tragedy, but a consequence of a certain form of social organisation, the gay underworld, breeding ground of blackmail.

The second example is also the turning point of the film. As Kurt and Franz struggle, Paul rushes in, separates them and starts fighting with Franz. Rather than stay with this, however, the film cuts to a head and shoulders shot of Kurt, his hand to his throat, an expression of profound shock in his face. This is a sufficiently distant shot for us still to be able to see Paul and Franz fighting behind him; the shot lasts a long time, so that Kurt's intense feelings of shock are counterposed to the struggle, between homosexual and blackmailer, that continues behind him. The struggle articulates and situates the dimensions of Kurt's horror at the revelation of Paul's involvement with the gay underworld. The close-up gives us the intensity of Kurt's feeling, but the camera position allows us to see what that feeling is about, its wider implications beyond Kurt's reactions.

The ambivalence in the story part of *Anders*, the pull of positive and negative elements, derives in part then from ambivalences built right into the Aufklärungsfilm genre, Veidt's image and contemporary film style. All of these made possible a serious social study in film of a personal, sexual matter, in the form of a story centred upon an attractive hero; but genre, star and conventions also made it easy to read the subject-matter, homosexuality, as itself the problem, inextricably tied to a way of life at once sinister and tragic. Yet the ambivalence is not only explicable in these terms; to it we must add the way different ways of thinking and feeling about homosexuality occur in the film. Kurt's shock, so powerfully rendered in the shot described above, is the shock of the loved one realising his lover has been untrue to him, but there is more to it than that: Kurt and Franz represent two different conceptions of homosexuality prevalent in the period, that may be characterised as in-betweenism and male-identification.

Male in-betweenism

In-between-ist conceptions of homosexuality saw lesbians and gay men as a kind of third sex. As is common in nineteenth- and twentieth-century thought about sexuality, notions of gender identity were conflated with notions of sexual identity. Thus a man was a heterosexual man, a woman a heterosexual woman, and it followed that people who were not heterosexual were therefore neither one thing nor the other, neither a real man nor a real woman but something in-between.

The most insistent proponents of this view were the founders of the German gay movement, going back to 1864 when Karl Heinrich Ulrichs published his first book on the 'riddle of love between men' and continuing in 1869 in the work of Carl von Westphal on 'contrary sexual feeling' and that of Károly Benkert, the first to use the term 'homosexuality' (Steakley 1975:3–17). Though there were different emphases in their work, all shared a view of gayness as natural, '"inborn" and ineradicable' (Silverstolpe 1987:213) and as in some sense androgynous, and their ideas inspired Magnus Hirschfeld and others in founding the sexual emancipation movement, the Wissenschaftlich-humanitäre Komitee (WhK – Scientific-Humanitarian Committee) in 1897.

Hirschfeld initially believed that lesbians and gay men were literally a third sex. The WhK's journal, *Jahrbuch für sexuelle Zwischenstufen*, even published in 1903 a sequence of three photographs demonstrating this: a very muscular youth holding a large fig leaf over his genitals represents the heterosexual male body type; a woman standing so as to accentuate the generous curve of her hips, with her pubic hairs either shaved or whited out, represents the heterosexual female body type; while the 'uranian' or third sex body is represented by a flat-chested figure wearing a scarf over its head and a veil across its face, standing so that its hip is less curved than the female type but still more pronounced than the male type, and with the genital area obscure, probably blacked out. Hirschfeld and the WhK officially abandoned this kind of literalism about gayness in 1910, but it persists in a relatively sophisticated form in his lecture in *Anders*. He shows some slides of 'men with the bodily and spiritual characteristics of a woman and women with every kind of masculine characteristic', admits that 'there are feminine men who are not homosexual, and homosexuals who give hardly any or even no impression of womanliness' but nonetheless avers that, following the research on gonad transplants in animals, it is certain that 'apparently merely spiritual intermediacy is bodily caused'.

The point of clinging to some version of these theories was to demonstrate that homosexuality was a fact of biology. If you could show it to be a part of nature, rather than an activity going against nature, then you could argue that society had no business trying to suppress it. Moreover, if it was part of nature it was not a sickness and therefore was not to be thought of in terms of cure – as the doctor in *Anders* tells Paul's parents, 'It is neither a vice nor a crime, nor even a sickness, but a variation, one of the borderline cases in which nature is so rich'.

If scientific theory and the WhK abandoned third sex ideas in their most literal form, they were too deeply rooted culturally simply to go away. There had been a fascination with the figure of the androgyne throughout the nineteenth century, in literature, painting and sculpture (Busst 1967). The androgyne might be an actual hermaphrodite, or a mythical or new kind of being, and was frequently seen as homosexual. S/he often represented a dream ideal, providing a wealth of celebratory in-between-ist imagery in which lesbians and gay men might recognise themselves. Even more important was the actual life-style of many people on the gay scene. Indeed, the third sex idea may well have been developed as a means of accounting for a predominant gay sub-cultural style, the Tante (literally, auntie). This could often take the form of full drag, as in the first love recounted by the anonymous author of *Wir vom dritten Geschlecht*, published in Leipzig in 1907:

> His figure was opulently slender (if that seems an oxymoron, it is nevertheless exactly right), and he was wearing a crimson morning-frock, and under the discreet outline of the bust the lustre of his skin was like alabaster. His blonde wig, tied in a Greek knot at the neck, was drawn in easy waves about his temple.
>
> (1985:25)

The oxymoronic opulent slenderness suggests the 'uranian' body type in the WhK photo sequence, and often the style was far less straightforwardly female impersonation:

> He received his guests in an indeterminate garment made by himself, a cross between a ball gown and a dressing gown.
>
> (Hirschfeld quoted in Theis and Sternweiler 1984:57)

Most characteristic perhaps was an effeminisation of male styles based on movie stars like Valentino:

> resemblance to the opposite sex is achieved through powder puffs and lipstick. They are somewhat profligate with perfume and coquettish in their pretty coloured silks. They have plucked eyebrows and crimped, sleek, shiny hair in soft quiffs. They look at you yearningly, dreamily, out of Belladonna eyes.
>
> (Curt Moreck quoted in ibid:70)

This Belladonna look was described by another observer as 'the febrile sparkle of eyes darkened by kohl' (Got 1923:673), a distinctive Tante fashion in the bars.

Both older and younger men might conform to this style, but there was also a liking for another, more butch type, the Bube or Bursch, the large, handsome, open-faced working-class lad, not a million miles away from the heterosexual male type in the WhK photo sequence. He figured with increasing frequency in the pin-ups in the gay magazine *Der Eigene* where by the early twenties he had displaced the idealised adolescent of earlier issues. In *The Scorpion* 1919, Anna Weirauch describes an obvious Bube: 'a broad-shouldered, bull-neck soldier, with a good-looking honest peasant's face, grinning, . . . but uncomprehending' (1975:227).

Quite apart from the aptness of the vampire as a metaphor for homosexuality (Dyer 1988), it is the contrast of Count Orlok and Thomas Hutter (figure 1.3) that so suggests *Nosferatu* 1922 as a film eminently readable as gay. They are a Tante and a Bube. Max Schreck plays Orlok with his shoulders permanently hunched and pinched, as compared to Thomas's shoulders broadened by a large cape. Schreck is thin, his face whitened with powder, his eyes heavy with kohl, a grotesque exaggeration of the effeminised male look. Thomas, played by Gustav von Wangenheim, is big, broad, with face only made up to the usual film conventions of the time. Orlok walks with mincing steps; Thomas strides about. And although Orlok is the sexual predator, it is Thomas, the sex object, whose genitals are on display in trousers that are loose everywhere but at the crotch. When Orlok goes down on Thomas as he sleeps, he is not just making do with male 'blood'.[3]

Paul in *Anders* is not exactly a Tante, yet he has something of it. For most of the time he is dressed in sober suits, yet at the gay dance he wears a sort of loose, satin robe with a hood, perhaps the kind of 'indeterminate garment' described by Hirschfeld. When he takes Franz home, he drapes the robe over his shoulder and slinks up behind him, his right hand hanging limp from his wrist (figure 1.4). Like the men in the bars, he has heavy kohl round his eyes, more than other characters in the film. And the casting of Veidt, with his cadaverous quality, is of a piece with the image of the Tante, present in much of the writing and in *Nosferatu*. Franz is his Bube, with broad, crude features, much less handsome than the pin-ups in *Der Eigene* and with a definite touch of lipstick round his mouth, but still recognisable as the working-class lad.

The in-between-ist idea of homosexuality is suggested in Paul, but

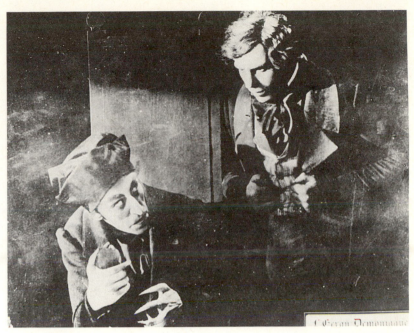

1.3 *Nosferatu* – vampire and prey, Tante and Bube? (National Film Archive)

1.4 Paul and Franz in *Anders als die Andern*: in-between-ist wrap and posture but male-identified statuary. (National Film Archive)

it is only fully present in the androgynous dancers glimpsed behind him and Franz at the ball. The milieu of the third sex exists more as a possibility or temptation for Paul. He strays into it and in so doing not only lays himself open to blackmail but destroys his relationship with Kurt, who represents a different, male-identified way of being gay.

Male-identified

If in-between-ism sees gay men as not real men, as somewhere between the sexes, male-identified gayness sees them as, on the contrary, the most manly of men. This too has its roots in the nineteenth century, perhaps earlier still than in-between-ism. Although the gay connection is not explicit, the most distinguished German art historian Winckelmann consistently celebrated the beauty of the male form in his work (1755–86) on classical art (Leppmann 1986) and much of the imagery and vocabulary of male-identification draws on and invokes classical example. Many writers and artists through the nineteenth century worked with a conception of 'Greek love', but it was not until the turn of the century that it was consolidated into a loose movement.

Although there were differences between them, male-identification can be seen in three main groupings. Firstly, there was the organisation, the Gemeinschaft der Eigenen (Community of the Special), founded in 1902, based round *Der Eigene*, the journal of one of its founder members, Adolf Brand. This ran, with occasional interruptions, from 1896 to 1931, and contained drawings and photographs, stories and articles, celebrating 'Greek' ideals of male beauty and 'manly culture' (Hohmann 1981). Secondly, there was the poet Stefan George and his circle, devoted to the life of the spirit as embodied in poetry, the beauty of male youth and friendship between men (Aarts 1983). They gave parties in Roman costume and made a cult of a dead youth, Maximin, along the lines of the Emperor Hadrian for Antinous, activities which, as much as the poetry, gave them a high public profile. Thirdly, there were the ideas of people like Gustav Wyneken and Hans Blüher on the homo-erotic dimension of male adolescent development, and in particular the importance of the erotic bond between pupil and teacher, boy and man. Wyneken put many of his ideas into practice in independent, experimental schools (Dougherty 1978, Maasen 1987); Blüher's writings concentrated on the youth ('Wandervogel') movement, whose leaders hotly denied his assertion of the valuable erotic attachments at the heart of their organisation.

1.5   Classical beauty, friendship and pedagogic eros in *Wege zu Kraft und Schönheit*.

The attitudes and feelings that hold these groupings together are
suggested in the first sequence of *Wege zu Kraft und Schönheit* (*The
Road to Strength and Beauty*). Set in a re-creation of a Greek
arena, its gay appeal lay not only in the sight of multitudes of
muscular young men clad in thongs and jock-straps, but in its whole
ambience, encapsulated in the opening shot (figure 1.5). There are
no women present – this is men together with men. The near naked
men against the pillars on left and right stand in classic Greek poses,
weight on one leg, the other slightly bent, one hand on the hip. One
of the two young men standing together just inside the arena puts
his arm round his friend's shoulder. The older man with a group of
younger men at his feet listening is a clear reference to Socrates and
his pupils. The framing of the scene not only creates a tableau
effect, invoking the perfection of art (as opposed to a more
documentary style), but also gives the display of the male body
male-identified gay inflections: the single figures suggest the ideals
of classical beauty, the two young men are in an attitude of
friendship, the Socratic grouping points to the notion of 'pedagogic
eros'. Each of these informs the imagery of *Anders*.

Taking its cue from how classical antiquity had been construed by
nineteenth-century arbiters of taste (Haskell and Penny 1981), gay
culture distinguished two Greek ideals of male beauty: the ephebe,

the boy poised on the brink of adolescence, and the older athlete. The former does not figure in *Anders*, but a statuette of an athlete, based on a classical original, features prominently in the furnishing of Paul's flat (see figure 1.4). It is sometimes argued that the cult of the athlete was just a cover for the desire to look at naked men. No doubt in some cases this was so, but the athlete was also the actual form that desire took. People were not pretending to be turned on by athletic features – they were the turn-on. The presence of the statue signals something of Paul's erotic imagination.

There is a high idealism in the rhetoric, both verbal and visual, depicting the athlete, and this is true too of the attitude towards friendship, which is seen as an essential means to personal growth in adolescence:

> The Community of the Special counsels the young man to have no contact with women before marriage, but rather to seek his highest social pleasure, his moral strength, his physical release, his spiritual calm, and his inner peace in the intimate company of a [male] friend.
>
> (Adolf Brand 1930; quoted in Hohmann 1981:324)

Such youthful friendship is often depicted in stories between an older and younger boy at school, with the joy of leadership and learning built into the eroticism of the relationship. Boys learnt to be men through this, as they did through the relation between pupils and teachers. Wyneken argued that true education depends on 'eros', the bond of love between an adolescent and his or her teacher or leader. (Although at heart only interested in boys, Wyneken did take girls at his schools and Sappho as well as Socrates was held up as an inspiration.) Joy in each other's beauty and wisdom makes this eros intense and enriching, a joy expressed in much gay fiction of the time. In 'Es schienen so golden die Sterne' by Walter Nitsche, published in *Der Eigene* in 1920, Heinz, following the death of his beloved schoolfriend Hannibal, becomes a teacher but is dismissed:

> The strict Headmaster had found out about his inclinations. About his secret, silent love for his friends [ie. his pupils]. About his great joy in their beauty and the dear masculine freshness of their youth, the very thing that had been the dream that had made him want to become a teacher.
>
> (1983:249)

In film, the ideal male homo-erotic master-pupil relationship is represented in the two film versions of Herman Bang's novel *Mikaël* (first published in Denmark in 1906), *Vingarne* (*The Wings*) and *Michael*. The earlier, Swedish version, directed by Mauritz Stiller, himself gay (as was Bang), is the more committedly homosexual, especially through the use of gay allusions in its title (the same as the Russian writer Mikhail Kuzmin's campaigning novel of 1904) and in the iconography of the central image of a bewinged nude male figure, evoking both Icarus and Ganymede (much used in contemporary gay art (Sternweiler 1984: 74–5) and specific works by gay artists such as Carl Milles (who provided the sculptures for the film) and Magnus Enckell (notably his painting *The Wings* (Hyvärinen 1988)). In the re-make this image is replaced by an altogether more classically 'straight' painting of 'The Victor'. Nonetheless *Michael* does acknowledge the relationship between Zoret and Michael, with Zoret pronouncing on his death-bed the words that are quoted at the start of the film, 'Now I may die content, for I have known great love'.

The ideals of friendship and 'pedagogic eros' structure the 'good' relationships in Paul's life. His friendship with Max at school is a 'spiritual unity', his relationship with Kurt a classic master–pupil one. Kurt has never missed one of Paul's recitals and comes to him begging him to take him as a pupil: 'If only you'd agree to teach me, then my dearest wish would come true'. Kurt's parents are uneasy about the relationship but recognise that his musical talent is being nurtured through love. Both relationships are presented as the highest expressions of Paul's personality. It is the Tante side of him that brings about the tragedy.

There is no physical expression of feeling shown between Paul and either Max or Kurt. The idealism of male-identified imagery meant that it was often ambivalent about sex. Much of the writing seems to advocate spiritual friendship between men of great erotic intensity yet without genital expression, as if sex, being material, is impure, even dirty. By contrast there is physical expression between Paul and Franz, Franz puckering his lips when he makes a play for Paul at the dance, Paul caressing him back at home. The 'good' sexuality in *Anders*, represented by Max and Kurt, as opposed to the 'bad' sexuality embodied in Franz, may on inspection not involve sex at all.

*   *   *

The fact that *Anders* does not take place wholly in either the in-between-ist nor the male-identified milieu in part relates to the fact that they were not as separate as may have so far appeared. The bar scene was the largest network of meeting places for gay men, whatever form their sexual desires took, and sometimes the ambience made a deliberate appeal to the male-identified:

> scantily clad boys doing Greek dances based on the pictures on excavated vases could meet the aesthetic needs of the 'pure' lovers of beauty, while it realised the sinful wishes of those clients who desired them.
>
> (Theis and Sternweiler 1984:57)

Even when no such concessions were made, it was still to the scene that the male-identified were obliged to go. Count Kuno, in Isherwood's *Good-bye to Berlin*, with his gymnasium re-creating attic ideals, has to trail round the bars looking for youths to use it. In John Henry Mackay's novel *Der Puppenjunge*, remarkable for its evocation of a love that is at once 'pure' *and* sexual, the older man Hermann, who falls selflessly in love with the street boy Gunther, sits day after day hoping to catch sight of him among the Tanten and Buben of the Adonis Lounge, a place utterly alien to him. With both Kuno and Hermann, what is stressed is the contrast – now comic, now tragic – between their ideals of love and the sordid reality of the scene.

The intermingling of the two homosexual worlds in *Anders* is characteristic, as is the implicit downgrading of the one (in-between-ist) at the expense of the other (male-identified). Perhaps this is not surprising. Male-identified notions were closer to many of the ideas of mainstream thought in the period than were those of Hirschfeld *et al.* Where he sought to establish the rights of homosexuals on medical and legal grounds, the male-identified worked on the terrain of 'respectability'. As George Mosse (1982) has argued, one of the ways that a bourgeois ideology of nationalism established itself in nineteenth-century Germany was through an imagery of the body beautiful. Greek models represented the ideal over against the materialism of the working classes and socialism; the cult of nature represented a rejection of the restless, febrile city, where the dangers of revolution and discontent fermented. In *Wege zu Kraft und Schönheit*, a stunning montage sequence of city life is intended to convey the pressure and restlessness of urban life as compared to the calm and health of country life. In a sequence in a museum, a group of people are shown gathered round a classical statue of a naked woman; the camera pans along them, revealing them as grotesques, deformed, sick-looking, looking lasciviously at the statue, in other words, corrupt modern people, unable to respond to the higher ideals of beauty.

The visual culture as well as the argumentation of male-identified gayness is astonishingly close to this main line of respectable bourgeois thought, whereas Hirschfeld's ideas disrupted bourgeois certitudes about gender and sexuality, about human nature (Hull 1982). Thus despite Hirschfeld's involvement and Oswald's un-doubtable liberalism, *Anders* comes down on the side of male-identified homosexuality, where there was a fit between the claims of pedagogic eros and the aims of respectability.

The last words of the film are nonetheless Hirschfeld's: 'We must all ensure that a time will soon come when such tragedies [as Paul's] are impossible, for knowledge will overcome prejudice, truth will overcome lies and love will conquer hatred.' But who could not agree on that? Not only are these broad sentiments, but the cause of the tragedy, as Hirschfeld sees it, is blackmail, a real enough threat to all gay men of whatever style as long as §175 was law (Theis and Sternweiler 1984). This gave the film its immediacy for gay audiences of the time, its campaigning edge. However contradictory and ambivalent its representation of how gay life was lived in the Weimar republic, *Anders als die Andern* was forcibly directed at some of the elements that determined the shape of that life. Forcibly enough to be banned.

MÄDCHEN IN UNIFORM

To turn from *Anders* to *Mädchen*, is to turn from archaeology to history. *Mädchen* exists in complete, at their best luminously beautiful, prints. Since its 're-discovery' by the contemporary women's movement, it has been widely shown in cinemas and on television, is available on video and has been the subject of major pieces of critical writing (Gramann and Schlüpmann 1983b, Rich 1984, Scholar 1979). It had, in any case, never been an obscure film. It was both a critical and a commercial success at the time, in Germany and abroad, and all standard histories of German cinema mention it. The two classic studies of the films of the period, Siegfried Kracauer's *From Caligari to Hitler* and Lotte Eisner's *The Haunted Screen*, both single it out for praise. It was never a film that had dropped from view.

Yet as a lesbian film, it did need to be re-discovered. While praising its artistry, historians, including Kracauer and Eisner, managed to downplay the film's lesbianism. For Kracauer it is a study of authoritarianism, whilst for Eisner it is both that and an admirably 'feminine' work. There is justice in both views, but the lesbianism is not incidental to the film's anti-authoritarianism and femininity: in many ways, it is what makes them possible.

> *Mädchen* centres on the relationship between Manuela von Meinhardis and Fräulein von Bernburg, pupil and teacher respectively at a private school for the daughters of army officers. Manuela's mother has just died. Like most of the girls at the school, Manuela adores von Bernburg, the only one among the teachers who does not believe in the Principal's approach of ruling with a rod of iron. For Manuela and von Bernburg, however, the relationship goes beyond a crush, though von Bernburg tries to deny it. Manuela takes the lead in a school production of Schiller's play, *Don Carlos*; it is a great success and at the party afterwards, when all the girls get a little tipsy, Manuela makes a speech declaring her love for von Bernburg. The Principal comes in on the end of it and, scandalised, has Manuela shut away in the school sick-bay and forbids von Bernburg to have contact with her. Von Bernburg confronts the Principal, but even as they speak Manuela has rushed from the sick-bay and climbed to the top of the deep stairwell in the centre of the school. She climbs on to the parapet at the top, preparing to throw herself off, but the other girls have realised what she is going to do and, together with von Bernburg, rescue her. The Principal walks off into the shadows of a corridor, defeated.

As is evident from this synopsis, lesbianism is pivotal to *Mädchen*'s plot, and the treatment both intensifies its romantic-erotic quality and suggests its subversive power. There are some shots of girls lying together bathed in a dappled light suggesting romance, but the greatest intensity is centred on Manuela and von Bernburg. The first time von Bernburg sees Manuela, the latter is standing above her on the stairs; she has on her new school uniform, with its large, white starch collar, and the light streams in from her right, so that the collar sparkles and she herself seems to glow; it is a shot from von Bernburg's point of view and the reaction shot of her indicates that she has caught her breath at the sight of Manuela, just as we are clearly intended to. In the scene in the dormitory, where von Bernburg kisses each of the girls good-night, Manuela, unlike the other girls, throws her arms round von Bernburg's neck. Von Bernburg removes them but then, in extreme close-up and with softly suffused light, kisses her, not on the forehead as with the other girls, but full on the mouth. For all the girls, von Bernburg's kiss is an erotic experience: a close-up shows one very pretty girl grinning in expectation, while the girl in the next bed to Manuela, Ilse, throws her head back in an ecstasy of anticipation. What is clear about both the first meeting and the dormitory scene however is that the feeling is as strong for von Bernburg as for Manuela, and that, in its use of lighting and camera position, it is to be seen as both romantic and erotic – it is not just a crush, and it is not only on the schoolgirl's side.

Lesbianism's power of subversion is suggested by the impact of Manuela's public declaration of her love for von Bernburg. Not only does she declare her own love, but she defies the Principal and hints at the place of von Bernburg in all the girls' affections:

> She gave me a present, a petticoat. I've got it on. I'm so happy because now I know for sure. She cares for me! Fräulein von Bernburg! Nothing else matters. She is there. I'm not afraid of anything. Nor [as the Principal walks towards her] anyone. *Our* beloved Fräulein von Bernburg lives! Long may she live!

The speech transforms the romantic-erotic intensity of Manuela's individual feeling into a shared, collective experience, uniting the girls; and it makes that experience public. It is a coming out. Equally, the excitement of the last few minutes is invested not only in the will-she, won't-she of Manuela poised on the parapet, but in the collective actions of the girls and von Bernburg to save her. Just prior to this von Bernburg pronounces the film's clearest defence of lesbianism: 'What you call sins I call the great spirit of love which has a thousand forms.' Up to this point she has still been working in the interests of the system, using niceness rather than rigid discipline to control the girls (Rich 1984: 104–7) and repressing her response to Manuela. Now, as she becomes aware of the girls' actions, she at last identifies with them, against the Principal, in the name of love.

Mädchen's lesbianism is so obvious that it is hard to believe anyone could downplay it. Nor was it lost on contemporaries. For many viewers, it was a turn-on. Carl Froelich, who supervised the production, in part invited this by rejecting the title of the play the film is based on, *Gestern und Heute*, because, he said, '[w]e want to get back the money we're investing, we'll call it *Girls in Uniform* – then they'll think, there'll be girls in uniform playing about and showing their legs' (Schlüpmann and Gramann 1981:41). Hertha Thiele, who plays Manuela, became a popular star, receiving love letters from male and female fans. There were also more hostile reactions. In the USA, the film was only granted a certificate after the excision of shots showing the depth of Manuela's lesbian emotions and von Bernburg's defence of lesbianism to the Principal. Thereafter, homophobic critics were free to argue that only perverts would see lesbianism in the film at all (Russo 1981:57–8).

The makers of *Mädchen*

In content and treatment, *Mädchen* seems obviously a lesbian film, but this is not such an easy label to apply once you start looking at the circumstances of its production. Only one of those centrally involved do we know to have been lesbian: Christa Winsloe, who supplied the source material. Even this is not straightforward.

Manuela's story went through four different versions in Winsloe's hands: two plays (*Ritter Nérestan*, produced in Leipzig in 1930, and *Gestern und Heute*, Berlin 1931), the film (co-scripted with F. D. Andam) and a novel, also called *Mädchen in Uniform*, published in 1933. There are significant variations: in *Ritter Nérestan* lesbianism was almost absent, whereas in all the other versions it is centrally present; in all but the film, however, Manuela does kill herself. Winsloe produced these four versions during a period of transition in her life. In 1930 she was still married to Count Ludwig Hatvany and well known about café society. It was not until the early thirties that she began to live openly as a lesbian and not until her short story 'Life begins' 1935 that she wrote a work exploring lesbian life directly and affirmatively (Reinig 1983:241–8). The absence of lesbianism in the first version and the 'negative' ending to all but the film seem to be accounted for in part by Winsloe's as yet unresolved feelings about her own sexuality.

What Winsloe provided was a story with the potential for being treated as more or less lesbian-identified. Was it then the director, Leontine Sagan, who was responsible for bringing this out? She was not so far as we know lesbian and on certain matters, notably title, casting and script, had less control than Carl Froelich, a well established director who had set up the collective that made the film (Gramann and Schlüpmann 1981:32–41); but in those aspects she did control, notably dress, performance and lighting, her influence does seem to have been decisive. Many, including Lotte Eisner, have considered the handling of these to be distinctly 'feminine' (1969:325–6) and it is in relation to this that one can speak of the film's lesbian identification.

The term 'femininity' in relation to art is notoriously difficult to use. Two of the things it may mean are having a particular inwardness with the situation and experience of women that only women can have and having many of the qualities traditionally considered feminine: delicacy, softness, feeling for detail and, in some theories, a preference for the rounded, centred and blurred over the angular, outwardly-directed and hard-edged.[4] Both can be argued to apply to *Mädchen*.

Many women feel that you can tell it was directed by a woman from the way the girls interact, the humour, the atmosphere. The lesbian magazine *Die Freundin* began its review in 1932: 'A woman (Leontine Sagan) is the director and there are only women acting under her sensitive direction' (quoted in Kreische 1984:195) and this is a common starting point in reviews. The fact that we know the film was directed by a woman with an all-female cast places us in a different relationship to the images on the screen and may make us feel very differently about such scenes as the girls getting ready for bed or Manuela and von Bernburg together.

On the other hand, the look of *Mädchen* may not at first glance appear particularly feminine, especially compared to *Olivia* 1950, another film about lesbian feeling in a girls' school also directed by a woman, Jacqueline Audry. In the latter everything is based on the curve: the spiralling hall staircase, the silhouettes of the head teachers' costumes, circling camera movements and a central visual symbolism of the oval window (Burrows 1981); whereas virtually the opposite is true of *Mädchen*: stairwell, costumes, lighting emphasise straight lines. But this is the difference between the schools: in *Olivia*, an intensely, self-consciously feminine world, nurturing values of grace and elegance, but in *Mädchen* an institution designed to subjugate the girls to the values of masculinity, discipline, rigidity. If the film has a feminine eye it must then be in the way it uses visual values – above all, straight lines – to suggest how inimical they are to feminine sensibilities. In this context, the extreme softness in the presentation of von Bernburg, lighting often softening the edges of her costume (even in her case quite severe) and blurring the contours of her face and body, could be seen as an especially meaningful celebration of the alternative feminine principle to the masculine one that rules the school.

If *Mädchen* is a 'feminine' film then, it is not because women will necessarily make a certain kind of film but because the known fact of a woman director informs our reading and because it can be related to features of traditional women's cultures. This femininity is part and parcel of the way *Mädchen* can be termed a lesbian film, for it asserts that lesbianism is nothing if not womanly. Before examining that however we need first to look at the way a less feminine definition of lesbianism also has a place in the film.

Female in-betweenism

In the Berlin production of *Gestern und Heute* von Bernburg was played by Margarete Melzer, in Hertha Thiele's words, 'a real butch type' (Schlüpmann and Gramann 1981:32). Melzer was a large woman with a broad, square face; for *Gestern*, she wore a collar and tie, a tailored suit which flattened her chest, and her hair cropped and combed with a parting. Dorothea Wieck, von Bernburg in the film, is by contrast (figure 1.6) exceedingly feminine: she has small, delicate features, wears dresses throughout the film which modestly outline her bosom and has her hair crimped in waves and decorated with a frilly cap.

This change of cast, Froelich's decision, is a rejection of a certain style of lesbianism. It was a style clearly related to 'third sex' ideas

1.6   Margarete Melzer (left) and Dorothea Wieck (right): two versions of Fräulein von Bernburg. (*Frauen und Film*)

(Lhomond 1985) and familiar on the lesbian scene: 'Seated at the bar there were women in dinner jackets, sipping cocktails, smoking an impressive number of cigarettes and carrying on like men' (from a memoir quoted in Vermij 1983:109). Jeanne Mammen's pictures of the milieu present many portraits of this 'Bubi' type, 'wearing ties, men's haircut, small "moustache"' and suggest that 'the ideal of the boyish woman obviously must have been as popular as the radiant appearances of the "femmes"' (Sykora 1983:541–2).

Discussion in the lesbian press, such as *Die Freundin* 1924–33 and *Die Garçonne* 1930–2, was divided as to the value of this style (Schlierkamp 1984, Vogel 1984). Some saw it as an expression of the character of women who wanted to be independent of men or simply to exercise their minds. In Aimée Duc's novel *Sind es Frauen?* 1903, about a group of such women, one observes:

> As a doctor I want to tell you that most of the hysterical, neurotic, so-called misunderstood women are married women who have almost without exception become victims of psychic disorders because the lack of productive, satisfying activity, of intellectual enlightenment, of mental training is taking its revenge. Strengthening of the will and education of the mind are the best prophylactic for avoiding hysteria.
>
> (1980:16–17)

Such strengthening and education had real consequences for relationships between women and men: the divorce rate rose in Germany throughout the twenties and there was a huge increase in the numbers of women competing with men for work, especially the newer, white collar jobs (Schenk 1980:63–7). This threat to male prerogatives was of a piece with the involvement of lesbians in radical politics, though both the socialist and women's movements tried to play this down. The latter responded to accusations that there were many lesbians in their ranks by denial rather than proud affirmation. In 1904 Anna Rüling complained at a WhK meeting that, considering

> the contributions made to the women's movement by homosexual women for decades, it is amazing that the large and influential organisations of the movement have never lifted a finger to improve the civil rights and social standing of their numerous Uranian members.
>
> (1980:88)

Still in 1931, even in the context of lauding the independent woman who has no need of men, a feminist could write: 'But it would be completely wrong, to suspect anything inverted or homosexual here.'[5] The appeal of the lesbian's financial and emotional independence was both threatening and yet had little political support, even amongst progressives. No wonder then that Melzer was not used as von Bernburg.

Yet, even with Wieck instead of Melzer, the Bubi does not go away; she comes back in, with special force, through the use of the Hosenrolle, the girl dressed as a boy. This motif was popular in Germany from the teens to the thirties in vehicles for major stars like Elisabeth Bergner, Lilian Harvey, Renate Müller and Asta Nielsen. Although usually light and comic, the films they made do not have the hysterical, farcical quality of most Hollywood cross-dressing films and nor, as with male to female cross-dressing, do the narratives involve humiliation for the protagonist. They presented images of women having adventures, going out into the world, being creative and along the way setting off complex plays of emotion and desire, that many women found attractive (Gramann and Schlüpmann 1981).

Der Geiger von Florenz (*The Violinist from Florence*), for instance, allows for all manner of sexual feeling. Bergner plays the tomboyish Renée, who disguises herself as a boy to escape from boarding school and is picked up by a brother and sister who take 'René' home with them. The brother is a painter and finds himself strangely drawn to his 'male' model (figure 1.7); he is disconcerted by this but when he learns the truth, that Renée is a girl, looks distinctly disappointed. Renée never gets back into women's clothes and the final shot is of the brother passionately kissing this person in boy's clothes. . . The sister too is attracted to René. Near the end the latter reveals to her that she is a woman by having her cup her breasts beneath her boy's costume and it is only now that the sister gives her a full, hard kiss on the lips, no sisterly peck on the cheek. It is the only physically intimate scene, between anyone, in the whole film, and takes place between two women who both definitely know the other is a woman.

The Hosenrolle image, its splendid spirit, its delicious ambiguities, resonate in Manuela when she plays the lead in *Don Carlos*. Even before being dressed as a man, she looks boyish by having her hair cropped and combed with a parting in the 'garçonne' style that had become quite fashionable in the twenties. Dressed as Don Carlos, one girl strokes her stockinged legs and breathes, 'How handsome you are!' (figure 1.8); shots of the audience at the

1.7 *Der Geiger von Florenz* – why is he looking at 'him' so intensely; why is 'she' looking so doubtful? (National Film Archive)

1.8 'What beautiful legs you have!' – Manuela in Hosenrolle backstage in *Mädchen in Uniform*. (National Film Archive)

performance centre von Bernburg, reconfirming her pleasure in Manuela, just as on the first time she saw her, with the light streaming on her hair newly pulled back to look boyish. The play is a classic, well known to contemporary audiences as a play of protest from the Sturm und Drang period of German romanticism, suggesting both youthful revolt and a critique of authoritarianism. The scene from the play actually shown is one in which Don Carlos declares his love for the Queen, who is in fact his father's new wife, and thus forbidden by, in Schiller's words, 'the world and nature and the laws of Rome'. As B. Ruby Rich (1984:109) argues, *Mädchen*

> clearly annexes this sentiment by choosing the scene in which Don Carlos proclaims his love for Elizabeth, the name of both the Queen Mother and of Fräulein von Bernburg. With Manuela cross-dressed as the passionate suitor (in a performance heralded by all for its remarkable sincerity!), the sequence represents the central theme of forbidden love encoded within the sanctity of German high culture.

It is while still dressed as Don Carlos that Manuela delivers her coming out speech, quoted above. This is the most direct statement of lesbian desire in the film and it is spoken by Manuela, not only dressed as a man, one associated with revolt moreover, but occupying a male space: it is a public act, it is proposing a toast (a male prerogative), it is under the influence of alcohol (ladies, as we see at the concurrent gathering with the Principal, sip coffee). It is also linked to the idea of modernity: the girls abandon waltzes for ragtime which also frees them to dance with each other and Manuela to make her speech. Modernity is associated with the 'new woman' and she in turn with lesbianism. This speech, this spirit of modernity, is seen and heard by both the Principal and von Bernburg. Through the one it calls down the wrath of the patriarchy but it inspires the other to have the courage of her feelings. It is explicit and effective – as, of course, was the Bubi style. This was the form that the public, visible declaration of lesbian identity took. Perhaps the, as Rich (ibid.:110) puts it, 'naming' of lesbianism in *Mädchen* could only be put into the mouth of someone who looked something like an 'out' lesbian.

Female-identified

Mädchen does not eliminate altogether the Bubi style, but does confine it to a short part of the film and in its least threatening form, the Hosenrolle garçonne, with connotations of the temporary, immature or merely fashionable. Yet it is not the limit of the film's lesbianism. The relationship between Manuela and von Bernburg may be stripped of in-between-ism, but this only heightens its female-identified elements, and these are the core of the film, in the central relationship and in the whole atmosphere between the girls.

The female-identified lesbianism of Weimar (and earlier) should not be confused with the women-identified-women lesbianism discussed in chapter four. Though there are similarities, especially in the sense of connection between lesbians and all women, there are also differences. In particular, female-identified lesbians were not separatist. Partly because of the less than whole-hearted support given lesbians by the women's movement, many preferred to work within the WhK and other mixed-sex homosexual organisations (Kokula 1984:149–50), which perhaps accounts for the presence of both in-between-ist and female-identified lesbianism in *Mädchen* without any sense of conflict between them.

Female-identified lesbianism did not celebrate new ideals of female strength, but rather stressed notions of femininity: lesbianism was not different from traditional ways of being female but on the contrary the most womanly form of womanhood. The focus of its imagery was adolescence and school days. The environment and ambience of the girls' school distinguishes the emotions shown from the two other predominant images of lesbianism. The schoolgirl could not be seen as an 'independent' woman, whose sexuality expresses or emanates from her independence from men; and, by virtue of her undoubtable innocence, she could not be seen in the terms of sickness and decadence found in much contemporary writing (Faderman 1981:254–94) or in the character of the Countess in *Die Büchse der Pandora*. The school story could express a lesbianism seen as natural, pure and intrinsically female.

The school story also relates to the importance of Sappho as a reference point. At least as far back as Johannes Flach's *Sappho: Griechische Novelle* 1886, Sappho had been used as a respectable image of female homo-eroticism (Foster 1985:218) and many women writers had taken possession of it subsequently (ibid.: 176–7). 'Sapphic' became a widely used synonym for lesbian and the fashion may have offered women 'their only possibility for a positive historical and cultural identity' (Sanders 1983:493). In particular her work provided what Elaine Marks calls 'the preferred locus for most fictions about women loving women', namely, 'the gynaecum, ruled by the seductive or seducing teacher' (1979:357) and Marks' account of the conventions of the gynaecum story (ibid.:357–8) is astonishingly close to *Mädchen*:

The younger woman [Manuela] . . . is always passionate and innocent [the intensity of her embrace of von Bernburg compared to the other girls, the spontaneity and directness of her feelings]. If . . . it is the younger woman who falls in love, the narrative is structured so as to insist on this love as an awakening [the contrast between Manuela's withdrawn state at the start and her blossoming of confidence as her love for von Bernburg grows].
The older woman as object of the younger woman's desire is restrained and admirable, beautiful and cultivated [almost a description of Wieck's von Bernburg].
. . . the exchanges between the older and younger woman are reminiscent of a mother-daughter relationship [discussed below]. The mother of the younger woman is either dead or in some explicit way inadequate [Manuela's has just died at the start of the film]. Her absence is implied by the young woman's insistent need for a good-night kiss [the dormitory scene].
The denouement . . . is often brought about by a public event during which private passions explode [Manuela's speech after the play].

The gynaecum tale provided a literary model and at the same time there was an interest in the phenomenon of the Schwärmerei, the schoolgirl crush, among contemporary commentators, including sexologists such as Havelock Ellis who published his 'The school-friendships of girls' in 1897. The growth of large boarding schools signalled a shift in the education of middle-class girls, making such intensities possible and even common (Vicinus 1985), and girls' Wandervogel groups, though less developed than boys' (Steakley 1975:55), may also have fostered such experiences. Käthe K., a woman in her eighties, recalled in 1984 joining the Jugendbund für Mädchen (Girls' Youth Group) in 1918 when she was fourteen and there, like many others, meeting her first great love, a young woman five years older (Tonbandprotokolle 1984:211).

There is often an implication in writings of the period that nothing that follows schoolgirl romance ever quite matches up to it. Marianne Weber, in a basically heterosexual study of *Die Frauen und die Liebe*, quotes Charlotte Bühler on the subject of Schwärmerei: 'Love rapt in wonderment and freely given obedience, such as is never again in later life experienced so delicately and so deeply' (1936:27). Elisabeth Dauthendy, in a study of the

'New Woman' and love, published in 1900, sees intense friendships between older and younger women now as a glimpse of what love will be between men and women in the distant future: 'The blooming young woman in the fullness of her beauty and the mature woman in the fullness of her experience and her immortal hope for the coming life . . . united in that devotion with which only women can love.' The 'new woman . . . cannot tolerate the love of man as he is' and so for the time being she 'must look for friendship with woman' (Faderman and Eriksson 1980:41–4). Dauthendy is at pains to deny there is anything unsavourily Sapphic about this friendship, but this may be because there is nothing in-between-ist about her idea of it – there is no doubting the erotic quality of the way she depicts it (Faderman 1981:156).

Schoolgirl lesbianism relates to the experience of all women, both by acting as a touchstone of feeling for later life and also by pointing backwards to the primary mother-daughter relationship. Freud's essays on female sexuality and homosexuality (1920, 1931) posited women's essential bisexuality and stressed the fact that the adolescent female had to learn to transfer her affections from her first love object, her mother, to its 'normal' object, a man. His ideas on lesbianism echoed those in contemporary women's writings (eg. Reuter 1895, 1921, Weirauch 1948 (1919–31)), not only the stress on the importance of the mother-daughter bond as the founding form of lesbianism, but also the patriarchally disturbing implication that, if lesbianism is always potential in women and if transference of affections to a man is so traumatic, why on earth do women bother? Why aren't all women lesbians? Although never so baldly expressed as this, Freudian theory combined with current imagery to suggest that lesbianism was a typical and profound experience for women.

It is sometimes argued that *Mädchen* is not 'really' about lesbianism, but about a young girl who is missing her mother: Manuela sees in von Bernburg a substitute for her recently deceased mother. There is no doubt that this further intensifies Manuela's need for von Bernburg, but, in the context of the gynaecum tale and contemporary ideas about Schwärmerei and lesbianism, the mother–daughter quality of the relationship only makes it more lesbian, not less. The film in fact heightens it in a number of ways. As Gramann and Schlüpmann point out, Manuela's first feelings for von Bernburg occur when the latter interrupts Manuela telling Edelgard about her mother; when Edelgard leaves, lighting and performance combine to suggest that von Bernburg is to replace that mother in Manuela's affections:

The camera observes on Manuela's face the shift from the silent bearing of grief to the upsurge of desire. The eyes begin to shine, the mouth opens slightly and twists, a flare of the nostrils signals that her features are getting out of control – she smiles and in a flash passion breaks forth. The lighting works to let the whole face appear to be suffused with this feeling.

(1983b:30)

The good-night kiss, a maternal ritual, is portrayed with the cinema's conventions for the representation of erotic love: 'halo' lighting of the loved one, soft shadows to create romantic atmosphere, the isolation (even, as here, in a dormitory) of the participants through editing and lighting, the extreme close-up on the kiss, itself the supreme signifier of love. When von Bernburg gives Manuela her own clothes (figure 1.9), this is both the act of a

1.9 *Mädchen in Uniform* – von Bernburg gives Manuela one of her own slips, as a mother to a daughter, a teacher to a pupil or one friend and lover to another? (Taurus Film)

mother's care for her child's need and an erotically charged exchange ('She gave me a present, a petticoat. I've got it on'). The scene from *Don Carlos* has Manuela/Don Carlos declaring his/her love on bended knee to his/her step-mother/queen/beloved; when the latter says, 'Do you realise that it is the Queen, your mother, to whom these forbidden words are addressed?', she exactly expresses the frisson of the film's construction of lesbian desire.

The focus of *Mädchen*'s female-identified lesbianism is the central relationship but it extends beyond this. There is an attempt near the beginning of the film to assure the viewer that the girls are 'really' heterosexual, giggling over pictures of musclemen and male film stars, but this is put aside for the rest of the film: there is no talk of boys, no sense of being anything less than satisfied with each other's company. What is strongly suggested is the sense of solidarity between them.

Other films around this time also extolled such solidarity and one of them, *Acht Mädels im Boot* (*Eight Lasses in a Boat*), is especially close to *Mädchen*, not only in the slight similarity of their titles, but also in its sense of what binds the girls together: solidarity against male domination and erotic feelings for one another. Both films evoke a world of men and male power that confines its female protagonists. *Mädels* concerns a women's rowing team that meets and most of the time lives together in its own club house by a river. When one of them, Christa, discovers she is pregnant, the others say that she should stay with them, have the baby, and they will bring it up together. Only at the end does Christa leave the team, returning to the outside world, as her father and fiancé want. The leader of the club, Hanna, is clearly seen as a rival to Hans, Christa's fiancé: not only are their names similar, but there are visual rhymes as for instance when Hanna, wearing a vest top like Hans, picks up Christa when she faints just as Hans does earlier. Away from the club, Christa has to submit to a chain of male authority leading from her father through Hans to the doctor, a friend of both men, who will perform an abortion on her. She has no say in the matter and the film prefers the group's collective and nurturing response to Christa's pregnancy to the men's controlling and destructive one. When Hanna goes to Christa's father, he threatens to call in the police to get Christa back, causing Hanna to remark later to Christa: 'I nearly forgot what fathers are like. They want to be tyrants. They are all the same, yours and mine.' The men do get Christa back, but it feels like a defeat and the last shot is of Hanna and the others diving into the water in the brilliant sunshine.

Mädchen does not show the world of men, but its presence is signalled throughout the film. The Principal spells out the school's function of servicing men early on: 'We are teaching the daughters of soldiers and by God we shall produce the mothers of soldiers'. The opening montage, to the sound of bugle calls, of pillars, a church tower and statues of men in uniform or fighting naked, links the values of order and discipline to the male regimes of the military and the church. A similar montage occurs immediately after the dormitory scene, suggesting the world whose rules Manuela is transgressing with her effusive embrace of von Bernburg. As Rich notes,

> [b]arred shadows cross the women's paths, a sternly overbearing staircase encloses their every movement, a frantic montage marshals their steps into a militaristic gait, and even the school songs reinforce the authority of a demanding fatherland with a handful of schoolgirls in its grasp.
>
> (1984:104)

Lesbianism is central to the anti-patriarchal feeling of *Mädels* as it is to *Mädchen*. Hanna is the charismatic leader figure, with her broad shoulders and athletic prowess; as she emerges glistening from the river in one shot, one of the women strokes her arms, commenting on how beautiful they are. Her gestures with the other women, particularly it seems the prettiest, are those of a lover – holding their chin in her hand, rubbing her cheek against theirs. But *Mädels* does not go so far as *Mädchen* – directed by a man, Erich Waschneck, there is something voyeuristic about the frequent shots of women taking showers or getting undressed for bed and it draws back from making the erotic intensity of the women's relationships too glowingly explicit. With *Mädchen* the lesbianism is explicit and its link with the struggle against authoritarianism clearly indicated. The moment of explicit declaration, of speaking for love against its silencing, has strong in-between-ist resonances, but the wider revolt against the law of the father is achieved through structures of feeling in which female bonding, mother-daughter relationships and lesbian love are indistinguishable from one another.

AFTER *MÄDCHEN*

Mädchen was not banned or censored in Germany until the Nazi period, but there is an indication of the damage that it might have been felt to have done in a follow-up film, *Anna und Elisabeth* 1933.

Using the same stars and making their relationship the selling point of the film, it nonetheless aims to show how sick and twisted such relationships are.

Wieck plays a crippled lady of the manor, Elisabeth von Salis. She hears that a village girl, Anna (Hertha Thiele), can work miracles and has her brought to her. In Anna's presence, Elisabeth does start to walk and she persuades her to stay with her, keeping her from her fiancé Martin, an Aryan-looking youth dressed in Lederhosen. When Anna later leaves her, she throws herself from a cliff; as she dies, she says to Anna, 'I am free. I am happy. You will be happy too' – by her death, they are both delivered from lesbianism.

The reference back to *Mädchen* is clear not only in the casting but in other details. The sick character who dies is Elisabeth, von Bernburg's name, but the young woman who escapes her power is called Anna, a sound German name, unlike the exotic, Latinate Manuela. The final sequence cuts back and forth between Elisabeth climbing the cliff to throw herself off and Anna talking with Martin, during which there is a sudden close-up of Anna as it comes to her that Elisabeth is about to destroy herself. This is exactly the same as during the climax of *Mädchen*, where von Bernburg breaks off her confrontation with the Principal in a purely intuitive, telepathic realisation of Manuela's intentions. The difference is that Manuela is saved from self-destruction, a triumph of personal and collective lesbianism, whereas Elisabeth does succeed in killing herself and freeing Anna from lesbianism.

Anna und Elisabeth's fetid atmosphere and hysterical conclusion feel like an attempt to batten down the hatches on the emotions unleashed by *Mädchen*. Yet those feelings do still come through, with if anything greater intensity and ardour. Elisabeth is able to walk through her belief in Anna, they do have a transcendent communion as suggested by Anna's intuitive sense of Elisabeth's suicide – even at plot level, the strength of lesbian feelings is not denied, and the filmic treatment enhances it. In one sequence the two are together on the night before Anna is to be interrogated about her powers by a group of priests. In an extreme close-up of them, their faces glow against a chiaroscuro night sky; Anna's face is on the left, lower than Elisabeth, looking up at her as she breathes out an ecstatic 'Tomorrow!'. This dissolves to another extreme close-up of them (figure 1.10), but this time with positions reversed – Elisabeth lifts her face up to Anna's and whispers 'To-day!'. The night has passed as the lovers dissolve into one another.

As Schlüpmann and Gramann (1981:46) put it,

> At this point the film is completely unrestrained and builds up an erotic tension, completely forgetting the plot context for a moment. . . . In such images the film expresses a relationship of unconditional devotion, which elsewhere in the narrative it denounces as enslavement.

Anna und Elisabeth is clearly in some sense an 'answer' to *Mädchen in Uniform*. The pull in the former between the delirious evocation of lesbian desire and the simultaneous condemnation of it suggests the presence and force of the latter, so much so indeed that the film was banned within a fortnight of its release. *Mädchen*'s lesbianism was something that needed to be negated, yet to give it expression at all was to set its powerful emotions in motion. *Anna und Elisabeth* suggests just how powerful, inspiring and intoxicating a film *Mädchen in Uniform* was, and is. Many of the principal figures involved in both *Anders* and *Mädchen* – Hirschfeld, Oswald, Sagan, Schünzel, Thiele, Winsloe, Veidt – had to leave Germany when Hitler came fully to power, their lives endangered by, among other things, their association with such boldly gay/lesbian films. Yet

1.10 Luminous intensity between *Anna und Elisabeth*. (National Film Archive)

for most viewers now, *Anders als die Andern* is a museum piece, touching, moving and testimony to the role of film in gay struggle, but needing an act of imagination to see beyond its fragments. But *Mädchen in Uniform* still stirs audiences with its sensual, moving, exciting and defiant assertion of lesbian love.

2   Shades of Genet

One of the standard items in any listing, season or festival of gay films is *Un Chant d'amour* (*A Song of Love*), a twenty-odd minutes long, silent, black and white film made in 1950 by Jean Genet. It survives in poor, scrappy copies[1] and was not given a commercial release. In many places it was confiscated, banned or simply not shown, on grounds of taste or simple heterosexism. (In the post Clause 28 climate, it was banned by Hull City Council in 1989.) Even now it is not widely shown outside of the gay season context. On the one hand, it is easily perceived as sordid: much of the footage shows men masturbating in grotty prison cells; there are scenes of whipping and of a gun being forced down a man's mouth; there are penises, armpits, toe-nails and other body parts in close-up. On the other hand, many of the sequences – two men frolicking in a sylvan landscape; men making love in careful poses, with idealising lighting, their genitals shielded from view – are lyrical, beautiful, 'artistic'. In marketing terms it is too arty to be porn and too pornographic to be arthouse.

Chant would be even more obscure were it not for Genet's fame. It is perhaps his fame more than his work itself that has been so influential – there is, as it were, Genet and 'Genet'. Genet is the person who wrote poems, novels, plays and essays; 'Genet' is the idea we have of what that man and his work are like, an idea cobbled together as much from blurbs, critiques and other artists' homages to him as from the works themselves. One can say this of any writer – we don't come innocent to Racine or de Beauvoir, Agatha Christie or Alice Walker, we read them through what we have picked up about them – but it seems especially true of Genet. His name evokes a flavour, a set of images, a world – you don't have to have read his works to know what sort of thing you're going to get when someone says such-and-such is Genet-esque, nor to be able to catch the allusions to him in so many novels, films and theatre pieces or to grasp the significance of the frequent references to him in the major intellectual trends of the post-war years. Equally 'Genet' is central to the construction of a major strain in gay culture. He is both a known set of symbols for a homosexual existence and a reference point for argument about what homosexual existence is or should be. *Un Chant d'amour* can be, and has been, read and reread in relation to all this, and equally these readings have themselves produced (or even been accomplished by) a number of Genet-esque films, embodying the shifts in what the gay 'Genet' has been taken to be.

This chapter looks at all of the above. I begin with *Chant* in itself and in its historical context. Part of that context is the presence of Jean Cocteau (at the filming of *Chant*, in Genet's life at that time, in French gay artistic culture), and his work, important in its own right to an account of gay film, also provides a first set of interpretive frameworks through which to read 'Genet' and *Chant*. I then move on to subsequent frameworks provided by the shifts in the construction of homosexuality, through homophilia to liberation and beyond. Throughout I am equally interested in relating these frameworks to rereadings of *Chant* and to later 'Genet' films.

UN CHANT D'AMOUR

Un Chant d'amour consists of four interweaving elements. In order of introduction, there are first the prison sequences, which form a rudimentary narrative – a guard comes to the prison and spies in on the prisoners' cells; he sees men masturbating and two prisoners communicating with each other through the walls (these may be identified as 'the murderer', from a sign over the cell door, and 'the Tunisian', since this was the nationality of the anonymous actor (Mekas 1972:165)); he goes into the Tunisian's cell, takes off his belt and whips him, but the Tunisian laughs when the guard goes while the murderer smiles as he listens; towards the end, the guard goes back into the Tunisian's cell and puts his gun in the man's mouth, but leaves without pulling the trigger; the guard walks away from the prison. Secondly, there are shots of a garland of flowers being swung from a cell window and eventually caught by a hand coming from the next cell window. Although part of the prison sequence, the way they are repeated gives them a presence of their own separate from the narrative of the guard and the prisoners. Thirdly there are sequences shot in chiaroscuro lighting of men (including the guard in some shots) making love. Fourth, there are sequences between the Tunisian and the murderer, away from the prison, chasing and playing with each other in a woodland before beginning to make love.

Structure

Chant has settings, characters and incidents and most people find themselves approaching the film as if its basic structure is narrative. Each of the four elements has a narrative dimension. The prison *poison* sequences are the story of the guard's voyeurism and frustration; the chiaroscuro sequences may be seen to follow, albeit inexplicitly, a classic pornographic narrative from kissing through fellatio to coition; the woodland sequences are a playful chase and capture; even the garland sequences are narrative in that there is the suspense of the hand repeatedly missing the garland swung its way before finally, satisfactorily, catching it. What is less certain is the narrative connection between the elements.

Some see the whole thing centred on the guard – his view of the garland and the prisoners masturbating, his fantasy of having sex with men in the chiaroscuro sequences, his imaginings of the relationship between the Tunisian and the murderer. Others see the chiaroscuro as his fantasy, but the woodlands as the Tunisian's fantasy, or perhaps memory. The editing does not give definite warrant to either of these. As the accompanying chart shows, the non-prison sequences do not consistently follow shots of the guard (which would by cinematic convention make them clearly in his mind), nor do the woodland sequences only follow shots of the Tunisian. The non-prison sequences are several times preceded by a fade, further cutting them off from the narrative/character flow of the prison sequence. Point-of-view is fascinatingly manipulated by the film, as will be discussed later, but it is not organised entirely and consistently through the guard's gaze. There is a constant, highly controlled shifting across elements and points of view that suggests narratives but never insists on them.

A different way of approaching the film is suggested by its title: a *song* of love. Its organisation is as much like a melody, with repetitions and refrains, as it is like a narrative. As the chart shows, there is an almost classical formality about the film's structure, such that laid out a kind of pyramid shape can be discerned. The guard/prison narrative never disappears, but there is a gradual

Table 2.1   *Un Chant d'amour*: shot breakdown

SHOT*	GUARD	GARLAND	PRISONERS**	CHIAROSCURO	WOODLAND
1 (credit)					
2–3	guard outside				
4		garland[1]			
5	guard outside				
6–28			communicating through wall		
29–84	guard spying on prisoners FADE				
85		garland[2]			
86–7				chiaroscuro[1]	
88–104	guard whips Tunisian FADE				
105–21					woodland[1]
122–3	Tunisian (122) and guard (123)				
124–7				chiaroscuro[2]	

128–30	Tunisian and guard			
131–47	Tunisian and guard FADE			woodland[2]
148–51	Tunisian and guard FADE			
152		garland[3]		
153–60			chiaroscuro[3]	
161	guard			
162				woodland[3]
163–5	guard puts gun in Tunisian's mouth			
166	corridor			
167	guard outside prison			
168		garland[4]		
169		Tunisian pacing cell FADE		
170	guard walking away			
171		garland[5] – – – –	(garland drawn into next cell)	
172–(credits)				

SHOT*	GUARD	GARLAND	PRISONERS**	CHIAROSCURO	WOODLAND
		1 guard's p.o.v. 2 follows shot of guard + fade 3 as 2 4 guard's p.o.v. 5 follows shot of guard walking away.		1 follows fade + shot of garland 2 follows shot of guard 3 follows shot of guard + fade + shot of garland	1 follows shot of prisoner + fade 2 follows shot of guard + fade 3 follows shot of guard

* given the state of prints of the film, this numbering should be taken as indicative rather than definitive.

** i.e. the murderer and Tunisian in prison when unseen by guard.

introduction of the other elements towards and then away from a central apex formed by the interweaved chiaroscuro and woodland sequences. The symmetry is not rigid, but the sense of the pyramid is reinforced by the placing near the beginning and end of the only two sequences showing the prisoners independently of the guard's seeing them. The balance and poise of this structure is only seriously disrupted by the very last shot – but this then gives that shot all the more force. Strict symmetry would require that the last shot be the guard walking away but in fact it is the garland being at last caught and drawn in. This links it with those few shots of the prisoners unseen by the guard, where they try to communicate with each other as well as dancing (alone) and caressing themselves. Equally the last shot draws the threads of the film together: the garland of flowers occurs in prison, chiaroscuro and woodland sequences and is highly charged symbolically, as will be discussed below. Ending on a shot of the garland, and of one prisoner finally catching it from another, means ending on a shot of the prisoners and one clearly linked with gay sexuality.

This kind of formalism is characteristic of Genet's early poetry ('Le condamné à mort' 1942, 'Marche funèbre' 1945, 'Un Chant d'amour' 1948 – the latter has no direct connection with the film). As Jean-Marie Magnan (1966:153) puts it, 'On the subject matter of his song – crime, pederasty – Genet imposes the most conventional system of weights and measures. . . . The structure is rigid, the metre strict and impersonal, formalism predominates.' Such classical form is traditionally associated with elevated subject-matter in moral, class and sexual terms: the ethical precepts and concerns of the ruling class and their heterosexual arrangements. Genet, as orphan, criminal and pervert, is beneath or without class, morality or the heterosexual imperative. The effects of this use of extreme formality and the canons of beauty in the evocation of degradation and perversity will be discussed in a moment.

Imagery

Two things characteristic of Genet's use of objects as symbols, in all his work, are the way any one object may symbolise many different, often seemingly incompatible things, and the way that they generally symbolise the opposite of what they do elsewhere, in poetry or everyday life.

Both these qualities are exemplified in *Chant* by the use of flowers, a favourite symbol in his work. Formed into a garland, they are a rosary – flowers as religious symbols are suggested by the titles of two of Genet's novels, *Notre-Dame des fleurs* 1944 and *Miracle de la rose* 1945. Also as a garland, they are the chains of imprisonment. This more unexpected symbolism also runs through Genet's work, as in this passage from *Miracle de la rose*, where the transmutation of one symbol into another, and its religiosity, is spelt out in the description of the condemned prisoner Harcamone:

> the fervour of our admiration together with the burden of saintliness which weighed on the chain that squeezed his wrists – his hair had had time to grow, its curls were tangled over his forehead with the knowing cruelty of the crown of thorns – made this chain transform itself before our not really surprised eyes into a garland of white roses. The transformation began at the left wrist which it encircled with a bracelet of flowers and continued along the length of the chain, from link to link, until it reached the right wrist.
>
> (1951:233–4)

Flowers in *Chant* may also symbolise the criminals themselves, as they do in *The Thief's Journal*: 'there is a close relationship between flowers and convicts. The fragility and delicacy of the former are of the same nature as the brutal insensitivity of the latter' (1949:9). Finally, they symbolise masculinity and the male genitals.

Unlike flowers as rosary, but like flowers as chains and criminals, flowers as masculinity run exactly counter to what we expect flowers to mean, yet the association is perfectly explicit in *Chant*. In the first woodland sequence, the murderer has a garland of flowers attached to his waist, hanging down over his crotch. As his lover looks on, he caresses the blooms gently. A little later in the sequence, he takes the garland off and gives the Tunisian a flower; in close-up, the latter presses it to his nose. The placing of the flowers on the murderer's body suggests that the flowers symbolise the genitals. Yet this is hardly a 'phallic symbol' as conventionally understood: phallic symbols are hard, thrusting, usually connoting power. Flowers on the other hand are soft, delicate, powerless. Genet's flower as penis imagery goes against the grain of how male genitalia are 'normally' described. As Jean-Paul Sartre (1952:82) puts it, in a passage full of regrettable assumptions, 'that same turgescence that the male experiences as the violent stiffening of a muscle, Genet feels as the unfolding of a flower'. Hence in *Chant* the come-on gesture of stroking the penis becomes a thumb playing lightly over flower blossoms and the beginnings of fellatio are holding a flower to one's nose. The flower as penis in fellatio recurs in the chiaroscuro sequence, where one man takes into his mouth a flower held in the other's mouth (figure 2.1).

This kind of representation of the delicacy of masculinity goes beyond the use of flower imagery. Fellatio in the film is also represented in the sequence where the Tunisian blows smoke through a straw in the wall into the mouth of the murderer in the next cell (figure 2.2). The fragile straw (penis) and billowing smoke (semen) are both rather blatant sexual symbols and yet surprising ones within the usual representation of male sexuality. Again the imagery is taken up in the chiaroscuro sequences where one man transfers a lighted cigarette from another's mouth into his own.

The men in the film are to be seen as beautiful. As in Genet's writings, they conform to certain notions of machismo that have long functioned as a turn-on: they are muscled, short-haired, often hirsute, often unshaven or bearded, often uniformed. Yet although it was common enough to find such men exciting, it was not common to find them beautiful. Beautiful men in French cinema might be the 'classical' athletic type (Jean Marais, Henri Vidal) or the clean-groomed, regular-featured type (Jean-Pierre Aumont, Louis Jourdan) or the delicate, romantic type (Michel Auclair, Gérard Philipe) but the perception of beauty in men did not usually stretch to rough, criminal types. In Genet however the rhetoric of beauty is applied to just such types, as in this description from *Miracle de la rose*, where aristocratic and classical references are used, as well as words like 'delicate', 'elegance' and 'beauty', to describe a man who is also heavily muscled, dirty and dangerous:

> Bulkaen was leaning his elbow against the wall, so that his arm was over his head and looked like it was crowning him. This arm-cum-crown was naked, for his jacket, as always, was simply thrown over his shoulders, and that enormous bunching of muscle, his baron's coronet. . . , was the visible sign of the ten years of banishment – ten years of beatings – that weighed on his delicate brow. . . . At the same time I saw his neck whose skin was a little bit shaded with grime. . . . His right ankle was crossed over his left, in the way Mercury is always shown, and on him the heavy frieze trousers had an infinite elegance . . . his waist was slim, his shoulders broad and his voice was strong with a confidence that came from his awareness of his invincible beauty.
>
> (1951:237–8)

Chant does not use classical or noble allusions, but it does

2.1   A flower passed from mouth to mouth in a chiaroscuro sequence from *Un Chant d'amour*. (British Film Institute)

2.2   The straw through the wall in *Un Chant d'amour* – obvious yet delicate fellatio symbolism. (British Film Institute)

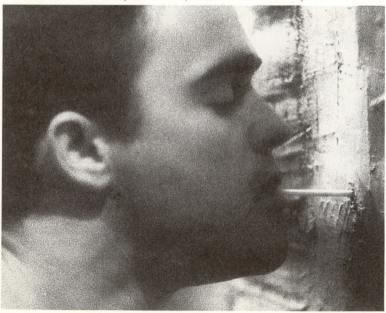

nonetheless present a similar beautification of a rough masculinity. In part this is achieved through the film's structure. Flowers link the men together, as has already been discussed, and the woodland sequences draw very directly on Romantic imagery of love. The chiaroscuro sequences in their studied use of lighting suggest a notion of the 'artistic': although sexually unambiguous, they do not show genitals or sex acts but a series of formal poses which stress, almost to the point of abstraction, line, shape, texture and surface.

Close-ups also allow us to dwell on the beauty of the men: the smoothness of the murderer's throat or the soft folds of another's trousers at the crotch. Some examples are more surprising still. There is for instance an extreme close-up of the murderer picking dirt out of his big toe-nail, which is poking through a hole in his sock. This is hardly the stuff that erotic dreams are made of, yet in Genet's writings such 'sordid' details are perceived as part of a man's beauty. In *Querelle de Brest* 1947, for instance, Querelle thinks over one by one Mario's 'diverse peculiarities', one of which is one of his thumb-nails: 'completely black, a very beautiful black, as if lacquered. There is no black flower and yet, at the tip of his crushed thumb, this black nail did make one think of a flower' (1953:195).

There are different views of how one should interpret this use of imagery and the structural formalism discussed above. One is that Genet borrows the conventions of what is beautiful and sacred in order to make the criminal and male beautiful and sacred too. Tony Rayns (1973:236) argues in similar terms when he writes of *Chant* having

> Genet's customary spirituality . . . the more remarkable in that the film is among the most intensely *physical* ever made, consisting largely of close-ups – faces, shoulders, crotches, phalluses, soiled clothing – all lent an almost Pauline purity by their isolation and the film's silence.

Others argue the opposite, that Genet negates the higher, holier values of conventional symbols by associating them with criminals, machismo and perversion. Richard Coe, for instance, suggests that Genet hates flowers, that his use of them requires us to see them and the value system they stand for as ugly, obscene, brutal (1968: 75–81). In this reading, it is not a question of transforming criminals and queers into good and respectable guys, but of seeing the straight world as itself criminal and queer. A third view is that there is no fixed moral valuation in Genet, just as there is no fixed point of view on the events in *Chant* and no fixed fictional world and story to be followed.

All three of these approaches can be applied to the structure and imagery of *Chant*, yet in many ways the first seems to come nearest to the feeling of the film. This is not necessarily because the other approaches are wrong about Genet's work in general, but because *Chant*, though undoubtedly very much a Genet work, is also touched by other gay cultural traditions, not least the figure of Jean Cocteau.

The immediate context

There was no publicly prominent gay scene, much less a gay movement, in France in the forties, the period in which Genet began writing. There was a memory of a highly developed scene in Paris from the turn of the century to the end of the twenties, with balls, cabarets and nightclubs, and celebrities such as the drag trapeze artist Barbette, the flamboyant aristocrat Robert de Montesquiou, and the writer and sometime actress Colette (Barbedette and Carassou 1981). Particularly famous was the grouping of well-to-do lesbians, many of them exiles, centred on the salons of Natalie Barney. It is characteristic of the French situation that figures such as Barney, Radclyffe Hall, Marguerite Yourcenar, Gertrude Stein, Renée Vivien, Djuna Barnes and Romaine Brooks should be celebrities, as well as – and because they were – highly esteemed writers and artists (Casselaer 1986; Benstock 1987; Jay 1988). The supreme example of the poet-as-celebrity is Jean Cocteau, who not only wrote 'poetry' in many media (writing, drawing, theatre, film, music) but was also involved in organising much of the entertainment and fashion of these 'années folles' (crazy years).

There was also an element of gay campaigning in the twenties, in the short-lived newspaper *Inversions* (four issues, from November 1924 to March 1925), the one issue of *L'Amitié* (April 1925) and André Gide's book *Corydon* 1925. The latter took the form of four dialogues in defence of homosexuality, arguing mainly from nature, though in terms of the fact of homosexual activity in the animal kingdom rather than third sex biologism. The title of the book (the name of one of the shepherds in the Pastorals of Virgil), its structure (recalling Plato's Socratic dialogues), and various references also invoke classical precedent for the acceptance of homosexual love. The use of nature and antiquity purify the subject of homosexuality, as does Gide's limpid prose style. This set the tone for the defence of homosexuality, up to and after the period in which *Un Chant d'amour* was made. Michel du Coglay in *Chez les mauvais garçons*, a book that protests its author's heterosexuality at many points, states the Gidean line as if it is obvious and common sense:

> Homosexuality, that attraction towards people of the same sex, has existed at all times. There's no point in making a great fuss about it, it will always exist. It is *in nature*, among animals just as much as among vegetables. Man cannot escape it. Those are the brutal facts.

> (1937:118)

The same position, with some other reasonable arguments, was taken by Paul Reboux in *Sens interdits* 1951 and this was to be the tone of the 'homophile' organisation, Arcadie, founded in Paris in 1954.

These voices were however quite isolated in the mid-century, with none of the glitter and display of the années folles to give their defence of homosexuality a wider public presence. This does not mean that there was no gay life. The writings of Maurice Sachs, Marcel Jouhandeau and Maxence van der Meersch, to say nothing of Genet and Cocteau, indicate the existence of a widespread, but now quite underground, gay scene, and not only in Paris. The second half of *Chez les mauvais garçons* is a rich catalogue of the cafés, restaurants, clubs, toilets, cruising areas and other meeting places of gay men in Paris in the thirties. Significantly, the first half details the lives of young male petty thieves and criminals. It establishes a link in terms of social status and perceived disposition between the criminal and the sexual underworld, not only by juxtaposing accounts of the two, but by dwelling on the sexual relations between the boys in the first half and pointing to male prostitution and stealing from clients as a major source of their income. As in the more literary work, there is an insistent linking of homosexuality with criminality.

In addition to the memory of the années folles, the isolated tracts and the continuing gay underworld, there was also an extremely prominent tradition within French literature of writing about homosexuality. In their study of gay and lesbian life in Paris in the twenties, Gilles Barbedette and Michel Carassou argue that

> as opposed to the German homosexual movement which was the creation of 'men of science', it is incontestably the case that

homosexuals in France experienced their first taste of freedom
when men and women of letters began to write on the subject.
(1981:102)

There was a lesbian and gay literature in Germany, as we have seen
in the previous chapter, but it was less influential there than the
legalistic and scientific lesbian/gay movement. The German gay
literary tradition differed from the French in at least three
significant ways, which also in part account for the decisive influence
of the latter in French life. Firstly, the German tradition was, from a
literary point of view, for the most part very traditional, even
conservative, whereas French gay writers were often at the forefront
of changes and experiments in literary form: varieties of symbolism
in Verlaine, Rimbaud, Huysmans and Lautréamont at the turn of
the century, explorations of the role of the narrator in the novels of
Gide and Proust, the involvement of Cocteau and Crevel in
surrealism. Secondly, much twentieth- and late nineteenth-century
gay writing belongs to a longer and not uniquely gay tradition of
French literature, so that the imagery of Genet, Verlaine and
Lautréamont can be linked to that of Baudelaire, de Sade, Villon
and others, writers, many of whom were themselves criminals, with
a facility for making poetry out of low life, degradation and social
damnation. Equally Proust can be linked to novelists like Balzac
and Zola, who, like him, used homosexuality as a telling part of
their panoramic account of contemporary society. The role of gay
writing in general literary innovation and its connection with more
deeply rooted French literary traditions together point to the third
difference from gay writing in Germany, simply that many gay
authors were considered also to be 'great' authors, good and
important figures on the literary scene. In other words, gay writing
had a general cultural prestige in France that it did not in Germany,
and that in a society which anyway traditionally accords particular
prestige to literature and the arts. The best example of this last
observation is Genet himself: it is hard to think of another country
where literary genius would be a sufficient argument to waive a
sentence to life imprisonment.

Genet's work in general belongs to that tradition mentioned
above that includes de Sade, Baudelaire, Lautréamont, Huysmans,
Rimbaud, Verlaine and others and was dubbed by Verlaine in 1884
'poètes maudits' ('accursed poets'). Three things place Genet here.
There is a fascination with evil, seen for instance as a source of
beauty (as in Baudelaire's *Les Fleurs du mal* 1857) or something for

abandoned, delirious worship (as in Lautréamont's *Chants de Maldoror* 1869). This fascination depended for its intensity on a strong consciousness of Christianity and, really, a belief in it: evil only retains its frisson if you actually believe in a metaphysics of good and evil, otherwise it is merely doing what other people consider evil and is little more than a desire to shock. If one does not grant them a strong belief in Christianity, the poètes maudits are merely a string of adolescent minded young men who wished to upset bourgeois and, often, feminine sensibilities. Secondly, there is an interest in criminality. De Sade wrote from prison, Isidore Ducasse (Lautréamont's real name) wrote as if he were a convict, Verlaine's imprisonment in 1873 (for shooting Rimbaud) was a cause célèbre. Even when there is not this direct or fake identification with the criminal, he or she symbolises in this tradition the outcast, a type of being beyond the pale of normal society, who throws the values and nature of that society into relief. Thirdly, homosexuality runs throughout all of this writing, even in writers with no indubitably gay identification. Lautréamont, for instance, who writes of 'you incomprehensible pederasts' with your 'shameful and almost incurable illnesses' (1966:286–7) also, as he writes, begins to be turned on by the excitement of that incomprehensibility and shamefulness:

> I have always experienced a wicked fancy for pale college youths and emaciated factory kids! . . . I even murdered (not so long ago!) a queer who didn't surrender himself sufficiently to my passion. . . . Why are you trembling with fear, you adolescent who's reading me? Do you think I'd want to do the same to you? You are absolutely right: beware of me, especially if you are beautiful.
>
> (ibid.:290–1)

The elements of evil, criminality and homosexuality are inextricably entwined in this tradition, and Gerald Storzer argues that this goes beyond the poètes maudits, so that even writers as apparently different as Balzac, Gide and Genet are similar in 'their obsessive preoccupation with the relationship between homosexuality and criminality' (1979:186).

Genet's work as a whole belongs in this tradition, but with a special intensity. The myth of his life emphasises his outcast state from the start by virtue of his being an orphan. He could have featured as one of du Coglay's mauvais garçons: he lived by crime, both theft and prostitution; he had spent years in prison. Christian imagery saturates his writings, and many critics argue, like Georges Bataille, that it is Genet's acceptance of the truth of the Christian moral order that gives his work its special intensity: 'He wants [abjection] because of a vertiginous propensity towards an abjection in which he loses himself as completely as the ecstatic mystic loses himself in God' (1973:150). Genet, in public perception, in what his writings claim about his life, is not playing at being the outcast, is not slumming – he *is* outcast, criminal, accursed, queer.

Not just in his personal circumstances but also by virtue of the period, Genet was even more the homosexual-as-criminal than any of the preceding poètes maudits: in 1942 homosexuality was made illegal in France for the first time since 1791 and remained so until 1982. Moreover, the various facets of gay existence mentioned above (the années folles, the tracts, the underworld, the literary tradition) should not lead one to think that the general climate for gays was easy and tolerant (cf. Lacombe 1988). Jouhandeau's *De l'abjection* 1939 and van der Meersch's *Masque de chair* 1958, roughly equidistant on either side of the making of *Chant*, indicate what social attitudes were and how deeply their authority could penetrate the soul. Jouhandeau ends with a 'eulogy' of the abjection to which his homosexual leanings have brought him because such abjection has in turn led to his seeking salvation in God. *Masque de chair* is a first person confession of the 'ignominy', 'evil' and 'defilement' of the narrator's homosexuality. When he writes of his outcast state, it is not in defiance or celebration, but in recognition of his worthlessness and his need for forgiveness:

> Who would still want this charred ruin, this thief, this drunkard, this adulterer, this committer of incest, this degenerate, this pederast, this invert, this monster, irremediably except for some miracle of grace caught in the toils of his vice? . . . . Rotten to the marrow, like a corpse, an object of disgust to others and to myself, there was no one left but God to save me from losing courage.
>
> (1960:158)

In various ways the writings of the poètes maudits are a rejection or an inversion of such attitudes, all the more intense for being produced in the context of them. Most write in a delirious style, words and images streaming across the page, heady, intoxicated. Genet is not like this. His writing, like *Chant*, has 'the beauty of a piece of jewellery' (Bataille 1973:165). The nearest one gets to the feel of the film in the poètes maudits tradition is perhaps Rimbaud and Verlaine's 'Sonnet du trou du cul'. This does not flinch from referring to excrement, wind, semen, all the while using the rhetoric of beauty. The very use of the sonnet form invokes an elevated tradition of love poetry stretching back through the great French sixteenth-century poet Ronsard to the Italian poet Petrarch:

Dark, puckered hole: a purple carnation
That trembles, nestled among the moss (still wet
With love) covering the gentle curvation
Of the white ass, just to the royal eyelet.
Threads resembling milky tears there are spun;
Spray forced back by the south wind's cruel threat
Across the small balls of brown shit has run,
To drip from the crack, which craves for it yet.

(1983:235)

This is comparable to *Chant*, even if the latter does not, beyond a very brief close-up of an erect penis, dwell on such conventionally 'obscene' details. Still we may relate it to the dirt in the toe-nail, or the close-ups of one prisoner's armpit, another's hairy chest, or another outlining with his hand the shape of his erection through his trousers, all the while associated with the visual poetry of garlands, woodlands and chiaroscuro lighting and held within a highly disci-plined formal structure.

One of the books Genet was on trial for stealing in 1943 was a rare edition of Verlaine's poetry. Perhaps it was *Hombres*, in which 'Sonnet du trou du cul' was published and which was not only rare but clandestine. Among those who attended the trial was Jean Cocteau who referred to Genet as Rimbaud (another link back to the sonnet), arguing that 'One cannot condemn Rimbaud'. As Milorad (1981–2:39) wryly observes, the judge 'who had just given a maximum sentence to a man who had stolen a bag of flour but who was not Rimbaud, acquitted Genet'.

Cocteau

Cocteau's intervention at Genet's trial saved the latter from life imprisonment (for persistent thieving) and brought him into the former's gay literary ambit. They had a brief affair and Cocteau got his publishers to publish *Notre-Dame des Fleurs* 1946 and did the illustrations for *Querelle de Brest* 1947. Genet wrote a play (*Héliogabale*, never published) in 1943 for Jean Marais, Cocteau's lover; *Les Bonnes* was produced by Cocteau's collaborator Louis

Jouvet in 1946 and closely inspired by Cocteau's 'spoken song' *Anna la bonne*; his scenario for the Roland Petit ballet, *'adame Miroir*, makes a Cocteau-like use of mirrors; and he wrote an unsparing eulogy of Cocteau in the Belgian magazine *Empreintes* in 1950, the year of *Un Chant d'amour*.

Genet had never made a film. Cocteau on the other hand was well established as a film-maker and just at the end of his most fruitful period of film-making. He had made *Le Sang d'un poète* in 1930, to great acclaim, but did not move back into films until the forties, writing scripts for several films including an adaptation of his play *Les Enfants terribles* 1950 and directing four films, including his most successful, *La Belle et la bête* 1946 and *Orphée* 1950. Although the producer, Nicos Papatakis, told Jonas Mekas that Cocteau had no influence on *Chant*, he was there 'almost every day' (Mekas 1972:164) throughout the shooting; given his charisma as well as his cinematic know-how, it seems likely that it would bear some of the marks of his work.

This does also seem to be a period in Cocteau's life where he was prepared to take more risks in the expression of homosexuality in his work than previously. That he was gay was an open secret, but most of his work presents homosexuality in a symbolic form that it is easy enough to miss. In the late forties however, several of his works are more explicitly gay. His illustrations for *Querelle de Brest* are frankly sexy, with exaggerations of nipples, body hair and genitals that are only slightly less extreme than in the gay porn images of Tom of Finland and others. *Le Livre blanc*, which had been published anonymously in 1928 but with a preface by Cocteau, was republished in 1949, and although Cocteau still did not explicitly claim authorship, the preface, and more sexy illustrations, clearly allied it to his work. The film *Orphée* is more homosexual than Cocteau's play, originally produced in 1926; as Al LaValley has argued, the heterosexuality of the Orpheus and Eurydice story is displaced in the film into a relationship between Eurydice and the angel Heurtebise, while Orpheus' passion is reserved for Death and the poet Cégeste, whom he has seen die in an accident. Although Death is played by a woman (Maria Casarès), it is a motif often associated with gay sex in Cocteau's work (as will be discussed below) and this is strengthened by the fact that Cégeste is also dead. Further piquancy is added by the fact that Orphée was played by Jean Marais, Cocteau's lover of thirteen years, and Cégeste by Edouard Dermit, his new lover of two years – gossip that was fairly widespread at the time.

Whether as direct or indirect influence, or because both men shared at the time the same gay culture (given its most extended expression in film by Cocteau), it is worth taking a look at Cocteau's film work, for its own sake and for the different take it offers on *Un Chant d'amour*.

Cocteau's work centres on the notion of 'poetry', the creation of beauty in works of art, regardless of medium. The question is, how to take this commitment to beauty. Cocteau often presented poetry as a sacred mission, the production of beauty out of the poet's imagination, a beauty that represents a higher truth than everyday reality. He drew on both myth and the unconscious (as conceived within psychoanalysis and surrealism) as sources of imagery unsullied by contemporary, contingent and conscious reality, enabling him, the poet, to create beauty. Yet Cocteau was also an entertainer and celebrity; much of his work, notably in film, draws attention to its own artifice and playfulness. So for many people Cocteau's views on the spirituality of poetry are themselves merely part of an elaborate and knowing charade, the conscious cultivation of the beautiful, of a glittering surface of manners, wit, style and form that is fully acknowledged as artificial and literally superficial.

Much of Cocteau's work uses the mythic figure of Orpheus as the embodiment of the poet and, as Arthur Evans (1977:68–9) points out, there is a strong tradition in classical literature linking Orpheus and homosexuality. The link between poetry and gayness in Cocteau is not however unique to him. The cult(ivation) of beauty has often been linked with male homosexuality. Marcel Eck, in his aspirantly objective psychological study of homosexuality, *Sodome*, averred that aestheticism is 'the great temptation for the homosexual' (1966:164) and takes Genet as the exemplar: since homosexuals by their nature live in a false world, they end up exalting the false as beautiful. There may however be other ways of understanding the link between aestheticism and homosexuality.

In various ways the link conflates different ideas and practices of sexuality and gender: manners became seen in the nineteenth century as the province of women and gay men are thought to be feminine; certain kinds of employment concerned with beautification (modelling, hairdressing, interior design) have been more congenial for openly gay men than have others; the widespread view of the aetiology of homosexuality in narcissism (discussed below) emphasises a concern with personal beauty. It may also be a resistance to the social place of homosexuality. Absorption in beauty is one strategy against, in Oscar Wilde's words, 'the sordid perils of actual existence' (which might include the dangers of outlawed gay existence); as an attention to surface and appearance, to getting these things right, such aestheticism is related to the need for gay people to pass for straight, to be adept at getting the appearances of normality right. Normality passes itself off as naturalness; the gay perception of the literal superficiality of normality has the effect of denaturalising the normal. At the same time, gay aestheticism doubts that there is any such thing as a natural way of being and thus the honest way of proceeding is to acknowledge the artificiality of reality. In this perspective the reality of appearance is always to be valued over the appearance of reality.

The ambivalence about Cocteau – transcendence or display? – is characteristic of Wilde and Genet too, and is perhaps itself a quality of that troublesome notion, the gay sensibility. It may well be that the ability to hold together a passionate belief in something with a concomitant recognition of its artificiality is a defining feature of much gay culture (Dyer 1986:154–5). Thus 'poetry' is both cult and cultivation.

The most obviously aestheticised parts of *Un Chant d'amour* are the chiaroscuro love-making sequences. They are in no way realistic and are strikingly different from the 'sordid' realism of the prison sequences. In the perspective of Cocteau's aestheticism, the chiaroscuro sequences are the 'truest' parts of the film. The prison merely shows the appearances of actual existence; the chiaroscuro presents the reality of poetry, the consciously chosen and constructed realm of the transcendent and the beautiful, not the unconsciously imposed constructions and restrictions of normality. This reading puts a different inflection to Eck's observation, made from within the citadel of unproblematic straight reality, that 'what is false and imaginary is for Genet richer than what is true, because the true transcends him whereas it is he who creates the false and imaginary' (1966:164).

Aestheticism in Cocteau is often realised through the image of the mirror. Mirrors aestheticise because they frame sections of reality and render them on a shimmering, one-dimensional surface: they make reality into beautiful pictures. The poet characters in Cocteau's films look at themselves in mirrors and then actually step into and behind the mirror into another world – they enter themselves and the magic of their imagination. In the second episode of *Le Sang d'un poète* (*Blood of a Poet*), the poet throws himself into a mirror through to another realm, represented as a corridor in a hotel, giving on to rooms in which a variety of strange and forbidden sights[2] may be spied through the keyholes; he is expelled from the mirror back into his room. Similarly Orphée steps through mirrors in pursuit of the beautiful emissary of Death and hence into the greatly to be desired realm of Death.

Mirrors also suggest narcissism, and this has been associated with homosexuality throughout the twentieth century. There are two logics to this association. Gay men fancy people like themselves (men) rather than unlike (women), therefore their sexuality must be an extension of their love of themselves. Or – women are naturally more narcissistic than men, and gay men are more feminine than straight men, therefore gay men are narcissistic. Guy Hocquenghem (1978:65–7) discusses the manifestation of the homosexuality-narcissism equation in psychoanalytic theories of the period. Freud, in his essay 'On Narcissism: an Introduction' had observed:

> We have discovered, especially clearly in people whose libidinal development has suffered some disturbance, such as perverts and homosexuals, that in their later choice of love objects they have taken as a model not their mother but their own selves.
>
> (1957:88)

In mid-century such ideas were common sense to the point of being thought self-evident. Reboux's *Sens interdits*, quite a sympathetic study of homosexuality, has a section on 'Their funny little ways', the first of which is narcissism (1951:153–6); similarly, Eck observes that homosexuals, 'when they are honest about it, are the first to recognise their narcissism, and even to boast of it' (1966:197). Milorad, discussing Genet's Cocteau-like ballet scenario '*adame Miroir*, describes the way the dancer (dressed as a US sailor) dances in front of mirrors, his reflection being danced by identically attired dancers until one of the reflections takes on a life of his own and 'leaves the mirror and dances an amorous pas de deux with the other, the whole thing forming a wonderful allegory of the relationship between narcissism and homosexuality, of the way in which homosexuality is born of narcissism' (1981–2:41). The equation of mirrors, narcissism and homosexuality can be traced in all Cocteau's works, even the least 'obviously' homo-erotic (cf. Susan Hayward's discussion (1989) of *La Belle et la bête*).

In the first sequence of *Sang* the poet is seen finishing a drawing of himself. When he looks at it, its mouth comes alive. He tries to wipe it off the canvas with his hand but instead it sticks to his palm. He presses it to his mouth – that is, he presses the mouth on his own self-portrait (his painting, his face) to his own mouth. Then his hand caresses his naked torso, before sliding down out of view of the camera; there is then a cut to his head thrown back, with eyes painted on his closed eyelids. The caressing hand with his own mouth in it disappearing below the waist, followed by a shot of his head thrown back, knocked-out but still wide-eyed, clearly suggests masturbation. As it stands, there is no particular reason to see it as specifically homosexual masturbation, but the context suggests it: not only that Cocteau was known to be gay but the dominant cultural perception of homosexuality as narcissism and narcissism as homosexuality.

Chant is narcissistic in the crudest sense: there are many images of masturbation in it. As the guard moves from spy-hole to spy-hole, he sees a series of men making love to themselves: the murderer does a little dance and caresses a tattoo on his right bicep; the Tunisian runs his hand inside his open-necked sweater over his hairy chest; a young white prisoner is first seen from behind, his body glistening with water, and then turns, simultaneously soaping his hair with one hand and his penis with the other; a black prisoner (in a sequence discussed below) caresses his penis hanging out of his trousers as he dances until he throws himself on to his bed.

Such imagery does not of itself make the prisoners' masturbation homosexual, and in fact the tattoo on the murderer's arm is of a woman. What makes the imagery homosexual first of all is the guard. We see what he sees, and see him playing with his penis beneath his trousers as he moves from door to door. In other words, what is homosexual about the sequence is its voyeurism, the fact that we are placed as a man being turned on by looking at men. At moments the prisoners play to this (the man washing turning round to the guard/us and displaying his soapy erection) or refuse it (the murderer stops masturbating and shields the bulge in his trousers from view). This voyeuristic structure is reminiscent of the corridor sequence in the second section of *Sang*. The poet spies through the keyholes into each room and sees a sequence of disquieting images suggesting clandestine activity, with sado-masochistic, lesbian and androgynous overtones. The possible gay dimension of such imagery is explicit in *Le Livre blanc*, where the narrator describes visiting a bath-house in Toulon in which it was possible to spy unobserved, though a two-way mirror, on 'young working-class men' bathing and masturbating. The description of them could be of the prisoner who is washing himself in *Chant*:

Standing up in the bath, they would look at themselves (and me) and begin by a Parisian grimace that bares the gums. Then they would rub one shoulder, pick up the soap and make it lather. The soaping turned into a caress.

(1983:65)

In *Le Livre blanc*, the man presents himself to himself in the mirror, it is only to the narrator because it is a two-way mirror. In *Chant* there is no mirror so the prisoner appears to present himself consciously to the guard/the camera/us. Perhaps the point in both cases is the playful ambivalence, blurring distinctions between narcissism, exhibitionism and voyeurism – do the men in the bath house really not know they are observed?; is the prisoner teasing the guard? In any case, the masturbating actor in *Chant* knows he is being watched, by the camera crew and potential audience, but he also knows that we, the audience, can never actually have him.

Part of the frisson of the film is that the guard – but, of course, not we – does cross the barrier (the mirror in the bath-house, the doors in the prison) and enter the masturbator's space. Yet once inside, he is unable to do anything sexually. He shoves his gun in the prisoner's mouth, which you could read literally as a substitute for his penis which he is too inhibited to put in the man's mouth, or symbolically as him putting his penis in the man's mouth but then unable to pull the trigger, suggesting that he cannot have an orgasm. One could relate this back to the timidity of the narrator of *Le Livre blanc* or more generally to the idea that the pleasure of voyeurism resides precisely in not making contact, in preserving the separation.

The masturbation in *Chant* only itself becomes homosexual when the Tunisian and the murderer are linked as lovers, through the straw in the wall and the woodland sequences. Details of this again recall other of Cocteau's works, situating it within the construction of homosexuality as narcissism. In particular there is a shot of the Tunisian, in the sequence near the beginning showing the two men unseen by the guard, in which he presses the side of his face against the wall, rubs it gently against the wall, kissing it (figure 2.3).

The positioning recalls a shot of Jean Marais in *Orphée* pressing his cheek against a mirror (figure 2.4) (cf. Harvey 1984:198, Lange 1983:292); it also recalls a particular incident with the two-way mirror in the bath-house at Toulon:

Once, a Narcissus who was pleasuring himself, brought his mouth up to the mirror, glued it to the glass and completed the adventure with himself. Invisible as a Greek god, I pressed my

2.3   Un Chant d'amour: 'the Tunisian' presses his cheek in longing against the wall. (British Film Institute)

lips against his and imitated his gestures. He never knew that the mirror, instead of reflecting, was participating, that it was alive and loved him.

(1983:65)

This man does not know (the narrator is sure) that there is someone on the other side of the mirror with whom he all but makes contact. The Tunisian on the other hand does know that there is someone behind the wall but does not make any sort of contact with him by this particular narcissistic act. It is only by breaching the wall, blowing smoke through the straw, that he is able to make contact. This sequence, moving enough without any contextual gloss, is all the more so when one sees it as an inversion of the voyeuristic consummation in the Toulon bath-house.

The other breaching of the walls, already mentioned, is the guard entering the Tunisian's cell. This has a further resonance with Cocteau's work in the association of sexuality with violence and death. René Galand (1979) argues that there is a sexual equation in Cocteau, whereby poetry = sex = death. The poetic experience is

2.4 *Orphée*: Orphée (Jean Marais) presses his cheek in longing against the mirror. (National Film Archive)

an erotic one involving a loss of self; the erotic apprehension of sexual beauty is poetic but also, in ecstasy (including orgasm), involves a loss of consciousness; thus both poetry and sex involve death, the loss of self and consciousness (albeit only temporarily). Galand traces this theme in Cocteau's work, showing how frequently love and death are associated for the poet figures and discussing such images as the hermaphrodite in the hotel room in *Sang* who lifts up its loin cloth to reveal a sign saying 'Danger of death'. Although Cocteau thus speaks of sex as 'fatal', this need not be read negatively: death is to be seen as a kind of transcendence, and the link of poetry and sex to death means that they too are avenues of transcendence.

Al LaValley suggests that the linking of sex with violence and death in Cocteau's work may be understood as a covert

> discourse of ritual sex, sado-masochism and taboo sexuality – the sleazy hotel corridor of *Blood of a Poet*, the labyrinthine world of male brothels and sleazy hotels in *The White Book*, Paul and Lisa's famous disordered room in *Les Enfants terribles* . . . the image of Dargelos subduing the young poet with the snowball, killing him, causing him to bleed profusely from the mouth in a shot held for a long time, with a horrible gurgling sound, in *Blood of a Poet*.
>
> (n.d.:12)

He argues that the slow pace of the latter may be understood as 'a kind of sado-masochistic ritual, probing into the self with religious and sexually taboo overtones that yield a peculiar form of erotic intensity in its very rhythms' (ibid.:15–16). Part of the eroticism of the female figure of death in *Orphée* resides in her bodyguards, a gang of motor-bike boys, helmeted and dressed in leather. They carry the beautiful Dermit (Cégeste) prostrate between them, his arms spread wide in the ecstasy of death. Such a view of sado-masochism is perhaps an example of that aspect of the 'gay sensibility' discussed above, whereby cult and cultivation happily co-exist. Here surrender to a heightened eroticism, believed in enough to be a turn-on, goes hand in hand with a full consciousness of the artifices of the role playing and ritual style involved.

Chant is also open to such a reading. Its rhythms are slow and deliberate, perhaps trance-like; the garland-as-rosary evokes religious observance. The guard beating the prisoner and later forcing a gun down his mouth can be seen as moments of pleasure. Will Aitken suggests that our identification with the guard may allow us to enter into 'the satisfaction that the guard finds in dominating'. He takes the woodland sequences as the Tunisian's fantasy and argues that their occurrence during the scenes of the guard's domination of him 'suggests that submission has its own secret powers' (1980:11). Our assumption that all the actors were gay (or, at the least, willing) might heighten the sense that these scenes of domination/submission are being played out for pleasure, the performers' and ours.

LaValley stresses that the taboo sexuality element in Cocteau is 'not fully articulated'. Certainly the reading of the guard's treatment of the prisoner as pleasurable sado-masochism goes beyond anything in Cocteau's work – even *Le Livre blanc*, the most sexually explicit of his writings, contains nothing like this. It is true that the narrator faints at the sight of the 'dark patches' on 'a young farm-boy' playing naked in a stream (1983:28) and is in awe of Dargelos, a boy at school, 'possessed [of] a virility far in advance of his age' (ibid.:32), but none of this amounts to sado-masochistic sex. Indeed, a sado-masochistic reading of *Chant* is far more Genet than Cocteau.

One of the most poignant episodes in *Le Livre blanc* concerns a sailor the narrator calls Pas de Chance, from a tattoo on his chest. He looks like a double of Dargelos and is described Genet-like as 'beautiful enough to move a flower' (ibid.:58). The narrator lets him wear his gold chain, which earlier he had recovered from his previous lover, Alfred. In the night, unaware that the narrator observes him, he takes the chain, 'kisse[s] it and rub[s] it on his tattoo'. He has fallen in love with the narrator. The next morning the narrator leaves, but returns, realising he has left his gloves behind. Before entering, however,

> I couldn't resist putting my eye to the keyhole ... PAS DE CHANCE had buried his face in my gloves and was weeping bitterly.
>
> I hesitated outside that door for ten minutes. I was about to open it when the face of Alfred superimposed itself with great precision on that of PAS DE CHANCE.
>
> (ibid.:57–8)

This feels very close to *Chant*. There is the imagery of a masculine-looking man caressing himself, including his tattoo, fantasising about the loved one, thinking he is unobserved (or at any rate acting as if that is what he thinks); a chain as a token of love; and the figure of the man spying through a hole on to a sexual scene. The poignancy in the novella resides in the narrator's exclusion from this, an exclusion deriving in part from the nature of voyeurism itself, in part from timidity (he feels that it would have 'ruin[ed]' his life to fall for such a man, though falling he was), in part because there is another man (who is, bitterest of ironies, his own previous lover). One could read a similar poignancy of exclusion in *Chant*: the guard observes the romance of others, albeit inferior others, a romance he cannot share in. His tragedy is that he is unable to express his desire except through violence (and even this is unconsummated) and has to walk away, leaving behind the final erotic consummation evoked by the garland at last caught and drawn slowly back into a cell. This is of course the most sentimental reading of the film, at the other extreme from the sado-masochistic reading. It makes the film far more Cocteau than Genet, or rather, far more Cocteau than 'Genet', the figure that emerged after Genet had disassociated himself from Cocteau and after the social and cultural construction of gayness had altered considerably from Cocteau's discreet, transcendent and playful homosexuality.

HOMOPHILE GENET

For the developing homophile movement of the fifties, Genet posed something of a problem. His growing fame meant that he could not be ignored, but the image of same sex relations in his work did not accord easily with that promoted by homophilia. He had either to be seen as a symptom of repression or else cleansed of his sordidness.

The term homophile was invented by Arent Van Sunthorst in Holland in 1949 and first used in France in the journal *Arcadie*, founded by André Baudry in Paris in January 1954. Just over a year earlier, in October 1952, the journal *Futur* had been founded, arguing for the acceptance of homosexuality on grounds of naturalness derived in equal measure from Gide and Kinsey, and identifying religious hypocrisy as homosexuals' main enemy (Girard 1981:31–8). *Arcadie* shared this perspective, but especially promoted the notion of homophilia rather than homosexuality. As Baudry put it in issue 71 of the journal:

> The word 'homosexual' describes sexual relations between partners of the same sex, while 'homophile' describes people who can only find erotic fulfilment (understood in the widest sense of the term: physical, psychological, emotional and mental) with someone of their own sex.

(Quoted in ibid.:49)

As with earlier third sex notions, the idea of homophilia was that it was natural and constitutive of personality. The problem with it, though, as Jacques Girard points out, was that it seemed to concede that sexuality is essentially sinful. Despite its recognition of church hostility, its tone savoured of the religious, as if it sought to cleanse gayness of sexuality, to stress instead the spiritual fulfilment of those people (homophiles) drawn to members of the same sex as themselves. Tactically it counselled discretion and non-confrontation and condemned effeminates; it made a virtue out of the necessity of concealment, proclaiming that gay people should be invisible to the rest of the world, promoting a 'dignified and virile secrecy' (ibid.:51). Cocteau, who contributed a drawing and message of support to the first issue of *Arcadie*, was, with his charm, covertness and literary standing, the model homophile, not Genet.

The homophile perspective on film is suggested by an article by Raymond de Becker in *Arcadie*, in which he argued for the need for 'un cinéma homophile'. This would consist of good films (not requiring the audience's indulgence), accessible to heterosexuals and not just dealing with 'l'amour des garçons'. He saw the latter as insufficient as a theme for a film, because

> homophilia cannot be reduced to love between men, and still less to sexual adventures of men with each other, it implies a general disposition, a particular view of life, an attitude towards the world which colours all thoughts and actions.
>
> (1960:98)

Chant is mentioned respectfully in passing, but it is too single-mindedly about 'l'amour des garçons' to count as a harbinger for homophile cinema. *Orphée*, rather, is the exemplary homophile film because it 'unveils an inner world to which homophilia is one of the doors' (ibid.:99).

In a later book *L'Érotisme en face* 1964, de Becker was again respectful of Genet, but saw his cult of evil and degradation as an expression of the oppressive situation of gay people in a Judaeo-Christian culture. Moreover, while Genet's cult may have a kind of purity, still 'it does not make any less sterile the hope all homosexuals have for seeing their particular characteristic admitted into society' (1967:129).

The homophile wariness of Genet is understandable enough. On many occasions his work has been a gift to homophobia, easily appropriated as the living proof of how sick, neurotic and degraded homosexuals are. One of the earliest pieces of writing on Genet, in the influential Catholic journal *Esprit*, refers to *Notre-Dame des fleurs* as 'a vile thing . . . on the edges of pornography', though it does have the grace to see Genet as symptomatic of society at large – if it is 'to the shame of our civilisation that it has suppurated someone like Jean Genet, among others' (Rabi 1951:741), still 'the shame we feel on reading these works is our own shame' (ibid.:745). Later writers have lacked even this perspective. Philip Thody (1969) argued that Genet's work is a systematic denial of the defence of homosexuality put forward by the Homosexual Law Reform movement (the British equivalent of the French homophile movement), to the point that:

> If this is what it is like to be homosexual and a rebel against society, one is tempted to say, then I'm jolly glad I'm normal. . . . Not only does [Genet] encourage the ordinary person to congratulate himself on his normality. He also provides valuable ammunition to those who would impose their own heterosexual norm upon society, and refuse to tolerate any deviations whatsoever.
>
> (72)

Thody manages to hang on to a notion of tolerance or pity; a more recent example illustrates how readily Genet is to hand to support still nastier twists in the homophobic litany. In the journal *Salmagundi*, Larry David Nachman (1983) focuses on Genet's supposedly relentless and anonymous promiscuity. He drags in C. A. Tripp's dubious study *The Homosexual Matrix* to provide empirical evidence of the typicality of this amongst homosexuals and then excitedly adds a postscript about the recent discovery (this is 1982) that all this promiscuity may have 'bombarded and undermined' gay men's 'immunological system' (372). Genet thus becomes the apostle of AIDS.

In *L'Érotisme en face*, de Becker traces the internalisation of such homophobia in homosexual cinema. He refers to *Chant* (which he grants 'a prevailing poetic quality') in the context of discussing another film, *Couronne d'or*, made by Gilles Velon (c. 1935) and presumably lost (cf. Limbacher 1983:523):

> It is full of magnificent imagery frequently spoilt by an over-emphatic sound track. The film presents the love of two boys who go to the extent of celebrating their wedding in a church. Death strikes down one lover whilst the other sees his face decompose and his body fade away as he lies in his arms.
>
> (1967:134)

De Becker sees it as very much a Christian work. Despite the intentions of its director, 'it makes death triumph over life, solitude over love, the sense of guilt over the positive act of will' (ibid.). In this way both *Couronne d'or* and *Chant* are seen as works scarred by the 'Judaeo-Christian scourge' (ibid.:135). It is not surprising that gay films, like other gay art, should produce such images of 'guilt, of disgust with life and society, the attractions of death, even perhaps the delight of criminality' (ibid.:134) in this society, but it is nothing to be enthusiastic about. Later gay films are open to similar interpretations, such as the 1980 Curaçaon 8mm film *Apocalypse – K – Distranjo*, with its guiltily ecstatic or ecstatically guilty images of a young man making love with Christ on the cross or the 1982 Greek film *Angelos* with its concatenation of the 'Genet' mix of sailors, drag, sado-masochism, prostitution, death, gifts of flowers, and Christianity.

Two of the earliest 'Genet' films, however, *Le Prisonnier* (*The Prisoner*) and *Possession du condamné* (*The Condemned Man's Possession*), suggest that it was possible to take much of the imagery of *Chant* and cleanse it of guilt and disgust, even endowing it with the spirituality that Girard detects in the writing in *Arcadie*. They suggest different aspects of homophilia, the former emphasising notions of camaraderie, the latter evoking transcendence through love. Perhaps neither is, by a strict definition, a gay film. The sexuality of their makers is unknown, perhaps discoverable through gossip or interviewing, but definitely not marked by the film text; equally, sexuality as subject-matter is either probably absent (*Prisonnier*) or in *Possession* inexplicit, unspecific, spiritual not genital. Yet these qualities are in part what suggest their closeness to a homophile perspective. The fact that they do not declare their makers' sexuality and are unclear about their subject-matter accords with the clandestine, equivocally erotic character of the homophile project, makes them more, not less, homophile.

Le Prisonnier is a film that was never produced. In 1949 Genet worked with Roger Vaillard on a script for it, to be made by Pierre Chenal (already a well-respected director); however, the chief backer withdrew, possibly because Genet had not yet become an acceptable name in artistic circles (and Vaillard had communist connections). Based on a novel by Hans Fallada, it told of a man who leaves prison but commits another murder and returns to prison and 'la chaude amitié qui y règne' ('the warm friendship which prevails there'). It was to open and close with the image of a piece of string with a screwed-up piece of paper on the end of it being swung back and forth from out of a prison cell window; in the opening sequence a hand catches it and draws it in; in the final section, the same happens, but this time the film cuts back to inside the cell and the man (the film's hero, Julien) unfolding the paper, finding a cigarette, match and the message, 'Les copains te souhaitent la bienvenue' ('Your mates say hello'); he begins to smoke the cigarette and '[s]on visage reflète enfin la sérénité qu'il n'avait plus connue depuis son départ de la prison' ('his face shows at last the serenity he had not felt since he left prison') (Virmaux 1986). This clearly recalls the swinging garland in *Chant*, here linked to a general sense of the camaraderie of prisoners, with the sexual symbolism possible but less insistent.

Possession du condamné was made in 1967 in Belgium, directed by Albert-André Lheureux, an avant-garde theatre director in Brussels and produced by Robert Malengreau, who went on much later to make several short gay films and help run the Brussels gay 8mm film festival. It is inspired by (rather than being a direct version of) Genet's poem 'Le Condamné à mort', and has a clear structure, strongly reminiscent of *Chant*.

> In the opening section the camera moves along rough stone walls, showing a series of men (about seven in all) alone or in pairs; for the most part they sit or stand still but occasionally interact, one giving another a piece of stone, one running his hand into another's hair above his brow. Suddenly the film cuts to an exterior location in a forest suffused with light, with two of the men from the previous section running after one another, ending on a brief close-up of one kissing the other's naked waist (figure 2.5). The film now cuts back to the earlier prison-like setting.

> The men move about and the camera at one point tracks around the whole group who look back at it. They begin to move forward, with one of the men featured in the forest sequence in the middle. They move in formation, suggesting the march to the scaffold and as they move the film cuts, so that they appear to move magically outside to a ruined church. When they stop, the two men from the forest sequence make love – one inhales smoke from the other's cigarette, one kisses the other's neck and rubs his cheek against his shoulder and, framed by a shaft of light in the shape of a vaulted church window, they lie naked on top of one another in a series of poses, almost still but for slight caressing movements of the hands. Then there are a series of shorter shots, with one man throwing his head back in langourous ecstasy, and a

2.5 A pure homophile kiss in *Possession du condamné*. (National Film Archive)

succession of close-ups cross cutting between one shaking his head ecstatically and the other looking up to the sky. This ends on a shot of one of the men laid out on the floor with blood trickling from his mouth. There is now a cut to him running through woods, out across cracked mud flats and finally off into a dazzlingly light horizon behind which he disappears.

The elements recall *Chant*: prison interiors, sylvan exteriors and the chiaroscuro sequences in *Chant* here suggested by the formally posed love-making towards the end. Yet their combination and treatment creates a very different atmosphere, and not only because there is no guard figure.

Chant is tightly structured with only the last shot of the garland disturbing its rigorous symmetry; the different sequences are organised as refrains with the overall structure and pace of the film determining their ordering, rather than one sequence calling forth the next. *Possession* on the other hand is organised as a progression from the confinement of the prison sequences to the release of total open space in the final shot. At the centre of this progression is the moment when the men appear to move out of the prison and into the church, as if miraculously freed of their confinement. The earlier, slight expressions of affection are now full-blown expressions of love. The woods appear twice: before the movement to the church they figure (as in *Chant*) as an idealised, romantic image of love and freedom which is striking for its utter difference from the prison world; after the church sequence they are a realm that can be entered on the way to the final release of the horizon in the final shot.

The ordering of the sequences creates a progression out of confinement and this is given a further élan by the transitions between sequences, which are always placed at moments of physical expression between men, each emphasised by the filmic treatment: repeated shots from different angles of one man running his hand in another's hair at the end of the first sequence; a sudden extreme close-up (following a series of fast-moving mid shots of men running) of a naked waist being kissed at the end of the second (the woods); and at the end of the church sequence, fast cross cutting between yearning gestures (one head shaking ecstatically, the other looking up to the sky) and a sudden cut to an overhead angle (never used before in the film) showing a man with blood trickling out of his mouth, suggesting orgasm or death or at any rate extreme physical experience. Each such moment calls forth the sequence that follows, each of which is a step closer to release: the woods, the movement out of the prison into the church, the release through the woods to the infinite horizon. There is no return to prison.

Not only the overall organisation of the elements but also the way they are treated are very different in the two films. The prison in *Possession* is from the start less rigidly laid out, less strictly like a prison, with the men not kept agonisingly apart. The camera movement (virtually absent in the prison sequences in *Chant*) and fluid editing create a loose space, with cells and corridors opening out into each other, while the vague, rather inexpressive relations between the men suggest at the least a sense of connection and identity between them. The space and relations make possible the 'magic' moment when the men all walk out of the prison into the church; nor does it come as a surprise when the men appear to act as a congregation for the lovers, undressing them, surrounding them. Thus love and freedom grow out of – and away from – the prison ambience.

Even more different from *Chant* is the use of light. *Possession* is a progress towards the light, with full religious overtones. The wood sequences in both films are brightly lit, but in *Chant* always shot at ground level, often slightly tilted down, whereas in *Possession* the camera often points to the sky, culminating in the final shot of the film. The love-making sequences in *Chant* are shot in studied chiaroscuro lighting, moulding the flesh; in *Possession* the couple are flooded with light almost to the point of being rendered translucent. The effect of a transcendent image of love is further heightened by the vaulted window shape formed by the shaft of light in which they lie, reminding us of the church setting. Here Christian imagery enhances a sense of the beauty of same-sex love.

The clarity of its structure, its rhythms of release, the emphasis on light, as well as the spareness of the artistic means employed, all also distinguish *Possession* from the poem by which it is inspired. 'Le Condamné à mort' uses rich, 'poetic' imagery and explicit sexual description; it expresses the yearning of a young murderer, his desire to make love, to be punished and forgiven, before his execution; there is a sense of delirium, with the poem ending on the realisation that today is not after all the day of his execution. The film by contrast has the men make love (not just yearn to do so), but without the genital celebrations of the poem, and they are released from confinement, not stuck with it.

Possession suggests the homophile perspective in its under-sexualised, religiose representation of same-sex relations and also in two ways in which it seems to disown the homo-erotic images it presents. It opens with a quotation from the Marquis de Sade (becoming an acceptable name in avant-garde circles in the sixties), asking when governments will come to prefer 'the science of understanding man to that of imprisoning him and taking his life'. The tone is at once set for a humanitarian protest. Perhaps this can be interpreted specifically in relation to imprisoning rather than understanding homosexuals (the latter a homophile demand, of course), but equally it allows the homosexuality to come across as merely a metaphor for the inhumanity of imprisonment. Secondly, the film is almost entirely lacking in point-of-view shots so that there is little sense of the camera/us entering the desires and emotions of the characters. *Chant* plays with this to implicate the film-maker and the spectator in its desires; by contrast *Possession* seems to hold back, as if making a point about imprisonment and, maybe, homosexuals, but not really owning homosexual desire as its own.

SEXUAL POLITICAL GENET

> Tout le monde y trouve son compte, du militant à la
> macho-queen.
> (There's something for everyone in it, from the
> militant to the macho-queen)
> (Yann Beauvais in *Gai Pied*, on the occasion of a screening of
> *Chant* in December 1980.)

Other Genets emerged out of the gay and women's movements from the early seventies onwards. These Genets themselves depended on radical shifts in the general perception of Genet, marked by the appearance of two books, Jean-Paul Sartre's massive biography *Saint Genet, comédien et martyr* in 1952, and Kate Millett's chapters on Genet in *Sexual Politics* 1969.

Sartre's Genet is an existentialist hero. In Sartre's philosophy the great enemy of human freedom and happiness is 'bad faith'. We are socially determined, that is, a product of our society and times; we are made by society. The existentialist issue is what we make of what we have been made. Bad faith consists in either denying the reality of what one has been made or, even worse, not taking possession of it, not owning it. Freedom consists in choosing to be, and living to the full, what society has made of one. Genet is an existentialist hero because he is what he is, because he is – fully inhabits and lives out – what he is – the position that social attitudes have accorded him. In the words of one of the chapter headings in *Saint Genet*, 'J'ai décidé d'être ce que le crime a fait de moi' ('I have decided to be what crime has made of me') (1952:64): crime is the social system that designates certain acts wrong and certain people 'criminals'; the existentialist hero, Genet, is the one who fully accepts this social designation and lives it out defiantly. This is not the contrite acceptance of what one is, nor yet pathologised ('I can't help it') apologetics for it; it is saying, 'You say that is what I am, OK, that is what I am, and I am going to be it to the hilt'. Hence Genet turns everything designated criminal – murder, theft, homosexuality – into things to be sought, desired, pursued and venerated, not to be avoided or disavowed. Even punishment and degradation are to be welcomed, the more extreme the better, because they allow one to taste to the full the reality of what one is and what one has therefore decided to be.

Millett's *Sexual Politics* was one of the books that seemed to relaunch feminism at the end of the sixties. Acknowledging Sartre's work, Millett sees Genet as the male writer who tells the truth about sexism.[3] The gay characters in his work are a metaphor for the state of relations between men and women in society because of 'the perfection with which they ape and exaggerate the "masculine" and "feminine" of heterosexual society' (1969:17); his work is an analysis and exposé of society's 'view of sex as a caste structure ratified by nature' (19). Precisely because everyone in Genet's work is male, the fact that they are playing out roles, and the exaggerated form that this takes, make one see the roles, and the notions of masculine and feminine nature they embody, as just roles, just notions. Moreover, while Genet may worship macho men he also exposes them for what they are, he shows that to be male 'is to be master, hero, brute and pimp. Which is also to be irremediably stupid and cowardly' (17). And while he asserts that '[m]asculine is superior strength, feminine is inferior weakness', still there is one exception: 'Genet has jealously reserved intelligence and moral courage for his queens' (340). Thus Genet both exposes the vicious reality of sexual oppression while at the same time indicating the strategies of survival and resistance in the feminine principle, exemplified in his work by the queens.

Neither Sartre nor Millett discuss Genet's film work, but what they discern in him – the sense of a defiant homosexuality in the former, an anatomy of sexual oppression in the latter – is the foundation of the gay and feminist appropriations of his imagery and tone, beginning with new and much extended readings of *Un Chant d'amour*.

Many of the themes of gay liberation as they apply to *Chant* are clear in Vito Russo's account of the film in *The Celluloid Closet*:

> [In the film] the need for fantasy grows from the cravings of men trapped in prison cells and driven to furtive homoerotic liaisons that desperately attempt to approximate tenderness and affection. Plaintive images of hands reaching through cell windows for symbolic union clash furiously with sadomasochistic visions of guards using dominance, submission, masturbatory fantasy and sex as power to get a little contact. [It is an] unforgettable reaction to the restrictions placed on the male role in society, told in almost pleading terms, on behalf of a subculture filled with unrequited passion and social despair.
>
> (1981:98)

Like the homophile de Becker, the gay liberationist Russo sees in the film evidence of the oppression of gay men ('trapped', 'driven', 'social despair'). Borrowing from Millett, however, this oppression is related to the oppressiveness of sex roles and, drawing on gay liberationist conventional wisdom, those who enforce gay oppression are seen as repressed gays (a point also made by Sartre), hence the guard acts as violently as he does to get the 'little contact' his role denies him. Within this situation of oppression, gayness remains an essentially benign sexual-emotional impulse ('homoerotic', 'tenderness', 'affection', 'passion'). It is the wider social analysis and the perception of a positive and alternative sexual identity within a context of oppression that makes this gay liberationist reading different from a homophile one.

Millett identified in Genet a process of denaturalisation and demystification of sexual oppression. This basic perception lies behind some still later analyses of *Chant*, influenced by developments in feminist film theory. The latter had initially concentrated on the way women were represented in film, but some theorists felt this was inadequate. The problem was not so much what was shown as how it was seen: it was how men looked at women, and how cinema reproduced that way of looking, that was significant. Looking and being-looked-at were part of the dynamics of sexual domination: in the act of looking at women, men put women in their place of subordination. Using ideas taken from psychoanalysis, mainstream cinema was argued to organise everything as if from a male point of view and, by playing on various psychic mechanisms, to massage the male spectator's ego, making him feel that he i̶s̶ control of the image, calming his subconscious anxieties, seeming t̶o̶ subdue the threat that woman poses him. Women figured in this process merely as images in the drama of the (temporary) satisfaction of the male psyche. In these ways, the organisation of looking in film is a kind of sadism, exulting in male control over women and disregarding the reality of women in the process.[4]

In this context *Chant* becomes a fascinating film, because it is so much about looking. The prison sections are organised around the guard. He looks into the cells and we see what he sees: not only does the film use the standard organisation of editing to establish a male point of view, but it draws attention to this as voyeurism by emphasising the peephole and by the fact that we are seeing intimate and private sexual acts. It is an act of looking that already goes against the grain of mainstream cinema by the fact that this is a man (who is supposed to do the looking) looking at other men (who are not supposed to have to be looked at, especially by other men). On top of this the film complicates the patterns of looking. At several points the prisoners look back at the guard/us, breaking the spell of pure voyeurism. We get shots of what they see, the guard's eye through the peephole, the instrument of gazing isolated and abstracted. Some of these shot/reverse-shot sequences are mis-matched, which Laura Oswald argues draws attention to their construction.[5] Finally the guard, the person doing the looking, is also in the erotic chiaroscuro sequences, whose posing and lighting most obviously offer him to us as a person to be looked at.

Several critics have observed these aspects of the way the film organises point-of-view, looking and being-looked-at, but their interpretations of how this works are significantly different. The theory had developed within feminism out of a desire to subvert and destroy the pleasures of male voyeurism. This clearly informs Oswald's article in the journal *Enclitic*, which argues that *Chant*'s shifts of viewpoint are threats to 'the hegemony of the male look as the organizer of erotic discourse' (1983:106). We are invited to share the guard's voyeurism, but are then forcibly reminded of what we are doing and of the fact that this is a cinematic construction – we are denied the pleasures of untrammelled voyeurism. Further the film links the implicit sadism of voyeurism to the explicit sadism of whipping and rape (the guard forcing his gun down the Tunisian's mouth). The manipulations of point-of-view mean that we both share but then are distanced from these pleasures, so that the film becomes 'an ironic reflection on the spectator's perverseness, on the

y of the look and on the sadistic origins of scopic
Jane Giles makes a similar point when she argues
)th recognises the powerful attractions of voyeurism
structures', but she also acknowledges that the film
he lovers who cannot see one another, 'the pain
1g unable to see' (1988:105). Oswald's account seems
to suggest that *all* looking is perverse, whereas Giles suggests that
much depends on the power relations between people: the guard
looks at the murderer differently from the way the Tunisian would
look at him. Both however suggest that the film enforces a reflection
upon, and disturbance of, the pleasures of looking. Gay critics have
seen it rather differently.

Will Aitken in an article in *Gay News* observes the same play with
point-of-view. The longish sequence of the prisoners unseen by the
guard draws us into their lives and feelings, all the more effectively
to wrench us into the guard's consciousness. We peep in on the
prisoners with the guard, until one of the prisoners sees him/us
looking and turns away:

> The guard backs away from the peephole, ruefully rubbing his
> own hardened cock. We in the audience have surely been
> similarly aroused long before this – the incessant concupiscence of
> the prisoners is calculated to produce that effect.
>
> (1980–81:11)

We, like the guard, have been turned on and then cheated because
we haven't been allowed to go on looking at the prisoner
masturbating. As a result, says Aitken, we share the guard's
frustration and so at 'some level we even understand when he
barges into the cell of [the Tunisian] . . . and beats him with his
belt, then pushes his gun down his throat' (ibid.). It is not however
to teach us a sexual political lesson that the film operates like this;
on the contrary the film's teasing form is a sophisticated kind of
sexual pleasure. The sadism and the distancing are all part of the
turn-on. 'The gun probing the throat' is 'the most disturbing' and
'the most fascinating' image in the film:

> it satisfies the anger we share with the guard at being deprived of
> the tattooed prisoner's orgasm and makes us fully aware of the
> satisfaction that the guard finds in dominating, while [the
> Tunisian's] response . . . suggests that submission has its own
> secret powers.
>
> (ibid.)

The shift in point-of-view, in this account, is at the heart of the film's eroticism: we are aroused by identifying with the prisoners, then by being a voyeur on them, so that when we (with the guard) come to punish them the film takes on a delirious erotic flavour:

> This dual identification with oppressor and oppressed, with the looming guard and the kneeling convict, makes for discomfort and confusion. . . . Neither role feels right on a moral or political plane . . . although Genet shows us that, at least in terms of arousal, they fit together just fine, like some libidinous dream of complete self-sufficiency: auto-erotic S–M.
>
> (ibid.:11–12)

What is perverse in Oswald is pleasure in Aitken, and what cuts across arousal in her is what heightens it in him. He acknowledges the challenge this poses to reason, but does not see it posing any problem to pleasure. This difference is not surprising – Oswald writes out of a tradition that is both normative and homophobic and which analyses pleasure in order to combat it, whereas Aitken writes out of a gay liberationism that embraces the exploration of all forms of sexual expression.

There is a similar feeling in Richard Kwietniowski's piece on the film, published alongside a shortened version of Giles' article in the lesbian/gay magazine *Square Peg* in 1988. He too sees it as breaking with mainstream cinematic conventions (though here those of pornography), in its treatment of the penis. Where in porn the penis '(the "star of the story") must always be *doing something*', in *Chant* it figures in isolation: the 'phallus, bald and wanting, becomes a sign for men aroused by themselves' (37). Yet this break with the pleasures of porn is clearly itself a source of pleasure, not the kind of reprimand that Oswald sees Genet administering.

'Genet'/*Chant* figures as a revealing reference point for the debates about politics and pleasure that have characterised feminist and lesbian/gay politics, in fact since their inception and with increasing clarity through the eighties. The impulse to be critical of pleasure (since its forms are the constructs of a patriarchal, homophobic society) meets head-on with the impulse to assert the rights of pleasure (sometimes seen as the return of the repressed, sometimes as turning back on society the objects, and persons, it has deemed 'bad'). I want to trace here two of the ('Genet' relevant) directions developing out of this – ethnicity and racism, sado-masochism and radical perversity.

If one moves beyond simply noting the fact of racial difference in

Chant in passing (as I have been doing), a whole new issue of the film's politics and pleasures emerges. There are two non-white men in the film: the Tunisian and one of the other prisoners spied on by the guard, a man of Southern African descent whom I will refer to as the Negro (an apparently descriptive term with an appropriately problematic weight of historical connotation). The presence of these performers would make a difference, even if the film did not treat them any differently from the white characters. Ethnic difference is always already signifying. As regards the relation between the guard and the prisoners, for instance, it might seem that the latter are all in the same boat, equally subject to the guard regardless of race, and that he treats them all in much the same way. Yet the moment one acknowledges the history of black subjection to white, any merely textual equality of treatment (were it there) evaporates. A white man subjugating a black man always gives off a different odour, intended or otherwise, from the reverse or two men of the same colour.

In any case, there are textual differences. It is the Tunisian that the guard selects to punish; there are no non-white men in the chiaroscuro sequences; the Tunisian is older, hairier and rougher than the murderer, perhaps calling up the stereotype of the black man as more virile. Perhaps these are accidents of casting, not 'meant' racially though still nonetheless inevitably bearing racial meaning. With the treatment of the Negro, one can go further. He is the last of the series of men on whom the guard spies (shots 29–84). Unlike the others, though he plays with his penis, it is not hard; and he dances his masturbation, rocking back and forth from the hips while still holding his penis, then flinging both arms in the air and moving in a more frenzied style until subsiding back to the rocking movement and finally throwing himself face down on the bed, gently grinding his hips into it. Clearly this is informed by an 'all blacks got rhythm' notion as well as 'the whole white European curiosity about black sexuality, black male sexuality in particular' (Mercer *et al.* 1988:30). Yet in a published discussion of the film between Kobena Mercer, Gayatri Spivak and others, this difference of treatment is not necessarily seen as negative. If for Mercer any 'image of identity [is] denied and excluded' by the film (ibid.:20), for Spivak and an unnamed speaker from the floor, the image of the Negro is the only one suggesting 'self-sufficiency', sexuality 'outside of the fantasy of coupling', with no participation in the 'power scenario at all' (ibid.:28). Presumably because Negro (outside 'society'), and despite the 'extraordinary objectification of the black male body within the pre-liberation gay community' (Spivak ibid.), this prisoner can represent something beyond the dependent relations obtaining for everyone else in the film. Either reading implies that ethnic difference (and indeed other social differences) always make a difference – there is no pure realm of 'the sexual' which exists apart from social realities.

Some of the renewed *political* interest since the seventies in perverse sexualities (pornography, paedophilia, fetishism, sado-masochism) does seem to yearn for that pure realm. When a white man advertised in the pages of the gay Canadian paper *The Body Politic* for a black slave, some of those who defended him against the charge that his desire was racist, spoke of the inviolability of desire, the sense of its existing untutored by social division. This position might be a logical development from earlier gay liberation-ist views, which on the subject of perverse sexualities were at least liberal ('it's up to you what you do as long as it doesn't hurt anyone else') and generally permissive and libertarian ('if it feels good, do it'). Sado-masochism, a litmus test of sexual attitudes, could not only be defended as a supremely consensual, not coercive, form of sexuality, but also seen as a celebration of human sexual diversity. There were also positions beyond such liberal libertarianism, positions close to some of the ideas about Genet I have been discussing. Just as Sartre's Genet wrested fulfilment in the teeth of degradation, so sado-masochism could be seen as the transformation of straight perceptions of sexuality: 'we select the most frightening, disgusting or unacceptable activities and transmute them into pleasure' (Pat Califia, *The Advocate*, December 1979; quoted in Weeks 1985:237). Genet is for Sartre a hero in his implacable hatred of bourgeois society, and similarly sado-masochism can be seen as an assault on the repressive restrictiveness of conventional morality. Again, just as Millett's Genet reveals the roles of sexuality, so sado-masochism can be seen as providing 'unique insights into the nature of sexual power, therapeutic and cathartic sex revealing the nature of sex as ritual and play' (Weeks 1986:85).

There is thus a shift from a merely permissive, tolerant attitude towards sado-masochism and other taboo sexual practices to a celebration and even advocacy of them, and then a further shift from a view that sees sado-masochism as a given potential of human sexual nature to one seeing it as an exploration of the social relations of power that constitute sexuality. In the first view, pain and the dynamics of domination and submission are of the essence of sexuality – getting into sado-masochism is simply getting into human nature. In the second view however, influenced by the writings of Michel Foucault, sexuality is seen as a form of power that has been socially and historically constructed – sado-masochism allows one to explore and confront the realities of power which lay hidden behind more romantic, idealised or sanitised views of sex. Ideas like this inform films such as *Querelle* 1982 and *Verführung – die grausame Frau* 1985.

Querelle

Querelle, adapted in 1982 by Rainer Werner Fassbinder from Genet's 1947 novel, is at the opposite end of the scale from *Chant*. It is full feature length and in colour, with, for a movie of its kind, a large budget and a cast of international stars including Brad Davis, Franco Nero and Jeanne Moreau. It was an immediate critical success, shown to acclaim at several film festivals, widely distributed on the international arthouse circuit and almost immediately available on video.

> *Querelle* takes place in the port of Brest, where the favoured bar among sailors is the Féria, run by husband and wife Nono and Lysiane. One of the rules of the Féria is that the (exclusively male) clientele have to play dice with Nono – if they win, they have the pick of the whores; if they lose, Nono fucks them. Lysiane brings together Querelle, a sailor docked at Brest, with his own brother, Robert, with whom she is having an affair. Querelle has opium to sell and Robert introduces him to Nono and Mario, the cop who hangs out at the Féria. Querelle smuggles the opium ashore with the help of another sailor, Vic, whom he then kills. He goes and plays dice with Nono, loses by cheating (as Nono in fact sees) and thus gets fucked. This is the first time he has had sex with a man. When Robert next meets Querelle, he fights with him for being a 'filthy queer letting that man touch you'. When later they start to fight again, Mario stops them and takes Querelle aside, questions him and then fucks him. Two of Querelle's ship-mates, Gil and Theo, quarrel when Theo sees Gil in conversation with a young man, Roger, at the Féria, and Gil kills Theo. Gil goes into hiding and Roger takes Querelle, at his request, to meet Gil. Querelle persuades Gil to disguise himself (such that as a result Gil looks like Querelle's brother Robert) and to steal money for his get-away from Seblon, the ship's captain. Gil is to cruise Seblon in a toilet and then rob him, which

he does. Querelle, who has fallen in love with Gil, arranges his get-away and kisses him passionately good-bye. He then tells Mario (the cop) where Gil is. Querelle discovers that Seblon has been in love with him all this time, knew that he'd murdered Vic but did not betray him to the police. Querelle and Lysiane become lovers. Captain Seblon intervenes when Querelle gets involved in a drunken brawl and they make love. Lysiane discovers, from the tarot cards, that Robert has no brother and the film ends with a voice over saying that Querelle feels that his death is not far off.

It is possible to treat *Querelle* as an abstraction of the erotics of power. It is shot entirely in the studio and there is no attempt to make it look like a slice of reality. The few sets look like sets, vividly lit in acid yellow with either red or blue. It is, literally but also in the way it feels, studio-bound, an hermetically sealed world, airless and listless, characters and scenes posed as tableaux or set-pieces. The play of power and desire between the characters seems to take place in isolation, divorced from any of the reference to social relations that a more naturalistic style would bring in. Yet *Querelle* is also a post-Millett, post-gay liberation production: its apparent abstraction and separation is less total than might appear.

Fassbinder's work is in any event always marked by an awareness of the way social structures impinge upon private worlds and experiences. His two earlier films centring on homosexual relation-ships, *Die bitteren Tränen der Petra von Kant* 1972 and *Faustrecht der Freiheit* 1975, display the operation of power within gay relationships, the power, in these cases, of class. This is perhaps clearest in *Faustrecht*, where the working-class protagonist, Fox, is taken up as a lover by a middle-class man, Eugen, on the strength of the former just having won a lottery, only to be dropped again when the money runs out because Eugen and his family have spent it all. There are implications that what Eugen and Fox find attractive in each other is class based – the former is piss-elegant, the latter is rough trade, gay subcultural modes with clear class connotations – but this examination of the class structuring of desire is less prominent than the unfolding of the way class power operates in the destruction of relationships. *Querelle* is different. Unlike *Petra von Kant* and *Faustrecht*, it examines the way power structures desire itself rather than the progress of relationships and it does not focus on class power but social sex power.

The direct embodiment of this in the film is fucking: the person who fucks is powerful and the person who is fucked is powerless. Fucking and being fucked are the means by which power is asserted or relinquished. Both may provide pleasure, but the pleasure of being fucked is the pleasure of humiliation. It is in fucking that the social realities of sex power – of gender, of heterosexual status – enter into gay desire.

To take gender first. Though there are no queens in *Querelle* (the feminine principle in Millett's reading of Genet), there is a marking of the characters in terms of masculinity/femininity, above all through the equation fucker=male, fuckee=female. Mario and Nono fuck, and they are also the most heavily marked in terms of stereotypical masculinity, both with short hair and moustaches, Mario in leather cap and vest, Nono in black singlet showing enormous arms and pectorals, with wide leather wristbands. The casting of a black actor (Gunther Kaufman) to play Nono links up with a thread of fascination with the exotic, foreign, super-virile male in Fassbinder's work, and besides it is a common complaint among black gay men that white men want them to play the black stud or topman.

The question of Querelle's place in this schema is at the centre of the film's drama. He is signalled as macho as compared to Seblon: in the first scene on board ship his singlet shows off his oiled muscles and the hairiness of his chest, while Seblon gazes at him from afar; later Seblon comes across him as he emerges from the boiler room, glistening with sweat and covered with dirt, and tells him how beautiful he is. Muscles, hairiness, sweat, dirt are conventional signs of masculinity and this is heightened by the contrast with Seblon, always neat and clean in his white captain's uniform, showing nothing of his body. Yet for all that, Querelle is not macho as Nono and Mario are. He is clean shaven, with a young, pretty face; he wears throughout his sailor's cap with its nice pink pompon; he doesn't wear leather, chains or any of the accoutrements of the macho gay sex scene. So he is available as both a masculine and a feminine figure, as both fucker and fuckee. Part of his humiliation is that he winds up the latter, in the feminine position.

Querelle's gender status is further developed through the notion of narcissism. Part of Querelle's sexuality is seen in terms of his desire for himself and for his like. He is first shown sitting on board ship, stripped to the waist, while Seblon, who has been looking at pictures of classic male nudes (that is, men *not* like himself), tells us in voice over, 'Querelle's great passion is his own body in repose. As he says, he is reflecting himself in his own image'. The first time

Querelle kisses a man (Mario), a title tells us that he found it 'like kissing himself'. This self-love can be transferred to those like himself: Robert (like him by virtue of being his brother) and Gil (like him because they are both murderers). These two likenesses are heightened when Querelle gets the one (Gil) to dress so that he looks like the other (Robert). (They are, of course, played by the same actor, Hanno Pöschl.) Sexuality figures differently in the two cases, but in both Lysiane is important. As a woman, virtually the only one in the film, she is the figure of difference that makes clear the sameness of narcissism.

In the case of Robert, Lysiane affects the two moments when one brother is sexually aroused by the other. In a scene with Robert, Lysiane complains of how similar he and Querelle are: 'All you look at is yourselves, I don't exist for you'. As she speaks of their alikeness, Robert masturbates. Later she and Querelle are together and she talks to him about Robert, comparing their penises, and he plays with his penis as he listens to her describing his brother's (his like's) penis. In both cases, a male narcissism of resemblance is mobilised through the figure of difference, a woman. In the case of Gil, this is less direct, but it seems significant that Lysiane is part of the way Querelle betrays Gil, the man he actually loves. The act of betrayal enacts Oscar Wilde's words that Lysiane sings repeatedly throughout the film, 'Each man kills the thing he loves'; it is after betraying Gil that Querelle becomes her lover; the poignancy of his betrayal of Gil, his other like, is heightened by the presence of Lysiane, the figure of difference.

Still more important than gender in *Querelle* is heterosexuality. Homosexual desire in *Querelle* is mobilised by means of hetero-sexuality. Not always – many of the characters in *Querelle* could be described as gay-identified, thinking of themselves as gay without reference to heterosexual norms: Seblon, Nono, Roger (who resembles the younger of the two main prisoners in *Chant*) and Mario (who is dressed out of the pages of a seventies US gay porn magazine). Yet for two of the main characters, Gil and Querelle, awareness of heterosexuality, as norm and as status, structures their homosexual desire.

Both deny that they are gay. Gil says to Roger, just before he starts kissing him, 'I'm not a queer'. Later, when Gil is in hiding, he cannot stop talking about Roger's sister, Paulette, much to Roger's sadness; but still Gil kisses him, assuring him that he is 'as pretty as a girl'. Gil's desire for Roger is established from the first scene of them together, as Gil talks of what he would do sexually with

Paulette while all the time caressing Roger. Thus, Gil always manifests homosexual desire when asserting heterosexuality. Part of the irony of this is that Gil dresses as a construction worker, another type found in seventies gay porn, even to the extent of men wearing construction worker's helmets to discos and one of the singers in the gay group Village People being dressed as a construction worker. This image connoted masculinity and straightness, but by 1982 it was also an established gay icon. Thus Gil's insistence on his straightness is all the more gestural, for a gay audience anyway, because he so embodies a gay fantasy of straight masculinity.

In Gil, straightness is a mask to gay desire. For Querelle, on the other hand, it is the means by which he experiences such desire. In his case, this desire is masochistic, its pleasure resides in humiliation.

When Querelle loses at dice to Nono, he insists that there be no kisses: 'All I give is my arse' (figure 2.6). In much gay male culture, kisses signify feeling and emotional response, but the penis and anus are mere instruments of pleasure: the hustler does not feel his masculinity is compromised, a partner in a gay couple does not feel he is being unfaithful, as long as feelings – kisses, embraces – do not

2.6   *Querelle* and the power politics of sex – black, gay-identified Nono, who has established the rules of the game, gets to screw white, straight-identified Querelle, who has deliberately played the game to this end. (National Film Archive)

enter into casual or paid-for sexual encounters. Here Querelle's refusal of kisses signifies that he is not to be thought of as gay. The irony is that he has cheated in order to lose and therefore be fucked, and Nono knows that he has cheated. Thus the act retains the appearance of a straight man being fucked by a gay man, with the humiliation that that implies, and yet is signalled as a humiliation that the straight man in fact desires (since he cheated to get it).

The same pattern holds for Querelle and Mario. When the latter questions him about having sex with Nono, Querelle insists 'I'm no fairy', and immediately, as if involuntarily, turns round to be fucked by Mario. As with Nono, the humiliation involved can only be experienced as humiliation if, instead of simply desiring to feel a penis in his anus, Querelle firsts asserts his heterosexuality, someone for whom anal penetration would be humiliation. Anal penetration is only humiliation if it signifies a loss of status and that can only be achieved if one has status, the status of being heterosexual, in the first place.

Heterosexuality structures Querelle's homosexual desire right to the end of the film, when he gives himself to Seblon. He has throughout despised Seblon. When he sees him gazing at him adoringly early on in the film, he simply looks back insolently; later, after Gil's arrest, he listens to the tape recorder into which Seblon has confessed his love for him. This establishes Seblon as 'weak', because he is in love, and accords with Querelle's perception of him, expressed in his encouragement to Gil to attack Seblon for money because 'he won't fight back – he's a queer'. Unlike Querelle, who betrays Gil to the police, Seblon does not betray Querelle (whom he knows to have murdered Vic), an act of love which is also further confirmation of his weakness. Surrendering to such a man makes Querelle feel, a voice over informs us, 'serene'. This serenity is not the discovery of true love but rather that of the final humiliation, the straight man possessed not by macho gays like Nono and Mario but by the queer, Seblon.

Querelle's drama of humiliation is decked out with many of the trappings of s/m – leather wristbands, peaked caps, bondage ropes, belts – and may readily be interpreted in the light of pro s/m arguments. By ritualising power and violence, it confronts and examines the generally unacknowledged dynamic of power present in all relationships. The fact that Querelle engineers his being fucked suggests that the humiliation involved is consensual as it is in s/m sex.

Particularly interesting here is the use of religious imagery. In his contributions to a forum on s/m, Ian Young stresses the importance of humiliation play as 'a way of stripping away the ego and its defenses and pretensions – becoming aware of different levels – . . . another way to achieve what religion or drugs attempt' (1979:91). (Compare the discussion above of Cocteau's equation of poetry with sex with death and loss of self.) Querelle's search for humiliation is accompanied at points by Christian imagery. When he goes ashore with the opium (an act which leads to his murdering Vic), the voice over tells us this is 'comparable to the Visitation' (the revelation of his destiny); his fight with his brother, who accuses him of being a queer, is accompanied by a Calvary procession (Querelle, like Christ, humiliated in the name of redemption); when Querelle gives himself to Seblon he says that he'll never find peace until Seblon has taken him and 'after, I'll lie across your thighs like a Pietà' (his apotheosis accomplished by his sacrifice of himself to Seblon). In addition to these direct Christian references, the general trance-like tone of the characters' movements, the almost intoned quality of their speech, the use of a male chorus for background music that is a cross between plainsong and the *Carmina Burana*, all give a quasi-religious tone to the film. Querelle's attainment of humiliation could thus be read as transcendence, s/m as the means to achieve nirvana, that loss of self that is the mystic's aim.

The problem is that the Christian moments in the film have a perfunctory, postmodern feel to them, there because they are in the original, but not meant and believed in as they are in Genet. Moreover, as I have tried to show, Querelle's pleasure/humiliation depends upon the real power relations of society, beyond the asocial space of a theatre of sex. His pleasure/humiliation can only be that if homosexual acts are accepted as indeed inferior and degrading in comparison to heterosexual ones. Querelle's transcendence affirms the hetero/homo hierarchy – only this can ensure that being fucked is indeed to be humiliated. If in gay s/m a loss of self is sought in mutual, consensual sex acts, in *Querelle*, the self is annihilated through the internalisation of heterosexual norms.

Verführung: die grausame Frau

Verführung (Seduction: the Cruel Woman), made in 1985, is an obvious point of comparison with *Querelle*: it even opens with a very *Querelle*-ish shot of a figure in a sailor suit leaning over a ship's rail. Already there are two important differences, however. The figure looks somewhat androgynous and is in fact a woman, and the predominant colour is clear, cold blue, as opposed to *Querelle*'s acidic combinations. From the start the difference from *Querelle* is clear even while it is being recalled: *Verführung* is a lesbian film and is as cold as ice.

Verführung centres on the character of Wanda, who runs a gallery in Hamburg specialising in s/m performance art. Apart from the shows, people also come to her to enact their desired sexual scenes; one man, Herr Mährsch, poses as a journalist to get an interview with her but reveals that what he really wants is 'to be her toilet'. Wanda has three lovers: her ex-husband Gregor; a live-in lover Caren, a shoe fetishist who runs a small, chic shoe boutique; and Justine, a woman visiting from the US. The film consists of a series of encounters, performances, fantasies involving these characters and others, which are organised not according to strict narrative connnections but rather as they illustrate the film's concern with illusion and reality in (s/m) relationships.

Throughout the film Wanda maintains an attitude of cool, ironic detachment. As the impresario for the s/m gallery performances, as the paid dominatrix, she treats all encounters as theatre. When Mährsch, in his initial interview with her, starts talking about s/m as a need and as therapy, she ridicules him – to her it is performance. Even when taking a bath by herself, she theatricalises the scene, decorating the room with candles in clam shells and posing in the bath like some sea goddess. The problem for the other characters is that they want things to be for real; their problem is Wanda's insistence that all is role. Justine has come from the States to have a relationship with Wanda, not just to take part in s/m scenes with her. Caren thinks that she is the special lover, yet Wanda tells her, 'Your talk of freedom and love sickens me'. Gregor too wants to be the special one, but Wanda excludes him, putting her lesbian encounters before him and finally dismissing him for ever. All three want to push their relationship with Wanda beyond acting to something 'real', which Wanda resolutely resists. Much of the play and humour of the film turns on this.

In one scene Justine complains to Wanda that she hates all this role playing and then roundly slaps Wanda on the face. 'Wunderbar!', exclaims Wanda. Justine does not wish to role play yet Wanda perceives that the slap is not really a spontaneous, involuntary act but is really a bit of role playing performance. So she thrills to it, albeit ironically: her 'Wunderbar!' indicates to Justine how she has been caught in the very theatricality she claims to want to eschew. There is even greater irony in the treatment of Gregor. When he comes cringingly to Wanda, after backing away from watching her make love with Justine, she tells him she hates him because he is always play acting. This sounds like a reversal of what has been said before, but it relates to Wanda's perception of Justine's slap. Gregor thinks what he is doing is for real, he cannot see that he is play acting, that all is performance – it is his inability to see this that Wanda despises. In revenge he tries first to shoot himself and then, during a performance, to shoot her. When he merely succeeds in grazing her, she bursts out laughing, as do all the audience. There is no escape from performance for Gregor (or anyone). Whatever we do is caught in the realities of roles and conventions and theatre. Wanda's strength is her ironic recognition of this; her s/m performances consciously embrace artifice, while the others still seek for the illusion of authenticity.

As I have already noted, there is a contradiction in much thinking about s/m, on the one hand arguing that it explores 'the political construction of sex' (Ardill and Neumark 1982:8) while on the other putting forward 'an essentialisation of sex, power and pleasure' (Weeks 1985:239), a celebration of the vital force of sexual desire. My reading of *Verführung* stresses the theme of the constructedness of sex, but Jayne Melville's review of it in *Square Peg* (and her contribution to a panel discussion at the Piccadilly Film Festival in June 1986) focuses on the way the film celebrates power, and especially in women. It is one of the few films that actually shows/celebrates active female desire: 'Female, and particularly lesbian, sexuality in the film is at once aggressive, animal-like, powerful and seductive. The women are capable of acting out fantasies and shaping their own sexualities' (1986:33).

We have moved a long way from Genet, if only because women, lesbian or otherwise, are for the most part absent from his work (even *Les Bonnes*, an all-female cast, was intended to be performed by men). Yet many of those lesbians defending or advocating an embrace of perverse sexuality have acknowledged the inspiration of gay male sexual culture. As Peg Byron observes in a review of some lesbian s/m and porn magazines 'Gay men also get credit for this explosion of lesbian bravado. Lesbians looked to gay men's porn for material taboo in their own circles – sex *sans* romance in its endless variations' (1985:48). And the terms of the debate, theatre versus essence, condemned to perversity or choosing it, have been central to the fortunes of 'Genet', if not Genet.

*   *   *

Genet's work has provided a storehouse of imagery and tone for gay and even lesbian cinema. There is a Genet iconography – flowers, prisons, drag queens, dirt, melancholy unshaven criminals and sailors, crucifixes, crotches, tattoos and scars – and a Genet flavour – guilt and defiance, crime and catholicism, the sordid and the sublime, all at once. The simultaneous presence of these elements is of the essence, especially in understanding the constant gay return to Genet. In 'Genet' constructions of gayness, it is not possible to think of spiritual union between men without thinking of cocksucking, nor to think of fucking without thinking of true love. The difference between the films discussed in this chapter, including the various readings of *Un Chant d'amour*, lies in what they make of the juxtaposition. The presence of spiritual imagery may promote, as in *Possession du condamné*, a feeling of transcendence through physical love, or may be something like a nostalgia for a belief in the transcendent, as in *Querelle*. The persistent image of the desirable virile man may just be a turn-on in some readings of *Chant*,[6] or a reflection of such a turn-on in others. Yoking together desire and confinement (in a literal prison or the prison of masculinity and taboo sexuality) may be seen to make a point about the repression of homosexuality or else to make confinement one of the conditions making homosexual pleasure possible – *Possession* is clearly the former, but does the intensity of *Chant* or *Querelle* (or, probably, *Le Prisonnier*) derive from the triumph of love against repression or the masochistic pleasures of repression itself?; is such intensity only possible now, as *Querelle*, *Verführung* and 'perverse' readings of *Chant* may suggest, in games, role play and substitutes for oppression?

Though 'Genet' is not to every lesbian and gay person's liking, the fruitfulness of his distinctive mix of imagery is not a marginal or specialised taste. The constant return to Genet has a little to do with his literary quality or prestige and the way he has figured so prominently in political-intellectual life in the post-war era, but for gay people it also has to do with the fact that 'lesbian'/'gay' is a sexual identity in a culture in which even heterosexuality is at best an unfortunate drive and at worst a kind of bestiality. The proclamation of gay/lesbian identity is thus always troubled by the fact that this ineluctably entails sex – no matter how hard one tries (homophile, feminist, liberated), one cannot escape from the way the whole of society has constructed sexuality. The return to Genet is a constant reworking of this trouble, a return to a point where homosexuality is always affirmed but never without an insistent acknowledgement of the degradation of (homo)sexuality for us. Part of the endless fascination is whether that degradation is to be thought of as inherent or socially enforced, whether it is to be rejected or welcomed. 'Genet' makes it possible to say any of these, to mull them over, or even to assert them all at once.

APPENDIX: GENET AND FILM

In addition to the films discussed in the chapter, Genet himself had some other involvements in film-making and his work has been a source or inspiration for many other films.

Genet contributed a scenario (little more it seems than a story and brief treatment (Billard 1966)) for *Mademoiselle* GB 1966, directed by Tony Richardson, but all the other films he worked on were either unmade or unshown. In addition to *Le Prisonnier*, described above, he was involved in a projected film on his childhood *La Révolte des anges noirs* in 1947 (Webb 1982:516), worked on a scenario called *Le Bagne* in 1955 (which included the image of a guard having his eye put out by a needle as he spies on prisoners (ibid.:518)) and in 1977 wrote a treatment for a film about a young Moroccan in Europe called *La Nuit venue* (Genet 1983; Webb 1982:540). He appeared in a 1948 film, *Ulysse ou les mauvaises rencontres*, directed by Alexandre Astruc, which was never released (ibid.:529), and sometime in the forties in a film with Violette Leduc, playing her baby (ibid.:535). He is in the documentary footage of *Prologue* Canada 1969, a film about revolution directed by Robin Spry; and was interviewed in *Saint Genet* 1985 in the BBC TV *Arena* series.

In terms of adaptations, there have been versions of the plays (*The Balcony* USA 1963; *Deathwatch* USA 1966; *The Maids* GB 1975), the second of which was probably 'the first film whose advertising was directed specifically at a gay audience' when it ran at the Bleecker Street Cinema in New York in 1967 (Russo 1981:150). There was talk of a film of *Miracle de la rose* in 1951 (Rabi 1951:744) and in 1962 a never-released version of *Pompes funèbres*, called *Le Tireur des toits*, from the credits of which Genet had his name removed (Webb 1982:529). Guy Gilles' television film *Jean Genet: Saint, poète, martyr* France 1975 used elements of 'Le condamné à mort', *Journal du voleur*, *Notre-Dame des fleurs* and *Miracle de la rose*. A projected film version of the theatre piece based on Genet, *Flowers*, by Lindsay Kemp, Celestino Coronado and David Haughton, was never made.

Other films not mentioned above that have the Genet flavour include *Flowers of Asphalt* France 1951 Gregory Markopoulos, *L'Amour à la mer* France 1965 Guy Gilles, *Bara no soretsu* Japan 1970 Matsumoto Toshio (set in a gay bar in Tokyo called the Genet), *L'Homme de désir* France 1970 Dominique Delouche, *Le Carnet rose d'un homosexuel* France 1971 Anthony Smalto, *Fortune and Men's Eyes* Canada 1971 Harvey Hart, *Pink Narcissus* USA 1971 anon., *Amen* Belgium 1974 Roland Mahauden, *Sept Images impossibles* Belgium 1979 Robert Malengreau (producer of *Possession du condamné*), *Casta Diva* Netherlands 1982 Eric de Kuyper, *Das Geräusch rascher Erlösung* BRD 1982 Wieland Speck, *Blauer Dunst* BRD 1983 Klaus Keske, *Haltéroflic* France 1983 Philippe Valois, *L'Homme blessé* France 1983 Patrice Chéreau, *Stadt der verlorenen Seelen* BRD 1983 Rosa von Praunheim, *De Vierde Man* Netherlands 1983 Paul Verhoeven, *Jean Genet is Dead* GB 1988 Constantine Giannaris and many more. One might also note that the Genet repertoire of imagery even gets into Hollywood movies, as for instance in the treatment of the gay prisoner who helps the heroes escape from prison in *Papillon* 1973 (Dyer 1980–1).

3   Underground and after

Underground films were short, low budget films, made outside the
mainstream film industry in the USA from the late forties to the late
sixties. They range from films full of obscure symbolism, hectic
cutting and vivid colours to others shot in grainy black and white
with next to no cuts and not much going on beyond random, banal
conversation. Their 'undergroundness' was partly their refusal of
Hollywoodian qualities of finish and clarity, and partly their
breaking of (mainly sexual) taboos, so that production and
screenings were socially, economically and sometimes legally
marginal and questionable.

Underground films were always recognised as a very gay
tradition. Jonas Mekas, one of the first to perceive their existence at
all, characterised them disparagingly in 1955 in terms of an
etherealised image of women, sado-masochism, homosexuality and
adolescent frustration. Eleven years later, when the underground
was in full swing, Andrew Sarris, one of the most eminent film
critics in the USA, observed during a public discussion at the New
York Film Festival:

> When you get some of these films that deal quite frankly with
> things like homosexuality I think the majority of the people are
> very violently opposed . . . and I think this is one of the issues
> that keeps coming up all the time, of subject matter.
>
> (quoted in Wellington 1967:44–5)

People could hardly be blamed. By far the most newsworthy
stories concerning the underground were the raids on screenings and
subsequent trials of *Flaming Creatures* in New York and *Scorpio
Rising* in Los Angeles (together with *Un Chant d'amour* in both
New York and San Francisco), all within months of each other in
1964, all overtly gay films. Many of the best known underground

film-makers were gay and gay subject-matter suffused not only their work but that of many others who did not identify themselves as gay. Even forerunners of the underground indicated the possibility of a gay cinema, and it has had an extraordinary impact on a wide variety of subsequent films, including art cinema, midnight movies and pornography. All of this is the subject of this chapter.

Underground films, even if one just takes the gay ones, do not constitute a unified, homogeneous body of work. *Fireworks* (Kenneth Anger 1947) is a tightly organised film, every cut highly disciplined, with a coherent, decipherable symbolic structure. It plays with space and time, but rigorously and in a manner that is only possible on the basis of understanding the rules of mainstream film-making. *Flaming Creatures* (Jack Smith 1963) is loose and languorous, with only the vaguest of underlying structures, and without esoteric symbolism. Its use of dissolves and superimpositions does not so much organise as dispense with co-ordinated time and space. *Couch* (Andy Warhol 1964) uses a series of long takes and in a sense respects real time and space: the camera is in one place for a set length of time and records what goes on in front of it. The action is a series of listlessly sexual encounters of one kind or another, with no apparent connection or development. Though there are common elements to these films – the use of camp, of gay sexualities – and they are more like each other than they are like conventional movies, still the similarities hardly convey what any one of these films is actually like.

These three films are characteristic of different phases of underground film-making (though the approach of the earlier phase persists well into the eighties, just as the later phases were already anticipated in films as far back as the thirties). The shifts in style – from rigorous construction through dissolving sensuousness to minimalism – parallel shifts in attitude and subject-matter, especially towards the self. The films from the late forties take the film-maker as subject-matter, her or his inner life, revealed by dreams, released by ritual, universalised by myth. The later films on the other hand are utterly impersonal as far as the film-maker is concerned – Warhol is said on occasion to have walked away from the camera once he had set it rolling and simply allowed to happen whatever took place in front of it. In between, films like *Flaming Creatures* show not the film-maker as inner personality but the performer's outer persona. While *Flaming Creatures* may have the stamp of Smith's personality on it, it is not an exploration of his psyche; but nor does it attempt to reveal the inner selves of its drag queen performers, they are presented as a show. There is a shift then from the personality of the film-maker to the personality of the performer which is also a shift from personality as an inner reality to be explored to personality as a outer surface to be observed.

These shifts are not unique to the gay underground, but it is no accident that gays were so central to the development and definition of the tradition as a whole. Underground cinema provided a space and an opportunity for gay men and, as is discussed in the next chapter, lesbians to represent themselves in films in a way that mainstream film-making (where many covert lesbians and gay men worked) did not. There had always been links and overlaps between the gay scenes and the artistic avant-gardes in the USA, and homosexuality was perceived at various times as a form of instinctual rejection of the narrowness and repressiveness of mainstream US life in general. The concerns of the underground – with personal identity, with self disclosure, with gender roles, with subversiveness – have a particular urgency in a lesbian and gay context, and even more so in the context of the development of newly assertive gay identities in the period. What makes underground cinema even more fascinating, however, is the way it also seems to problematise those identities. This chapter then is about the emergence of a gay cinema tradition, at this time and in this form, and its relation to the construction, and dissolution, of contemporary homosexual identities.

The first gay underground films were made on the West Coast, mainly Los Angeles, in the late forties; then there was a break until the early sixties in New York. In between, and despite (or in reaction to) the restrictiveness of the fifties, homosexuality had come to a new and vivid visibility in US cultural life and a vigorous US avant-garde in the arts was fully established. The next two sections look in turn at these two moments, in each case tracing first the mix of elements, cinematic and sub-cultural, that came together to provide possibilities for gay underground cinema and then discussing the film-makers and their key (gay) work. A third section considers the continuance and influence of this cinema into the seventies.

FROM THE WEST COAST

The first phase related to older elements within gay culture, particularly the overlap with artistic milieux, as well as to earlier examples within European and US avant-garde film gay imagery.

The time and the place of its emergence also seem propitious – the Second World War had had a general impact on the situation of homosexual people in the USA, and strengthened deeper rooted gay traditions; equally the particular mix in LA of developed gay and film (in and outside Hollywood) cultures made gay film a possibility and in part determined the shapes it took. These are the two sets of elements dealt with here.

Gays and the arts

The social space allowed art in the USA and that allowed homosexuality have long overlapped. Emmanuel Cooper points to various specific instances of this in his history of homosexuality and art,[1] and it is vividly evoked in *The Young and the Evil*, a novel published in Paris in 1933 but set in Greenwich Village, New York, and written by Charles Ford and Parker Tyler. Ford, a poet and artist, made a late underground film, *Johnny Minotaur* in 1971, and Tyler worked as a film critic, celebrating, in very undergroundish ways, the subconscious appeals of Hollywood, writing criticism of underground films and, in 1972, the first book on gays and film, *Screening the Sexes. The Young and the Evil* concerns, in a very free-wheeling style, a group of young men who lead free floating lives, writing poems, hustling, hanging out, sleeping with women but mainly with each other. Not only are they half-in, half-out of art circles themselves, it is clear that they are accepted, glamour star eyebrows and all, by the straight art scene and also by those on the left, who share their social marginality.

A particular view of the art/gay nexus was offered by Robert Duncan in his article 'The Homosexual in Society', published in the left-liberal journal *Politics* in August 1944. The article, basically an argument for homosexual rights, takes it as a given fact known to all that the arts and intellectual life are full of gay men. This fact, he argues, is used against homosexuals 'in private conversation, at every table, at every editorial board' – 'modern art' is seen to have been 'cheated by what almost amounts to a homosexual cult' (209). However, Duncan goes on, the equally deplorable fact is that many homosexuals do participate in 'a cult of homosexual superiority to the human race', cultivating 'a secret language, the *camp*, a tone and a vocabulary that is loaded with contempt for the human' (210). Two of the specific inflections of this 'homosexual cult' are startlingly evocative of aspects of underground films.

One inflection is witchcraft. Duncan refers to

new cult leaders whose special divinity, whose supernatural and visionary claim is no other than this mystery of sex. . . . Like early witches, the homosexual propagandists have rejected any struggle toward recognition in social equality and, far from seeking to undermine the popular superstition, have accepted the charge of Demonism.

(ibid.)

It is hard to know how literally Duncan means this, but the general sense of an affinity between homosexuality and the occult is widely attested, not least by the films of Kenneth Anger. There is a long historical association of homosexuality and witchcraft (Evans 1978, Grahn 1984), and fringe or outlawed cults may often provide a space for marginal or forbidden sexualities. The occult not only provides a space for the expression of sexual identities that are repressed or despised elsewhere in society but may also exalt them (cf. Fry 1986).

A second aspect of the cult is the idea of there being 'special worth in suffering, sensitivity', in 'isolate sufferings that [have] been converted into the poet's intangible "nobility"' (Duncan 1944:209). Even if not explictly claiming specialness, early underground films do dwell on the isolated, suffering figure, whose sensitivity is contrasted to the cheerfully playing athletes or crowds at whom he gazes. Sensitivity may be a curse but it is also a sign of greater aesthetic and moral refinement.

The idea of gay men being sensitive may also be a case of 'accepting a charge' levelled against us. The term 'sensitive' was often used as a code word for homosexuals in popular novels, plays and films in the period, no doubt deriving from the idea that gay men are more like women who are of course more sensitive. Often the term was spoken sarcastically, especially by male characters, whereas women characters were more likely to indicate a feeling of affinity with the man in question – see, for instance, the opposed attitudes of Spencer Tracy and Katharine Hepburn to the character of Kip, played by David Wayne, in *Adam's Rib* 1949 (Russo 1981:67–8). It is then not surprising that some gay art should not only accept but affirm that homosexuality is a condition of sensitivity.

To this general notion of homosexual sensitivity needs to be added the influence of Freudian ideas, widely spread in various forms among artists and intellectuals in the USA since the twenties (Hale 1971). The twin planks of popularised notions of homosexuality were homosexuality as a form of narcissism and homosexuality as a result of maternal domination, motifs that recur throughout underground films and, even more, straight critical accounts of them. Homosexuals in this psychoanalytical discourse are 'inevitably' unhappy and guilt-ridden: narcissism is immature and therefore unfulfilling, to desire one's mother violates the incest taboo and anyway they know it's unnatural. The whole feeling – mother fixation, guilt, homo-eroticism, inevitable unhappiness – is suggested by this description of an East Coast underground film, Willard Maas's *Images in the Snow* 1948:

> The hero . . . is haunted by dream images of youths in muscular poses, dashes his worn-out mother's lovingly proffered breakfast-egg to the floor, and rushes out through grimy New York streets, until in the cemetery, he identifies his mother with the Virgin and his own suffering with Christ's, wallowing in the snow, between the graves, as if life were burial alive in some numb cold pain.
>
> (Durgnat 1972:252)

A similar Freudo-religious guilt informs the image of homosexuality in such later films as *The Voices* (John Smitz 1953) and *Line of Apogee* (Lloyd Michael Williams 1968).

Freudian ideas not only provided aetiologies of homosexuality, but formal qualities as well. The importance of the Oedipal phase accorded well with a society in which the notion of 'adolescence' as a distinctive life phase was already being emphasised (Springhall 1983–4) and it provided the central dramatic motif of the young man passing through a tormented rite of passage, issuing in both a formal structure, the journey in search of the self, and a character type, 'the sad young man' (figure 3.1). More important still were the Freudian notions of the structures of the unconscious. Early underground films are often constructed along lines similar to the way that Freudian analysis construes dreams: unconscious thought processes seen as reworking elements from conscious perception; objects and incidents becoming highly charged emotionally and, especially, sexually; things being substituted for other things, places suddenly becoming other places; unexpected juxtapositions of images.

Such a vocabulary for the cinematic rendering of dreams had already been developed in the European avant-garde of the twenties and thirties. These had been made available through the touring film programmes put out by the Museum of Modern Art starting in 1937 and the 'Art in Cinema' series put on at the San Francisco

3.1   Downcast eyes and the urban nightscape – elements of the iconography of the homosexual as sad young man on the cover of *The Gay
Year* 1949. (Castle Books)

Museum of Art from 1947 on. Two of the most widely seen were *Un Chien Andalou* 1928 and *Le Sang d'un poète* 1930, both of which have homosexuality as part of their cinematic vocabulary. *Sang* in particular seems to be a model for many of the West Coast films: its title suggests the stance of taking oneself as subject, one's subjectivity as subject-matter; its structure is a series of journeys into the self; the sequence in the hotel corridor is evoked again and again in the corridors, stairways, doors and rooms of the houses through which underground film protagonists wander in search of themselves; and the film welds personal and oneiric concerns to mythology, invoking notions of eternal and universal archetypes in human (un)consciousness. This last may have been particularly appealing for gay film-makers in the period – in part it argues for the (always everywhere) naturalness of homosexuality; it elevates its cultural significance; it swallows up self-doubt and self-hate in higher realms of perception. More generally, myth brings a healing unification to the fragmented self presented in underground films, a general feature of these films but, like the journey structure, one with special resonance for gay people.

Lot in Sodom

Another film shown in the museum series was *Lot in Sodom*, from an earlier, isolated moment of avant-gardism in the US itself, and I want to end this section by considering it in some detail. It was made in Rochester (New York State) in 1930 by Melville Webber and James Sibley Watson, university lecturers who had already made another film together in 1928, an adaptation of *The Fall of the House of Usher*. Whether either or both of them were gay is not known, but it is hard not to assume one at least of them was on the evidence of *Lot in Sodom*. It shows Sodom destroyed for its gayness and thus may appear morally conventional, but it feels like a celebration of gayness (cf. Fischer 1987–8:44).

Lot in Sodom contrasts the life of Lot and his family with that of the exclusively male townsfolk of Sodom, a contrast of frenzy and stillness. The townsfolk are luridly painted queens and handsome young men shot in soft chiaroscuro lighting; all leap and writhe about and are presented as if in permanent sexual play, without specific narrative incidents and with extremely rapid editing. Lot and his family, on the other hand, are plainly dressed and made up; they stand still or make slow and deliberate movements; it is through them that the story of God sending an angel to destroy

Sodom is told, edited to a slow, deliberate pace. This could be a contrast between the confusion, chaos and disorientation of the gay sequences and the calm, order and piety of the Lot sequences – that the gay sequences seem colourful and fun and the Lot sequences dull and dreary might be just a personal response. Yet there are other ways in which the film seems to encourage this response.

There is a contrast between the way the gay men are presented in the film and the way Lot's daughter is. The film gives us the men's bodies, often half naked, caressingly lit, but the daughter's beauty is presented in symbolic, non-sexual terms. The chief sequence concerning her beauty is her giving birth. She opens her dress, but we do not see her body and the film cuts away to a title telling us that 'Mulier Templum est' ('Woman is a temple'), followed by a shot of her with a temple superimposed over her hips, then shots of doves and of flowers opening, symbolising birth. We would not expect to see the birth directly, but one might expect, from a heterosexual film, some celebration of the daughter's bodily beauty. As it is, the image of woman in the film is ethereal, conveyed without the erotic conviction with which the men are shown. It feels as if the film is consciously presenting woman, and therefore heterosexuality, as morally and aesthetically superior, but unconsciously betraying the excitement and sensuality of men, and therefore homosexuality.

This ambivalence is heightened by the appearance of the angel (figure 3.2), a handsome young man, with large, sad eyes and sensual mouth, lit in the same soft chiaroscuro as the gay young men of the city. He is an archetypal 'sad young man', beautiful but melancholy. At the end he does destroy Sodom, yet the affinity between him and the gay men is striking. If the film morally condemns what it is nonetheless attracted to, then perhaps the angel represents the gay believer's destruction of his sexual self in the name of the morality to which he subscribes.

This is necessarily speculative, but certainly *Lot in Sodom* anticipates the gay underground not just by its direct use of gay subject-matter and imagery (itself virtually unheard of in the USA up to this time and until the mid-forties) but by its use of expressionistic lighting and non-narrative editing to evoke experience, its ambivalent attitude towards women, its use of the sad young man type and the way that one can discern elements of splitting and fragmentation in its presentation of psychic and sexual states.

3.2 The angel as sad young man in *Lot in Sodom*.

The forties/Los Angeles

Historians of homosexuality in the US are agreed on the absolute importance of the Second World War in the widespread emergence of gay and lesbian identities (D'Emilio 1983:23–39, Costello 1985:153–74). The war involved mass mobilisation, throwing men together with men in the military, and women together with women in both the military and on the home front. It created conditions in which homosexual experience became almost commonplace and in which people might easily realise they were gay and be well known to be so. Thus despite the uproar that greeted the publication in

1948 of Kinsey's *Sexual Behavior in the Human Male* (which gave figures to show that 37 per cent of men had had some homosexual experience and 4 per cent were exclusively homosexual) and the public harassment and denigration of homosexuality focused by McCarthy's witch hunts (D'Emilio 1983:41–53), personal experience of homosexuality and acquaintance with gay people were widespread, perhaps accounting for why the fifties was to be a period of both increasing tolerance of gays and growing gay communities as well as a period of vicious anti-gay propaganda and repression.

The war also associated gay eroticism with the military. Tom Waugh notes in his study of imagery in gay pornographic photos 'a huge proliferation of military-themed erotic photos' in the forties (1984:31; cf. Sokolowski 1983:13–14). As he observes;

> Sailors and khaki had always been part of gay iconography – think of Walt Whitman's Civil War experiences or of Paul Cadmus's ribald paintings of sailors from the Thirties – but during the War, a previously marginal cultural tendency centred in seaports and bohemian undergrounds took the shape of a mass cultural phenomenon.
>
> (1984:31)

Soldiers and sailors were no longer straight-identified men seen from afar by gay-identified men, they were gay – or at any rate sometimes queer or homosexual – themselves. Perhaps here began the process which culminated in the seventies' gay macho clone look, whereby gay men no longer saw themselves as intrinsically different from their objects of desire but made themselves into those objects of desire.

Sailors have especially figured in gay erotic tradition (figure 3.3), for a number of possible reasons: longer enforced periods spent in enclosed single-sex environments suggests they may have greater homosexual experience; their rootlessness accords with the anonymity and fleetingness of much gay sexual contact and means they are not 'tied down' to marriage, family and conformity; their knowledge of the world makes them seem either exotic or broad-minded; the rigours of sailing produce well-developed physiques. Even their clothing, perhaps by association, seems more erotic – open-necked tops suggesting broad chests; trousers worn tight at the crotch and made of moulding serge; the flap fly; bell-bottoms which emphasise, by their oddity, naval costume as costume.

Whether as a result of the war experience or not, the post-war period saw what Roger Austen calls a 'burst of novels with gay

3.3 Sailor imagery in early beefcake mail order. (Thomas Waugh Collection)

themes. . . .by the end of the decade a *New York Times* reviewer complained that [gay fiction] was getting to be a "groaning shelf"' (1977:93–4). Among those to make an impact at the time were *The Fall of Valor* (Charles Jackson 1945), *The Sling and the Arrow* (Stuart Engstrand 1947), *The Gallery* (John Horne Burns 1947), *The City and the Pillar* (Gore Vidal 1948), *Other Voices, Other Rooms* (Truman Capote 1948), *The Gay Year* (M. de F. 1949) (figure 3.1), but Austen's list is much longer than these few. Most depict homosexuality as a disturbing eruption of 'different' desires in otherwise ordinary men, something the war had made widespread and known about.

In *The City and the Pillar* one of the characters remarks, 'I'll bet they got more pretty girls and crazy people and queers in LA than any other town' (Vidal 1965:36), a view that subsequent chapters confirm. Certainly Los Angeles was very gay, enough to have well-established gay places. Henry Hay, one of the founders of the Mattachine Society, refers to the 'notorious' Pershing Square (1976:407; also documented by Donald Vining in his diary (D'Emilio 1983:27)) and to the 'Gay beach in Los Angeles, in Santa Monica' (Hay 1976:411). Even before the founding of the Mattachine in 1950, there were the beginnings of activism in Los Angeles in the form of the gay inter-racial group, The Knights of the Clock (founded in 1949) and Lisa Ben's lesbian magazine *Vice Versa* (June 1947–February 1948) (D'Emilio 1983:32), suggesting that Los Angeles had an atmosphere more congenial than most to gay initiatives. Hay refers to going to 'a beer bust at the University of Southern California, run by some Gay guys I knew' (1976:408), where the idea of a gay group was drunkenly mooted; USC was where the gay underground film-makers of the late forties, Curtis Harrington, Kenneth Anger and Gregory Markopoulos met.

Further evidence of LA's gayness of particular importance here is the growth of gay porn film and photography in the city. Two of the first regular photographic studios producing male physique studies and running a mail order service supplying them were Bruce of Los Angeles and the Athletic Model Guild (AMG), both of which started in the early forties. AMG was set up by Bob Mizer, who had no difficulty getting models in a city characterised by film-making, body culture and rootlessness:

> Bob did all his initial recruiting personally, visiting local gymnasiums and muscle beaches, setting up his tripod in the athletes' sporting hang-outs. . . . [The models were] dedicated bodybuilders. . . husky men muscled by hard labor, movie star hopefuls, drifters and an assortment of boy-next-door types.
>
> (Lewis 1983:5)

The earliest example of regular gay erotic film-making (though probably not intended for commercial release) is the work of 'AT', who produced eighteen (extant) 16mm films between the mid-thirties and the mid-fifties, if not specifically in Los Angeles then at any rate in Southern California (Waugh 1983:31–2). The region seems thus, by the standards of the time, to have been quite a concentration of gay photo arts production.

Los Angeles is also Hollywood. Quite apart from the presence of gay men behind and in front of the cameras, Hollywood was a purveyor of potentially gay images – glamorous men, camp costumes, excessive fantasy worlds. As Charles Boultenhouse observed in 1963 of his fellow film-makers:

> In a sense, we all grew up on Hollywood, and, for many of us, our first experiences of the Marvellous is enshrined in the tacky trappings of Hollywood glamor. But, at the same time that these films aroused, they also failed to satisfy. Hollywood is the tease of all time.
>
> (1970:137)

The use of the word 'marvellous', complete with capital letter, suggests an awareness of the French surrealists' view of popular cinema, namely, that it in some way tapped the 'convulsive beauty' of the unconscious. Consciously, Hollywood, as popular cinema par excellence, might try to control and tame the libidinal forces its imagery set in motion, but none the less it did let them loose on to the world.

A surrealist approach to film was to go randomly to the cinema, not knowing what was showing, never seeing the complete film, and thus releasing the imagery from the shackles of narrative (Breton 1978:42–3). The possibility of doing this within a film itself was suggested by *Rose Hobart*, made in 1937 by the sculptor Joseph Cornell. This takes a 1931 film starring Hobart, *East of Borneo*, and cuts it up and reassembles it so that what we get are

> those random moments of dramatic affectivity that impress the viewer on a non-narrative level (e.g. the stance of the figure, the flair of a gesture, the texture of the light) but that are swallowed up in a conventional context by story sense.
>
> (Ehrenstein 1984:38).

The effect both heightens the visual beauty of many of the kitschy images and emphasises the fake orientalism of the whole thing. As with many underground films, there is a knife-edge between Hollywood as repository of the popular unconscious and Hollywood as camp. Both uses are to be found in Kenneth Anger, but it was not until the New York gay underground of the sixties, so much further removed from the presence of Hollywood as industry, that they became a defining feature.

Quite apart from its unconscious marvellousness, Hollywood also had its own underground in the late forties, the film noir. Not a term in use in Hollywood at the time, films noirs were convoluted pessimistic thrillers centred on jaded male protagonists drawn into seedy or decadent worlds characterised by sadistic criminals and femmes fatales. Many made use of 'expressionist' techniques – chiaroscuro lighting, unbalanced compositions, dislocating cuts – and of dream sequences that draw on the Freudo-surrealist conventions for the representation of dreams. It is in film noir that homosexuality, usually on the margins in the form of decadent queens and predatory dykes, reappeared in Hollywood films for the first time since the early thirties (Dyer 1977). Hollywood thus associated homosexuality with quasi expressionist/surreal styles just as Harrington, Anger and Markopoulos did more concentratedly in their work. Film noir and the forties gay underground alike sought to convey inner, often conflictual or disruptive, experiences, which can be taken as symptomatic of anomie and malaise or, alternatively, as a kind of revolt against the bland conformities of mainstream US life. Underground films go much further than film noir in eliminating depiction of the everyday, 'normal' world (usually still present as a reference point in film noir), in attenuating narrative to the point of incomprehensibility, in submerging in unconscious, subjective and dream states, in dislocation of both space and time.

Though the forties and LA were a more likely time for the emergence of new gay expression than earlier, still in a Hollywood dominated city (and society) even to imagine the possibility of another kind of film-making in the USA was remarkable. It was Maya Deren, who made her first film, *Meshes of the Afternoon*, with Alexander Hammid in 1943 in Los Angeles, who pointed the way. Deren is often referred to as the 'Mother of the Underground Film', because she was the film-maker who both through her own films suggested what was aesthetically possible and who also set up many of the conditions that made underground film-making practically viable. Her films were the first to be made directly in 16mm, indicating what could be achieved in this cheaper, lighter medium, and they took the film-maker herself, her own preoccupations and anxieties, as their subject-matter. She realised the potential of colleges, universities, schools and museums as places to show non-commercial film and found theatres and cinemas ready to put on screenings of them. In 1954 she established the Creative Film Foundation to help other film-makers with problems of obtaining grants and raising money (Cornwell 1979:186–7). It was at her funeral (at the age of 44) in 1961, that several of the film-makers she had helped and inspired discussed and eventually, under the aegis of Jonas Mekas, set up the Film-makers' Co-operative, a mutual support organisation for the distribution of underground films. Gay film-makers' debt to Deren is in these general terms much the same as everyone else's, but, as is discussed in the next chapter, although Deren was not lesbian, her films also suggest aspects of what a lesbian underground might be.

The elements discussed in this and the previous sub-section made a gay cinema possible and provided approaches and motifs out of which it could be fashioned. Three film-makers – Curtis Harrington, Kenneth Anger and Gregory Markopoulos – seized the opportunity. Although they produced most of their work away from Los Angeles and in subsequent years, they made key gay films there in the late forties before going on to produce work still marked by and developing out of the nexus of features sketched above. It is to them that I now turn.

The films

Kenneth Anger and Curtis Harrrington were born and brought up in Los Angeles; Harrington and Gregory Markopoulos studied film there, at the University of Southern California, one of the few universities offering it; Anger, slightly younger, sat in on classes. Anger and Harrington were friends and, according to the latter, 'started making films pretty much about the same time in 16mm' (Gow 1971:16); Harrington and Markopoulos lived in the same university residence as well as being in the same department and working on each other's films. All three had had a go at making films before they met but the work which has survived and for which they are known was produced after.

It is not clear that Harrington belongs in this book, but his best-known film, *Fragment of Seeking* 1946–7, has often been interpreted as a gay one. In it, a young man wanders corridors, aware of young women, one of whom he embraces only to have her turn into a skeleton; he runs into a room 'where, seeing himself, he is made to face the realization of his own nature' (Jacobs 1968:568). Given the cultural perception of male homosexuality as a combination of narcissism and the repulsed rejection of woman, a gay reading is possible. Again, given the widespread notion of gay men as mothers' boys, you could, as Michael Wade does, read *On the Edge* 1949, 'showing himself physically roped to his mother' (1982:31), as a pessimistic view of homosexuality. His later films do not appear to offer such possibilities, though some of the features, after he formally renounced underground film-making in the pages of *Film Culture* in 1963, are pretty campy (eg. *What's the Matter with Helen?* 1971) and one may feel that his graduation to director of episodes of *Dynasty* on television pretty well clinches the argument.

Kenneth Anger

Kenneth Anger's films are organised according to 'Magick', the esoteric system of pagan belief and ritual elaborated in the life and work of Aleister Crowley. Magick rituals invoke vital forces, sometimes symbolised, sometimes embodied in gods and goddesses, the ultimate purpose being to put the ritualist in touch with 'the

Holy Guardian Angel (the aspirant's higher self)' (Rowe 1982:75).
The forces invoked are often forces of chaos and disruption,
joyously celebrated but also in the course of the ritual mastered or
used by the ritualist, Magick being, in Crowley's words, the 'science
and art of causing change to occur in conformity with the Will'
(quoted in Rayns 1969:27). The films are structured according to
Magick ritual: characters or the film itself invoke the Magick spirits
by various means (drugs, dressing up, the use of occult objects and
words and so on) and master them in transcendence (symbolised by
gestures or images signifying wholeness and completion). This
transcendence is also the realisation of the 'higher self'.

Magick is not an exclusively or specifically gay system, but it has
strong gay connections, in addition to those generally true of
witchcraft discussed above. According to Rictor Norton (1977:20),
Crowley is best considered as 'ambisexual', open to all sexual
practices and objects, though Colin Wilson suggests that Crowley
practised homosexuality more out of conviction than inclination.
Whatever the case, Magick lays great stress on sexuality as one form
of access to the spirits of chaos, and the more perverse the sexuality,
the more it strays from the norms of a hidebound society, then the
more potent it is liable to be, the more disruptive of thought
patterns inhibiting the release of vital forces. The idea of dressing
up as the assumption of an identity may be related to Jack
Babuscio's discussion (1977) of the 'gay sensibility' which stresses
the absolute importance of mastering appearances and assuming
identities in a gay life where passing for straight (assuming a straight
appearance) is so critical. Finally, the fact that the purpose of the
ritual is the realisation of the 'higher self' may be especially
significant for persons whose sense of self is so battered and assailed
by the realities of sexual oppression.

Anger had made several films before *Fireworks* 1947, the earliest
of his films in distribution and the most directly gay (see below). It
was one of the first gay films to be internationally acclaimed (at the
Festival du Film Maudit in Biarritz in 1949) and one of the first to
be seized by the police (at a public screening in San Francisco in
1960). He followed it with *Puce Moment*, part of a projected longer
film, in which a woman gets dressed up in an extravagant outfit and
trolls about with a pair of long-haired dogs in a homage at once real
and ironic to the Great Ladies of Hollywood.

The Biarritz festival had been organised by Cocteau, who greatly
admired *Fireworks*, and in 1950 Anger moved to Europe. His first
work there made explicit links with Cocteau and the poètes maudits

whom the title of the Biarritz festival so evidently invoked. Thus in 1951 he made a film of Cocteau and Roland Petit's ballet *Le Jeune Homme et la mort*, whose title suggests *Fireworks*' own imagery, and in the same year he prepared, but never made, a version of Lautréamont's *Les Chants de Maldoror*.

His next finished and released film was *Eaux d'artifice* 1953. Using parts of Vivaldi's *The Four Seasons* as soundtrack, it shows a dwarf dressed in an extravagant eighteenth-century frock and elaborate feather headdress, moving about a baroque water garden. In Magick terms, the dwarf is pursuing a vital force which she[2] finally becomes: at the end, through editing, she is turned into a fountain. In a Magick, but also Freudian and/or gay context, water is also a sign of desire. Semen is an obvious symbolic possibility, though, given the overall pee-green colour of the film, it could be 'water sports'. The film is full of shots of stone mouths spewing fluid and near the end there is a long held close-up of a (stone) male face with water running continuously over it, which ends on a cut to the dwarf covering her face coyly with a fan. The coyness suggests the previous shot is a 'naughty' one, but this is also the moment of transubstantiation: the fan is hand tinted a brilliant chartreuse (the apotheosis of pee-green?) and at once, through editing, the lady becomes a fountain. The campy coyness at male fluids is also the fulfilment of the Magick ritual.

Inauguration of the Pleasure Dome was begun on a visit to Los Angeles in 1954 and has existed in at least four different versions (see Sitney 1979:104–5). It is a film of jewel-like richness, with a sybaritic, not to say queeny, central Magus figure, a fair bit of camp imagery and one of the participants, a blond Pan, 'gorgeous beyond words' (Rayns 1969:29) with a bunch of grapes at his hips. At one point Pan passes the Magus lying on a bed, holding a bunch of grapes to his mouth, which recall those at Pan's hips. The Magus's tunic is pulled back so that one can just see his testicles peeping out, creating a visual rhyme with the grapes, a characteristically witty solvent of the seriousness of desire.

Scorpio Rising, Anger's next completed film and undoubtedly his best known (see below), was made in 1962–3 on his return to the USA to live in New York. He followed it with *Kustom Kar Kommandoes* 1965–6 (in fact a mere fragment of a project), which is much like a sequence from *Scorpio Rising*: a young man in jeans and T-shirt caressingly polishes a custom car with a giant white powder puff, to the accompaniment of 'Dream Lover' sung by the Parris Sisters. Characteristically, butch imagery is sent up yet still sensuously filmed in gorgeous pastels. *Invocation of My Demon Brother* 1969 is Anger's most satanic film, with shots of US soldiers disembarking in Vietnam disconcertingly played over shots of naked boys, one black, one white, watching and wrestling. Since then, apart from revising earlier films, Anger has worked on various versions of *Lucifer Rising* (Rayns 1982).

Apart from their relation to traditions of witchcraft, the main gay interest of Anger's films lies in their treatment of desire. They use much of the iconography of twentieth-century US gay eroticism (sailors, bike boys, muscle men) and symbolise gay sexual pleasure, acts and orgasms, vividly and intensely. At the same time they have a humorous view of desire, so that images are sent up even while they remain keenly desired. This mix of intensity and irony in the treatment of gay desire is most fully illustrated by *Fireworks* and *Scorpio Rising*.

Fireworks

Fireworks has a narrative of sorts. A young man fondles himself in his room before going out cruising; he picks up a sailor; later, a group of sailors appears, chases him and beats him up; the first sailor reappears and masturbates over the young man; he too has an orgasm and the film ends with a shot of him and a man lying in bed together. This simple narrative structure is however overlaid with elements of Magick, dream and humour. These really organise the film, and I use them as the basis for this discussion.

Gayness is inseparable from *Fireworks*' Magick purpose of invoking the vital force of 'fire'. When the young man goes cruising, he asks the sailor for a light and gets it in the form of a bundle of burning sticks; the sailor's orgasm is symbolised by his lighting a roman candle sticking out of his flies and the young man's by a burning candle on the tip of a Christmas tree. Thus gay sexuality is the invocation of fire: cruising is asking for a light (fire), coming is the ejaculation of fire. (A close-up on the young man doing up his button-fly jeans is similarly both a gay and a Magick dressing up ritual.) This network of ritual symbolism is suggested by the voice over at the beginning: 'Inflammable desires dampened by day under the cold water of consciousness are ignited at night by the libertarian matches of sleep and burst forth in showers of shimmering incandescence.' This also suggests dream, which in Magick gives access to occult forces. *Fireworks* is not a literal rendition of a dream,[3] but it is, in its use of sexual symbolism and handling of space and time, dream-like.

The first sexual symbol in the film is an African statuette. The young man lies in bed with, apparently, a huge erection pushing the sheet up like a tent pole, but he removes a statuette from beneath the sheet which falls back into place. This is an obvious gag, which also deflates any expectation that there will be preoccupations with penis size in the film. On the other hand there is massive exaggeration in the symbolisation of ejaculation: the light the sailor gives the young man is from a huge bundle of sticks (a flaming faggot, a visual pun?); a stream of milk is poured over the young man's chest after the group of sailors have beaten him up; the sailor's orgasm is a spectacular roman candle, the young man's a Christmas tree candle. Though not in any usual legal sense pornographic (we see no actual penis or semen), this resembles gay pornography in two regards: the emphasis on the male orgasm as something seen, as spectacle, and the exaggeration of how much fluid it produces and how long it lasts. In actual pornography this is achieved by such devices as repeating the same shot of the ejaculation, or editing together different, coterminous shots of the same ejaculation, or slow motion, or intercutting shots of the ejaculator's face in orgasmic ecstasy, all devices making something more and longer of something less and shorter. The endless stream of milk, the lengthy roman candle display, the slow-burning Christmas tree give the same message.

In pornography the imperative to show orgasm (nearly always involving withdrawal) is often interpreted in terms of 'value for money' – the spectator needs to know that he has really seen an orgasm, it wasn't just faked – but this is clearly not the case here where the question of actual orgasms does not arise. What *Fireworks* suggests is the importance within gay sexuality of the orgasm as something to be seen, an importance that may be accounted for in a number of ways – as a sign that the other is excited by one's presence, as a present (a giving of a part of oneself), as part of the importance of the visible in the construction of male sexual desire and so on. (These might also be important in understanding why the imperative to show orgasm also characterises heterosexual pornography.) Equally the exaggeration of ejaculation may express the great psychic importance of so slight a physical reality or also be an example of erotic utopianism, lengthening and heightening the moment of (visual) pleasure so regrettably brief in reality. (Interestingly the longest, most delirious symbolic ejaculation on film is that of the bull in *The Old and the New* 1929 whose

semen floods the land in a wild, ecstatic montage. It was directed by
Sergei Eisenstein, with whom Anger has often been compared, and
who was also homosexual.)

In addition to its use of sexual symbolism, *Fireworks* is also
dream-like in its handling of time and space. As Sitney (1979:100)
observes, its 'repeated sudden changes of locale . . . are standard in
the cinematic vocabulary of the dream'. The young man leaves his
bedroom via a door marked Gents; cut to him in the street cruising,
suggesting he walks through the toilet door (into it or out of it?) to
the street; standing in the street he looks off camera left and there is
a cut to what, by editing convention, he sees, namely, the *interior* of
a bar; asking for a light from the sailor in the bar he is roughly
repulsed, but then there is an immediate cut to the two of them
back in the young man's room with the sailor lighting the cigarette;
moments later, the young man is back in the streets and after he has
been beaten up there are shots of urinals and him lying on the floor
in front of them – behind him the door marked Gents (the same one
as in the bedroom) swings open and there is a cut to the sailor, so
that it looks like the door swings open to reveal him; the sailor lights
the roman candle sticking through his flies, and then, via an almost
subliminally brief shot of a lighted paper floating on water, the film
moves to the young man in his room holding the Christmas tree
over his head; finally it cuts to him asleep in his room next to
another man. Details emphasise the non-realist feeling of all this.
The bar is obviously a painted backdrop, as in a theatre; the side of
the door marked Gents (which should mean we are seeing it from
outside the toilet) is on the inside of both the bedroom and the
toilet. This last case suggests that bedroom and toilet are the same
space, and the fluid, illogical transitions also suggest that one space
is simply being substituted for another throughout the film, that all
spaces are equal and equally sexually charged.

This is especially suggestive in gay terms. One of the commonest
ways of thinking about gay men's lives is in terms of a public (non-
sexual) face and a private (sexual) face. Yet this public:private
dichotomy is in many ways misleading when one considers gay
sexuality. On the one hand, much gay male sex is had in public
spaces – street corners, public conveniences; and on the other, gay
fantasy life is full of imagery (such as sailors) from the 'straight'
public world. *Fireworks* reworks these structures of gay sexual
reality in its shifting spatial transitions. It also indicates the dangers
– the delicious dangers – of this reality. Gay men are beaten up
and/or arrested in these sexual spaces but *Fireworks* neither

documents nor protests this. Rather, it turns it int?
pleasure. Orgasms in the film take place after th
been beaten up and many have ascribed a masoc'
film (notably Howard 1961).

Fireworks' complex imagery is further held together by
image of the sailor holding the young man prostrate in his arms.
track-in on this opens the film (figure 3.4), but it is next seen as a
photograph in multiple copies lying on the floor of the young man's
room; he gathers them up and throws them on the (unlit) grate
before going out cruising. After the candle orgasms he sets fire to
the pictures in the grate and the camera dwells on them slowly
consumed by fire (figure 3.5). The image itself combines two
elements with gay resonances: the erotic iconography of sailors
(figure 3.3) and Christianity. The latter is suggested by the young
man's Pietà-like position. Christ is the supreme instance of a ritually
significant sad young man in Western tradition. The shot-become-
photo thus condenses various of the Magick-erotic strands of the
film and is centrally involved in the invocation of fire/desire. It also
emphasises film itself, this film, as Magick eroticism – it is a
photographic image that sets everything in train, that is gathered
together and later lit in a final consummation. All this suggests
masturbation to porn, but intensified not only by its Magick purpose
but also by the highly charged significance of gay images when gay
practices are taboo, the (then) recent availability of gay beefcake
and the special force of photographic erotica, its elusive, tantalising
relation to the real.

Amid all this talk of Magick and dream-like constructions of
sexuality, it is easy to lose sight of the film's humour. This too is
both specifically gay and specifically Magick. Some gags have
already been noted – the statuette, the flaming faggot, the sailor
flexing on a stage set of a bar. Then there is the moment when the
sailors tear open the young man to reveal his heart as a meter, a
'ticker', and the absurd exaggerations of the milk and firework
orgasms. This humour does not undermine the ritual import of the
film – humour also unlocks the unconscious (as in Freudian theory)
and releases spiritual forces through its sudden associations (in gags
and puns) of what the rational mind keeps separate and through its
wild, anarchic, nothing sacredness, not even the sacredness of one's
own desires.

The ability to hold together intense devotion to something with a
simultaneous irony or even derision towards it is characteristic of
much gay culture. Thus the muscle display is both keenly desired

3.4 Fireworks: the image of the young man in the sailor's arms.

and lightly mocked, the masochistic ecstasy of death is revealed as a put-on in the 'ticker' gag. This is at its most delirious in the Christmas tree image. The tree is a symbol of Christianity, a spiritual force that has caught fire; the young man, in the shot-photo a Christ figure, wears the tree as a headdress (dressing up, assuming a Magick identity); the lit candle at its tip suggests orgasm; perhaps too there is a joke, in that the tip of Christmas trees is traditionally

3.5 '. . . catches fire'. (National Film Archive)

occupied by a fairy, and here is a fairy caught fire; and the tinsel and tat of the tree's dressing is a campy, queeny look. The tree thus condenses all the symbolic meanings in the film, with a wealth of gay connotations and as if with a shriek of laughter. It is both meant and sent up, and the irreverence of the latter, like the wild laughter of screaming queens, has a vitality and bezzazz that gives a further anarchic force to the film's magickal gay ecstasy.

Scorpio Rising

Like all Anger's films, *Scorpio Rising* is extraordinarily dense and complex yet rigorously structured. Thirteen more or less self-contained sequences are fitted to rock tracks and organised into a four-part ritual progression (see chart, p. 127). It is intensely homo-erotic but, apart from some lewd horse-play in 'Party Lights', this is not so much in the form of sex acts as in the way the film invites us to look at these boys, as desirable and unknowingly homosexual, the two dimensions discussed here.

Much of the imagery of men in the film is that of the gay porn magazines of the period, notably *Physique Pictorial*. The camera dwells on both physiques (huge back muscles, tautened abdomens and hard flesh) and fetishistic clothing (leather jackets, jeans, studs, belts). The songs direct us to see them with desire. 'Fools Rush In' enjoins us to fall in love with the biker we see cleaning and preparing his bike; when he walks towards the camera with his leather jacket open to reveal his torso, Rick Nelson sings, 'Open up your heart and let/This fool rush in'. The fact that this is the love of a 'fool' does not undermine it – Magick is about releasing the craziness to be found in such love, to which only those the world deems 'fools' are open. 'Blue Velvet' celebrates in words the sexy glamour of blue velvet while showing us one biker zipping up his jeans, another pulling on a T-shirt, another putting on chains and another just lying on a bed showing the smooth skin of his chest. The camera glides up or over the bodies, smooth as the hard, unhairy, probably lightly oiled flesh itself, smooth as velvet. 'Devil in Disguise' opens with Elvis singing 'You look like an angel' to the biker lying on his bed – he is gorgeous but also 'the devil in disguise', perhaps because the response his beauty elicits unleashes (welcome) satanic spirits. In 'He's a Rebel', a sensuously lit head and (bare) shoulders shot of a man in a bike cap smoking a cigarette (still sexy in the early sixties) is accompanied by the words 'Just because he doesn't do what/ Everybody else does,/ That's no reason that/ I can't give him all my love', suggesting, as Ed Lowry puts it, the 'surrender of self to an attractive figure of rebellion' (1983:44).

Most of the singers are men ostensibly singing to women, but the film has them appear to sing to other men. Montage further suggests the homo-erotic dimension of the images. In 'The Devil in Disguise' many seemingly heterosexual images are rendered gay (and devilish). Dean and Brando were already gay pin-ups (and the subject of gay gossip), but comics were thought innocent. Lowry (ibid.:43) details the way selection here brings out their latent gay potential:

> The pederastic undercurrent of 'Dondi' . . . [is] overt in this context: Dondi invites an attractive older man to share his room with him. The cartoon of the two boys with their arms around one another from the 'L'il Abner' comic strip may clearly be read as homosexual; and the title of the strip, 'The Sons Also Rise', suggests the boys' arousal to erection.

The use of cut-ins of an old film of the life of Christ, *The Road to Jerusalem*, draws Christ into the gay erotic circle. When he restores the blind man's sight, the latter goes down on his knees before him and there is an almost subliminal cut-in close-up of an erect penis,

Table 3.1   Scorpio Rising

BOYS AND BOLTS*: physical preparations		
'Fools Rush In'	Rick Nelson	uncovering, cleaning, assembling bike; biker posing in jacket
'Wind-Up Doll'	The Ron-Dells	watching toy bike revolve
'My Boyfriend's Back'	The Angels	skeleton hanging over biker polishing bike
'Blue Velvet'	Bobby Vinton	biker dressing up

IMAGE MAKER: psychic preparations		
'Devil in Disguise'	Elvis Presley	biker lying in room, reading comics, stroking cat, Brando on TV, pictures of James Dean on wall; lights cigarette
'Hit the Road Jack'	Ray Charles	biker gets up; boy rides round fairground on bike
'Heat Wave'	Martha and the Vandellas	taking cocaine; images of Dracula, Westerns, skull and crossbones, etc.; kissing a scorpion in glass
'He's a Rebel'	The Crystals	biker walking along, Christ and disciples ministering

WALPURGIS NIGHT: releasing powers		
'Party Lights'	Claudine Clark	party, sex play
'Torture'	Kris Jensen	party, pouring mustard over boy; church, images of Christ, Nazis, Brando

REBEL ROUSER, THE GATHERING OF THE DARK LEGIONS: final rites of destruction		
'Point of No Return'	Gene McDaniels	climbing on altar; starting off bike race, Christ enters Jerusalem on donkey
'I Will Follow Him'	Little Peggy March	Christ on donkey, Puck; standing on altar, peeing into Nazi helmet and offering it up; Nazis; skull
'Wipe Out'	The Surfaris	bike race, ending in crash, death, police lights.

* titles in capitals are from Anger's published notes (Sitney 1979:116).

suggesting the man fellates Christ. At the party, there is a shot from the Bible film showing a man laying out jewels on a table before Christ, followed by a shot of the man at the party baring his arse, his jewels, to the crowd. In the same sequence, there is a cut from Christ looking off camera to what he sees, namely, the bikers' orgiastic party, suggesting that he is, as Anger puts it, a 'wallflower at [the] cyclers' party' (Sitney 1979:116). Christ may have homo-erotic possibilities but his religion is repressive and, in Magick terms, a spent force, so that, though in the previous song 'he's a rebel', he cannot participate in the Magick sexual rite.

Scorpio Rising invites us both to look at the bike boys with desire and to consider the homo-erotic undercurrents of their rites and relationships. These in turn are linked to the desirability of death – 'My Boyfriend's Back' opens with those words over a close-up of a skull; 'Heat Wave' starts with the biker putting on a skull-and-crossbones ring; s/m pleasure is linked in 'Torture' with shots of Christ and his crown of thorns. The reference to Christ is not mere irreverence but a reference to the central feature of the Christ story, namely that he died and was born again. In 'Wipe Out' this is brought together in an image of a skull wearing a blonde wig and smoking a cigarette marked 'Youth'; in the eye sockets appear identical pictures of Christ pointing the way for an adolescent boy. The obvious interpretation is that death is the way forward for the boy, his youth is running out (burning away) and his death will be, like Christ's, a moment of renewal. As Lowry (1983:45) suggests, it is also 'bursting with implications of pederasty'. The cigarette, associated with butchness in 'The Devil in Disguise', 'clinched between the teeth of the skull becomes overtly sexual'. Youth is literally being sucked off by Death. Thus when the biker dies, the effect of swirling lights, rapid cuts, sudden changes of perspective and a welter of imagery is 'orgasmic; the orgasm is death' and this 'ritual death signals . . . ascension'.

The forces invoked by *Scorpio Rising* – sadism, male sexuality, immaturity (Puck, the bikers as boys), Nazism – are not ones widely approved of, but it is not at all clear that the film disapproves of them. They are not offered, as Lowry in a rather Freudian move seems to claim, as the malignant results of repression, but rather as the wild, transcendent forces that convention represses. The point is that most people disapprove of them (just as conventional morality disapproves of homosexuality, and probably sexuality, in general); their disapprovableness is a sign of their fitness for Magick invocation. If they were not conventionally wrong they could not be Magickally right.

Such wilfulness is at the heart of the difficulty of coming to terms with Anger's work. If I'm in the right mood, the intensity and brilliance of his films convey a feeling for gay desire as part of an elemental system of powers that defies and disrupts strait-laced conventional views of the world. At other times, it just seems like a lot of silly people getting dressed up in silly clothes and playing at evil, with little grasp of what cruelty and wickedness really are. But then perhaps this is the point – the 'silly', giggly, *naughty* quality of Anger's films is a spirit which at times feels irritating, unhelpful to the cause of gay rights, but at others is a tonic refusal to grow up into the drab oppressiveness of normal straightness.

Gregory Markopoulos

The films of Gregory Markopoulos suggest narratives that are never quite grasped. Titles often invoke Greek myth, many of the films are based (very loosely) on literary works, mainly French, and even without these pointers, the films do have characters and events, filmed with enough of the conventions of mainstream cinema to make you feel that there is a narrative in there somewhere. This is reinforced by the use of sequences consisting of brief shots from earlier in a film, very rapidly edited together and functioning as a kind of recapitulation of what has gone before. Sometimes these sequences replay the shots in the order in which they have already occurred in the film, at other times the order is different and seemingly jumbled. Such sequences suggest that there has been a narrative, a sequence of connected events that can be referred to and repeated, but the rapidity of the sequences and the jumbling of narrative order make it hard to pin down just what that narrative is. This elusiveness is heightened by lip movements on screen whose speech we don't hear, speech on the soundtrack that is often fragmented and only in a 'poetic' sense related to the images it accompanies, striking but obscure imagery and vivid visual textures, the fascinations and pleasures of which distract you from the business of 'following' a narrative. This multi-layered, open, ambiguous and confusing feel of the films is important in understanding their approach to homosexuality.

Markopoulos's first three films (aside from those he made as a boy) form a trilogy called *Du sang, de la volupté et de la mort*. The first part, *Psyche*, was made in 1947–8, the second and third, *Lysis* and *Charmides*, in 1948. *Psyche* has been interpreted (Mitry 1974:29, sometimes Markopoulos (Sitney 1974:142)) as representing lesbianism; *Lysis* and *Charmides* are more evidently homosexual. (They appear cryptic on this point today, but an editorial in *Films in Review* 2(7):2–3 tut-tutted of a screening at New York University in May 1951 that 'there were quite a few suggestions that abnormal perceptions and moods are desirable', reminding us of the scandalousness of even these esoteric films.)

Lysis, the title deriving from Plato's dialogue on friendship of that name, cross cuts between two young men, one dark, shot outside in industrial landscapes, parks and a graveyard, the other fair, lolling about a bedroom or hanging from his wrists in some possibly sado-masochistic scene. The two men could be embodiments of different facets of homosexual existence in the period. The dark man is the troubled, 'sensitive' young man: opening sequences associate him, first as a child, then as an adult, with a welter of feminine imagery (lace, candles, porcelain figurines, flowers); thereafter his moody wanderings in bleak settings cast him in the mould of the homosexual as outsider, the epitome of alienation. The fair man on the other hand could be termed 'gay-identified': in the bedroom his feet play lazily with streamers, his languorous movements perhaps suggest queeniness; the s/m sequence, if that is what it is, indicates particular sexual practices and is followed soon after by shots of him wandering about a Greek-looking temple dressed in a toga, suggesting the association of homosexuality with classical antiquity.

The two men never appear together, yet the drive of the cutting suggests they should, setting up an expectation of coming together which never happens. Between shots of the dark man wandering in a graveyard (the isolated homosexual) and the perhaps s/m sequence (the practising homosexual) the screen is blank and a voice refers to a 'we' who are 'retranchés du nombre des hommes' ('cut off from the mass of men'). Towards the end there is a sequence of the dark man sprawled by the sea beneath the moon, symbols of change and renewal, into which are cut two brief shots – one of the fair man, the representative of homosexuality, and the other a book illustration of a man chained to a rock with a male figure coming to his rescue. The press of the editing towards union, the reference to a collective identity, the image of someone coming to the rescue of a man in chains all suggest need and desire for change in the situation of the homosexual.

The title *Charmides* refers to another Platonic dialogue, this one a discussion of the attractions of the youth who gives it its name. Again there is cross cutting between two men with an even stronger sense of connection, even identity, between them. They are brought together in one shot, where the camera moves from one man across and down a tree to the other: both stand bare chested in the same pose with their arms held up in the air. The camera movement stresses their separation, but the similar pose and their being in the one take suggests a close affinity. Many of the camera angles and set-ups in the cross-cut shots of the two men likewise imply their similarity, including at one point shots suggesting martyrdom, one of them pinned to the ground by a network of wires, the other staked by the branches of trees. They are also shown to be objects of desire for one another. In one sequence one of them walks through a wood and joins a group of youths by a stream; there is a cut from him looking to what he is looking at, the youths and, downstream from them, the other man; the precise eyeline matches mean that it is clear that the first man is looking at the second. The youths, as groups of young men earlier in the film, may represent a kind of male bonding not available to the first man, but the other man is someone who could be. Thus far the possibility of connection and consummation between two men seems stronger than in *Lysis*, but the final sections have a more turbulent quality. The setting is a kind of pit, the music is agitated, most of the imagery connotes doom, and the film ends with the virtual obliteration of the scene by the use of superimposition. If the possibility of gay association seems closer in *Charmides*, so does the anxiety and trauma that may be attendant on it.

Several of Markopoulos's next films or projects refer to famous works of gay French literature: he planned a film of Gide's *Les Faux-monnayeurs*, dedicated *The Dead Ones* 1949 to Cocteau, named *Flowers of Asphalt* 1951 after Genet. His 1950 film *Swain* is organised around a flight which is generally taken to represent 'a subconscious rejection of the stereotyped masculine role that society and women insist upon' (Weinstein 1974:28), its wild quality embodying the '"insanity" to which society condemns those who do not bend to its sexual norms' (Noguez 1985:101).

His next completed and extant film is *Twice a Man* 1962–3. This centres on the tension between a central character, Paul, and both his lover and his mother, the latter incarnated in a younger and an older woman. This tension animates the narrative: Paul and the lover take, separately, the ferry from Manhattan to Staten Island; Paul wanders about his mother's house, cross cut with him walking in the park with his lover and visiting his house; finally in a ballroom, Paul dances but in a final shot seems to disintegrate. This structure is complicated by interpolated sequences: in the ferry section, there are shots of Paul climbing on to a roof and seeming to be about to commit suicide until his lover puts his hand on his shoulder and stops him; within the house section there are several other sequences showing Paul, cutting off a lock of his hair and posting it in a post-box in the street, caressing a tree trunk, being 'born' in the heavens, stretched out naked over his mother's lap on a rock by the sea. There are also two instances of the kind of recapitulation sequence described above.

Gay icons are briefly shown – Paul and his lover visit the Greek sculpture room of a museum, Paul walks before a painting of a sailor – and Paul is astonishingly handsome in a neat, square-jawed kind of way. The lover is slightly older than Paul, perhaps evoking the classical ideal of male lovers. The film's feelings about homosexuality are however uncertain: the relationship between Paul and his lover is evoked with a luminously calm intensity, but there remains a strong sense of torment in the film.

Throughout the film there is a contrast between the imagery of Paul with his mother and with his lover. The former often has a wild, hysterical edge to it, down to the very splitting of her into older and younger versions of herself, suggesting unresolved feelings of desire for the mother (standard in the sub-Freudian aetiology of homosexuality in the period). The scenes with the lover on the other hand are much straighter. Particularly powerful are simple close-ups, held for some time, which contrast in their visual simplicity, stillness and length with the fast movement and rapid editing characterising most of the film. The first of these close-ups occurs in the 'suicide' sequence – Paul's right shoulder fills most of the screen, with just part of his chin and neck showing in shadow; the lover's hand is posed on his shoulder, just the fingers visible. The intensity derives not only from the contrast with the rest of the film and from the shot's narrative significance (the lover has just stopped Paul from committing suicide), but also from qualities of the shot itself. The hand does not grip the shoulder but simply rests there; there is a slight turn of the jaw towards the hand, suggesting the momentousness of the touch. The long take allows us to dwell on the image, the texture of the cord jacket, the brilliance of the light on the hand, the dark redness of Paul's jaw and neck. It is a beautifully balanced composition – Paul's jaw, neck and jacket take up all of the right side of the frame but this is balanced by the luminosity of the hand on the left of the frame. A similar shot towards the end of the film, of the lover taking Paul's hand, again suggests intensity through qualities of stillness, balance and simplicity, the virtues of classicism. The camera holds on it, though there are repeated cut-in shots of the mother's house and her voice is heard on the soundtrack. The film seems to contrast the serenity of homosexual relations with the torment of mother-son ones.

Yet from the start the representation of Paul and his lover also draws on the 'sad young man' image. The first shot of the lover shows him seated on board the ferry, his gaze cast downwards, half his face in shadow. When Paul enters his mother's house, there are shots of a group of young men crying on the stairs; a close-up of one shows a tear rolling down his cheek and his lips appear moistened or lipsticked, a dwelling on and sensualising of a handsome young man in sorrow. Many of the shots of Paul in his mother's house show him wistful, sad, lying with his chin to his hand, turning disconsolately on a bed and so on. At the end of the film he seems to be destroyed. First he is shown both collapsing and rising in the same setting, as if no clear resolution is possible; then in the final ballroom sequence, before Paul's face cracks and disintegrates, there are shots of him fast cut with shots of the two mothers in bed with him, his lover kissing him and a coloured drawing of a bird, not shown complete but broken down into wings, beak, claws and so on. The bird in pieces and the subsequent disintegration of Paul's face suggest that his personality fragments and disappears under the pressure of the tension in the film.

Markopoulos's next film was *The Illiac Passion* 1964–6, in which a young man crosses the Brooklyn Bridge into Manhattan and there encounters various figures who represent both his many selves and the gods and goddesses of Greek mythology, played by many of the stars of the by then established underground cinema, Taylor Mead, Jack Smith, Clara Hoover, Gregory Battcock, Andy Warhol and others, the gods and goddesses of this Manhattan scene. As with others of Markopoulos's films, the homosexual elements remain unresolved, the conflict remaining within the central character. The same appears true of *Himself as Herself* 1966, described by Tony Rayns as exploring 'the bisexuality of a young man, by intercutting shots of his male and female personae and symbolising the fragile barrier between the two with close-ups of fluttering fans' (Rayns 1968:9). *Eros O Basileus* 1966 consists of a series of tableaux of a naked young man in a variety of poses, the man played by Robert Beavers who has himself made a number of films and now lives with

Markopoulos. With *Ming Green* 1966, *Bliss* 1967 and *Gammelion* 1968, Markopoulos moved away from films with such homo-erotic content towards a more purely formal or abstract kind of film, in this following developments within avant-garde film-making in the period.

THROUGH THE FIFTIES TO THE SIXTIES

The burst of gay film-making activity in the late forties did not continue through into the fifties. Anger and Markopoulos made few films and most of them in Europe. It was not until the early sixties that they returned to film-making in the States to join a new wave of gay film-making, such as *Flaming Creatures* and *Blow Job*, both made in 1963. By this time underground cinema itself had arrived.

The term 'underground cinema' itself had come into use round about 1960 (Noguez 1985:161–2), along with the infrastructures for such a cinema: distributors, places of exhibition (museums, galleries, schools, as well as cinemas and film clubs), criticism and journals, sources of funding beyond the film-makers' own pockets. The use of the term signalled that the underground had become something more than a series of scattered and isolated films and film-makers. The importance of gay film-makers was now fully acknowledged, Jonas Mekas writing more positively in his *Village Voice* film column in May 1963: 'The homosexuality because of its existence outside the official moral conventions, has unleashed sensitivities and experiences which have been at the bottom of much great poetry since the beginning of humanity' (1972:86).

The gay underground films of the sixties were very different from those of the late forties. The earlier films were carefully made studies of an inner gay consciousness that was taken to be the film-maker's own; the later films were apparently artless depictions of the exterior forms of gay life. The troubled young men in *Fireworks* and *Twice a Man* give way to the incandescent drag queens and sullen hustlers of *Flaming Creatures* and *Couch*. This change has to do with both the social perception of homosexuals and with the convergence of new ideas in the arts and the gay sub-culture.

Homosexuality was becoming seen as something present and significant in US society. Gay activism had begun to make homosexuality felt in public life, while a number of high profile writers – the Beats, novelists like James Baldwin and John Rechy – were constructing the homosexual as a figure symptomatic of contemporary society. The drag queen and the hustler, key figures of this writing and of the sixties gay underground alike, were no longer weird side-shows but symbols of the state of the nation. At the same time many of the formal qualities of sixties underground films – their apparent artlessness, the cult of spontaneity and chance, the use of pop material and pastiche – while they can be related back to internal developments within the visual arts have clear affinities with gay culture. Once again gay and artistic sub-cultures converged, notably in pop art and in the development of off-off-Broadway. These are the elements discussed in the following pages.

The fifties is often thought of as a period of sexual repressiveness before the permissiveness of the sixties. For gay people it was a period in which Joseph McCarthy extended his witch-hunting activities from 'commies' to 'queers', in which the police stepped up raids on lesbian and gay meeting places, in which the press discovered, or invented, the homosexual scandal story (D'Emilio 1983:40–53). Yet, as D'Emilio points out, this also indicates that there were homosexual communities there to be attacked, and the publicity attendant on the attacks drew them to the attention of other lesbians and gay men. Moreover the roots of the sixties' more open attitude towards sexuality reach back into the fifties.

The fifties saw an increase in the direct and single-minded attention paid to sex in popular culture. The two Kinsey reports, on men in 1948 and on women in 1951, were immediate best-sellers and the magazines *Confidential* and *Playboy*, with first issues in 1951 and 1953 respectively, gained very rapidly in circulation. Many of the best-selling novels, most of them made into successful films, centred on questions of sexuality, and Hollywood films began to break many of the taboos on what could and could not be dealt with on film (Dyer 1986:24–7). *Playboy* most clearly articulated the view that sex was both urgent (you had to have it) and benign (it was good for you) and that only the suppression of sex did harm. Though this was generally understood to be within heterosexuality, and indeed within marriage, it did provide an attitude and a space for alternative, and thus homosexual, voices.

There had been sporadic attempts at setting up gay rights organisations in the late forties, in Boston, New York, Los Angeles and probably elsewhere but the Mattachine Society, founded in Los Angeles in 1950, and the Daughters of Bilitis, founded in San Francisco in 1955, were the first really successful groups (D'Emilio 1983:57–125, Licata 1985:165–73). They worked at establishing a respectable culture and network for lesbians and gay men and

educating heterosexuals through publications and example. However, in New York in the early sixties, the style and approach began
to change (D'Emilio 1983:149–75). Randy Wicker, a member of the
New York Mattachine, tried leafleting and recruiting in the bars,
and although this was not directly successful ('"There's Miss
Mattachine", they would say' (quoted in ibid.:158)), it did force a
mutual awareness between activists and the gay scene. More
important, Wicker courted mass media publicity, appearing on a
radio programme which itself became a media controversy skilfully
milked by him, with substantial coverage in *Newsweek*, the *New
York Times* and other journals. This led to more general coverage
of gay life in New York, notably in the *Village Voice*, the alternative
newspaper in which Jonas Mekas had had a regular column covering
independent film since 1958. Gay rights was now a live media issue
and for the first time gay people themselves were speaking as gay
people, not deferring to or hiding behind a mask of professional
expertise.

In San Francisco in 1961 José Sarria, a drag artiste at the Black
Cat bar, ran for city supervisor, the first openly gay person to run
for a political appointment (ibid.:186–188). Sarria's drag acts often
directly expressed outrage at the situation of gay men:

> Donning an outlandish hat to sing *Carmen*, for instance, he
> reworked the script for his audience and its milieu. The heroine
> would be in Union Square, a gay cruising area in downtown San
> Francisco, scurrying through the bushes in an attempt to avoid
> capture by the vice squad. An overflow crowd of 200 or more
> cheered Carmen's escape.
>
> (ibid.:187)

Sarria was not elected supervisor but the act of standing gave a
politically explicit edge to the potential for defiance that he found in
drag.

Sixties gay underground films were not gay activist. They appear
politically indifferent and although drag is ubiquitous, for the most
part it just seems fun, not an expression of defiance. Yet they
appeared at a moment when homosexuality was now firmly on the
public agenda and, with Sarria, in its most flamboyant form. Even
where the films appear listless and inconsequential, they have
behind them the force of these new interventions by gay men in the
political arena and, like the activists, were howled down for their
pains.

Gay activism was part of a widespread conviction that to be

sexually progressive was also to be socially progressive. At an intellectual level there were new versions of Freudianism: Herbert Marcuse's *Eros and Civilisation* (hardback 1956, paperback 1962) and Norman O Brown's *Life against Death* (hardback/paperback 1959) played down Freud's insistence on the need for repression and stressed rather the essentially bisexual, genderless, 'polymorphous perverse' nature of human desire. The body and the unconscious were inherently free of notions of male:female, straight:gay and so on, and a society which imposed these categories was destructive of its people; to get back in touch with the body and the unconscious was to begin the transformation of society. The notion of polymorphous perversity, and therefore the embrace of homosexuality as part of the range of libidinal activity, informs such underground films as *The Bed* (see below), *Amphetamine* (Warren Sonbert and Wendy Appel 1966), men making love as part of the high of drug taking, and *Lovemaking*, made by one of the most highly regarded of all underground film-makers, Stan Brakhage, in 1968. Brakhage's films explore a range of sexual and mystical experiences, including masturbation, childbirth and, with *Lovemaking*, male homosexuality, which is placed as one of four sequences alongside heterosexuality, dogs copulating and children playing together naked, thus making homo and hetero equivalent and both as natural as 'nature' and innocent as 'childhood'.

Such views – the essential benignity and polymorphousness of human sexuality, the assertion of this as a demand for social change – were not confined to intellectuals and the avant-garde. In the twenty-fifth anniversary edition of *Playboy* (January 1979) it is suggested that the magazine was very much part of a general mood of dissent in the period:

> *Playboy* came out of aspects of the same energy that created the beat crowd, the first rock-'n'-rollers, Holden Caulfield, James Dean, *Mad* magazine – and anything else that was interesting by virtue of not eating the prevailing bullshit and being therefore slightly dangerous.
>
> (267)

Many would demur at this yoking of *Playboy*'s glossy, antiseptic pages to that alienated crowd of misfits, but it is not clear that there would in the period have been so great a feeling of inappropriateness.

From a gay point of view, an even more interesting, and surprising, example of such a connection being made is a speech by the father of the 'sensitive' male protagonist of *Tea and Sympathy* in the 1953 film version. He is expostulating to a friend on how shaming it is not to be able to talk to his colleagues about what his son is going to do for a living because he cannot tell them that his son wants to be – and here there is a long pause and we surely anticipate 'ballet dancer' or, a fifties favourite, 'interior decorator', but what he actually says is, 'a folk singer'. From the thirties folk music was associated with socialism in the USA and in the fifties everyone knew that commies and queers were bedfellows. The reference may be this precise or it may be a general nod in the direction of the fecklessness of those who don't have proper, male, bread-winning jobs. In the period it was the Beats who most fulfilled that role.

The Beat writers were 'beat' in the sense of beaten, frustrated, 'right down to it, to ourselves' with 'a weariness with all the forms, all the conventions of the world' (Jack Kerouac quoted by John Clellon Holmes in Cook 1971:6). Their poetry broke with the tidy, neat, carefully wrought work of the time, it sprawled, it abandoned obvious or self-conscious technique, words and images tumbled over each other in splurges of feeling. They identified middle-class America with conformity, restriction, lack of spirituality, domesticity, in short, dullness. To it they opposed a cult of authenticity, of being 'real' and one's 'self' over against conforming to social and moral convention. Drugs and sex helped free one from the sickness of normality, as did a loose way of living that was not tied down by a nine to five job and a house and family.

Many of the poets of the Beat movement were gay, Allen Ginsberg, Robert Duncan, Jack Spicer and others, and many lived in San Francisco in the same neighbourhood, the North Beach, and used the same bars and cafés as the developing gay and lesbian community (D'Emilio 1983:176–95). Others, such as Kerouac and Neal Cassady, thought gayness was 'cool' and were open to it on occasion. From early on, with the reading and publication of Ginsberg's long poem *Howl* in 1956, beatness associated homosexuality with revolt against bourgeois convention and identified in gay sex, vividly and unflinchingly evoked, the sources of a new holiness.

The Beats' stress on the spirituality of sexuality is not to be found in the sixties gay underground, but it is there in the work of the San Francisco based poet and film-maker James Broughton. His films, the first of which was made in 1946, show a progression from a rejection of homosexuality through an acceptance of it as part of the spectrum of sexuality to a total embrace of it. In *The Adventures of Jimmy* 1950 the hero seeks love in San Francisco and at one point even in a Turkish baths, but this is rejected along with other alternatives in favour of marriage. *The Bed* 1968 shows a series of naked people (alone, in couples or more) outdoors on an old fashioned bedstead. Filmed in bright sunshine, with humour but without ridicule, it constructs a sense of sexuality as natural and polymorphous, though this is less open than appears: most of the people are white, the one black woman treated exotically and in a faintly kinky context; there is no lesbian sexuality; gay male sexuality is introduced by a track back from a close-up on one man's face revealing that he is in the bed with another man, clearly something we are meant to be surprised at, not simply take for granted. *Dreamwood* 1972 is a quest-for-the-self movie, mainly heterosexual but including a Whitmanesque sequence where the searching protagonist meets a beefy woodsman and after an initial struggle goes into the forest with him; they emerge naked and the woodsman points the way for the protagonist, who heads off for more heterosexual self discovery. *Together* 1976 (made with his lover, Joel Singer) is Broughton's first whole-heartedly gay film, consisting of two images of his face which gradually merge, while on the soundtrack a poem celebrates the idea of coming together, meaning at once merging one's male and female selves, coming out and perhaps the harmony of simultaneous orgasm. *Hermes Bird* 1979 has a close-up of a penis filmed in slow motion so that one sees 'every small pulse and throb of it as it slowly opens into flower, growing in thrust and assurance, elevating toward heaven' (Broughton 1982:36), a spiritualised delight in the penis, that links to the Beats' phallic worship without their masculinist hang-ups (Stimpson 1982). *Devotions* (with Singer) 1983 does for the variety of gay sexuality what *The Bed* sought to do for human sexuality in general. Shots of men in leather, of male nuns on roller skates and other icons of the urban gay male culture are intercut with shots of Broughton and Singer together. As in *The Bed*, there is humour without ridicule, and the imagery of spiritual things, together with the film's title, indicates that this is a spiritual embrace of the range of contemporary gay sexualities.

More influential on the sixties gay underground than the Beats' 'heartfelt, populist, humanist, quasi-heterosexual, Whitmanic, bo-hemian, free-love, homosexual tradition' (Ginsberg 1974:9) were the novels of urban alienation such as *Another Country* (James Baldwin 1962), *City of Night* (John Rechy 1963), *Midnight Cowboy*

(James Herlihy 1965) and *Last Exit to Brooklyn* (Hubert Selby 1965). Here poverty, prostitution, drugs and street life are represented as the condition of America, with homosexuality seen as both symptomatically anomic but also sometimes a genuine grasping after human contact. This is well suggested by the film *Echoes of Silence* (Peter Emmanuel Goldman 1962–5), a series of fifteen vignettes of life in Greenwich Village shot in rough, grainy black and white, in one of which two boys, Viraj and Robert, 'return home after a frustrating Saturday night' (voice over) and begin tentatively, unpremeditatedly to touch and caress one another until the film fades to black. Although presented as two straight boys turning to each other for want of a woman, lighting, the hesitancy and delicacy of touch and interaction all suggest an acceptance of homosexuality as an option among others. The much later film, *Corner of the Circle* (Bill Daughton 1972) uses New York more bleakly as the expression of a gay man's hatred of being gay, of fruitless cruising and lonely evenings in grotty surroundings (see pp. 267–8).

The key figures of the novels, as of the sixties underground, are the hustler and the queen. The central character of two of the most successful, *City of Night* and *Midnight Cowboy*, is a hustler and hustlers figure importantly in *Another Country*, *Last Exit to Brooklyn* and other less acclaimed novels such as *The Messenger* (Charles Wright 1963) and *Naked to the Night* (K. B. Raul 1964). If the sad young man of earlier novels is in search of his 'self' and his 'true nature', the hustler is by contrast testing himself; if he is in search of anything, it is 'America'. The structure of the earlier novels hinges on discovery and revelation: the character discovers 'what he is'. There is no such introspection with the hustler. The tension derives more from the uncertainty about his masculinity and heterosexuality. It is not that he wants to find out if he is gay or what that means, but that he wants to prove that he is masculine. He does this by making it with women and only having sex with men for money. Heterosexuality proves he is a man, and manliness has not to do with inner feeling but with performance, acting like a man.

The novels explore the emptiness and hopelessness of the hustler's aspirations. In the section about him in *City of Night*, Chuck, 'one of [the] best-liked citizens' (Rechy 1963:126) of the Los Angeles hustling scene, recounts his aspiration to be a cowboy, though he was born in Georgia, and how he hitched out West and got a job on a ranch, but 'it was not like I figgered. I jes work aroun

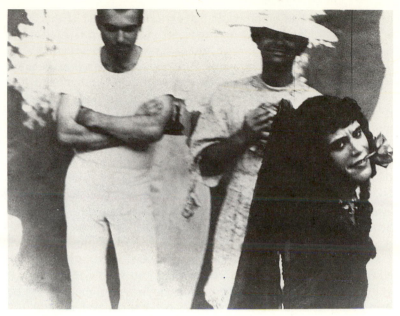

3.6   Some of the *Flaming Creatures*. (National Film Archive)

the place, doing, you know, odd things' (ibid.:140). When he tries to take a horse and ride on it, he is turned in to the police: 'And when I left, I think: Well, hell, it ain like in the movies' (ibid.:141). As he speaks to the narrator, 'his eyes search the park, as if wondering where the West of his imagination twisted into the West of Los Angeles' (ibid.:140). To be a cowboy is to be a man and to be an American; the hustlers' various macho outfits all attempt to embody this dual ideal, and yet time and again this is shown to be based on illusion, often explicitly the movies. At their most ambitious, and certainly in how they were widely received at the time, these novels suggest that the hustler's experience tells the truth about America, its obsession with masculinity and effeminacy, its identification of maleness with Americanness, the emptiness of all definitions of Americanness.

The other major characters in the novels are the queens, who also figure in a minor capacity in practically all fifties and sixties novels with a gay theme and are important to such literary successes as *Giovanni's Room* (James Baldwin 1955) and *The Gaudy Image* (William Talsman 1958). The latter, written entirely from within a queen perspective, was itself a kind of underground novel, published by the Olympia Press in Paris and seized by US customs.

The queen too could be taken as a symptomatic figure of the USA: 'her' hysterical affectation could be seen as another product of the obsession with effeminacy, with the exaggeration of sex difference in US life, and 'her' very being as a 'fake' woman, 'her' excitement when a man thinks she is 'real' (i.e. a woman), 'her' modelling of herself on movie stars, all suggest a life lived on the basis of illusion. But the queens also have tremendous energy, courage and conviction. Unlike the hustlers, they are not faced with the shattering of their illusions when they discover that one cannot be what one aspires to be – the queens know they are not real women and never can be, they know they are giving a performance and choose to do so up to the hilt.

The queen, especially at his/her most screaming, is curiously placed in relation to the shift at the end of the sixties from the 'authenticity' of the Beats, and other contemporaneous aspects of the art world such as abstract expressionism in painting and the Method in acting, to the impersonality and artificiality of such developments as off-off-Broadway and pop art. The queen could be appropriated to both these seemingly antithetical tendencies.

In his *Gay Sunshine* interview Ginsberg suggests how the queen can be seen as authentic, with spiritual roots that mean he can be seen as outside the inauthenticity of mainstream culture: 'the old shamanistic transvestite that we see running up and down Greenwich Avenue. . . . The screaming young queen – there's something very ancient and charming about that' (1974:19). This perception of the queen is suggested by the film *Chumlum* 1964 Ron Rice, a series of sequences, full of superimpositions, of men making up, trailing about parks in diaphanous drag, playing on swings, lounging in hammocks, all to the accompaniment of 'Eastern' sounding instruments. The latter are campy, a bow in the direction of Hollywoodian Arabian Nights movies, but also part of a beat interest in mysticism and the 'otherness' of the East.

Queens might thus be perceived as spiritual, but equally they are the supreme instance of role play and artifice, of a purely material play with the signs of social life. The queen can undermine all certainty as to what could be labelled authentic or real. *Portrait of Jason* 1967 Shirley Clarke has Jason Holliday, 'a black queen' as he calls himself, talking direct to camera about himself and his affairs, hustling, pick-ups and so on. As Dwoskin observes, it is not clear what kind of film this is – is it just a documentary record of a street queen or is it something else: 'Is Jason acting? Is he real? Jason loves it; he entertains – showbiz baby – but he is real. There before

your very eyes is Jason, laughing and crying. Fact or fiction?'
(1975:227).

This perception of the queen is more in line with new sixties art.
Beat writing, abstract expressionism and Method acting all shared a
commitment to authenticity and masculinity that resulted in
sprawling, ranging, apparently undisciplined and artless art, the
untrammelled exteriorisation of the self. Susan Sontag, in her
review of *Flaming Creatures* in 1964, saw this as 'an old cliché of
European romanticism' which persisted longer in the USA than
anywhere else, a belief that 'neatness and carefulness of technique
interfere with spontaneity, with truth, with immediacy' (Sontag
1967:228). Something of 'artlessness' remains in off-off-Broadway
and pop art, and sixties underground cinema, but no longer
connected to notions of authenticity and self-expression.

The development of off-off-Broadway, starting at the Caffé Cino
in 1959, meant not only new venues for theatre but a new kind of
theatre: 'Twice each night, and sometimes three times, the Caffé
Cino presented the outrageous, the blasphemous, the zany, the
wildly poetic, the embarrassingly trite, the childish, and frequently,
the moving and the beautiful' (John Gruen, Joe Cino obituary, *New
York Herald Tribune*, 3. 4. 67, quoted in Poland and Mailman
1972:xviii). The major reference point for off-off was mass culture,
recognised as illusion and seen as extravagant, ludicrous, baroque
and wild, in other words, as camp. There was mockery, but no
desire to undermine. Such theatre replaced authenticity, which
retains some notion of the fidelity of a representation to what it
represents, with intensity, a commitment to incandescent performance that burns away any lingering concern with so-called realism.
Hollywood movie stars, especially the women with their devotion to
glamour, especially in films set in, for instance, Arabia or
Transylvania, places that owe nothing to geography and everything
to the imagination – these are the stuff of off-off, and the cheaper
and tackier the better, for then the triumph of intensity is all the
greater.

This feeling is present in the films made in the early sixties in Los
Angeles by the Gay Girls Riding Club, a group of friends who met
on Sundays for horse riding, brunch and home movie making.
Shown in the Los Angeles gay clubs, they were a series of campy
film parodies, including *Always on Sunday*, *Roman Springs on
Mrs Stone*, *What Really Happened to Baby Jane* and *All About
Alice*. The same sensibility informs the films of the Kuchar brothers,
an amazing outpouring of wild trash parodies with titles like *I Was a*

Teenage Rumpot 1960, *Lust for Ecstasy* 1963 and *Sins of the Fleshapoids* 1965. Some of George Kuchar's solo films are on the cusp between the two gay undergrounds. One of his earliest, *Eclipse of the Sun Virgin* 1967, has many of the motifs of guilt and furtive homo-erotic longing of the first gay underground, as well as the intense colour and clean-grained image quality. Yet its sense of the outlandish banality of middle-American conversation and style, its use of an extravagant (popular, classical and Hollywood derived) music collage soundtrack and its loose, unhurried structure bring it much closer to both Jack Smith and Andy Warhol, as will be apparent in the discussion of their work below.

By the sixties camp, manifest now in fringe theatre and film, was becoming a known quantity beyond its roots in gay subcultural entertainment, partly thanks to Susan Sontag's influential article in *Partisan Review* in 1964. She presented camp as part of pop art, though where off-off is all intensity, Warhol's silkscreens of Campbell's Soup tins or movie stars' faces (Marilyn Monroe, Elizabeth Taylor) seem all cool and detachment. What they share is the use of imagery drawn from mass culture and their 'lack of moralism' in relation to it. Where some see pop art as a critique of US society (eg. Poland and Mailman 1972:xiii, Rowe 1982:35–9), Sontag stresses its refusal to criticise: 'The best works among those that are called pop art intend, precisely, that we abandon the old task of always either approving or disapproving of what is depicted in art – or, by extension, experienced in life' (1967:229–30).

Yet if camp and pop art are without moral or political 'position', they are not, especially from a gay perspective, socially inexpressive. They may embody a gay strategy for dealing with the world, as Bruce Boone suggests in his article on the work of the poet Frank O'Hara. O'Hara was a curator at the Museum of Modern Art in New York and much involved with the development of abstract expressionism and 'Action Painting', even writing a monograph on Jackson Pollock. He was also a gay man. He was thus influentially at the intersection of the art and the gay sub-cultures, in this case the sophisticated, less street-based gay milieux of up-town New York. It was this inflection of gay tradition that came to influence the art world. Boone sees at the centre of this a gay way of handling language that he calls 'trivialisation'. On the surface, seen from a straight perspective, this is simply taking nothing seriously, treating everything as trivial. Boone detects more specific formal strategies in O'Hara's poetry, which derive from gay men's speech patterns and give a particular edge to trivialisation. O'Hara's poems, like gay gossip, work 'paratactically', that is, 'events, observations, etc., are simply enumerated: "I do this, I do that"' with all connectives left out (1979:81). What this bespeaks is the fact that 'connection' for gay people may be 'dangerous'. All situations hold potential disaster for gays, straight ones because you don't belong, gay ones because they are outlawed – better then not to spell out connections. At one level such an approach expresses 'a sense of a life lived as continuously imperilled and unfulfilled in its essential social needs by virtue of membership in a community whose existence is always in question' (ibid.:83). At another level, writing, speaking, like this is also a strategy for survival, skating along over the perils and uncertainties of community.

Sixties gay underground films belong with camp and pop art, in various ways exploring surface, role, artifice and the detritus of mass culture. Their formal strategies may be seen as part of the denaturalising, trivialising impulse of some forms of gay language. But their imagery – homosexual acts, hustlers, queens – also had resonances because it seemed a harbinger of the importance of sexuality, expressing now the hope for a libidinal transformation of society and now a sense of the USA's destruction of all such hope. This combination of strategies and imagery is most fully exemplified in the work of Jack Smith and Andy Warhol.

Jack Smith

What all [Smith's] movies have in common are Jack Smith, wild and perverse sexuality, prankish improvisation, costumes related to all previous elements, and camera work loose as a goose.

(Kelman 1963:4)

The work of Jack Smith cannot be pinned down. Elusiveness, flux, transience, transformation seem to be its essence. It is not just that Smith has taken so many roles (performer, scriptwriter, theatre piece maker, film-maker, writer on films), but that most of what he has done has not stayed in one fixed form for long, and even the major exception to this, *Flaming Creatures*, feels impermanent, fluid, mutable.

He was a performer in films made by Ken Jacobs (*Little Cobra Dance* 1957, *Star Spangled to Death* 1957–60, *Little Stabs at Happiness* 1958–61, *Blonde Cobra* 1962) and a nightclub show, *The Human Wreckage Review*, which they put on together in Provincetown in 1961. Jacobs used a monologue Smith had recorded as the soundtrack for *Blonde Cobra*, and there is a good deal of improvisation by Smith in all the films he made with Jacobs. Apart from appearing in his own films and theatre pieces, he also appeared in, among other things, *Queen of Sheba Meets the Atom Man* 1963 and *Chumlum* 1964, both directed by Ron Rice, *Batman Dracula* 1964 (Smith plays the former) and *Camp* 1965 by Andy Warhol, and Markopoulos's *The Illiac Passion* 1964–6. In many of the films Smith appears in tacky drag; in *Queen of Sheba* he plays Hamlet. The quality of the performance veers between a wild-eyed, hysterical intensity and a lolling-about playfulness: in the opening sequence of *Little Stabs*, he gobbles at a plastic doll's crotch before gleefully stubbing a lighted cigarette into its eye, yet in the final section, 'The Spirit of Listlessness', he dawdles about in Pierrot costume, itself redolent of floppy inconsequentiality, idly sucking on or playing with different coloured balloons.

Smith's soundtrack for *Blonde Cobra* is a scabrous monologue involving necrophilia, burning a little boy's penis with a match and a long sequence about Madame Nescience, a Mother Superior who lashes one nun with a rosary and beats the convent girls with the cross for using a plaster cast of Jesus as a dildo. These shriekingly violent passages, with their vein of misogyny, are however preceded by a camp languidness ('Gloria Swanson had a pair of shoes for every dress') and followed by languidness shading off into despair ('Why shave when I can't even think of a reason for living?') and a reference, at once witty and uncomfortable, to gay sex ('Sex is a pain in the ass').

Smith's first film, now lost, was called *Buzzards over Bagdad* 1951–6; in 1960 there was *Overstimulated* and in 1961 *Scotch Tape*, described by Stefan Brecht as 'various faggots cavort[ing] in . . . what appears a rubble-strewn ground' (1978:23). *Flaming Creatures* (discussed below) was made in 1963 and thereafter Smith's films have appeared in constantly changing forms, the same footage being reassembled, with new bits added, different soundtracks and changing titles, often only shown once. David Ehrenstein (1984:20–1) gives some of the titles: *Normal Love* 1963–4 (later *Tales of Cement Lagoon* and *Normal Fantasy*), *No President* 1969 (aka *Slave President* and *The Kidnapping and Auctioning of Wendell Wilkie by the Love Bandit*), *In the Grip of the Lobster Claw* c. 1966, *Loathsome Kisses of Bagdad* 1969, *Zombie of Uncle Pawnshop* n.d. and *Lucky Landlordism of Lobster Lagoon* 1981. I find the titles evocative, even without having, alas, seen the films. Hollywood is raided, especially for horror and Arabian fantasy imagery, but juxtaposed with imagery inimical to such escapism (buzzards, cement); there is the suggestion of social comment (normality, the presidency, landlordism) though even to name it as social comment is being too heavy. The most intriguing title is *Overstimulated*, almost suggesting the effect of the films as registered in the films themselves, rich, heady imagery that collapses under the weight of its own excess, the way that a bout of shrieking camp ends up in febrile exhaustion.

In 1962–3 *Film Culture* published Smith's article 'The Perfect Filmic Appositeness of Maria Montez'. Montez was the star of minor forties adventure movies put out by Universal Studios, such as *Bombay Clipper*, *Arabian Nights*, *Cobra Woman*, *Gypsy Wildcat*, and *Siren of Atlantis*. The titles suggest films of opulent spectacle and vivid excitement, but in reality the sets are cardboard, the acting wooden and the story negligible. Much of the appeal resides in the films' failure to live up to their promise – they are examples of camp as 'failed seriousness' (Sontag 1967:287). What is important about them for Smith is Montez's 'convictions of beauty/her beauty'. She is not acting, which is after all 'hoodwinking', she is displaying her belief in the films'/her aspiration to the creation of magic, beauty. This gives an intensity to the films even while the crappy acting and sets cut across any potential viewer involvement in the plot. Smith finds the convulsive beauty prized by the surrealists in the gestures, clothes and props of films whose controlling, explaining narratives can be ignored (cf. the discussion of *Rose Hobart* above). It is this quality that is evoked in his most celebrated film, *Flaming Creatures*.

Flaming Creatures

Flaming Creatures consists of a series of sequences loosely hung together, performed by a group of people who are sometimes clearly male or female but more often ambiguous – transvestite, hermaphrodite, hormone assisted. It was shot on outdated raw film stock, giving the image a washed out, overexposed or occasionally murky look. Clothes, props and music all refer to Montez's notions of Hollywood glamour and femininity and of what Spain, China and Arabia are like. The bleachy, grainy look and the Hollywoodiana all make it look like an old B-movie that has been run too many times through projectors. At the same time, it is nothing like a Hollywood movie.

In the opening sequence, the handwritten credits are accom-

panied by *Scheherazade*-style music and a voice repeating 'Ali Baba
is coming!'. Various indistinct figures flutter about and there are
close-ups of a flower being slid along a bare arm and a shell being
placed at a crook in someone's body (between the legs? on the
inside of a bent elbow?). All the feel of the film is there: you can't
quite work out what or where anything is, yet the music and voice
evoke a familiar world of the imagination and the image insistently
suggests a languorous eroticism. Nor can you work out where the
film is going. 'Ali Baba is coming!' sets up narrative expectations,
but of course he never comes, the narrative 'hook' is never picked
up – like the flaming creatures of the film, we are left to languish in
the moment, abandoning the pleasures of tension and development,
of 'following', that characterise mainstream feature films.

The first scene after the credits has a transvestite in white, holding
white lilies, meet, kiss, and play about with a woman[4] with swaying
hips, wearing black. This is accompanied by a fake South American
pop song and at one point is shot through lace. Next there is the
lipstick sequence. A voice over reads out from an advertisement for
a 'heart-shaped lipstick'. At one point a male voice asks, as if
writing to a women's magazine advice column, 'How does a man get
lipstick off his cock?', to which comes the reply, 'A man is not
supposed to have lipstick on his cock'. Meanwhile various creatures
are putting on lipstick, including a man with a beard and another
with a penis resting on his shoulder.

A long-held shot of a group of the creatures sitting perfectly still,
until one of them starts to wiggle his/her toes, seems to introduce
the more or less central and longest sequence. With Chinesey music
on the soundtrack, the creatures from the scene after the credits
chase one another back and forth (and off) the screen, until the
transvestite grabs the 'woman' and forces her to the ground. Other
creatures descend and rape her, the camera moving hectically
about, loud screams on the soundtrack. There are extreme close-ups
of her wobbling breasts and at one point her dress rides up to reveal
her vagina. The rape somehow develops into an orgy which itself
seems to be accompanied by an earthquake. But no-one shows
much alarm, petals are scattered over everything and 'things quickly
dissipate, disintegrate, and collapse into inertia' (Ehrenstein
1985:24). In the following sequence the raped 'woman' gets up and
is kissed, comforted and petted by another woman. They too are
scattered with petals.

Next a coffin opens and out of it comes a transvestite in a blonde,
Monroe-esque wig, to the accompaniment of honky-tonk music.

'She' dances and rubs calla lilies over herself, before vampirising an androgynous creature.

> In pained rapture, the vampire, whose wig is slipping and whose breast-padding is falling out, pulls down her own stocking and desperately wiggles her limp genitals with one hand as she clutches the androgyne's still breast with the other.
>
> (Packman 1976:55)

It is a characteristic moment. Her femininity is coming apart, she pleasures herself, and she doesn't have an erection. It is 'failed seriousness', the drag unconvincing, the vampirism no turn-on. Yet, in the final group of inter-cut sequences, the ecstasy of acting out imagination and desire are reaffirmed. Everyone, including a black transvestite and a hustler type, dances to tango-like music, with many close-ups of armpits; the vampire and a transvestite in Spanish drag (figure 3.6) dance together; a group of Arab men and a large-breasted woman recline together, one of the men stroking the woman's breast, to the accompaniment of 'Bebopalula'. The film ends on a close-up of a wobbling breast.

In *Queer Theatre*, Stefan Brecht suggests the nature of *Flaming Creatures* beauty in terms which rework Smith's appraisal of Maria Montez:

> the images . . . are all cast in the artwork's searing gesture of irony, an adoration neither of the tawdry, nor of beauty, but of the aspiration toward beauty, the purer for its immersion in the tawdry, a more fond, defiant and compassionate respect for this aspiration, than an adoration of it.
>
> (1978:26)

What is lacking in Smith on Montez but apparent in his film work is the sense of pathos Brecht implies. It is as if Hollywood's successful attempts at beauty produce a rationalistic, controlling beauty, but all other attempts are bound to fail because of their marginality and cheapness, so that all that is left is the aspiration to beauty. This aspiration is bound to fail, just as drag queens will never be women, which evokes in the films a mood of 'fond, defiant and compassionate respect'.

Andy Warhol

Andy Warhol may have been the most famous openly gay artist who ever lived. He was a world-wide celebrity, his doings known to millions who had never seen, much less admired, his work. Like movie stars before him, he was famous for what he was taken to be rather than what he did; but unlike previous stars, he did not give the illusion that he was sharing or revealing his 'self', his inner person. With Warhol, what you saw is what you got, the appearance of stardom was the limit of it. If the first gay underground was obscure and concerned with inner reality, with Warhol it was ultra famous and concerned with self as surface.

Warhol was a well-established artist when he made his first film, *Tarzan and Jane Regained . . . Sort of* in 1963. He had made his name in the fifties as an illustrator, notably of shoes and short stories. In 1962 he had exhibited silkscreens of Campbell's Soup cans, flat poster-like reproductions of one of the most familiar domestic objects in US homes. It was the cheek of it that drew media attention: the skill required was no more than that of the person who had designed the cans in the first place, there was no sign of the ineffable touch of an Artist; the object was mass culture trash, not worthy as a subject for Art; and it wasn't as if the work seemed to be criticising consumer society or something. Much the same might be said of the films that he began to make a year later.

Between 1963 and 1967 Warhol made upwards of eighty films. Many are lost, others were incorporated into longer films. There is no definitive list.[5] They are commonly divided into four groups. The first, from *Tarzan and Jane* to *Mario Banana* (November 1964), consists of silent, black and white films. The camera is generally perfectly still and a take lasts as long as there was film in the camera. In some of these nothing apparently 'happens': *Sleep*, six hours, a man asleep shot from different positions; *Empire*, eight hours, the Empire State building from 8 p.m. till dawn; *Taylor Mead's Ass*, just that for an hour and a bit. As so little happens, the spectator may nonetheless notice what does happen, in what is filmed – the sleeper's body registers his breathing, night wears on – or in how it is filmed – Mead's buttocks are overexposed at first but become gradually more palpable. Some of the other films in the period are positively eventful by comparison, but there is still the effect whereby minutiae of body movement or camera placement become enormously noticeable. With both *The Thirteen Most Beautiful Women* and *The Thirteen Most Beautiful Boys*, the camera just gazes at the subjects as they pose, increasingly uncertain of what to do, embarrassed, turning away, even crying. In *Haircut* one man has his hair cut by another, while a hustler type preens and poses, prepares pot and strips; in the last third, the man having the hair cut stares fixedly at the camera and at the end the other two men also stare at it, before everyone bursts into giggles. *Blow Job* consists of a close-up of a man's face, while below off screen he is being sucked off by another man; the fellatee's face registers various heights of pleasure until, just before the end, before the final can in the camera ran out, it contorts in the pleasure of coming. A more detailed account of a film from this period, *Couch*, is given below.

The last film of the first period anticipates the first of the next. *Mario Banana* shows Mario Montez eating a banana and this is the substance of *Harlot*, December 1964, but here there is also a soundtrack, consisting of three queens off camera talking about movie stars. The films in this group are again black and white, with, mostly, still camera and long takes, but they have sound and often a script by Ronald Tavel (who subsequently worked with the Theatre of the Ridiculous (Smith 1987)). Again there are no events or incidents, people sit about and witter on; the forms and styles of femininity and masculinity seem, in a desultory way, to be what the films are about. Femininity is perceived principally through Hollywood, with references to Hollywood stars (Harlow in *Harlot*, Hedy Lamarr in *Hedy* (aka *Hedy the Shoplifter* after the scandal involving Lamarr to which the film alludes), Lana Turner in *More Milk Yvette* (why? why?), Lupe Velez in *Lupe*) or, failing that, either invented stars (*The Life of Juanito Castro*) or else the business of becoming a star, as in *Screen Test #1*, where Mario Montez, already becoming an underground star, is on screen in drag answering questions and reading lines given him by an off-screen voice, and finally admitting that he is a man. Masculinity takes centre screen in *Horse*, a parody of the Western, and in *Vinyl*, based on *A Clockwork Orange* and focusing on the protagonist's attack on a book-reading passer-by and his subsequent punishment, bound to a chair and tortured, surrounded by others in the throes of sadomasochistic encounters.

Probably the last film in this second grouping would be *Hedy*, but already in July 1965 came the first of the third grouping, *Beauty #2*. Still mainly in black and white, the films now begin to make greater use of camera movement, while the scenarios by Chuck Wein are less camp, with no elements of fantasy, more fly-on-the-wall documentary in feel. The best known is *My Hustler* (see below).

The Chelsea Girls summer 1966 is often seen as the transition point from the third grouping to the last. The footage is much like that of *My Hustler* or *Beauty #2*, but now there is colour and the film was designed to be shown on split screens, different episodes unfolding side by side in arbitrary sequence. Further 'expansions' of cinema followed, comparable to Hollywood's move into wide screen and stereophonic sound in the fifties: ****, which lasted twenty-five hours and was shown only once (in New York on December 15–16, 1967) consisting of various films made over the previous year, projected randomly two at a time on top of each other; *The Exploding Plastic Inevitable*, a rock event with overhead projection of films. *The Chelsea Girls* was also the first big success of the underground. It was transferred from the small, independent Film-makers' Cinematheque in New York to an up-town, first-run cinema and ran continuously for nearly a year, meanwhile getting cinema screenings all over the States. *Newsweek* ran a story on it; the big distributors began to take an interest. The other films of this final grouping were marketed as commercial movies, part of their success being the promised frisson of seeing something come up and out from the underground.

The Chelsea Girls consists of a number of sequences, whose only connection is that they were filmed at the Chelsea Hotel. They include: a blond young man, caressing himself, tripping on LSD and stripping; a high camp 'Pope' hearing confessions; a hustler and his client, serenaded by Mario Montez in drag; two women making love. Other films in this last grouping include *The Loves of Ondine* (featuring Ondine, the most 'unapologetically and adamantly homosexual' (Berlin and Bruce 1986–7:57) of Warhol's stars), *I, a Man, Bike Boy, Nude Restaurant* and *Lonesome Cowboys* (1967), which is discussed below.

In June 1968, Warhol was shot and wounded by Valerie Solanis, a former member of Warhol's entourage and author of the manifesto of SCUM (the Society for Cutting Up Men), one of the earliest voices of a new, separatist feminism. He may have made one film after this, *Blue Movie* (aka *Fuck*), but most writers seem to think that this is really Paul Morrissey's first film as director, though like his subsequent films for the next few years sold under Warhol's name. Morrissey had become part of the Warhol entourage round about *My Hustler* and Koch credits him with the move towards greater narrative coherence in Warhol's work (1973:62). After *Blue Movie* he made three films centred on Joe Dallesandro as a hustler: in *Flesh* 1968 his lesbian wife pushes him out on to the streets to earn money for her and their child; in *Trash* 1970 he is a heroin addict who cannot get an erection and therefore cannot earn any money; in *Heat* 1972 he tries to make it in Hollywood. The drag queens in these films played *Women in Revolt* 1972, which can be seen as a critique of female stereotypes by having 'transvestites enact other people's fantasies of "the feminine"' (Gidal 1981:1299) or else as saying, 'Life is a camp – and this means *your* life, too, lib ladies!' (Tyler 1972:231).

One way at looking at these groupings of Warhol films is as an ironic, knowing recapitulation of the history of the movies, a history at once technical-aesthetic and commercial (James 1985). The first films are fascinated by the process of filming itself; gradually spectacle and performance become more important, and are then organised into increasingly coherent and planned narratives. Concurrently, the films reach beyond the fine art world, first to the subworld of gays, prostitutes, addicts and so on, who stand in this history for the fairground and immigrant audiences of conventional histories, and finally achieve mass media success with stars and a studio set-up ironically named The Factory.

Warhol's stars were drawn both from other underground films (Taylor Mead, Mario Montez, Frances Francine) and from the denizens of the 'interlocking subcultures of the late 1950s – artistic, sexual, sometimes even criminal' (Koch 1973:3) who hung about his loft in New York. These stars are representative figures of the gay underground: the gay-identified men, camp but not in drag (Ondine, Mead); the drag queens (Montez, Francine, Candy Darling, Holly Woodlawn); the hustlers (Paul America, Joe Dallesandro); figures like Gerard Malanga and Eric Emerson, who play at being butch but undercut their play with camp; and, ambiguously placed, the real women such as Edie Sedgwick, Viva, Nico, Brigid Polk and others. Berlin and Bruce (1986–7:53) point out that all these figures are the kinds of people 'on whose backs Hollywood was built, both on screen and off (closeted gay actors, actresses, and directors, set designers, wardrobe and make-up people, mistresses and gigolos, etc.)', yet who were portrayed on screen 'as tragic or indecent figures'. The Warhol films put them centre screen, and what's more have them then ape Hollywood's onscreen images, precisely, as in the references about Lamarr, Turner, Velez, Montez, or more generally in the transvestites' appropriation of glamour and the hustlers' approximations of the sullen hunkiness of Brando, Dean, Presley and co. So here were these perverts, who were always anyway the unspoken part of Hollywood's history, now openly in the movies and putting on the very put-ons of glamour and sexuality that Hollywood had been peddling for so long. Then, a further irony in the Warhol recapitulation of movie history, they actually got taken up by the industry proper, really did become stars, featuring in magazines, guesting on chat shows. They then sometimes proceeded to undermine the cosy, nice 'n' normal assumptions of the success machine. Berlin and Bruce describe the effect of Nico's appearance on the Merv Griffin chat show:

> Merv started his show biz chatter, but Nico refused to talk. She said not one word. Merv, live, began screaming on camera to someone off-screen, 'Who is this woman? Who booked her on the show?'. He was reduced to a blubbering idiot, and Nico had made her point. The facade of happy Hollywood had given way to reveal a man screaming at a woman who sat very still.
>
> (ibid.:57)

This simultaneous buying into and debunking of Hollywood was done by those groups of people closest to it in terms of sensibility (producing sensuousness and glamour and/or trading in sex) yet most rigorously excluded from it at the level of representation.

Yet this makes Warhol's films sound too critical, whereas the overall tone is a detached embrace of what Hollywood stands for in full recognition of its phoneyness. One of Warhol's best known quotes catches the stance: 'I love Los Angeles . . . I love Hollywood . . . Everybody's plastic – but I love plastic. I want to be plastic' (quoted in Koch 1973:23). In the educated middle class's vocabulary of the fifties and sixties, 'plastic' was a by-word for all that was wrong with Hollywood, itself the epitome of contemporary civilisation: artificial, cheap, disposable, available, in a word, inauthentic. Warhol's statement, and his work, do not deny this; on the contrary, they affirm it and get off on it, to the point of wishing to be it. The early gay underground films sought authenticity in the self, often with recourse to metaphysical systems that would heighten the sense of self. By the time we get to Warhol notions of the authentic self have been discarded, to be replaced by the desire to be as inauthentic as possible.

Oscar Wilde had been there already. In the preface to the *Portrait of Dorian Gray* he wrote of the great virtue of being 'as artificial as possible'. He too was coming at the end of a movement that had concealed its perverse well-springs in a display of splurging emotional authenticity. Not only does Warhol recapitulate the history of Hollywood, the underground recapitulates the history of romanticism and decadence, as well as that history, which echoes it, of modernism and postmodernism.

Couch

Couch was made in July 1964, though not shown until April 1966. It consists of eight sequences, each the length of a roll of film, each ending as the film whites out at the end of the roll. It shows various people doing various things on an old couch. Though there are no credits and one would not necessarily recognise them, part of *Couch*'s frisson is that it stars, in addition to some Warhol regulars, Malanga, Mead, Ondine, some celebrated Beats, Corso, Ginsberg, Orlovski, Kerouac and various other people.

The first sequence has two men lying together on the couch, one naked; through the sequence they get into various positions, including fellatio. Meanwhile in front there is a young man talking, soundlessly but clearly campily, off screen, presumably to the film-maker; he gets up, strips. Meanwhile two other men, one of them only half on screen, start dancing. The man who stripped walks towards the camera, almost blotting out the image, then drops down, so that we can see the naked man on the couch being stroked by the other, until the image whites out. In the second sequence there are again two men on the couch, snuggling up together; two men in front pick up something bright which shines into the camera, then one sits on the edge of the couch, pointing off screen while he chats; meanwhile, another man has come in and leant over the back of the couch, looking at the two men snuggling on it. In both sequences, the camera is at a right angle to the couch and there is a single source of harsh, white light, coming from over the back of the camera and creating a ring of light across the couch.

Heightened by the subject-matter, the stark rudimentariness of the technique draws attention to the simple but essential excitement of film: what you see and what you don't see. On the one hand, we are getting to see what is not normally (especially in 1964) seen: male nudity, gay sex. The centrality of the sex, centre screen, where the one bright light falls, on the eponymous prop, emphasises it as the thing seen, and having someone come in and look emphasises the fact of looking. Yet it may also emphasise what we don't get, a close-up, and elsewhere the two sequences obstruct our looking with people walking into camera or lights shining into it. They also draw attention to what we don't see. Some men are only half seen, characters talk to and point off screen, the sense of there being a space beyond the frame is not concealed but emphasised. It is an interesting and gay space too: the half-seen men look like they may be sexy, the chatter is obviously campy, and what is that queen

pointing to? We're seeing flesh and sex, but we're also missing
things too. In this way the film can be seen, with the rest of the early
films, as an 'investigation of the technological and social mechanisms of the recording apparatus' (James 1985:25), because it
explores the bare mechanics of lighting, framing, having the camera
run; but, because of the subject-matter, it also shows this is never
just mechanics but inextricable from our investment in the pleasure
of looking.

This play continues through the film. The third sequence is shot
from another angle, 90 degrees to the first two shots, lengthwise
across the couch, making noticeable the fact that we are seeing from
a different angle, seeing two men, one white, one black, making
love to a white woman. Next shot, another angle, a naked woman
on the couch, adopting glamour poses, while a man on a bike fiddles
with it, indifferent to her apart from saying 'hello'. We look
uninterruptedly at what he seems not to be interested in looking at.

Sequence seven marks a startling break: the couch is no longer
seen whole. The camera is closer in, and about a third of the frame
on the left is taken up by a woman, smoking, shifting about in her
seat, looking ahead; behind her, along the top of the couch, a man
is lying, but we can only see his brilliant white jeans; kneeling
behind the couch, we see a man in a black T-shirt and dark glasses,
who leans over, unzips the man's jeans, takes out his penis and
sucks it. Once again, a play on what we see and don't see. We don't
see the rest of the man in the white jeans, yet, in terms of light, he
is the most noticeable thing on screen and we do see what we are
normally least likely to see, his penis being sucked. The man doing
the sucking, on the other hand, wears dark glasses, part of his posey
look, but also drawing attention to eyes. Meanwhile, the woman
does not look at the fellatio. In part, her refusal to look and the
spatial dominance of this person not looking, emphasises that we *are*
looking; but also, she is a woman, she looks awkward, self-
consciously pecking at her cigarette. Gay sex excludes women, but
her awkwardness suggests something more, either a testing of
traditional feminine sensibilities (cast as reactionary in much sixties
sexual rhetoric) or witness to the denial to women of the right to
look, especially at men.

The last sequence reverts to the first camera set-up and shows
three men on the couch, falling about each other, getting undressed,
kissing, scattering drops from a bottle over each other. It is the most
straightforward episode of all, the kind of sequence that earned
Warhol's films their reputation for matter-of-fact acceptance of gay

sex. But the looking on at it is not straightforward. *Blow Job* makes the point still more teasingly – we are watching a man being sucked off to orgasm, and there's no doubt about it, except that we don't see his penis being sucked and is he really having an orgasm or just acting? We see and we don't see what the film's title has invited us to see (cf. Koch 1973:47–51). *Couch*, *Blow Job* and the other early films are thus not just about breaking the taboo on seeing gayness, but exposing some of the aesthetic mechanisms of the proscription and the lifting of it.

Kitchen

Filmed in May 1965, *Kitchen* records in two 35-minute takes a script by Ronald Tavel set in a modern, domestic kitchen, with fridge, blender and streamlined units. In the first half a woman, Jo (Edie Sedgwick) sits on the table, doing her make-up and bickering with a bare-chested man, Micky; in the second half, the bickering continues with another pair, a man called Joe and a woman called Mickie. Behind them, unheeding, a young man potters about the kitchen, and at various points a man enters from behind the camera and takes photos of the characters.

The play on the processes of film concentrates here on the construction of what is filmed, rather than, as in the silent films, how it is framed and lit. The film opens with someone reading out a description of the set from the scenario: what we see isn't just there being filmed, it was assembled or selected to be filmed. We are then told that copies of the script are concealed about the set: we are going to see people playing lines, not just, as may appear, being in front of the camera. The fact that this is a space for a performance is emphasised by having all the characters enter from somewhere behind the fridge, but having the photographer enter from behind the camera, from the space outside of the performance. The play on what you see and what you don't see is shifted, in this sound film, to what you hear and what you don't hear. The chat covers all sorts of things, including gay sex in a shower, men's underwear and Bette Davis imitations, but you can't make it out a lot of the time, it is poorly recorded, and for a long period the blender is running, drowning out what is being said.

This emphasis on the fact that the film has been constructed, despite its fly-on-the-wall look, does not just deconstruct the film as fiction but also domesticity itself. The dialogue deals in the banal, the everyday, the clichéd, but the repetitions, inconsequentiality and flat delivery betray a camp pleasure in the styles and forms of ordinary conversation. Much of the opening conversation is about a 'litter basket', Micky repeating the words meaninglessly, then telling Jo she should 'rummage around in it', her sharply saying that she does so because 'that's how I found you', him complaining that she has thrown his 'undergarment' in it. This undercutting by heightening of domestic chit-chat is given a further twist by employing the psycho-babble that was the standard, middle-class mode for comprehending the tensions of domestic life. So Micky goes on about how he likes to wear another man's clothes so that he can understand the other's personality even though he cannot understand his own, while at other points more specifically Freudian discourse is parroted ('I've failed you. Both as a mother and lover I've failed you'; 'Isn't a mother a boy's best friend?').

It is partly in the language that the normal world of the kitchen is denormalised, but also in the way that what happens undercuts the heterosexuality that is the bedrock of domestic normality. One of the first things Micky tells Jo is that he has had sex with Joe, to which she indifferently replies, 'How nice'. Later, just before Joe and Mickie join them, a voice reads from the script that Jo/e should be played as high camp and Micky/ie as a dumb blonde. So far we have only seen Jo and Micky and don't know there are other characters to come. Certainly when he arrives, Joe is a full-blown queen, but hasn't Jo's chatter also been a witty camping of domesticity? As for the other two, neither is blonde, both are witless, and it is the man, Micky, posing about in levis and bare chest, who most resembles the sex object suggested by the term 'dumb blonde'. This confusion, names and roles no longer clearly sexed, muddles up the certainties of heterosexuality, until Joe says 'Why does everyone have to have the same name? How is one to know who to have sex with?'. Jo points out that 'You don't have sex with a name, do you?', but perhaps the point is that one does, that one has sex with the social image of male and female as much as with men and women apprehended in pure biological terms. The sexual and gender certainties that underpin domesticity evaporate, leaving the charade of playing at being domestic.

My Hustler

My Hustler has a plot, a situation which has the audience asking, 'what is going to happen?'. It also, in its first half, makes very noticeable use of camera movement, creating a strong contrast to the still camera in the second half.

The first half consists of a conversation between a man, Ed Hood, and his guests (a woman, Genevieve and Sugar Plum Fairy, an ex-hustler) on the verandah of his beach house about a blonde man, Paul America, away out on the beach, whom Ed has hired from Dial-a-Hustler. The whole is shot in three longish takes, with the camera intermittently panning and zooming sometimes fast, some-times slow, between the house and the beach. The talk is about Paul, the object of desire; every so often we spend time looking at him while we hear him being discussed. The effect of the zooming and panning (and the rather jolting two cuts) is ambivalent. Like Hollywood, they give us the sight of the object desired, give us the pleasure sought by the man, but they also draw attention to the devices that are permitting the object to be seen and establish distance, so that when Paul is in frame we may nonetheless be aware that only we the audience, and not the speakers, can gaze so closely. The frisson, especially for the mid-sixties audience, is also that we are able just to sit there, in a public place (a cinema) rather than secretly at home, and look with uninterrupted lust at a man.

Ed realises that the other two are out to seduce Paul away from him; he makes a bet that they won't be able to. During a long camera hold on Paul, Ed starts on the soundtrack to wonder where Genevieve has got to and she enters the frame and at once starts chatting Paul up and oiling his back. The disjunction between voice and image maintains the sense of separation between the desirer and the desired, making the woman's entry into the space of the desired all the more disturbing for the desirer (the male speaker and the gay men in the audience).

The moving camera of the first half emphasises distance. The second half takes place in the bathroom in the client's house, occupied by Paul and Sugar Plum Fairy. The still camera keeps the confines of the space rigidly in place. It is now proximity rather than distance that is emphasised. This does not mean there are no barriers to desire. In part what we see are the rituals of 'straight' butchness, showering, shaving, haircombing, oiling, exhibitionism and voyeurism that don't recognise themselves as such. This is intensified by the hustler's straight identification. The excitement of the proximity of their bodies is evident, but the old hand can only make a play for the newcomer by treating it as a professional matter, making out that he just wants to teach Paul some of the tricks of the trade. Homosexual desire could be openly spoken when the object of desire is at a distance, but in circumstances of proximity requires an elaborate manipulation of male codes of 'business'.

The sequence ends with first Genevieve, then Ed, then Genevieve again coming in and telling Paul what financial inducements they can offer him. He remains oblivious, grooming himself gazing in the mirror, while Sugar Plum Fairy still lurks in the background. The central narrative hook – who will get him? – remains teasingly unresolved, while the camera keeps him gorgeously central frame.

Lonesome Cowboys

Lonesome Cowboys consists of a string of incidents, loosely threaded together but with much left unexplained or disconnected and with many camp diversions from the central Western set-up.

> Ramona (Viva) and her 'nurse' (Taylor Mead) are hanging about some Western street set when a group of cowboys rides into town. There is an immediate, but ambivalent, hostility between the two groups, with Mead at one point running to ask the Sheriff for protection from one of the cowboys who, he says, has a big bulge in his pants, is smoking hashish and wearing mascara. Two of the cowboys, Joe and Eric, hang about town discussing gunplay and hair-dos. Mead approaches another, Julian, to ask him to come and meet Ramona, and shows him how to dance a Lupe Velez number. One of the boys slaps Ramona, who is rescued by Mead and the Sheriff. The scene shifts to the cowboys camping out in the country. Eric wakes his bedfellow Joe to discuss newcomer, Julian, who is sleeping with the oldest 'brother', Mickey. Eric runs over to the others, who get up, play about, spraying each other from beer cans. They all go off to Ramona's bordello, where they rape Ramona and Mead. Joe tells Julian he'd like to go off with him to California, where there are 'lots of women, lots of beautiful men'. The Sheriff, who has refused to interfere in the goings-on, gets dressed up as a woman for one of Ramona's clients. The other cowboys join in, dancing, putting on women's clothes, faking sex. Ramona and one of the cowboys, Tom, make love. Mead joins them and gives them a fatal leaf to take, but only Ramona takes it. She collapses over Tom and Mead kisses them both. Mead and Joe dance to a Beatles song. Tom and Eric ride off to California together.

Lonesome Cowboys operates with an opposition, between the group of cowboys and the townspeople (Viva, Mead, the Sheriff), that is characteristic of the Western: country versus town, the range versus the settlement, East versus West, male bonding versus heterosocial arrangements. This is generally how the film has been perceived, though there is disagreement about where the film's sympathies lie. Peter Gidal (1971:124–32) sees the boys as representing an unrepressed, natural, sweet form of sexuality, as opposed to Viva, Mead and the Sheriff, who represent sex for money and law 'n' order. Berlin and Bruce, on the other hand, see 'Viva, the sexually self-determining female, and Taylor Mead, the affirmed gay male' as the positive figures in the film; by contrast the boys' 'unstated homosexuality – bathing and sleeping together, but retaining a heterosexual stance – is repressed and contained, and results in a rigid patriarchy' (1986–7:60). The rape scene is crucial to these arguments. For Gidal it is 'sexual parody' (126), the boys acting out the sexuality the genre requires of its men, but their real sexual interest being in each other, whereas for Berlin and Bruce it is real (even to the point of Viva not knowing it was going to happen), 'the male unit using rape to protect its power and assert its hostility toward the female' (60). After it, they suggest, the male group falls apart.

The film is probably a good deal less coherent and critically conscious than either of these readings suggests. For instance, neither Gidal's sweet sexual freedom nor Berlin and Bruce's patriarchal unit quite seem to catch the film's attitude towards the boys, which may doubt the value of their manliness but fancies them all the same, playing with the signs of masculinity but turned on by them too.

When Ramona and Taylor Mead first see the cowboys riding into town, Ramona says, 'Maybe they're real men', to which Mead replies, 'Oh not real men! Ramona, I must protect you'. The levels of irony in the delivery of these two improvised lines are so unresolved as to defy analysis. Does Ramona want them to be real men? Does Viva already know they are not? How insincere is Mead's shock-horror at the prospect of real men? How could he protect Ramona, and would he be protecting her in order to have the boys to himself? Just where is the irony directed – at the very idea of 'real men' or at the idea that these gay boys might be it? And would their being real men make them more or less desirable?

For desirable, to the film, they certainly are. In a series of sharp cuts, Mead's voice repeats 'Look at' and we see a different part of each of the boys in turn, the fragmenting of their bodies suggesting the appraising look at their attributes. Throughout the film there is far more emphasis on the male body than the female, most memorably in a long take on Julian washing, stripped to the waist, the camera moving over his body, the whole sequence even less narratively motivated than anything else in the film, just an excuse to look at his body.

The focus, in all this desiring, remains on the boys' maleness, but by no means contained by the idea of the real man. A real man might be defined by his being heterosexual or else by his having traditionally masculine qualities. Gay desire may find either or both a turn-on, but the boys in *Lonesome Cowboys* overturn all that. In the conversation between Joe and Eric as they hang about the town, Eric first of all compliments Joe on his 'sexy jacket' because 'it makes you look butch', before going on to tell him he should do something about his hair. Then he advises him that he should do some exercises to build up his legs so that they will hold up his gun. The exercises turn out to be ballet pliés, with the hitching post used as barre. Eric reveals that the real value of this exercise is not its help in gunslinging but because 'it puts meat on the buns'. The conversation is camp, cowboys talking about their hair and doing pliés, but it also acknowledges that strain in US gay culture that came into its own in the Nautilised seventies, the conscious creation of a hunky look – so the jacket is good because it 'looks butch' and the exercise is good because it tones and builds up the arse. 'Male' qualities are being stressed, but there is no intention of passing for straight.

Ater having sex with Tom, and because it was so beautiful, Ramona makes the grand romantic gesture of committing suicide; but Tom is too impassive to do likewise. At the end of the film he rides off to California with Eric. Grand gestures are for heterosexuals or women – riding off to a hedonistic land where there are 'lots of women, lots of beautiful men', a utopia of free floating sexuality, is the boys' ideal. Pace Gidal, there is nothing particularly right-on about this, especially from a feminist perspective, but nor, pace Berlin and Bruce, does it suggest an ultimate identification on the film's part with Viva and Mead. What it conveys best, genially or insidiously, according to view, is Warhol's 'complete refusal to assume critical consciousness' (Koch 1973:108).

AFTER

 The lack of both anxiety/guilt and 'critical consciousness' in the later gay underground is a measure of the arrival of homosexuality in, at any rate, certain circles in major metropolitan centres. Only when homosexuality is seen as a fit subject and sensibility for art and when gay scenes and organisations are well developed, can art be produced which takes gayness as a starting point, just gets on with being camp, can afford to investigate the mechanics of men looking at men in the ways indicated above.

One can get a sense of this context from the film *Gay San Francisco*, made by Jonathan Raymond between 1965 and 1970, in part a record of gay life in the city, but with affinities at moments to sixties underground film in its style. The extensiveness of the San Francisco gay scene is documented in footage of cruising places, parties, clubs, bookshops and so on. Intercut with this are interviews with three pairs: two drag queens, confident in the rightness and, to a large extent, acceptedness of their life-style; a clean-cut gay couple, distancing themselves from queens and hustlers, sure of the normalcy of gayness; and a lesbian couple, talking unembarrassedly about their relationship. The interviews suggest the confidence with which lesbian/gay people were beginning to live their lives in such environments. Much of the footage is conventional home movie/documentary, but there are more undergroundish moments. On the one hand, there are (gay male) sex scenes, shot with a hand held camera close to the bodies, so that the effect is blurry and uncontrolled; on the other, much of footage of the gay scene is accompanied by a travelogue style voice over, scandalised at the goings-on it so gleefully presents, while some of the parties have the kind of atonal music accompanying them that Hollywood and television used to connote perverse weirdness – examples of the gay instinct for pastiche so evident in sixties underground film.

Much of the confidence evidenced in *Gay San Francisco*, and implicit in the stance of the sixties gay underground, underpinned the development of a newly militant gay movement, discussed in chapter five. As a cohesive phenomenon, the underground as such fell away during the seventies and yet, throughout that decade and since, gay underground film bequeathed a number of possibilities that have been the point of departure for a large proportion of gay cinema. A good starting point for surveying this is *Pink Narcissus*. Released in 1971 (but probably made over the previous seven years) and credited to 'Anonymous' (though generally now ascribed to Jim Bidgood), it manages to combine most of what the underground was and what would become of it.

Pink Narcissus opens and closes with sequences in a forest, the

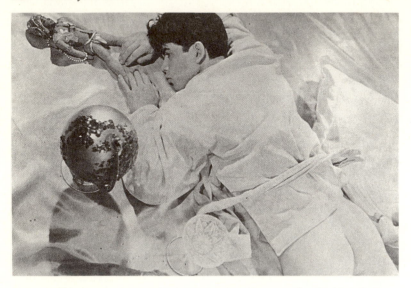

3.7   Bobby Kendall in *Pink Narcissus* – underground, kitsch, softporn.

camera tracking past plastic foliage shot against a sheer full moon.
In between the film centres on a soft-faced, dark-haired, full-lipped,
well-endowed young man (Bobby Kendall) (figure 3.7) in a variety
of settings: in his room, looking at himself in rococo framed mirrors,
taking his clothes off repeatedly, pouring champagne on himself,
masturbating; out in the sleazy streets and lavatories; as a Roman
slave; in a bullring, a forest during a storm and an Arabian Nights
style male harem. The movement between these sequences is
described in a synopsis accompanying the original release as
between the man's fantasies and the intrusions of reality (the street
scenes), though now the latter too seem like fantasies, with their
men in construction worker helmets or sailor shirts, naked from the
waist down, and a sexual encounter in a lavatory leading to
violence, all part of the standard repertoire of gay porn. Equally the
more obviously fantastic sequences contain s/m elements: dragged in
as a slave in one, watching a near naked dancer felled by a scimitar
in another (the latter followed by orgasmic imagery, streams of
white beads superimposed on an extreme close-up down on to the
glans of a penis). Only two things take the edge off the delirious
stream of erotic fantasy. One is the image of a butterfly, breaking
out of its cocoon in the opening sequence and flying to the young
man, later held in his hands and at his crotch but later still crushed

to death by him, following a street sequence of him hustling. The other is a moment near the end in which an older man comes into the young man's room and turns round to reveal that he is the young man, now himself become a hustler's client; a pane of glass in front of the scene shatters, forming a broken cobweb pattern which then becomes a cobweb as the final sequence begins, the sinister cobweb contrasting with the butterfly emerging from a cocoon in the opening sequence.

The film has imagery from most phases of the underground: the sensitive young man, a visionary use of nature, intensified B-picture Hollywoodiana, hustlers and sailors. The only thing missing is drag, though there are demented ladies in the street scenes and harem boys, different aspects of the use of drag in Smith and Warhol. Stylistically, the use of 8mm blown up to 35mm gives the film both the iridescent colour of Anger and Markopoulos and the graininess of Warhol. The structure, oneiric, mythic, masturbatory, with a moment of terrible self-discovery towards the end, suggests the forties underground, but the looser, languorous shifts from one sequence to another also recall *Flaming Creatures*. The enjoyment of artifice, the embrace of seediness, the unremitting eroticism all suggest the sixties underground imposed on more personal, obsessive and tormented forties underground structures. All that is entirely absent is Warhol's detached, observational mode.

Pink Narcissus stands somewhere between continuing elements of the underground and new developments that both exaggerated particular aspects of the underground and also in the process moved it some way above ground. As much as anything this has to do with changing patterns of exhibition during the seventies. At one extreme, there are film-makers whose small-scale, highly personal, even hermetic, work is largely shown in the original underground spaces, galleries, art schools, collectives devoted to avant-garde film. Some of these film-makers have been able to move into the art cinema circuit, but the real commercial success has lain in those highly profitable fringes of the industry, 'midnight movies' and pornography. These different institutional spaces do not fit entirely smoothly with different kinds of product: all of these films would be considered pornographic by some people, all of them have elements of the 'personal' about them.

Among those working at the avant-garde end of the scale are Tom Chomont (see below), Jim Hubbard (*May 21–22, 1979* 1980, *Homosexual Desire in Minnesota* 1981–5), Roger Jacoby (*Kunstlife* 1975, *How to be a Homosexual* 1978), Curt McDowell (see below),

Warren Sonbert (*Divided Loyalties* 1978, *Noblesse Oblige* 1981), Jerry Tartaglia (*Lawless* 1977), Michael Wallin (*The Place between Our Bodies* 1975) and two poets from previous generations discussed above, James Broughton (see above) and Charles Henri Ford.[6] The latter's *Johnny Minotaur* 1967–70 concerns a man making a film based on the Minotaur legend and the mainly homosexual and masturbatory sexual activity off screen. It is probably the last underground film to make use of classical Greek reference in its treatment of homosexuality and the fact that it is about making such a film, which is moreover never completed, together with the image of a crumbling papier-mâché Minotaur mask at the end, perhaps suggest how little currency there was still in such classical allusion. The work of Chomont and McDowell, on the other hand, indicates the potential of other aspects of the underground.

There is a stronger feeling of the personal in Tom Chomont's films than in even Markopoulos or Smith. These are films drawing on the film-maker's personal circle: a lover in *Oblivion* 1969, a group of polymorphous perverse men, women and children in *Love Objects* 1971, a soldier friend in *Minor Revisions* 1979, a man head-shaving and tying up his lover in *Razor Head* 1984 and so on. The images have an intimacy conveyed by the use of close-up and repetition, suggesting the cherished importance to the film-maker of, say, this moment of peeling an onion (*Minor Revisions*) or this way that a loved one takes his underwear off (*Oblivion*). The sense of the specialness of these otherwise banal images is often heightened by a certain strangeness in the filming, much use of negative reversal, superimposition or remarkable set-ups such as that in *Minor Revisions*, a man's genitals glimpsed from beneath in a hand mirror laid on a grey towel. The images, seldom held for more than a few seconds, are repeated and recombined with a strong rhythmic sense, so that the overall effect is both of evanescence and intensity, the intimate moment slipping from grasp yet registered with great tenderness. There is neither anguish nor camp in this work, no felt need to interrogate or assert a gay identity, just getting on with being homo-erotic among other things. Chomont's films seem one of the few cases where gayness is incidental without being in the process marginalised. Perhaps now this can only be achieved in such a highly personal and intimate mode, where the questions of effect and representativeness, necessarily entailed in more public modes, do not insistently obtain.

Some of Curt McDowell's films also appear very personal, but are far more self-conscious about themselves as films and the act of going public with such personal material. The films present, but also take to pieces, the film-maker's sexual desires. *Confessions* 1971 has him talking to camera telling his parents about childhood thefts and fibs and about having been in love several times, once with a woman. This monologue is cut up and interrupted by people playing at burglary and confession, making the stream of confession seem less transparent and authentic. *Ronnie* 1972 is the first of his films to explore his fascination with straight-identified men, here a hustler who poses about in front of the camera while on the soundtrack boasting of his macho straightness. *Nudes: A Sketchbook* 1974 shows a variety of people, male and female, in couples and alone, including one sequence where a delivery boy is observed by the camera – when he suddenly falls to the ground, the camera moves in and we see McDowell's hands reach in and pull the boy's trousers down as the film goes black. The play with voyeurism is fascinating and/or discomforting: the boy seems to know he's being filmed, but you're not sure; McDowell oversteps the boundary between watcher and watched, but we, the other watchers, cannot. *Loads* 1980 shows a series of men undressing and masturbating, while on the soundtrack McDowell talks about how he picked the men up and how attracted he is by straight men. The different encounters are loosely edited together to suggest a repeated erotic structure – the men hanging about, undressing, playing with themselves, coming – but the voice over moves from coolly intimate delivery to stumbling, excited stuttering until, his mouth full of cock on screen, there is no more speech. The attempt to render a verbal account of sexual desire goes awry in the excitement of recall; the assumption that the person behind the camera has power over the person in front of it is thrown into confusion by it being a gay man looking at straight men, by the range of embarrassment and pleasure the men evince and the question of class (the men are working-class, some Hispanic; McDowell is a poor but college-educated film-maker). *Taboo: The Single and the L.P.* 1981 focuses on an Arab youth, Fahed Martha, hanging about outside with a friend or in McDowell's apartment, staring at the camera, 'no more than a graphic presence – an empty centre, a hook of flesh for desires not his own' (Ehrenstein 1985:113).

With films like these, Chomont and McDowell remained underground film-makers in a classic sense, but others have succeeded in establishing a niche in the field of relatively well-financed (often state-subsidised) feature films shown on the international art cinema circuit. Of these, the British director Derek Jarman is the best example.

There are two strands to Jarman's film work, strands initially identified with differences in technology and institution and which come together in his later work (O'Pray 1985). On the one hand there are short films shot on super-8 (such as *Fire Island* 1974, *Duggie Fields* 1974, *Picnic at Ray's* 1975, *Gerald's Film* 1976) and on the other 35mm feature films (notably *Sebastiane* 1976, *Jubilee* 1978, *The Tempest* 1979). The former have a home movie feel in terms of subject-matter, records of friends, visits, parties and so on, but shot and edited[7] to create a distinctive erotic texture. The dark, grainy, gentle, washed-out yet palpable look of the films, together with the kinds of boys and settings featured, give a somehow very English inflection to the underground tradition. The features on the other hand are lit and shot in a relatively conventional art cinema style, though tending to play down narrative drive in favour of lingering on tableaux which are painterly both in their visual texture and in their clear evocation of famous paintings. The subject-matter is tougher, notably in *Jubilee*, which depicts a future state of England characterised by punk-style violence, in which, among other things, policemen who have sex with each other destroy or beat up beautiful young men. The gentleness of the super-8 films is largely absent but not their homo-eroticism, here explored in sado-masochistic guise. The two sides of Jarman's work have begun to come together more recently: *Imagining October* 1984 explores the homo-erotic appeal of soldiers but softened, literally stripped of their violent accoutrements; *The Angelic Conversation* 1985 is a 35mm, feature length film originally shot in super-8, consisting of loving images of men set to readings of Shakespeare's sonnets; *Caravaggio* 1986, his 'biggest' film to date, is also the fullest exploration of the historical and social complexities of the imagery found throughout his work.

Sebastiane was one of the first independently gay-made feature films to get a wide showing (including, astonishingly and fortuitously, a commercial release in Britain). It tells of the banishment of the Roman soldier Sebastiane, once the favourite of the Emperor but now a Christian, to a remote outpost, where he refuses the advances of the captain, Severus, who finally has him shot to death by arrows. The film uses this story to lay out some of the forms that 'eros' (love, desire) can take. At one extreme, there is the character of Max, endlessly spewing lewd talk of women while initiating evidently homosexual horse-play between the men; at the other,

Sebastiane, representing an etherealised, spiritual love, embodied in poems and dances to the sun as well as his Christianity. In between there are: Severus, whose desire for Sebastiane is frustrated; Justin, Sebastiane's selfless friend, beaten up by Max for his attempt to protect Sebastiane from Severus; and the lovers Anthony and Adrian. The latter provide an image of untrammelled eros in the beautiful central sequence of them making love, in the open air and in a pool. Slow-motion photography caresses their limbs and in the pool shows mesmerising streams of waterdrops glancing off and haloing their glowing bodies. The use of water to convey this dreamy eroticism links it to, but also distinguishes it from, the violent sexuality of horse-play and frustration. In an earlier sequence, Max leads the crude verbal by-play as the men cavort in the sea playing ball; when Anthony tackles Adrian, the latter, recognising it as an advance, backs off and refuses to play any more; yet later we have the love scene between them, now whole-heartedly sexual, not uglified by the others' need to declare a heterosexual fuck mentality. Their love-making is observed by Severus, standing at a distance with Sebastiane. Earlier Severus had looked longingly at Sebastiane as he poured water over himself in the early morning, a sequence shot in the same besotted slow motion. Now Severus looks at Anthony and Adrian, but when he puts his hand out to Sebastiane, has it brushed away. Sebastiane rejects Severus in the name of a higher love ('Poor Severus. You think your drunken lust compares to the love of gods'), but this love is expressed in vividly homo-erotic terms ('. . . his blue eyes . . . his golden body . . . I love him, I want to be with him'), and first in an ecstatic delirium after Severus has tortured him. His Christian love is sexual, but fixed on an impossible love object, stimulated by pain, unable to realise itself in the loving sensuality represented by Anthony and Adrian. *Sebastiane* recognises the fascination of the morbid eroticism of the St Sebastian figure, notably in the final execution which makes reference to many of the paintings of his martyrdom, evoking an art tradition long recognised for its homo-erotic appeal (cf. Castillo 1983). Yet even while acknowledging this fascination, the film also evokes in Anthony and Adrian an alternative to it.

If Jarman can be seen as moving on from the forties underground, the gay contribution to the 'midnight movies' phenomenon is clearly rooted in the sixties underground. 'Midnight movies' were 'a distinctive strain of subterranean moviegoing' and programming (Hoberman and Rosenbaum 1983:1), developing during the seventies, usually late night, often all night, a heady mix of avant-gardism, B-pictures and youth movies which was a continuation by other means of the cultism already associated with the cinema in the forms of fandom and buffery. Some gay underground films (*Scorpio Rising*, *Lonesome Cowboys*, *Jubilee*) were part of it as were many films with pronounced gay content (*Fellini Satyricon*, *Beyond the Valley of the Dolls*, *The Rocky Horror Picture Show*) but the key gay contribution grew out of the off-off-Broadway brew of drag, kitsch and schlock, which flowered through the late sixties and seventies in the Theatre of the Ridiculous (Smith 1987). Films like *Luminous Procuress* 1972 showcased drag performers, in this case the San Francisco group the Cockettes; the continuing work of George Kuchar (including his script for Curt McDowell's *Thundercrack!* 1975) upped the delirious banality of melodrama, soap opera *and* cinéma vérité. The films of John Waters went still further. Much of the content of his films (*Mondo Trasho* 1969, *Multiple Maniacs* 1970, *Pink Flamingoes* 1971, *Female Trouble* 1975, *Desperate Living* 1977, *Polyester* 1981) is not in any obvious sense gay: most of the characters are heterosexual, or sometimes lesbian, and mostly concerned with self-advancement, filth, hair-dos, killing, eating and fucking. It is the perspective that is distinctly gay. In *Female Trouble*, Edith Massey declares 'The world of the heterosexual is a sick and boring life' and it is just this that the films show, but with a gleeful sense of the gross that makes them intoxicating. Waters' star is Divine, an enormous drag queen who often seems the only really positive person in the film, full of energy, fun and lust for life. 'She' (Glenn Milstead) always plays definitely female characters in the films, yet every viewer must know she is a man. In sex scenes, the scraggy or self-obsessed quality of her partners evokes joyless heterosexual screwing, but Divine's magnificent lust is a paean to gay desire.

While many would consider Waters' films obscene, they are not pornographic ('I would never want to film hardcore pornography because it always looks like open-heart surgery to me' (quoted in Samuels 1983:120)), but this is the third direction in which the gay underground moved. There has been gay film pornography almost as long as there has been straight (the earliest examples in Waugh's researches date from the twenties), and it has generally followed straight porn in becoming gradually more publically available, first through mail order and then finally in cinemas. Paul Siebenand (1980:2) gives the Park Theatre in Los Angeles in June 1968 as the date of the first public screening of gay porn films in the USA. Such films were short and artisanal, but industrialisation swiftly followed with films such as *Stud Farm* 1969, *The Fraternity*, *Hang Loose*, *Meat Rack*, *One Touching One* and *Sticks and Stones* 1970 and in 1971 *Boys in the Sand*, generally reckoned to be the breakthrough film, Hollywoodian in both its camera work and its production of the first gay porn star, Casey Donovan.

Films like *Fireworks* and *Un Chant d'amour* had been deplored or welcomed as porn and when porn as business took hold it often remained, and remains, startlingly close to the conventions and concerns of these earlier films. (*One Touching One*, for instance, was marketed as portraying male homosexuality as 'one of the life forces of the 20th century'.) Many of the structures of underground film, formal analogues of psychic states, organise gay porn: dreams (*Song of the Loon* 1970, *Boys in the Sand*), memories (*Nights in Black Leather* 1972), hallucinogenic visions (*Destroying Angel* 1975) and conscious fantasising (*Boys in the Sand*, *American Cream* 1972, *Adam and Yves* 1974), all always sexual, often intercut, Chinese boxed or not clearly distinguishable from one another. Porn films are offered to the audience as fantasies, but these structures show a self-consciousness about the process, in some cases authenticating the fantasies as fantasies, in others drawing attention to their fabrication. The latter tendency is even more evident in the common reference to film itself, in plots about making porn films (*Bijou* 1972), in pastiches of films (of *A Star is Born* in *The Light from the Second Storey Window* 1973, of Cocteau, Garbo and Brando movies in *Adam and Yves* 1974, of gay porn itself in *Catching Up* 1975, of *American Graffiti* in *Cruisin 57* 1979) and in films in which people watch films, in some cases having sex in cinemas showing porn films (*The Back Row* 1973, *Passing Strangers* 1977), a scenario which of course is itself a reflection of what actually went on in gay porn cinemas.

Two early films illustrate porn's relation to the underground, *The Song of the Loon* and *L.A. Plays Itself* 1972. The former, based on a best-selling novel by Richard Amory (published in 1966), is still softcore, telling the story of a young man, Ephram, in frontier times and his discovery of (homosexual) love through contact with Native Americans and Whitmanic woodsmen. The imagery of nature, the recognition of Native American values, the talk of free love and spiritual values, the unfetishistically manly coupling, all root the film firmly in beat/hippy culture and the film culminates in a visionary sequence, induced in Ephram by the wise man, Bear Who Dreams, in which Ephram discovers the truth: his love for the woodsman Cyrus and his rejection of his attachment to Montgomery, symbol of the repressed, restrictive mores of the white man. In content *Song of the Loon* lays out many of the informing ideas of one part of the gay underground, yet technically it is straightforward, even the visionary sequence clearly signalled as such as in a Hollywood film. *L.A. Plays Itself* also uses hippyish imagery in its first half, a sexual encounter between two men in the countryside near Los Angeles. Long-held extreme close-ups of flowers, fossils, butterflies are intercut with those of the two men making love, accompanied now by Orientalish flute music, now by Beethoven's Pastoral Symphony. Towards the end of this sequence images of a tractor are superimposed over the love-making, a disruptive incursion of the mechanical which segues into shots of down-town LA and the second half of the film. Here s/m, bondage and fist fucking are intercut with a welter of images from popular culture to the accompaniment of rock music, more hectically cut than *Scorpio Rising* but very much evoking the feeling of that film, which is more explicitly evoked in director Fred Halsted's next film, *Sex Garage*. Both films suggest aspects of where gay porn would mainly go, towards conventional film style and macho sexuality, while also retaining the visionary, playful and self-reflexive qualities of underground cinema.

*   *   *

Underground film was the space in which gay cinema could emerge, at that time, in the USA. Gay films could be made in that space, partly because of the overlaps of avant-garde and gay milieux and the importance of homosexual imagery in what informed the underground (Freudianism, the novel of alienation, camp and pop art) but above all because of underground cinema's definition of cinema as 'personal'. Being personal meant not making films as impersonal, routine or official as mainstream cinema. It also generally meant being open about sexuality, since this was seen as constitutive of the personality, a view which it was especially hard for 'a homosexual' to resist. If the point of underground cinema was to be personal, then any gay man making a film was liable to include gayness: being 'personal' inextricably entailed being gay.

In the underground film gay expression thus emerged through self expression. The films suggest shifting definitions of the self: disturbingly fractured in the early examples, unless, as in Anger, healed through ritual; sheer surface and performance in Warhol or Waters; fragmented, numinously in Smith or Chomont, excitedly in porn. What they did not present was the unified, affirmative self suggested by the films of the lesbian/gay movements discussed in chapter five. Indeed, gay underground films did not claim to be gay at all, they claimed to be personal. Such a stress on the individual self is anathema to collective notions of identity. The point about 'the individual' is his/her difference from everyone else, not what he/she shares with others. Moreoever, the obscurity of underground films in every sense – difficult to understand, technically deficient (judged by mainstream criteria), hard to get to see – meant that many gay people did not recognise themselves in them. Yet it was perhaps only a convinced, and for that very reason idiosyncratic, individualism that allowed gay cinema to emerge at all in the period – this was the form that progressive ideas took. Besides, the variations in the underground's constructions of the gay self suggest conundrums of personal identity that the lesbian/gay movement had to ignore but which will not go away. Lesbian/gay identity is a paradox: it makes defence and promotion of homo-erotic relations possible, but it also depends on the illusion that 'gay/lesbian' is a unified sense of self held in common amongst lesbians and amongst gay men. The fragments and surfaces, authenticity and theatricality, control and abandon, of gay underground cinema suggest some of the disturbing and exhilarating instabilities of the necessary fiction of identity. In its attention to film as film, especially in Warhol, McDowell and some porn, it also counsels caution about connecting selfhood and cinema at all.

4   Lesbian/woman
Lesbian cultural feminist film

In Maya Deren's third film, *At Land* 1945, a woman, played by the
film-maker, emerges from the sea, encounters the land and returns
to the sea. On land she steals chess pieces, first off a banquet table,
then from a pair of women playing chess by the sea. She steals the
piece from the women through seduction, stroking their hair until
'they lay their heads back rapturously in a kind of self-forgetting
orgasm' (Brinckmann 1984b:81); then she takes the chess piece and
runs off, but comes back and again caresses the women and all three
turn their bodies in unison before Deren runs off to the sea.

This is the only sequence in Deren's work that is in any obvious
sense lesbian. It anticipates a body of lesbian film work that could
only begin to emerge twenty-five years later. Like this work, *At
Land* relates female sensual bonding both to the alienation of
women within a male-defined society and to time-honoured notions
of the feminine. The chess pieces seem to symbolise Deren's/
women's relation to the world. She finds the first piece at the end of
a banquet table that she has to crawl along, quite ignored by those
sitting at it; she loses it/him and has to chase him through various
landscapes and then has a conversation with a man who keeps
changing into other men. These developments are part of the film's
use of chess as, in Judith Higginbottom's words, 'a traditional and
potent symbol of patriarchal processes of power and domination';
from this game she steals a pawn, perhaps, as 'the lowliest piece in
the game', it 'represents herself' (1983:7). The pair of women,
however, play this 'men's game . . . in their own way – quickly,
light-heartedly, continually communicating to each other, apparently not taking the rules very seriously' (Brinckmann 1984b:81);
from this game, Deren steals a queen, the most important female
piece. Through sensual involvement in a women's way of handling
culture, she can possess an important symbol of female power and

return to the sea, itself 'a conventional symbol of the female and the womb' (Higginbottom 1983:7). The title of the film and its structure, emerging from and returning to the sea, suggests the idea of being 'beached', the woman out of her element; the return to that element is effected through erotic contact and identification with women and women's culture.

A less obvious lesbian moment occurs in a later Deren film, *Ritual in Transfigured Time* 1946. Here a woman, 'the Widow', runs from a man's sexual advances and finally leaps into the sea. At the point of leaping the film is negative reversed, so that the Widow's black clothes become bridal white: 'The woman has returned to the sea, the domain of instinct and the unconscious and the female. Perhaps she has married the sea; perhaps a part of herself has returned to be reborn' (ibid.:9). The sexuality is less sensually presented here, but is suggested by the idea of being a 'bride' in order to return to 'the female', lesbian eroticism as the entry to the feminine.

Deren's work is not 'really' lesbian, but these moments can be seen as part of what Adrienne Rich in 1980 would call 'the lesbian continuum', the sense of connection between all forms of experience in which women know themselves as women beyond male definition. Such notions have always been controversial: many women feel that they have hijacked the definition of lesbianism at the expense of most actual lesbians (eg. Clark 1982, Echols 1984:61–2) and presuppose an essence of 'womanhood' existing outside of the social and historical production of womanhood as a category in the discourse of a male-dominated society (eg. Barry and Flitterman 1980). Yet it was these notions that informed a coherent body of lesbian films made during the seventies in North America,[1] work developing in but away from the space of underground film as part of the growth of the wider phenomenon of what became called cultural feminism.

Underground cinema by 1970 had established the possibility of this kind of film practice, and although women as directors remained few, still there were more than in mainstream production. Their work provided some of the forms for the seventies lesbian films: Deren, Constance Beeson, Storm de Hirsch, Marie Menken, Gunvor Nelson, Carolee Schneemann and, in Canada, Joyce Wieland, all explored specifically female experiences; Menken and Wieland used traditionally feminine spaces and crafts (Hammer 1981:122–5), and Schneemann in *Fuses* 1965–8 presented a flowing, blurring evocation of female (hetero)sexuality.

The male gay underground, especially in its West Coast variant, was also important. There are links of imagery and structure between Barbara Hammer's early films and those of Anger and Markopoulos (cf. Zita 1981:30); the Canadian film *Labyris Rising* Margaret Moores and Almerinda Travassos 1980, with its title and women with push-bikes dressing up in boots and denim, all set to women's rock tracks, is a friendly parody of *Scorpio Rising*. Even where there are no such specifiable links, there are general similarities between the two. Yet their different contexts give such similarities radically different significance. Both use symbols that at first sight seem purely personal, but which can be related to both psychic and mythic schema. The difference lies not just in the schema themselves – feminine spirituality and archetypes as opposed to Freud, Magick and Greek myth – but in the use that is made of them.

The gay films are individualistic, using psychoanalytic and mythic imagery as means to express, explore and heal the self. The lesbian films are no less personal, but much less individualistic: the personal becomes the intimacy and inwardness shared by women, to which the spiritual and archetypal give access. This emphasis on the personal as collective rather than individuated means that the quest structure of Deren, Markopoulos *et al.* is not used. What are formally similar are: the use of fast, often subliminal, editing, with many films seeming to be a rush of images hard to pin down; the use of superimposition, which further breaks down the space-time continuum of conventional film-making; much hand-held camera work; and, often, an apparent lack of finish and precision, a feeling of spontaneity and immediacy. For both the lesbian and the earlier films this has in part to do with what Sontag castigates as 'the old cliché of European romanticism – the assassin mind versus the spontaneous heart' (1967:228), but given a new inflection by the lesbian feminist suspicion that the mind is an assassin because it is male, that to recover the heart may be a way out from under patriarchal consciousness. Moreover many of the editing and camera techniques which express anxious feelings of fragmentation and lack of control in the male films embody feelings of merging and blurring that are welcomed in the lesbian films as aspects of a specifically feminine aesthetic.[2]

This aesthetic emerged from the resurgent feminism of the early seventies, and especially from the notion of the 'woman-identified woman'. This notion, always controversial within the seventies sexual political movements, led in one direction towards radical separatist politics but in another towards the idea of rediscovering and developing a distinct and alternative women's culture (Zimmerman 1985). Part of this endeavour was the creation of appropriate modes of film. In what follows I describe some of the underlying principles of cultural feminism as it developed out of the women's movement before considering how these principles relate to the characteristic iconography and form of lesbian cultural feminist film. (This label is not one much used in the criticism of these films, but I hope this chapter makes clear that it is an appropriate one.) The chapter ends with a discussion of the work of the most prolific of these film-makers, Barbara Hammer, and a consideration of an issue raised by all this work, the possibility of *lesbian* lesbian erotic film.

PRINCIPLES

In 1970 the New York Radicalesbians published a manifesto entitled 'The Woman-Identified Woman'. In it they argued that male power maintains itself by preventing women from associating with each other and, potentially, standing together against men. As they saw it, the term 'lesbian' was used by men to disparage women who try to be strong and independent or who try to associate with each other; in other words, 'lesbian' is a term of abuse directed at women who don't accept subordination and don't help to maintain male power. Radicalesbians spied in this abuse a reality: women who live independently of men and bond together *are* a challenge to male power, and therefore women who recognise that women are oppressed by men should be lesbians, should be among those whose way of living challenges male power. Hence they proposed a definition of lesbians not as a purely sexual category, but as women-identified women, identifying with each other as women, but also identifying with themselves individually as women, refusing the negative sense of self that male domination instils in women.

One of the ambiguities of this definition of lesbianism was whether it entailed sexuality. In 1970[3] Ti-Grace Atkinson defined lesbianism as woman identification, regardless of sexuality:

> There are women in the Movement who engage in sexual relations with other women, but who are married to men; these women are not lesbians in the political sense. . . . There are other women who have never had sexual relations with other women, but who have made, and live, a total commitment to this Movement. These women are lesbians in the political sense.
>
> (1974:132)

This was always a controversial move. Older lesbians or women who did not come out as lesbian through the women's movement were often, as Sidney Abbott and Barbara Love put it, 'both surprised by, and leery of, women with little or no sexual experience with other women who call themselves Lesbians'; they felt that such women lacked 'a gay consciousness' or 'any recognition of society's hostility towards homosexuals' (1972:153). Other feminists argued that it was not enough just to identify and live with other women, sex was important too. The Gay Revolutionary Party Women's Caucus in 1971 argued against 'self-identification and affirmation [as] solely a head-trip', for

> a woman can never comprehend herself in sensual isolation. It is only through sensual communication and association within her sexual peer group that she can hope to do this. The process of physical and psychic self-affirmation requires full relation with those like oneself, namely women.
>
> (1972:179)

In the films discussed below lesbianism does entail sexuality, but within the wider sense of woman identification, as is made explicit in *Labyris Rising*, where one woman has 'Woman Identified Woman' sewn on her jeans and another reads the radical feminist magazine *Off Our Backs*.

To identify with each other and to build a new sense of self already imply the need for a women's culture, that is both a space separate from men where association between women can develop freely and also a wholly different way of thinking and feeling. Radical lesbianism emphasised the importance of 'creating a space for women-loving-women separate from the homophobic and misogynistic culture of the patriarchy' (Arnup 1983:53), which in practical terms meant setting up women's publications, cafés, bookshops, record companies, festivals, contact networks and so on, all well established by 1977 (Zimmerman 1985:257). It was in such spaces that lesbian film-makers could show their work (Wolf 1979:78). In this cultural space, women themselves could determine women's consciousness. Radicalesbians saw the ways women in a male-dominated society habitually think and feel as male-derived, male-serving modes of thought and feeling which have to be rejected: 'irrespective of where our love and sexual energies flow, if we are male-identified in our heads, we cannot realize our autonomy as human beings' (1972:175). Such a process of altering consciousness is achieved through relating to women, for '[o]nly women can give each other a new sense of self' (ibid.:176).

The need for a change of consciousness, for a *new* sense of self, seems to imply something entirely new in the way of cultural forms. Yet since about 1974 'cultural feminism', as it was first (critically) termed by the Redstockings in 1975 (Echols 1984:67), has tended to explore traditional aspects of femininity. Just as Radicalesbians took possession of the notion of lesbianism as the rejection of men, so cultural feminism looked to what patriarchal societies had labelled 'feminine' and saw there alternatives (or a space for the creation of alternatives) to the destructive values that patriarchal society promotes. Thus although cultural feminism came out of radical feminism, it also marks, according to Gayle Kimball, a distinct break from it: radical feminists 'advocated entirely eradicating gender-linked roles of men and women' and hence were uneasy with the promulgation of a women's culture, which is by definition based on notions of the specificity and distinctness of gendered identities (1981:3).

The idea of a gender specific culture suggests, though does not necessarily entail, a notion of inherent differences between women and men. In principle Kimball and others leave open (or 'demonstrate a cavalier disinterest in' (Echols 1984:51)) the question of whether the different ways women and men think and feel are socially or biologically determined, but they are often drawn to nature-based arguments about women's consciousness and culture. Kimball suggests that women may have developed the right hemisphere of the brain (associated with the 'relational, artistic, integrative, intuitive and imaginative') while men have developed the left hemisphere ('analytical, linear, intellectual, and logical') (ibid.:4);[4] and even if this is not so women 'project their own way of relating to nature because they feel that they are more closely allied to it' (ibid.:5). Similarly Estella Lauter argues that a woman's

actual or potential experience of menstruation, penetration, pregnancy, birth, lactation, and menopause may leave her more open to a 'story' of human relationship with nature which is non-hierarchical and less compartmentalized than the one to which we have become accustomed.

(1984:170)

Such formulations are careful not to be biologically determinist but they do embrace modes of feeling and expression that arise out of the specificities of women's situation in the world. Other feminists have argued that these modes do not arise but are 'imposed on women through oppressive social conditions or prejudice' and therefore 'should not be made part of our definition of women's art and thus be further perpetuated' (Ecker 1985:16). Yet this is just what cultural feminism set out to do, arguing that such work wrests the definition of femininity out of the hands of society (men), rediscovers female traditions long hidden or denigrated by history, by his story, and/or invents new forms in this traditional space of the feminine.

Kimball maps out in the introduction to her book (to which Barbara Hammer contributes the section on film) some of the features of women's art that flow from these ideas of women's culture. In the next section I use her breakdown as points of departure for describing the recurrent characteristic imagery, or iconography, of lesbian cultural feminist cinema. Ecker argues such cataloguing in fact excludes much of the art produced by women (ibid.:17), which is why I have used throughout 'cultural feminist art' (rather than 'women's art' favoured by cultural feminists themselves) in order to locate the work within this specific context of its production. The section ends with an account of the film *Getting Ready*, in many ways a summation of both the principles and iconography of this cinema, before turning to a discussion of lesbian cultural feminist film form.

ICONOGRAPHY

Kimball lists first the importance of images of power, of female power countervailing that of men, which leads to the rediscovery and use of such past icons of female power as goddesses, figures in Biblical and Greek mythology, 'evil' women now seen as powerful ('Eve, witches, and Lilith' (1981:11)) and famous historical women. Examples in lesbian cultural feminist films include a witch in *Psychosynthesis* Hammer 1975, Amazons in *Superdyke* Hammer 1975 and (in the shape of a double-headed axe pendant) *Labyris Rising*, and a reference to Artemis/Diana in *Luna Tune* Carol Clement 1977. Like *Scorpio Rising*, *Labyris Rising* also invokes figures from the mass media who can be appropriated for lesbian consciousness, notably Janis Joplin and women blues singers. Kimball also suggests that simply by choosing themselves as subject women have explored 'their own identity and strength' (ibid.:12) and have felt a power in relations between women, as friends, siblings or mothers and daughters. Several lesbian films have a clear autobiographical element – *I Was/I Am* Hammer 1973, *Cumulus*

Nimbus Virginia Giritlian 1973 (about a young woman wondering if she is lesbian), *Women I Love* Hammer 1976 and *Lebisia* Jere van Syoc 1979. *Moon Goddess* Barbara Hammer and Gloria Churchman 1976 brings the iconographic and autobiographical together with its final image of women merging into one another in a mythically suggestive landscape, the merging suggesting 'finding the mother within one's self, a step beyond the external mother search' (Hammer 1982:62).

Secondly, women have explored alternatives to the nuclear family. This aspect of women's culture is implicit in lesbian underground films but more fully explored in documentary work coming out of the women's movement and discussed in chapter five. Thirdly, cultural feminist art may be grounded in women's experiences, taking, exploring and celebrating experiences specific to women, whether these be bodily ('menstruation, childbirth, and sexuality' (Kimball 1981:17)), to do with women's traditional roles (imagery of food, craft, clothing, jewellery) or grounded in 'the daily experiences of women' as recorded in 'journals, diaries, letters and oral statements' (ibid.:18). Each of these is important in lesbian underground films. Sexuality is explored directly and explicitly in *Cumulus Nimbus*, *Dyketactics* Hammer 1974, ('the first lesbian lovemaking film I am told to be made by a lesbian' (Hammer 1982:60)), *Dura Mater* Lainard E. Bush 197?, *Exotica Numero Una* Winona Holloway and Marcia Still 197?, *Multiple Orgasm* Hammer 1976, *On a Cold Afternoon* Barbara Jabaily 197?, *Wheel Dream* Jabaily 197?. (Sexuality is by contrast for the most part absent from non-avant-garde feminist films (Rosenberg 1983:72).) Menstruation is the subject of *Menses* Hammer 1974. The eroticism in *Dura Mater* is mixed with scenes of daily life and in *Wheel Dream* flows out of a woman's involvement with making pots, often considered a traditional female craft. *Women I Love* includes all these elements: sexuality (lesbianism and masturbation), menstruation, food, crafts and such everyday activities as washing up and gardening.

Everyday life also forms the basis for *Cool Hands Warm Heart* Sue Friedrich 1979 though here rather more ambivalently explored than in cultural feminist celebrations. Habitual women's tasks are rendered violent, most notably in the opening sequence in which a woman shaves her legs and armpits on a podium set up in a busy street – close-ups suggest the razor's destructive potential, while the setting wrenches an intimate, private act, one that is both banal yet taboo to mention, into a public arena. This sense of violence in women's lives is counterposed to the interactions of a black and a

white woman, including one giving the other a rose which she tucks
into her jeans, suggesting other dimensions possible in life among
women. An even stronger sense of women bonding over against
male exploitation is suggested in *Chinamoon* Barbara Linkevitch
1975, in which four prostitutes murder their clients in a pagan choral
ritual. (This suggests the possibility of a different tradition, that of
lesbian separatism, which only really began to emerge in film in the
eighties, most notably with *De Stilte rond Christine M* (Netherlands
1982 Marleen Gorris) (Murphy 1986).)

Kimball's fourth characteristic, women's bodies, is in some ways
the most controversial. Though she states that it is 'the woman's
body' that is at 'the core of the female experience' (1981:18), most
of her discussion emphasises the vagina, as both sexual and
generative. What is at stake is not just reclaiming women's genitals
for women, but freeing them of the actual dislike, even disgust, at
them that many feminists argue is what men really feel about female
genitals. Lisa Tickner (1987) begins a discussion of such 'vaginal
iconology' with a quotation from Germaine Greer's *The Female
Eunuch* (1971) evoking the general distaste which little girls are
taught to take in their genitals, while Rozsika Parker and Griselda
Pollock point out that for all its obsessive interest with the female
nude, the Western art tradition never actually represents female
genitalia, because they are the sign of women's difference from men
and thus provoke 'men's fear of sexual difference' (1981:126).
Vaginal imagery in cultural feminist work both looks head-on at
female genitals and sees them as beautiful. *Multiple Orgasm*
Hammer 1976 starts with an extreme close-up of a vagina, with a
finger playing the clitoris; the use of imagery and colouring (see
below) insists on the beauty of this startlingly direct image. *Women
I Love* uses a variety of vegetables that open out (cabbages,
artichokes, cauliflowers and so on) as vaginal images; the first is a
red cabbage, starting from an extreme close-up, when one cannot
identify that it is a vegetable but only has before one an image of
red, veined lips creating a half-diamond, half-circle shape surrounded by membranous folds. In its abstraction, its vivid colour
and elliptic patterning, this is the cinematic equivalent of the vaginal
imagery (figure 4.1) in the work of contemporaneous artists such as
Judy Chicago, Miriam Schapiro and Hannah Wilke and traceable in
the work of perhaps the most widely revered US woman artist,
Georgia O'Keefe. The fact that it can be traced in work by women
who were not declaredly woman-identified, much less cultural
feminist, gives credence to those, like Lauter (1984), Chicago and

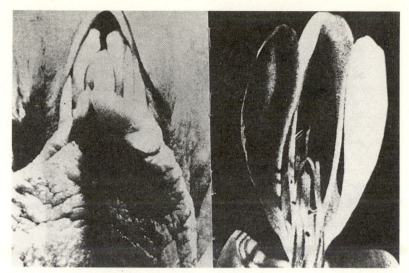

4.1   Vaginal iconography: Suzanne Santoro from *Towards New Expression* (1974)

Schapiro (1973) or Sandra Roos (1981), who would argue that this is intrinsic women's art, rather than only a specific political-aesthetic project.

Lesbian use of such imagery insisted on its sexual – rather than its procreative – significance, and such imagery is even more significant for lesbian sexuality than for hetero. If it is true that female genitalia are figures of disgust within male consciousness, then for women to treat them as figures of beauty and a fit subject for celebration is not only to stop thinking in male-identified ways but also places delight in female genitalia within an all-female circuit of pleasure. This is women looking with pleasure at other women's sexuality. *Multiple Orgasm* shows solo masturbation not sex between women, yet it is a (cultural feminist) lesbian film, not just because Hammer is known as a lesbian but because this is a sexual image offered by a woman to women.

Kimball's final characteristic is the controlling role of the right hemisphere of the brain in cultural feminist art, emphasising intuition and emotion, the unconscious, receptivity to nature and openness to mysticism and spirituality. Accordingly cultural feminist art draws upon the female unconscious (defined in Jungian rather than Freudian terms), nature (assumed to be directly knowable, without the interference of cultural perception) and forms of women's spirituality. This is seen as in part getting back in touch with ancient ways of being a woman: women's closeness to nature in part gives rise to their spirituality. Kimball quotes the anthropologist Elizabeth Gould Davis:

> Throughout the ancient world the tradition prevailed that women held the secrets of nature and were the only channel through which flowed the wisdom and knowledge of the ages. [Hence the] priority of female oracles, prophets, priests, sybils, pythonesses, maenads, Eringes, shamanesses, and so on.
>
> (Davis 1972:32; Kimball 1981:5)

Because unconscious, natural and ancient, these sources of imagery are, in cultural feminist theory, beyond the reach of male definition.

Diane Nelson, a Jungian psychotherapist, has analysed the use of images of the 'Archetypal Feminine' in the works of six women filmmakers. This has two aspects: the Elemental, with both 'life-promoting and death-devouring' qualities; and the Transformative (1978:495). An example of the first, life-promoting aspect is *Near the Big Chakra* Anne Severson 1972, consisting of 'a silent and stately color presentation of the vulvas of thirty-six women', the title referring to the Hindu 'mulaharachakra', 'the primary energy center at the base of the spine where the life force serpent Kundalini lies coiled' (ibid.:496). Nelson relates the film's imagery to both the 'primordial memory . . . [of] the tunnel, the cave, the spiral, the call of the womb-sea, the realm of down and in' and to the ancient worship of the moon goddess, not seen up in the sky, but from the same position as the camera in the film, 'legs spread open with the sexual aperture the focal point of adoration' (ibid.). Although a more erotic film, *Multiple Orgasm* involves similar feelings: the cave imagery in the middle of the film very much suggests 'the realm of down and in', and the camera never wavers from keeping 'the sexual aperture' its 'focal point'. What makes it different is its emphasis on clitoral imagery (described below). The clitoral orgasm had been 'rediscovered' by the women's movement, largely through the enormously influential article by Anne Koedt (1973) 'The Myth of the Vaginal Orgasm', first presented at the US national women's liberation conference in 1968 and published in 1970. It needed 'rediscovery' (literally, for astonishing numbers of both women and men) because of the persistent attempt in official discourse in mid-century to locate true female sexual experience in the vagina. The significance for feminists of its rediscovery was the assertion of an autonomous female sexuality, not inextricably tied to either men or procreation. In practice, it has been *lesbian* cultural feminist cinema

4.2 A frozen moment from the ever shifting sand animation of *Luna Tune*. (Women Make Movies)

that has insisted on the clitoral as much as (though by no means to the exclusion of) the vaginal dimension of female genital imagery.

An example of death-devouring Elemental imagery discussed by Nelson is *Silverpoint*, the only one of the films she discusses to have any obvious lesbian content. This has a narrative element ('[a] young woman dancer loves another woman and loses her to a third' (Weiss 1981a:22)) but the treatment uses symbolism (a razor blade, the sound of sirens) and 'a rather chaotic, tumbling, agonizing style of mood-collage' to convey 'the ambivalent Shadow side of relational life' (Nelson 1978:501). Desire is symbolised in 'night sky imagery . . . glittery star-and-crescent-bedecked veils', portraying 'moon lure romanticism' (ibid.). Nelson claims that there is nothing specifically lesbian about the death devouring imagery in *Silverpoint*, but moon imagery does figure as part of the construction of lesbian desire in some cultural feminist work. *Luna Tune* illustrates this as well as Transformative imagery.

Luna Tune (figure 4.2), an animation of shapes formed out of sand, consists of transformations. A white shape becomes a woman becomes a moon becomes a woman; she becomes two women, with heart shapes at their crotches; there are more transformations, a bird becomes a woman, her vagina becomes a bird becomes spirals become flames; a woman shoots an arrow at the moon; a line of women holding hands become spirals; a heart-shaped vagina becomes a bird and flies into the moon. In these rapid transformations – the film is only two minutes long – women are identified in archetypes: the moon (privileged in cultural feminism because it is 'inexorably related to women's menstrual cycles and childbirth on earth' (Nelson 1978:495; cf. Shuttle and Redgrove 1978)), the spiral ('the down and in') and, in the image of a woman shooting at the moon, the goddess Artemis/Diana, who was both a huntress and identified with the moon. This is given a lesbian inflection by the image of two women together, their emotional and sexual bond suggested by their heart-shaped vaginas; and this lesbianism is part of woman identification not only because of the archetypes but because they are linked to a line of women holding hands. The use of bird and flame imagery perhaps suggests the untrappable essence of womanhood, something also suggested by the use of dry sand as the medium of figuration and the pace and fluidity of the film as a whole.

Even where archetypes are not directly used in these films, nature in general is. Women bare breasted in nature is a common image, as in the sequence at the Michigan Womyn's Music Festival in *Labyris Rising* and throughout Hammer's work. As Jacqueline Zita puts it:

> Just as the spiritual side of lesbianism is one mode of counter-currency present in the new lesbian cultural movement, so the material side seeks its exuberance and legitimation in the world of nature. It is here that Barbara is most at home. Images of nature proliferate in her work, most with the effect of fitting the lesbian body into the libidinal flow of life, in its coming and going.
>
> (1981:29)

The insistent association of lesbianism with nature goes against the dominant tendency in Western thought to consider homosexuality the epitome of the unnatural. Yet, as Zita points out, there are problems here. For one thing the spiritualisation and naturalisation of lesbianism may obscure the reality of lesbian oppression and of the class, race and cultural differences between lesbians. Images of oppression are left off screen and though a black woman figures briefly in *Superdyke* and Native American imagery is used in connection with one of the *Women I Love*, the over-riding impression of these films is pretty white. Moreover, there is a danger, especially in much cultural feminism's attachment to procreative imagery, in falling back into a patriarchal and heterosexual division of the world, binding women to their 'natural' function of reproducing for men.

Lesbian work does sometimes go beyond this. Hammer's genital imagery emphasises the clitoris (*Multiple Orgasm*) and sexual pleasuring (*Dyketactics*, *Women I Love*) as much as the labia. The sororal commune, which some believe characterised ancient human societies and in which 'female collectivity, not matriarchy per se' shaped culture and religion (Nadeau 1983:38; cf. Shinell 1982), may be evoked as in the images of collective female rites and bonding, without reference to procreative femininity, in *Superdyke* and *Luna Tune*. Such female togetherness is celebrated in *Labyris Rising* in the choice of Ma Rainey singing

> Went out last night with a crowd of my friends,
> They're most of 'em women 'cause I don't like no men.

(Rainey, one of the greatest of all blues singers, was lesbian, a fact that was beginning to be widely known; her repertoire included this 'Prove It on Me Blues' as well as 'Bull Dyker's Dream' (Katz 1989)). Another possibility is presented in Judy Grahn's book *Another Mother Tongue*, where she suggests that the 'special knowledge' of the oracles, priests *et al.* derived from their special place, because lesbian/gay, outside conventional society and from their transgression of the gender boundaries that keep conventional thought in place.

> One of the major homosexual/shamanic functions in any society is to *cross over* between [the] two essentially different worlds [of female and male sub-cultures] and reveal them to each other. . . . Access to worlds inaccessible to most people has always been a Gay cultural function; we have always had underworlds of every description.
>
> (1984:47–8)

Grahn's use of the word 'underworld', with its criminal connotations, is no accident: it suggests the degree to which lesbians and gay men are outlaws, which also means, in this perspective, untouched by the rigidities of conventional society.[5] This observation comes at the end of Grahn's discussion of the traditional dyke image, and throughout the book Grahn is interested in cross-over, androgynous images of lesbians and gay men. Here then is an argument for lesbian/gay universal archetypes, mining a very different tradition from the feminine procreativity archetypes discussed by Nelson, Lauter and others. Yet though there are dykes (with dildos and motor-bikes yet) in *Superdyke* and plaid shirts and a montage of boots in *Labyris Rising*, lesbian cultural feminist films do not generally use such imagery. They are woman, not androgyny, identified.

Getting Ready

The qualities discussed so far are really to do with content – they can be present in a film that is formally conventional. This is the case with *Getting Ready* Janet Meyers 1977, a film which in some ways sums up what has been said so far. It concerns two young school friends, Val and Diana, who gradually realise their love for one another. This involves an explicit rejection of the world of men, an awareness of an alternative, female culture and some sense of the continuousness of lesbianism with other relationships with women.

The film establishes the idea of male control of the female body, and hence of women, from the start. A series of photographs of women from different cultures (suggesting the universality of the situation of women) is accompanied by sounds of appreciative male noises – women are seen through the eyes of men, and the film begins by reproducing that, all the better later to wrest us and the central characters away from it. There are images of women being looked at by men and then a shot, freeze-framed, of a woman's shadow on the pavement; it unfreezes, starts to move and there is a cut to the young woman whose shadow it is. She is one of the main characters of the film, Diana; the montage introduction suggests her universal significance, and her introduction via her shadow suggests the issue of identity.

From this point on, the system whereby men seek to control women through their bodies is established within the narrative of the film. Diana passes a school friend, Bobbie, on the street and they smile at each other, but a male voice off screen calls out 'Hey, Bobbie, over here' and Bobbie at once goes off in the direction of the voice – the command of the invisible male, and of the heterosexual imperative, is more powerful than the greeting of the two women visibly present to one another. In the next shot, Bobbie is led past Diana by the man who has claimed her, his hand on her neck. Male control is not only established through heterosexuality: it is Diana's father who comments intrusively on the fact that she is growing up ('You're really getting to need that bra') and has started her period; it is a male teacher who lectures the class of girls on menstruation. The alienatingness of male culture is further suggested, first by the bike-boy film that Diana sits through, petted by Chuck on a date that her parents have more or less forced her into, and then later by a bearded layabout who pesters her and Val.

Gradually though a woman-identified way of being asserts itself. The idea that relationships with other women are less important than those with men is presented, ruefully acknowledged by Diana in the decline of her friendship with Bobbie since the latter has got a boyfriend, asserted as a principle by Diana's mother after Diana has tried to be physically affectionate with her much to her dislike. Yet that idea is rejected by the film. The possibility of a female sense of the female body is suggested in sequences of Diana alone. In one, immediately following her father's 'bra' remark, she looks at and caresses herself in her bedroom mirror, suggesting her appropriation of her body for herself. At several other points she caresses and turns over in her hands a cowrie shell, a vaginal icon which is also part of the way that a woman-identified lesbianism is established between Diana and Val.

In the last narrative sequence in the film, Diana and Val come out to each other as friends. They do not use the word 'lesbian' but by saying that they are 'admitting' to the desire to be 'friends' they clearly indicate something beyond casual, non-erotic friendship. The sequence mobilises many of the ideas and symbols of cultural feminism. Womanhood is stressed. Val asks Diana what she wants to be when she gets older:

Diana: A woman.
Val : What do you mean – a good woman?
Diana: No – just a woman.

Diana reads an Emily Dickinson poem out loud, invoking a famous, creative woman from the past, whose love for women had only recently been identified by feminists (in for instance Myron and Bunch 1974). The sequence opens with Diana wailing into the wind, practising what she had earlier said she would like to be, a professional mourner, a traditional women's occupation.

Womanhood, Dickinson, wailing all place Diana and Val within specifically female traditions; the setting gives this a further mythic inflection. They are sitting by the sea, long a symbol of womanhood. Diana buries Val up to her neck in the sand and dances hollering around her, doing what she has earlier said older women did with menstruating girls in Australian Aboriginal culture as a celebration and rite of passage to womanhood. Thus menstruation is taken back from attempts by men to define and announce it, through an ancient women's rite which connects what these particular young women are doing to deep rooted women's traditions that transcend cultures. However, the fact that Diana refers to the source of the rite as 'Indians in Australia', while narratively excusable as adolescent ignorance, may also alert one to this as a Western construction and appropriation – cultural feminism's use of images and symbols from colonised cultures as markers of an authentic otherness betrays its embeddedness in white Western culture (cf. Smith and Smith 1981).

Finally Diana shows Val the cowrie shell, a further sea symbol but also, as Diana tells Val, a powerful object, for out of it came the goddess Aphrodite and it is the symbol of the Great Mother. Earlier the shell's vaginal symbolism was suggested. Now in the narrative, the women handle it as they declare their friendship. The shell thus unites the womanly, spiritual, sexual and loving imagery together. It only remains for the film to show another set of images of women of all ages, from all periods (though only whites) but now without the sounds of male response.

FORM

Getting Ready expresses many of the ideas of cultural feminism, making explicit their connection to a critique of patriarchal society, a critique often only implicit in other films. It is, however, formally conventional. Most lesbian cultural feminist films break with mainstream (felt as male) ways of looking and seeing as well, in particular in terms of physicality and of merging and interweaving.

The sense of physicality means both an emphasis on the sensuous properties of the art work itself and the use of forms and structures felt to be analogous with women's bodily experience. All art uses the physical properties of the media employed, but often either to represent the physical properties of what is being depicted or, in much modernist work, to draw attention to the medium *qua* medium. Cultural feminist art on the other hand emphasises physical properties in order to express the subjective experience of the physical world: not the inherent properties of objects or art media, but how they both hit the senses and are extensions of the artist's body. Composition is not concerned with creating the illusion of an objective three-dimensional space, hierarchically organised so that everything is in its allotted place, but is rather spread across the surface, using the immediate and subjective qualities of texture and colour, rather than shape and line, as the main concerns (Brinckmann 1984a:4).

There are precedents for this in some of the US art discussed in the previous chapter: the rolling language of the Beats, the squirts and washes of abstract expressionism, the use of subjective camera in some underground films, but these are based on constructions of male physical experience (driving, ejaculating, probing and so on), whereas cultural feminist work is based on the female. Joan Snyder speaks of the 'softness' of women's work (in Lippard 1976:86), while Lucy Lippard notes 'a new fondness for the pinks and pastels and ephemeral cloud colors that used to be tabu unless a woman wanted to be accused of making "feminine" art' (ibid.:49). This very much characterises the cloud imagery in *Cumulus Nimbus* or *Double Strength* Hammer 1978, with its soft sepia sequences alternating with gently coloured ones. Much of Hammer's work is based on the sense of touch, the sense that most directly links the body with the world and one especially valued in women's cultures (its role in mothering or in such woman-associated activities as massage, kneading dough or arranging flowers). This may simply involve insistently showing touching, as in the carefully named *Dyketactics* (figure 4.3), where every shot (110 in four minutes) involves the sense of touch: feet walking through grass, hands holding hands and objects, kissing, caressing, cunnilingus; even the title credit is shown just after being painted on a wall, another tactile act. Equally a film may suggest that the act of filming is itself tactile, the camera as an

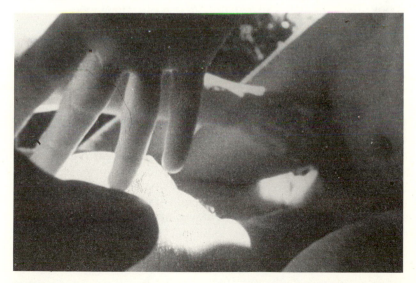

4.3   One of the 110 shots of touch in *Dyketactics*. (Barbara Hammer)

extension of the body, as in *Women I Love* where we often see the film-maker herself (her shadow, her reflection, part of her body) as she films, physically involved in the enjoyment of filming and celebrating the women she loves.

What are taken to be the shape and structure of female bodies and bodily experience may also form the basis for aesthetic properties. Vaginal imagery may extend beyond specific symbols to a general interest in compositions characterised by 'circular forms, central focus, inner space' (ibid.:49); menstruation suggests a use of cyclical structures while female orgasm suggests an open ended series, 'excitement and ebbing, excitement and ebbing – seemingly without beginning or end' (Jay 1978:56) in contrast to the male organisation around a single climax. Both in composition (spatial structure) and sequential organisation (temporal structure), 'instead of a division into major and minor elements (with the major at the centre), or a structure which gradually leads to a high point then falls away, there are more centres, more or less equal, next to one another' (Brinckmann 1984a:4; cf. DuPlessis 1985:278). Compositionally, this does not seem to be especially true of lesbian underground films (less uterus, more clitoris oriented?), but sequentially many are indeed based on multiple and equal centres: *Women I Love* is a series of equally arresting film portraits; *Luna Tune* has no climax, merely a sense of emerging out of a blob and into a moon. Even *Double Strength* and *Silverpoint*, which have elements of narrative, are not organised around narrative high spots. The former parallels different stages in a relationship, showing its demise alternatively (one segment after another) or simultaneously (sound and image out of synch) with its good times, not showing one 'leading to' the other. *Silverpoint* uses its intricate editing to show 'not the structured pain of the accident, the suicide or the funeral, but the diffuse, bleeding-out-of-boundaries pain that is characteristic of the meandering ways of the feeling function' (Nelson 1978:501).

The qualities discussed in the last paragraph point towards the other general way of characterising this work, in terms of merging and interweaving, the use of 'layers, or strata, or veils, an indefinable looseness or flexibility of handling' and 'striation' (Lippard 1976:49,81). Where the emphasis on physicality is based on a perception of the inherent nature of the female body, merging and interweaving have been seen (including by Brinckmann and DuPlessis) to relate to women's socialisation. Here Nancy Chodorow's work has been especially important. Chodorow stresses the fact that both boys and girls in this society form their first bond with a woman, the mother figure, and this is fundamental in establishing gender identity. Boys learn their anatomical difference from the mother and hence notions of autonomy, separation and uniqueness are central to male identity, whereas girls know their anatomical identity with the mother, and so notions of connection, relatedness, fusion and blurring characterise female identity. Many writers see in cultural feminist art forms analogous to this female identity formation. Lauter speaks of '"permeable boundaries" between the female self and other phenomena' (1984:215) and concludes her survey of women's literary and visual art: 'The images and forms presented in this body of work depend upon a different conception of appropriate boundaries between things – a conception that does not erase the boundaries altogether but allows for easements' (ibid.:216).

Some also see in this a different way of thinking, one which rejects rigid dualisms and categorisation. DuPlessis writes of 'both/and vision. . . the end of the either-or, dichotomized universe. . . [a vision] born of shifts, contraries, negations, contradictions' (1985:276). Kimball similarly suggests that what characterises women's art is 'wholeness', a refusal of 'the patriarchal view that splits conscious/unconscious, humans/nature, spirit/body, friend/stranger' (1981:21), to which one might add 'friend/lover, lesbian/straight'. Kimball sees this expressed even in purely abstract qualities, the revaluation of quilting, for instance, an art that makes fragments into wholes.

In film, these qualities may be present in what is selected to be filmed: the medium of dry sand in *Luna Tune*, which is formed into clearly recognisable figures but without sharp edges; the ease with which, in the same film, one figure becomes another; the selection of objects and fabrics in Hammer's films. It can be achieved through lighting, as in the complex play of soft shadows over women's bodies in the central sequence in a tent in *Superdyke*; or the use of a camera that refuses to keep its distance, hand held and in extreme close-up, involved in and connected to what is being filmed; or in compositions that do not frame, and thereby box in, what they show. It is most evident in rapid editing, interlacing images so fast that they fuse in the mind's eye; in dissolves between shots, one bleeding into the other rather than crisply cutting; above all in superimpositions, often multiple, layer upon layer of merging imagery.

Merging and blurring may characterise all cultural feminist art, but it has a special significance for lesbian work. Though certainly not the intent of her work (which some would consider homo-phobic), Chodorow's arguments are very close to those of lesbian theqrists as different as Charlotte Wolff (1971:52–60) and Adrienne Rich (1980:638–9), who see the mother–daughter bond as funda-mental to lesbianism and besides as women's primary emotional and sensual experience. Lesbian feeling becomes what is most natural or characteristic of women and, conversely, what is most fundamental to female experience (physical and emotional connectedness) comes to characterise lesbian feeling and sexuality.

Barbara Hammer

Barbara Hammer has produced the largest body of lesbian cultural feminist work. With at least fifty films since 1973, the quantity of her work is several times that of all the other films discussed in this chapter put together. There have been retrospectives of her work at the Berlin Film Festival, the Pompidou Centre in Paris, the Museum of Modern Art in New York and elsewhere, and she has won prizes and awards at several festivals. All this from someone who did not make a film until she was gone thirty.

Thematically there are four major strands in her work: auto-biography, sexuality, lesbian collectivity and spirituality/nature. Something of each is present in most of the films, but one generally predominates. Since about 1980 the content of her films has been much less 'obviously' lesbian, but these four elements have not ceased to characterise them. Here I trace these strands in turn through her work in the seventies, before looking in detail at four characteristic examples: *Superdyke*, *Multiple Orgasm*, *Women I Love* and *Double Strength*.

Her earliest films are among her most autobiographical. Her first, *I Was/I Am* 1973, together with *X* 1974 and *Psychosynthesis* 1975, form a trilogy, with, as Zita points out (1981:27), a psychodrama element close to that in Deren, Anger *et al.* Through the trilogy there is a shift from anger and bitterness to a feeling of serenity. *I Was/I Am* draws together elements of women's oppression experi-enced directly in the film-maker's life (the only woman in a film class, being refused treatment for a bullet wound because as a woman she might complain if it left a scar) with pain at the death of her mother. *X* has images of carcasses, disembowlment and meat being sliced up, expressing the pain at the end of a relationship. In one sequence, however, the film-maker is shown masturbating behind a large window, observed by mothers and children passing by, a defiant claiming of her own sexuality. The shift is underway. *Psychosynthesis* represents the inner self in four figures: a child, a witch, an athlete and a film-maker. The aggressive tone suggests that these are 'the splinters of a fragmented psyche caught in a chaotic phase of life'; but suddenly at the end, 'we are transported into an altogether new tranquility and peace', conveyed through silence and gentle nature imagery (ibid.).

Even when not self-evident from the films themselves, the viewing context suggests their autobiographical dimension. Though anyone might see these films, most viewers will know they come out of a lesbian context, in which women as subject matter are not held at a distance as biographically other. Hammer has written about her work and been widely interviewed, and probably audiences for the special screenings of her work are familiar with some of this. Besides, most of the screenings are special, frequently put on by lesbian/gay or women's groups, or if in cinemas, seldom just a routine part of a cinema's repertory, but accompanied by extracts from Hammer's writings and interviews or by her in person.

The representation of sexuality is also strongly autobiographical. With *Women I Love*, this is evident from the film itself: the title announces the film-maker's feelings for the women we see, and in various ways the film shows the presence of the film-maker in the sexual scenes on screen. With others, *Dyketactics* or *Multiple Orgasm*, this would once again be inferred from the viewing context. *Women I Love* and *Multiple Orgasm* show individuals, the film-maker herself and/or those she loves; *Dyketactics* also shows women together, public group experience as an extension of private love experience, the one indissoluble from the other.

With the films that emphasise lesbian/women's collectivity, the viewing context acts like a reflection, the (usual) audience's own lesbian/women's collectivity one with that on the screen. Some of the earlier films (*Sisters!* 1974, *A Gay Day* 1974 and *Superdyke*) show liberationist collectivity, lesbians defiant and having fun together in public as a group; *Menses* 1974 explores menstruation as an experience common and unique to women; other films are of women's collective rituals (*Women's Rites* 1974, *The Great Goddess* 1977, *Sappho* 1978). Just as sexuality cannot be separated off from collectivity, so, as the last titles indicate, neither can collectivity be separated off from spirituality. *Moon Goddess* has two women, lovers, exploring a landscape for ancient sites; *Arequipa* 1981 is shot in a convent in Peru, evoking spiritual collectivity in an exploration of doors, walls, passages and courtyards, 'dissolves and translucent blue and mauve paints . . . pull[ing] us deeper into its recesses' (Leduc 1982:35); *Stone Circles* dwells on these prehistoric format-ions, which can be associated with women's religion (Grahn 1985:37–41). With other films (*Eggs* 1976, *Pools* 1981, *Pond and Waterfall* 1982, *Pearl Diver* 1984), it is aspects of nature alone that suggest a spiritual dimension.

Hammer's films also have many of the formal features of cultural feminist film. The 'permeable boundaries' of her work are not confined to the use of superimposition, the film-maker in the shot and so on; she has sought to move beyond the limitations of film itself, beyond, that is, film conceived as a thing made by one person in one place, and then moved about the place to be screened separately from the film-maker. Though most of her work does inevitably remain within this framework, she has found ways of breaking out of it. She has made films with other people (*Moon Goddess* with Gloria Churchman, *Superdyke Meets Madame X* with Max Almy, *Pools* with Barbara Klutinis) and in 1982 inaugurated a project, as yet unrealised, called *Eros, Women's International Erotic Art Film*, which would be 'a compilation of film shot by women all over the world depicting what they think/feel is erotic to them' (Leduc 1982:34). If this would break down the boundaries between women as isolated artists, Hammer's ongoing *Audience* breaks down the separation of who is on and who looks at the screen. It consists of a series of interviews and discussions (so far in San Francisco, Toronto, Montréal and London) with audiences at screenings of her work; when shown to another audience, there is the possibility of a sense of connection between people on the screen and people in the auditorium.

Hammer's most thoroughgoing assault on the limitations of film is *Available Space* 1978. The implicit subject-matter of this film is autobiographical, 'the suffocation of a tight relationship' (Hammer 1982:63). There are shots of constricted spaces, with the frame itself emphasised as a further constriction. When the film is shown, it is projected from a revolving table and at the end, while on film there are images of Hammer cutting through the screen, Hammer in person stands by the screened image and appears to push it round the room. The cutting and pushing, the presence of the film-maker both in and with the film, break the boundaries of film at several levels: who sees (cameraperson) and is seen (performer) merge; the film-maker, generally absent once the film is made, is present; revolving the image blurs its rectangular boundaries, while creating a strong sense of a centred circularity emanating from the centrally placed projector. Hammer's presence thus both personalises the film, makes explicit its biographical lesbian content, and simultaneously, through its form (on screen and in projection), embodies a cultural feminist aesthetic of centredness and diffusion.

Superdyke

Superdyke shows a group of women romping about San Francisco (wearing Superdyke T-shirts that were top sellers at the women's bookstore in San Francisco (Wolf 1979:115)), then together in the country and finally returning to the city. It connects elements of dyke style and liberationism with sexuality, spirituality and nature; and it is fun and funny.

The women are part traditional dykes, cropped hair, jeans, some on motor-bikes, but crossed with lesbian feminist images of powerful women, carrying shields emblazoned 'Amazon', like Diana shooting with bow and arrow. Aspects of the dyke image are referred to humorously: two women try to squeeze into a telephone box labelled 'Closet'; in a department store, women grab various objects and mime using them as dildos. The Amazon image too is seen as fun: the shields are obviously cardboard; a woman flexes her muscles like a macho man; another wears a T-shirt with the Superman logo on it.

While they remain in San Francisco, these Amazon dykes zap the place with instant street theatre. They are enacting coming out, bursting through a crowd with their shields and dancing together in a public square. At an art exhibition and a department store, they are outrageous, not only by being so openly lesbian but by miming a lesbian response to the places. The art exhibition is of erotic art, including vaginal imagery, and the women stand before the images and play with their crotches, exaggeratedly miming opening them out to view. In the store, all manner of objects become potential dildos until one is grabbed and borne aloft out into the shopping mall.

In the country the women are naked and the imagery is less dykish/Amazonian, more 'Archetypal Feminine'. Collective imagery merges into and out of love-making imagery. They dance together in a circle, with braids of flowers in their hair, before falling to the ground, and the camera swings in an echo of this movement to 'discover' two women rolling over together on the ground; in the following sequences, it is night and the women kiss, massage and caress each other. Daylight again and the women are outside, naked in nature; then inside, a group of women in a semicircle, holding each other round the waist, caressing themselves and each other with bones; they scatter sand over one woman lying on the floor before leaving the tent and, outside, walk along through grass in a chain, each putting her hand on the shoulders of the one in front. This section is rich in spiritual significance. Circles and chains are basic forms of ritual; the sand burying is reminiscent of the ancient women's ritual alluded to in *Getting Ready*; bones were part of the equipment of divination and shamanism, and they may be felt to be the ground of animal being (cf. Lauter 1984:150, 160). Throughout this sequence collectivity, sensuality and spirituality are not separable, and this feeling lingers over the final section of the film, the return to the city, the women disappearing together into the night.

The fun of the film is not only in the antics of the women, but in the filming. The sequence in the store is pixillated, a traditional comic device where editing makes the actions frenetic and jumpy, reminiscent of wrongly projected silent movies. Music, a piano accompaniment played by Margaret Moores, often provides comic counterpoint: a biker accompanied by that male action cliché, the *William Tell* Overture, rather falteringly played; Tchaikovsky's piano concerto, a high point of lush Romanticism, accompanying fooling around at the erotic art exhibition; cod 'Red Indian' music with the beginnings of the country sequence; 'vamping' underscoring the kissing and massage. This use of humour, especially the music, might have something of the 'gay sensibility' about it, simultaneously humorous and serious, ironic and intense, but without the corrosive, defensive edge of gay male humour. It feels more joyous than that, more fun than funny, a celebration of the geniality at the heart of collective, erotic and spiritual experience.

Multiple Orgasm

The few silent minutes of *Multiple Orgasm* consist of the continuous superimposition of two elements: rock formations and a woman masturbating. Together they construct a sense of the experience of female orgasm.

The rock formations are both external and internal, cliff faces and caves. The patterns in both are analogous to female genitals, and there is a sense of movement between outer and inner genitals, the camera moving over the cliff face but into the space of the cave. In cliffs and caves, outside and in, the camera discovers both the whorls and folds of 'central core' vaginal imagery and also buds and protrusions that suggest a clitoral imagery. The latter are the more remarkable, partly because rock formations have long been used as a source of phallic imagery. The camera in *Multiple Orgasm* scans the skyline and finds not rearing, thrusting shapes, but knobs and nodules; peaks and boulders nestle into the tucks and grooves of both cliff face and cave walls; camera angles make even stalactites look clitoral.

The shots of the woman are first of her vagina, then her face. The film opens with an extreme close-up of the vagina, fingers parting the labia, then rubbing the clitoris. After a while, the film cuts to and remains on the woman's face, sometimes thrown back in ecstasy, sometimes calmer, smiling. The predominant colour of both rock and body shots is reddish/pinkish, though a bright. blue in the rock shots occasionally serves to set this off, heightening its body/blood colour qualities. The rock formation element uses many cuts and a constantly moving, hand-held camera, whereas the vaginal and face shots are long takes with a static camera, the only movement coming from the subject herself. Though there are technical reasons for this (Hammer was filming herself masturbating) it has the effect of anchoring the diffuse rock imagery, the analogue of experience, in the physical presence of the body.

The film is sequentially, not randomly, structured, but not towards precise moments of orgasm. The first few minutes superimpose cliff shots over the vagina; round about the time the face replaces the vagina, the cave shots are introduced; after a bit, both superimposed elements momentarily freeze on a frame. Up to this point the camera movement has been quite slow and steady, though the finger's movement has been fast and the head has been jerked back quite violently; now the camera movement, still on internal imagery, is much faster, only slowing, very considerably, when the film returns to external, cliff imagery. Finally the film ends on another freeze.

The structuring does suggest periods of greater frenzy or calm, but it does not pinpoint the orgasms as events in the way that *Fireworks*, for instance, does (to say nothing of male porn). The treatment of lesbian love-making in *Dyketactics* similarly avoids such constructions of orgasm. The women undress each other, kiss and caress all over, manually and orally pleasure one another, but all of this is shot from many different angles and with no sense of coming to a final climax. This contrasts with Constance Beeson's film of lesbian love-making, *Holding* 1971. Beeson is an experimental film-

maker and *Holding* is one of three films by her depicting love-
making, the others being *Unfolding* 1969 (heterosexual) and *Stamen*
1972 (gay male). Interestingly a similar perception of sexuality runs
through all three. Beeson uses many of the aesthetic qualities
associated with cultural feminism: sea imagery in *Unfolding*, flowers
in *Stamen*, woodlands in *Holding*; soft, blurry composition, much
superimposition and interweaving editing, with things shot from
many different angles. Where they differ from *Multiple Orgasm* or
Dyketactics is in the sense of a gradual building up to a climax,
conveyed partly through music (crescendo, introduction of ever
more and varied instruments and sounds) and through faster cutting
and dissolving. The multiplication of sounds and images means that
this is still not the orgasm as isolated, one-off event as in men's
films, nor is there any emphasis of the visible moment of orgasm.
Nonetheless there is not the sense of open ended orgasmic pleasure
as in Hammer, and Zita feels that there is still a feeling of 'eroticism
reduced to "getting the orgasm"' (1981:28).

Zita also suggests that *Holding* remains at a distance from what is
being filmed, maintaining 'the voyeuristic alienation between the
spectator and the event' (ibid.). *Multiple Orgasm* avoids this not
only because we are likely to know that the film-maker is also the
woman we are looking at, but also by at one point including the
film-maker as film-maker in the film. Near the beginning her shadow

4.5

4.6

Three of the *Women* Barbara Hammer *Loves*

falls across the cliff face being filmed; superimposed over the vagina shot, it looks as if she is also filming the vagina, as if the labia are being parted for her to see. The woman is a sexual image for herself as well as for her audience.

Women I Love

Women I Love (figures 4.4, 4.5, 4.6) is a series of portraits of women, single or in couples. It makes the most sustained exploration of both vaginal imagery and showing the film-maker in the film of any of Hammer's work, while also in effect presenting an account of a certain kind of seventies lesbian life-style.

Vegetables are used throughout the film as a source of vaginal imagery. The opening shot (described above) of a red cabbage, is followed in quick succession by lettuce, broccoli, artichoke and cauliflower, the camera pointing straight down from overhead, slowly zooming back, one shot dissolving into another – vaginal imagery and boundary-less technique. Thereafter such shots punctuate the film, generally separating one portrait from another. Most of the vegetables are obvious choices: those already mentioned, and used again, all fold out; others introduced later, oranges, lemons and onions, peel open. A corn cob, an archetypally phallic vegetable, is more surprising, yet this too is rendered vaginal: it is shown still wrapped in leaves, then, through stop-motion animation, is unwrapped, with the silvery, ribbony strands that cover it laid out around; because it is shot from overhead, it seems less phallic, less big and jutting, more jewel-like; and a tiny zoom in and out on it suggests it quivering. The film stock used brings out the glowing colours and intricate shapes of the vegetables, while the animation, zooms and dissolves give the whole film a celebratory élan.

There are other sources of female body imagery in the film. Spiders' webs towards the end of the film have vaginal (core centred) qualities, in addition to their long cultural association with women. The title is given against a shot of water dripping down in front of a sunrise, suggesting perhaps vaginal wetness and/or the association of women and water. Flowers too are used in the film, though in a different way and in relation to particular women. One woman is shot standing close to a lilac bush, then in fir trees, then behind hanging orchids. In another portrait sequence, the woman is associated with daffodils, to the point that they seem to characterise her existence. There are shots of opening a dish washer to find daffodils inside, a broom gently sweeping daffodils along the floor, a rubbish bin moved to show daffodils lying behind it, daffodils lifted out of the washing-up suds and rinsed under the tap. This domestic association then gives way to sensuousness: daffodils, shot from several different angles, lie on the pillow in the bedroom, in the garden, the woman smells daffodils and caresses them with her lips. In between these sensuous shots there have been shots of daffodils in a back pocket, in a plastic holder, held in the hand.

At several points, particularly the most intimate, the film-maker is visible as she makes the film. One woman's body is explored by the camera in extreme close-up; the camera is hand held and bounces a bit, reminding us of the presence of the film-maker; at one point we see her filming her naked reflection in the mirror, thus drawing her explicitly into the sequence. At another point, we again see her naked in a mirror; a clothed woman passes in front of it; the film-maker turns the zoom handle and as a result the shot zooms in on her, finally focusing on her vagina. The normal situation of film-making is reversed: here it is the film-maker who is naked and revealed, not the performer; and we see the mechanics of achieving a shot, the zoom consciously, personally directed on to the most taboo part of the anatomy. Later, with another woman, the naked film-maker filming is reflected in a window behind which another woman caresses and kisses herself; the film-maker approaches the window until finally we can no longer see her, only the other woman. Again we are reminded of the film-maker's involved and connected presence; both women are equally vulnerable because equally naked; and at the end the film-maker merges into the image of the other woman.

Such sequences both show the film-maker's connectedness to what is being filmed and dissolve the strict boundary between who films and who is filmed. Another sequence achieves this even more directly. It is a quite long sequence of cunnilingus, shot from the position of the woman being pleasured; at the end the other woman looks up, laughs and rests her head on the pleasured woman's thigh, smiling. Here the film-maker, as one being genitally pleasured, could not be more bodily connected to the image, and her lover's smile at her/the camera/us also stresses the lover's happy participation in being filmed. In the other sequences it is Hammer's presence and movement into the scene that crosses the boundary between filmer and filmee; here the lover's smile to the filmer is a movement back across that boundary from the other side.

Because of its portrait album quality, *Women I Love* does also have a dimension as a record of a lesbian life-style. All the women are white, though the last might be Native American if the head-dress she wears is not just a cultural borrowing. The film is *not* a documentary and is not concerned with, for instance, what these women do for a living or what their political views are; but it does nonetheless construct a not unfamiliar milieu of a rural life-style with all mod cons, with domesticity, art production and spirituality all inseparable from this rural base. We see only wooden houses, porches, gardens, countryside, the sea, no urban imagery; there is washing and washing up, gardening and cleaning, writing and reading, and filming. In one shot a smiling woman twirls a blood red tampon from a string, an open and celebratory inclusion of another facet of womanhood – but the tampon reminds us of modern conveniences. Spirituality could be read into the vaginal and nature imagery throughout, but it really comes to the fore in the final sequence, which draws together images of all the women in the film with imagery of webs, the moon, the sea, the Native American head-dress, a galaxy.

The final sequence also seems to have strongly sexual rhythms. An extreme close-up of clitoral manipulation is superimposed first over a woman's face, then over the sea. The redness of the vagina makes the sea red too. Then following a series of shots of a spider's web finishing on its centre, there are a series of shots of the spiritual elements listed in the previous paragraph, each one faded into and out of, ending on a shot of the masturbating hand, now still; there is then a final shot of the moon ending the film. The fade-in, fade-out editing makes the sequence throb; while the ordering of shots frames the spiritual within the sexual imagery.

At one level the structure of the film suggests a cultural feminist reading, whereby the individuality of the women in the different sequences is finally merged into a mystical-orgasmic sense of womanhood in the final sequence. Hammer's programme notes make clear that the film was shot over a period of years, as the varying quality of the film stock betrays, and this suggests another dimension. The film explores not only lesbian sexuality but also alternative forms of lesbian relationships, based not on the model of the monogamous, once-and-for-all couple but on successive couple relationships (or 'serial monogamy') and a desire to embrace them all in the memory, not seeing the latest as *the* one which denigrates the value of all that went before. Andrea Weiss sees this as a weakness of the film, since the representation of the relationships is based on romantic conceptions of love (long a target of feminist criticism before its 'revaluation' by some in the eighties). As she says, there is (daffodils apart) rather little differentiation between the women and Weiss sees this as idealising each woman, effectively casting her into a certain mould of the desirable woman. She suggests that the succession of women implies that each relationship is a failure, and that the structure is both a refusal to recognise this, always passing on to the next one, preserving the idealisation intact, and a mere repetition of the same relationship (idealisation and failure) without 'progression' (1981b:30). Yet, taking the film as it stands, there is no reason to conclude that the relationships must have been failures, nor would it be wrong to preserve in an album images only of the good times. Weiss's argument is part of a wider concern, that Hammer's imagery remains caught within a patriarchal repertoire of romantic images of women, which no more tells the truth about women and lesbianism than do the more overt denigrations of both.[6] These are arguments familiar from the general critique of cultural feminism indicated above, and there is no easy intellectual reconciliation between those that see that world view as an inflection of patriarchal ideas and those who see it as an alternative to them. Perhaps here the boundaries are impermeable.

Double Strength

Double Strength is probably Hammer's most critically praised film: 'One of Barbara's most beautiful films' (Zita 1981:28), 'the most exhilarating of the . . . films' (Leduc 1982:35), 'one of Barbara's best films' (Springer 1980:35). It shows a relationship between two women, Hammer and a trapeze artist, Terry Sendgraff; it both celebrates the relationship while registering its break-up.

The film alternates sepia and colour sequences, showing the women, mostly naked, exercising on a trapeze bar, cartwheeling, doing handstands, climbing a tree. For the most part it is Sendgraff not Hammer doing these things, but Hammer is still characteristically connected into the scene. In one shot the camera follows a piece of rope along the floor and up a ladder until the film-maker's leg comes into the image; in another the camera zooms back from a close-up on Sendgraff's face and the film-maker's feet come into frame; in another the camera looks down on Sendgraff turning the trapeze in her feet and then letting go, so that the image spins into a blur as the trapeze swings round. These sequences do not only show Hammer's connection to the image, but also signify her participation in her lover's art, trapezing.

Already on the soundtrack there are hints of the end of the

relationship: the sound of a telephone permanently engaged, then a voice saying it has been disconnected; a voice speaking about death, not gloomily but in terms of completion and sleep. As the film proceeds, images also begin to suggest the end: stills of Hammer's face in rage; one woman's movements superimposed harshly, not mergingly, over the face of the other. In the last few minutes there is a loud, urgent heart-beat on the soundtrack; and the fast cutting between elements becomes a violent flicker effect before slowing down to the end of the film.

As Weiss notes, although these elements showing the end of the relationship are clearly present, it is somehow easy not to take them in: 'each time I've seen the film, audiences have stated that they missed all the signs, had no idea that the relationship was deteriorating' (1981b:30). This was my own impression. Weiss argues that the film uses idealising, romantic imagery that is far more powerful than its attempts to break such imagery down through juxtaposition and editing. A different explanation is possible. Probably what one remembers most of the film are the images of Sendgraff trapezing. They are remarkable for celebrating a woman's beauty in terms of strength and athleticism, and they continue throughout the film – Sendgraff's beauty and strength is never forgotten or turned into something hated. Moreover the use of sepia suggests images from the past, memory and nostalgia. The film wants to hang on to a good memory of the loved one and the relationship, an impression reinforced by the voice over speaking of death (the end of a relationship?) in positive terms. Not surprisingly then, what abides is the impression of love rather than the pain of separation.

TOWARDS LESBIAN EROTICA, OR PORNOGRAPHY

Lesbian cultural feminist films celebrate and often directly show lesbian sexuality but it was not necessarily part of their purpose to turn women on. Yet to communicate an erotic delight in women's bodies and to show acts that a film-maker finds sexually pleasing is at the very least liable to give a pleasure to the viewer that can be categorised as erotic, sexual, sensual or pornographic. Much of the problem, of course, is which of those words you use. Two films made in 1979, *Three Short Episodes* GB Rachel Finkelstein and *Sweet Dreams* USA Honey Lee Cottrell, opened up, in very different ways, the question of this pleasure. I want to look at them both here before considering their relationship to one of the most remarkable developments in the mid-eighties, the emergence of avowedly pornographic lesbian film.

Three Short Episodes contrasts male constructions of female sexuality and the erotic with, in its third episode, female constructions of the erotic. The first section makes fun of the idea of penis envy with pixillated images of women frantically searching between their legs or forcing a banana down their throat then sicking it up; the second uses old heterosexual porn film, keeping it at a distance by running it fast or filming it being projected, conveying a mucky, hole-in-the-corner feeling. The third episode opens with the title, 'Towards a New Female Sexuality'. Its central image is an oval hole torn in cardboard with the bowed figure of a woman superimposed below it; as the episode develops this figure raises her arms in a parabola, thus seeming to embrace the hole. Circular shapes form the basis for the montage of images that accompanies this: a woman looks at her vagina in a round hand mirror; buttocks are shot to emphasise their roundness and caught in a pool of light; hands caressing another's hair outline the head as a sphere; batik (a fabric associated with women in African tradition) provides further curving shapes and even the music, solo flute arabesques (by Kay Gardner) is, we learn at the end, entitled 'Moon Circles'. The whole episode is an evocation of 'central core imagery', its cool, languorous tone constructing an eroticism quite other to what had gone before.

Sweet Dreams also draws on some of the cultural feminist repertoire, notably in an opening sequence where a woman's hand plays softly over the shape and texture of blossoms, feeling the stems, fronds and heads of daffodils and lilies. A cactus, its soft, furry texture suggesting pubic hair, is shot from one angle to evoke the clitoris, while in another shot a finger probes into its core. After this however the film presents female sexuality more directly. There are four main sections: a white woman masturbating; a black woman caressing herself; the white woman masturbating again and finally the two women making love. Though the imagery is plain, there are differences of cinematic treatment. The black woman's solo sequence, shot in sepia, uses more editing of close-ups of different parts of her body; the two white woman's sequences are in colour, with much less editing. The first sequence in particular starts with an extremely slow zoom back from a close-up of a woman's hand masturbating, back and back until her whole body and environment are in frame. In both her sequences, she speaks about masturbating, about fantasies, about tasting and smelling her vaginal juices. In other words she is much more fully present to us than the fragmented and unspeaking black woman. The final sequence of the women making love is cross cut with shots of the white woman masturbating, suggesting that this is her fantasy; near the end a long hold on her face in spasm and a repeated keening phrase of harmonica and violin on the soundtrack convey orgasm, but we do not see the women together coming to orgasm. At the end of the film, the white woman smiles slightly at the camera and her name, Pat Califia, comes up.

Three Short Episodes signals a need for imagery of female sexuality, to enable women to feel beyond heterosexual, male constructions of sexuality; to do this it has to eschew existing aspects of sexual representation that might seem too contaminated by those male constructions: sex as narrative, the importance of orgasm, an address which elicits the viewer's excitement. *Sweet Dreams* has no such problems. Pat Califia is one of the best-known spokespeople for forms of sex, including s/m and pornography, that were long identified with male constructions of sexuality; she has contributed a regular column to the gay journal *The Advocate* (thus acknowledging a link with male gay sexual practices (cf. Byron 1985:48)) and in 1980 published *Sapphistry*, a celebration of the diversity of sexual practices open to lesbians. With its floral opening and diffused treatment of the black woman, *Sweet Dreams* shows its roots in cultural feminism, but the insistent signalling of orgasm, Califia's presence (and final look at the camera) and the direct reference to smelling and tasting juices suggest a very different direction for lesbian erotica.

In 1985 two US companies put out films (available straightaway on video) that for the first time[7] were made by lesbians and aimed to provide for profit erotic entertainment for lesbians. In other words, the first lesbian pornography for lesbians. These were *Erotic in Nature* Tigress Productions and *Fun with a Sausage*, *L'Ingénue*, *Private Pleasures* and *Shadows* Blush Productions.

Tigress in fact refused the term 'pornography', insisting that their work was 'erotica'. As Kate Millett suggested in an interview with Chris Bearchall, however problematic the distinction, many women preferred to think in terms of erotica because pornography is associated with exploitative imagery rooted in misogyny and at root 'all the old attitudes of a puritanical and prurient society' (Bearchall 1983:31; cf. Lorde 1984:55–6).[8] Bearchall herself however remained sceptical, preferring to stick to pornography, partly because of the class connotations of 'erotica' ('the rich person's pornography'

4.7 Cultural feminist or standard straight porn imagery in *Erotic in Nature*? (Tigress Productions)

1983:33), partly because of the unhappy hard:soft core distinction that seems to flow from it. This embrace of the pornographic is of a piece with the development or reclamation among some lesbians – or, as they would as likely say, dykes – of such practices as butch:femme role play, sado-masochism, the use of dildos, all of which are explored and celebrated by Blush Productions' films. Blush is affiliated to the magazine *On Our Backs*, whose title is a deliberate provocation of the radical feminist newspaper *Off Our Backs*, seemingly reclaiming the pleasures of the missionary position. *Erotic in Nature* is more tentative. An opening sequence has a woman masturbating with an translucent, amber-coloured dildo; in a central sequence, the two lovers wear clothes suggestive of butch:femme roles; and the high colour gloss look of the film is reminiscent of *Playboy* or *Penthouse*. The latter also do spreads shot in natural surroundings, but the emphasis here from the title through the opening shots of a bare breasted woman chopping wood to the sex sequences by a river and in a clearing in a wood, also evokes cultural feminist iconography (figure 4.7); and the fact that the 'sex is variations on Vanilla' (Rodgerson 1986:33) shows that *Erotic in Nature*, though a commercial turn-on proposition, eschews the 'dirty' sex of the new lesbian pornography.

*   *   *

Lesbian cultural feminist film put the possibility of an erotica for women on to the lesbian film-making agenda, though many of its proponents would certainly not recognise this impulse in the likes of Blush Productions. The division that these new initiatives have opened up, between varieties of not easily reconcilable definitions of lesbian desire, are only a more recent version of a problem that always confronted lesbian cultural feminism: its appeal to an essential core of womanly/lesbian identity in which in practice many women and lesbians did not recognise themselves. Some would see this as a telling indictment of lesbian cultural feminism, passing off as universal a particular, rather white, rather vanilla version of lesbianism. Yet if many lesbians' often pretty fierce rejection of this work does invalidate its claims to universality (unless one were to argue that a lesbian's inability to recognise her essential identity is itself an effect of patriarchal domination), its particularity does not invalidate it as a construction of lesbian identity and desire. All lesbian/gay identity images are culturally and historically particular, but this does not make them less real, it merely makes them particular. Cultural feminist lesbianism is no more invalidated because it took its particularity for universality than any of the other constructions of lesbian/gay identity in this book. It was one way that some women forged from what was available a construction and unequivocal celebration of lesbian desire.

5   From and for the movement

In 1949 the Dutch gay rights movement, the COC, produced a short silent film entitled *In dit teken*, directed by Jan Lemstra. Made thirty years after *Anders als die Andern*, it was the first film to be made directly by and in the name of a gay organisation.

The films discussed so far were rooted in the gay/lesbian culture of their times, which had more or less strong links (as did the film-makers) with the concurrent gay/lesbian movements. The latter may even have been necessary for the films' existence: they created a public space and climate of self-confidence for lesbian/gay cultural production. Without the movements, lesbian/gay films would often have remained home movies in the closet. Yet no film so far in the book was clearly part of and speaking for the organised movement of lesbians and gay men. Even the shots of Hirschfeld addressing a meeting in *Anders* are only moments in a conventional feature film that neither deals directly with the gay movement nor declares itself to be part of it.

The films in this chapter are grounded in the iconography and rhetoric of the lesbian/gay movements, ally themselves with these and were for the most part funded and produced by them. I have divided them into three groups, corresponding to different forms of politics which I shall designate institutional, confrontational and affirmation. The first group, consisting in fact only of *In dit teken*, belongs to an approach concerned with establishing gay organisations and promoting change through existing mechanisms of reform. The second group, still only a handful of films, comes out of the libertarian impulses of late sixties politics. The last group, outnumbering the other two combined by something like forty to one, are from the gay, lesbian and women's liberation movements of the seventies, concerned to affirm the worth of gay/lesbian existence.

These distinctions have to do not only with different analyses of society but also, built into those, with different assumptions about how change is brought about, how a given kind of politics can bring it about. The films are part of the politics, not only presenting political content but also placing the viewer in relation to the processes of change the politics advocates. Not just what they say but how they address the viewer is central to the politics: who they imply the viewer is, how they want her/him to react, what they want her/him to *do* and also who they imply the film-makers are, their place in the political process. The differences at this level are also differences of film form – the mode selected, the use made of it – and it is this relationship, between kinds of political practice and of film form, that is especially at issue in what follows.

INSTITUTIONAL POLITICS

The COC[1] was founded in Amsterdam in 1947 in the spirit of the pre-war gay magazine *Levensrecht* (*The Right to Exist*). The earlier NWHK (Dutch Scientific Humanitarian Committee), founded in 1911 along the lines of the German WhK, had put most of its efforts into changing attitudes through influencing influential people, whereas *Levensrecht* had placed the emphasis on establishing a safe and respectable gay sub-culture. The COC contained both approaches, but the latter was its dominant emphasis (Tielman 1987:10–13).

In dit teken opens on a shot of the COC's logo, a man in silhouette raising his hat in a welcoming, slightly foppish gesture (figure 5.1), superimposed by the title reading, 'This sign has given hundreds of people the courage to go to the Keizersgracht'. The Keizersgracht was (is) the street in which the COC had its offices, and we next see shots of it and of Nick Engelschman, aka Bob Angelo, one of the founders of the COC, in the office. Two men are shown asking for directions, being greeted by Bob, given pamphlets, having a cigarette, becoming members. Having established the Centre's existence, the rest of the film is in two sections. The first warns of the dangers facing homosexuals: shots of a (well-known) public toilet in Amsterdam, of a queeny man in a bar; a title enjoining 'Don't go to. . .' followed by shots of a scouts club, a swimming pool and then a prison. The rest of the film presents the alternative, principally as provided by the COC: a cultural evening, mostly men singing to a piano or guitar, but including a one-man sketch sending up queeny behaviour; a 'bal masqué', with the

5.1 The COC logo in *In dit teken* (COC)

preparations of drag and decorating shown as well as scenes of dancing (including the only shots of women in the COC sections of the film). In between, there is a sequence showing the possibilities of going 'free in nature with your friends': shots of trees, rivers, pools, men and women sitting or wandering, and particularly pairs of men, riding horses, sitting outside drinking, giving each other piggy-backs.

No individuals speak in *In dit teken*. (Even a silent film may use intertitles to indicate what people say.) The only 'voice' in the film is the voice of the COC itself. This is in part because of the film's function, which is akin to advertising, the inter-titles working like slogans or headings in a leaflet. It also relates to the kind of politics represented by the COC. The Centre is established as an organisation that provides facilities, an already existing structure to which one can belong. The impersonal 'voice' of the film is part of the construction of a stable institutional identity.

In dit teken clearly assumes its audience will be gay men and, maybe, lesbians. It may be the only film in this book unequivocally addressed to a gay audience. Many others may imply or only really work for a gay/lesbian audience, but none proceeds as if what is being said could only conceivably be relevant to gay people. This is a gay organisation talking to gay people about being gay. Again this is a question of function – who but gay people would be potential recruits to a gay club? – but also of politics. As Tielman explains, the COC operated according to the characteristic Dutch principle of 'verzuiling' ('pillarisation'), whereby society is split into 'pillars', distinct, separate spheres of concern supported and legitimated by the state. The Dutch government came to treat the COC as a kind of 'mini-pillar', the agency for the regularisation of homosexuality. By presenting itself as an institutional grouping of homosexuals, the COC both established the existence of this 'pillar' and could speak on its behalf with other 'pillars'. Part of its strategy was then not only an institutional style, but the construction of a constituency of homosexual people. The film, with its deliberate address of a gay audience, is part of this strategy of building a 'pillar' of homosexuality in Dutch society.

This kind of politics appeared 'closetty' to later generations of gay and lesbian activists. The suspicion that straight values probably come along with 'verzuiling' might appear confirmed by the film's attitude towards the unrespectable aspects of homosexual existence: pederasty ('Don't go to scouts clubs'), public sex ('Don't go to toilets') and queens. The film does not waver on the first two, but it is more ambivalent about the last. The injunction not to go to bars shows a queen chattering with a group of men and there is the sketch sending up queeniness; yet the last third of the film is devoted to the bal masqué. Preparations are dwelt on. At a fitting one man parades about in the style of Queen Wilhelmina, a great camp moment. At the ball, the film shows the wide range of imaginative and outlandish costumes. It is as if with its mind the film says, 'Don't act like queens', yet with its heart wants to celebrate the exuberance and ingenuity of queening and camping.

At the end of the ball, the title 'démasqué' comes up and everyone takes off their masks, followed by the title 'Now only for this evening, but later in the future. . .'. Demasking symbolises a political point, suggesting that organising a club and 'verzuiling' are parts of a strategy towards the full participation of homosexuals in society. Demasking anticipates coming out, something longed for but not yet thought possible. Thus *Levensrecht* does not advocate the closet, and its moment of demasking/coming out is also the climax of its perhaps inadvertent celebration of the carnival of camp.

In dit teken is a modest and hardly insurrectionary film, yet is nonetheless an isolated example, without equivalents in other countries or follow-ups within the COC itself. Film was still an extremely expensive medium of which few people had experience as producers; film-making was bound within the institutions of the entertainment industry, the art world and the state or industry sponsored documentary. Few marginal pressure groups could afford or would probably even think in terms of film. Equally the spaces for showing films remained restricted, especially for propagandising gay or lesbian films – neither entertainment nor art, as conventionally defined, such films would not be part of the range of social issues favoured by schools, colleges, unions, women's groups and so on. By contrast the later movements benefited from the greater cheapness, accessibility and ease of use of new developments in film technology (lightweight cameras, 16mm film [itself lighter, easier to handle and cheaper than 35mm], light-sensitive film stock [not requiring cumbersome artificial lighting], portable synchronised sound-recording equipment) and from the increased use of film among radical movements at large. Indeed, the new lesbian and gay movements put a special emphasis on film, partly from the desire for high public visibility for gay people and partly as a consequence of identifying mass media film as a central aspect of lesbian/gay oppression.

CONFRONTATIONAL POLITICS

The protest movements of the late sixties in the capitalist countries managed to be both visceral and cerebral: 'zapping'[2] (demonstrations and sit-ins, storming and disrupting meetings and conferences, sabotage and mainly symbolic terrorism) went hand in hand with a readiness for, and often an insistence on, analysis and theory. Society was to be grasped in its totality, any particular oppression seen as an expression of the whole way in which society was structured; culture, including film, was as much an arena of political struggle as the shop-floor or university, as much the vehicle of power and control as the government or police, as ripe for zapping and analysis as anything else.

If everything was to be seen as political, it followed that gender and sexuality too should be put on the revolutionary agenda, though the act of doing so by women, lesbians and gay men was often experienced, by them as well as by straight men, as a break with the revolutionary left. The new sexual politics alarmingly acknowledged everything as politically loaded, including how you react to men and to women and what you do in bed. Zapping and analysis animated the early days of the gay liberation movement (see next section) and such short lived, tiny groupings as the Comité d'action pédérastique révolutionnaire in May 1968 in Paris. They remained moments or marginal tendencies within the seventies movement, but nonetheless a handful of European films furthered this politics by finding ways of using film both to analyse and to zap.

There are two main groupings: films made by Rosa von Praunheim in Germany and the USA and those made in France (and a few elsewhere), notably by Lionel Soukaz. I'll look at these two groups in turn, ending with a consideration of the most internationally commercially successful confrontational film, *Taxi zum Klo*. All this work mixes zap and analysis. The difference in emphasis lies partly in who appear to be the object of the zap, gays or straights, and partly in what they are being zapped with, the sordidness of gay oppression or the delight of gay perversity. Broadly speaking, von Praunheim is more given to confronting gays with the ugliness of their conditions of existence, the French work to defy the straight imagination with the wilder reaches of the gay libido.

Rosa von Praunheim

Von Praunheim made four films before 1980 dealing directly with the gay movement. *Schwestern der Revolution* (*Sisters of the Revolution*) 1969 and *Nicht der Homosexuelle ist pervers, sondern die Situation in der er lebt* (*It is not the Homosexual who is Perverse, but the Situation in which He finds Himself*) 1970 show and express aspects of post-68 gay politics, and screenings of the second are generally thought to have stimulated the formation of gay activist groups in Frankfurt, Cologne, Munich and other German cities (Holy 1985:184). *Homosexuelle in New York* 1971 is a record of a gay march and *Armee der Liebenden oder Aufstand der Perversen* (*Army of Lovers, or Revolt of the Perverts*) 1978 presents developments in the US gay movement since the early seventies, judged from the perspective of confrontational politics.

Schwestern and *Nicht der Homosexuelle* only deal in part with gay political activity as such. The former is in three sections, the first of which features members of the (fictitious) eponymous collective, described by a voice over as 'a militant group of homosexuals within the political left who fight for the liberation of women'. They are shown in a variety of tableaux – trailing through filth on a river-bank, struggling to climb ladders, running frantically down a street –

or in conversation with women; the text of the conversation and of the voice over accompanying the tableaux is taken from a contemporary women's liberation pamphlet. The second section is a story about a woman looking for her mother, with encouragement from her brother, and the third a discussion (effectively two monologues) between a married couple about whether change in their relationship must happen now (her) or wait for the revolution (him). The central thread of *Nicht der Homosexuelle* is a kind of gay Bildungsroman, the story of a man's moral/political growth told through a series of set pieces illustrating different aspects of gay existence. Daniel has an affaire with Clemens which peters out, is taken up by a group of highly cultivated men until he realises that they only want him for his looks, explores various facets of the Berlin gay scene (bars, beaches, leathermen in the park, toilets) and ends up with a gay commune that seeks to change social attitudes towards homosexuality and to rid themselves of sexual attitudes that ape hetero norms.

The groups at the beginning and end, respectively, of *Schwestern* and *Nicht der Homosexuelle* provide perspectives for the rest of the film. The Schwestern section voices a critique that informs the sections that follow; the commune in *Nicht der Homosexuelle* suggests a critique of, and alternative to, the forms of gay existence shown before. The critique in *Schwestern* focuses on gender. The opening voice over does speak of the Schwestern coming out of hiding and confronting 'the wreckage of a civilisation whose structure they despise', but thereafter the spoken ideology of the film, from the feminist pamphlet, deals with relations between the sexes. Within the first section the link between women's and gay oppression is not so much argued as willed: voicing ideas of women's liberation over symbolical images of gay men in struggle forces connections between them. Sometimes this is in terms of the idea of the politics of personal feelings – a man says to a woman (the words straight from the pamphlet): 'It is necessary to understand oppression in one's private life not as private but as politico-economic. It is necessary to alter one's private life qualitatively and to understand this change as a political action.' At other points the pamphlet's critique of relations between men and women is used to point up the way these are reproduced in gay relationships. A shot of two leathermen carrying a man in chains between them is accompanied by an analysis of the way men organise sexuality in terms of power and sacrifice, victory and pain, at the end of which the man in chains spreads his arms in an appeal for help, repeating direct to camera, 'I don't want to be a bunny, just because I am sensitive and in need of love'.

This sexual politics then informs the other two sections. The brother in the second is one of the Schwestern and urges his sister to find their mother in terms of the need for women to help one another and to separate from men. In the final section each partner expresses their version of sexual politics, but hers founders on her love for him, suggesting, as the pamphlet has, that women will never attain autonomy while locked in emotional thrall to heterosexuality. The critique of heterosexism is remarkably sharp, yet it is striking that, though gay men speak as gay men in *Schwestern*, they do not do so on their own behalf. Women's struggle is seen as the political priority, gay struggle as such is not referred to. This displaced relation to politics is reinforced by the delivery of the lines. On the one hand, the men speak the lines awkwardly, as if not in possession of them, signalling their separation from them; and yet it is they who speak, not the women, often at inordinate length, often directly lecturing the women, and it is the brother who urges the sister to go out and be a liberated woman. The Schwestern may champion the liberation of women above their own, yet the film's style reproduces women's subordination.

The other reference to homosexuality in *Schwestern* accompanies a shot of two men clinging to each other while trying to hang on to a steep ladder placed across water; the voice over says that 'they' lack solidarity because they have such low self-esteem and that homosexual relations never last because to commit oneself to them means committing oneself to a loss of social status. This view is echoed in *Nicht der Homosexuelle*, which paints an unflattering picture of homosexual life to show the 'perversity' of homosexuality in contemporary society. Every stereotype is evoked, bitchiness, predatoriness, piss-elegance, joyless promiscuity; the voice-over commentary is derisive, making liberal use of derogatory terms for gays.

The point of this is given in the title. How gay men live in this society *is* perverse, this is what oppression reduces them to; society does not just restrict homosexuality, but perverts its expression to the very core. This is what society has to be indicted with, and hence what must be shown. The film offers us a distance on this perversion by various means: the title; a dialectical use of image and sound tracks (a narrator tells parts of Daniel's story, the words and lip movements of characters in conversation are not synchronised,

sequences are accompanied by political disquisition on gay existence); vocal delivery, characters mouthing banalities in flat voices,
political discourse uttered in a somewhat ranting fashion; the
commune's discussion, rejecting the forms of homosexuality imposed by capitalism and male supremacy.

The formal qualities of both films relate to a kind of radical
cinema much canvassed in the wake of May 1968 and most
associated with the work of Jean-Luc Godard (Harvey 1978:62–9).
Ideas and images are not presented as self-sufficient and fully
worked out: the audience must actively participate in making sense
of the film's politics. *Schwestern*'s use of juxtapositions (of symbolic
tableaux and spoken theory; of three apparently unrelated sections)
requires the spectator to work out their inter-relations; *Nicht der
Homosexuelle* poses its title, sound-image dialectic and final
discussion sequence against a familiar narrative structure in a
titillating milieu, and again requires that we make the former
critique the latter.

As in Godard, the implicit injunction to the viewer to work it out
for him/herself is in part disingenuous – when one of the commune
in *Nicht der Homosexuelle* says, 'We gays must stop hating gays. We
must love them and not just deal with them as competitors', it is
clear that this is what we are supposed to think. Yet part of the
film's interest resides in what escapes this dictatorial impulse. The
fact that he refers to both 'we gays' and 'them' suggests a tension
between being both of and distinct from gay people. This replays a
familiar ultra-left dilemma, the divorce between the political
vanguard (drawn predominantly from the bourgeoisie) and the
masses, but one least easy to sustain with gay politics where laying
oneself on the line as gay was such a fundamental principle. A sense
of being both within and without gay existence runs through much
of the film, making it more open than the rather closed
pronouncements of the commune at the end might suggest. Thus
muscly posing is condemned and yet a hunky guy stripping to trunks
on the beach is dwelt on, with shots of Daniel's longing gaze and a
close-up of the hunk's crotch as he teasingly unbuckles, unzips and
lowers his jeans. Similarly, the narrator tells us that Daniel finds the
leathermen's silent choreography uncomfortable and the political
voice compares them to Nazis, yet the sequence showing them is
probably the longest, seemingly most captivated in the film – it is for
most of its length entirely silent, and it is by no means clear whether
this is simply to show the silence noted by Daniel or is hushed
fascination with the unsmiling manoeuvres.

Despite the welter of verbalisation and appeal to cerebration, *Schwestern* and *Nicht der Homosexuelle* are as much zap as theory. Moreover, as the commune member's quote suggests, it not just straights who are to be affronted. *Nicht der Homosexuelle*, by seeming to rub our noses in the sordid perversity of the gay underworld, is intended to provoke anger at the way gay men have to live, but as often as not provoked anger from gays at von Praunheim/the film itself for showing this side of gay life and feeding the prejudices of straight viewers. The film *Audience Response to 'It is not the Homosexual. . .'*, shot following a screening of *Nicht der Homosexuelle* at the Museum of Modern Art in New York in 1973, records this reaction and von Praunheim's defence of the film on the grounds that it provokes anger and therefore starts people thinking (Kelly 1979:116), a belief characteristic of late sixties radical politics.

Zap is at the heart of von Praunheim's political practice. In Keith Kelly's words, his

> mission is largely involved with provoking . . . a fight. The name Rosa (taken to force people to question sexual branding), his dress (almost always entirely in black), his public attitude (baiting his audiences through insult if necessary), and most of all, his films, are, in effect, weapons of confrontation.
>
> (ibid.:115)

Bryan Bruce similarly discusses von Praunheim's deliberately disconcerting self-presentation of a feminine name and macho look, heightened by a cultivated porno star image which 'is clearly intended to shock his audience, testing the tolerance of liberals who are sympathetic to gays as long as their sexual activity remains hidden and discreet, and challenging reticent gays to be more open and assertive' (1987:27). *Armee der Liebenden* continued this politics, although focusing on the US gay movement and its rather more affirmative politics.

Armee interweaves a history and survey of the gay movement in the USA. The history refers back to the pre-Nazi German movement and the post-war US movement but its main narrative is an oscillation between radical (confrontational) and reformist (accommodationist) moments in the post-69 US gay movement. Thus the Stonewall riot and foundation of the Gay Liberation Front gives way to a split between the Gay Activists' Alliance, keeping the spirit of Stonewall alive, and the National Gay Task Force, 'a conservative, élitist organisation' with besuited officers doing gay business through the established institutions of society. This moment of conservatism is reinforced by gay men's retreat into 'discos, baths and orgy bars'. What saves the gay movement is the anti-gay campaign launched by Anita Bryant in the mid-seventies, galvanising gay people back on to the streets. In particular, the murder of a gay man in San Francisco by a group of 'punks' shouting 'One for Anita!' mobilises a huge demonstration in the city. The final part of the film contrasts the New Orleans Mardi Gras with the Briggs initiative in Los Angeles (the attempt to have homosexuals banned from holding positions in schools). The initiative is defeated but the narrator warns against 'rosy passivity' and losing the confrontationist spirit again.

The survey aspect of the film suggests the diversity of the US gay movement (though the narrator acknowledges that the film deals more with gay men than lesbians because 'as gay men we are incompetent to deal with the whole range of women's points-of-view'). Not only are there interviews with representatives of all the forms of activism mentioned above (including Harry Hay from the Mattachine Society and Del Martin and Phyllis Lyon from the Daughters of Bilitis), but an astonishing range of people and points of view are also featured: Parents of Gays, the black, Asian and Native American Tri-Base Collective, a lesbianfeminist, a porn star, a gay Nazi, gay religious groups, human rights organisations, the 504 emergency coalition (for disabled gays), a nun, gays who support gay rights but don't belong to anything, the G40+ club for older gay men, Coming Out (a gay youth group in Boston), a pedophile and the novelist John Rechy, who lays out his philosophy of promiscuity.

These historical and survey elements are supplemented by two more personal sequences. Following the interview with the lesbianfeminist and her strong criticism of gay men's misogyny, there is a sequence of von Praunheim visiting gay cruising places, musing whether his increased understanding of women's oppression has really had any effect on his sexual practice; the sequence ends with him getting off with porn star Fred Halsted. Following sequences at a gay parade in San Francisco, there is a section showing von Praunheim's class in 1977 at the San Francisco Art Institute, who film him having sex with Glen, another porn star.

All three aspects of *Armee*'s structure promote the political value of provocation. The narrator's comments spell it out and are reinforced by the sequences of street theatre and demonstrations. These are very much part of the rationale of confrontational politics

– the point of the zap approach is a belief in, as Laud Humphreys put it, 'the symbolic success of melodramatic confrontation' (1972:112), in other words, in the political value of the filmable. Of the interviewees, the two people who seem to be given most space are those who advocate the more extreme politics: the lesbianfeminist, 'livid' and 'in a rage' at men's, all men's, attitudes towards women, and Rechy, insisting that the most perverse aspects of homosexuality are 'actually the most enriching', that homosexuality is 'revolutionary' because it 'confronts the archaic laws'. These two state confrontationist positions, but the very choice of some of the other interviewees is provocative. It goes well beyond the liberal range to include, unchallenged, a porn star (extolling sado-masochism), a neo-Nazi and a pedophile. The latter, Tom Reeves, presents himself as a revolutionary: he does indeed 'recruit' boys, the great fear of anti-pedophiles, 'I recruit [them] away from the middle-class, up-tight, violent family'. Perhaps most confrontational of all are the two personal sequences – showing cruising (at length) and gay sex (in extreme close-up) insists on gayness as sex, stripped of the more socially acceptable vocabulary of rights or relationships; having film students film gay sex challenged their liberalism, and filming them filming dares them not to be liberal; having the film-maker himself at the centre of these two sex sequences breaks with the comfortable sense of 'distance' that the documentary convention allows the viewer the rest of the time. The film ends on a confrontational note, the Gay Sweatshop company singing 'As Time Goes By', holding hands staring out to the audience and ending abruptly on the words, 'No matter what the future brings. . .'.

Armee illustrates well some of the problems of this form of political film-making. It makes analytical statements but does not analyse – a proliferation of instances does not amount to an analysis of the social situation of gay people. It both has a point of view (pro-confrontation, anti-accommodation) yet wants to be open, giving space to many voices, getting the viewer to make connections. It is caught between vanguardism (telling people what's what, urging them into action) and libertarianism (refusing to have a position or set oneself up as a leader). This was a contradiction running deep within late sixties politics which remained unresolved in von Praunheim's work and which gave it much of its bite.

France and elsewhere

Armee confronted audiences with the diversity of gay desire, giving a verbal space to the disreputable. Yet there is something grim about its visual presentation of desire and, as with *Schwestern* and *Nicht der Homosexuelle*, gay self-hate (diagnosed in other gays but also expressed in the films' contempt for them) comes across as strongly as delight in being gay. This is where they differ from (mainly) French confrontational cinema.

The history of the gay movements in France and Italy in many ways replays that decried in *Armee*. The Front Homosexuel d'Action Révolutionnaire (FHAR), started in Paris in 1971, was superseded in 1974 by the Groupe de Libération Homosexuelle (GLH), with both reformist (GLH-Groupes de base) and revolutionary (GLH-Politique et Quotidien (PQ)) tendencies (Girard 1981:81ff, 118ff); the Fronte Unitario Omosessuale Rivoluzionario Italiano (FUORI) started in Turin in 1971 and in 1974 joined a coalition of feminists, civil rights activists and others in the Radical Party (Adam 1987:87, Pezanna 1978:27). The revolutionary impulse did not disappear but continued alongside reformism, often finding expression in film.

FHAR's earliest manifestos, notably a four-page intervention in the left-wing paper *Tout* on 23 April 1971 and later that year the *Rapport contre la normalité*, went beyond simply demanding freedom for homosexuals. In *Tout*, they called for rights for 'all sexualities' and for children 'freedom of desire and its realisation' (quoted in Girard:83), demands rooted in a belief in the wild richness of libidinal desire that has been repressed and controlled in the form of the acceptable behaviour of adulthood. Demanding less than this, restricting oneself to homosexual rights, was a betrayal of desire. Drag, pornography and pederasty, insistent components of the films, were of particular importance. Each was something homosexuals had been taught was a shameful part of homosexuality, yet each in reality had been selected out for shame because of its subversive nature. Each poses a threat to the social order: drag as a refusal of male privilege, porn making present the polymorphous perversity of desire, pederasty undermining the authority of the bourgeois family. What is distinctive, however, is not these arguments in themselves, which had their counterparts throughout the international gay movement, but the way they are fuelled not by political correctness but by pleasure itself. Other pro-drag, -porn and -pederasty positions seem to imply that one should get into these things in order to smash male and familial power, but the French polemics start from wanting them. It is the power of desire, its unruly urgency, that is championed first, in its own right, not for its role in political agendas laid down elsewhere.

Drag, porn and boys are all eminently visual, but this is not the only reason for the role of film in this politics. The favoured form was not documentary or fiction but avant-gardism, for reasons part institutional, part to do with political style. As Alain Sudre (1983) argues, the development of a space for independent film in France and the assertion of a homosexual identity both happened in the wake of May '68 and were closely interconnected. Both occupied a marginal social position, avant-garde film having no more social status or economic security than open homosexuality, and avant-garde film's use of the idea of the 'home movie' had special significance for gays seeking to explore and develop new forms of intimacy and sexual community. Most of this work, referred to in passing in chapters three and four, is personal and experimental, only by implication political, but the mutually reinforcing sense of the marginality of both 'cinéma different' and lesbian/gay identity meant that it was here that an uncompromising politics of the edge was maintained. Moreover, the particular form of avant-gardism favoured – montage, based on a mixture of original footage and images from the mass and gay media – was particularly appropriate to a style of politics that sought simultaneously to analyse and celebrate the construction of homosexual desire.

Given that the starting point is pleasure, it is not surprising how full of humour and eroticism much of this work is. Both in terms of production and exhibition, these are films made and shown by gay groups or active members of gay organisations, yet they do not always contain content that would be evidently political to all viewers. The festivals organised by FHAR in Paris in 1977 and 1978 (and by the Circolo Culturale 28 Giugno in Bologna in 1982) included pornographic films, labelled and welcomed as such. *More More More* (Wallace Potts 1976) is described in the January 1978 Paris programme as 'half way between pornography and a critique of the family' and films such as *Hommes entre eux* (Norbert Terry 1977), *Homologues ou la soif du Mâle* (Marvin Merkins 1977), *Et. . .Dieu créa les hommes* (Jean Estienne 1978) and *Le Beau Mec* (Potts 1978) incorporated philosophical/political discourse into their hardcore scenarios. Similarly drag was accepted as part of the revolutionary gay repertoire right across Southern Europe (see, for instance, Mieli 1980:193–9), as in *Les Intrigues de Sylvia Couski*

(France 1974 Adolfo Arrieta), *Fatucha Superstar* (Portugal 1976 Joao Paulo Ferreira), *La Cité des neuf portes* (France 1977 Stéphane Marti), *Lisa and the Other One* (Greece 1977 Takis Spetsiotis), *Satan bouche un coin* (Belgium 1977 Jean-Pierre Bouyxou), *La Tasse* (France 1977 Michel Nedjar), *La Belle* (Greece 1978 Takis Spetsiotis), *Ocaña, retrat intermitent* (Spain 1979 Ventura Pons) and notably *Una Filma*, made by the gay collective Fioli Frochie Audiovisive Gotiche in Rome in 1977 and taking off from Andy Warhol's observation that women stars are so excessive and false that only a transvestite is adapted to playing their roles. One film – *La Banque du sperme* (France 1977, Pierre Chabal and Philippe Genet), in which men going to donate sperm are given a helping hand by gleeful members of FHAR – suggests in its anarchic sexual humour the simultaneous defiance and fun of this work, explicitly connected to a consciously political movement.

All this sounds genial enough, but the whole-hearted embrace of drag, porn and pederasty undoubtedly flew in the face of acceptability, pederasty especially, undoubtedly the sticking point for seventies tolerance and widely disowned by gay people themselves. Porn and pederasty are brilliantly and provocatively intertwined in three films by Lionel Soukaz: *Boy Friend 1* (1977), *Boy Friend 2* (1977) and *Le Sexe des anges* (1978). Soukaz in many ways embodies Sudre's observations on the interconnections of gay activism and 'cinéma différent'. On the one hand, he worked on personal films, such as *Lolo mégalo* (1974) and *Ixe* (1980). The latter begins with a man shaving and putting on make-up and escalates through a series of image and sound montages (e.g. shots of the Pope crosscut with men having sex, to the sound of the Singing Nun) to shots of an atom bomb exploding, ending on blackness and the sound of interminable maniacal, mechanical laughter. At the same time, Soukaz was involved with the GLH-PQ, including organising with them the film seasons in Paris, the second of which in October 1977 was forbidden by the Ministry of the Interior and physically attacked by fascist groups (Soukaz 1978:53–4). In 1979 he made with Hocquenghem *Race d'ep!* (see below), but it is in the two *Boy Friend* films and *Le Sexe des anges* that the politics and the 'cinéma différent' come together most clearly in work which Soukaz himself in an interview called 'provocative and generous . . . publicity films, manifestoes' (Garsi 1981a:51).

These films already provoke by their subject-matter. All three contain imagery taken from pornographic magazines, as well as new footage of gay sexual intercourse and masturbation; there is also much imagery of adolescent boys. This showing is then given intellectual weight, by means of voice over or editing: theoretical texts on pornography and pederasty by Hocquenghem, Tony Duvert, Gabriel Matzneff and Soukaz himself are read out; *Le Sexe des anges* is organised around the figure of an adolescent, Bruno, using montage to contrast the restrictive world of familial, patriotic and religious images that surrounds him, including that of the angelic asexual innocence of childhood, with his actual angelic sexual imagination. What however makes the films still more provocative is the way they elicit from the viewer a libidinal response to their pornographic and pederastic imagery.

They do this in part by editing the images to straight-identified music. Classic heterosexual love songs, notably Piaf singing *La Vie en rose*, accompany images of boys, crotches and cruising, in a way that casts them all in the pink glow of mainstream romance. *Boy Friend 2* ends deliriously with shots of a man masturbating over the cover of a porn magazine, with cut-in shots of boys, all to the sound first of the Internationale, then, as he comes, the Hallelujah! chorus, pinnacles of Marxist and Christian cultures respectively, neither of which have had much time for homosexual desire.

Beyond this use of straight celebration in the service of gay libido, the films also use the cinema's codes of subjectivity to encourage the viewer to experience pornographic and pederastic desire. The attenuated narrative structure of *Le Sexe des anges* resembles that of two other films of the period, *L'Hiver approche* (Georges Bensoussan 1975) and *La Chambre des phantasmes* (Jean-Michel Sénégal 1979). In the former a young man wanders about Paris at night, real encounters and visits to gay places being intercut with fantasy images culled from gay porn and mainstream media alike; in *Chambre* a young man fantasises on the basis of the pin-ups that he finds covering the walls of a maid's bedroom. Both films give us an identification figure through whom we can experience the pleasures of fantasising and shows the source of these fantasies in the mass media and urban life. Unlike the rather more puritanical Anglo-Saxon gay movements, there is no criticism here of porn, the media and the gay ghetto, but a celebration of the exuberant bricolage that the erotic imagination makes out of the images available to it.

Boy Friend 2 is still more challenging. By dispensing with an identification figure and placing the viewer directly in the line of desire, it denies us the get-out of not identifying, of associating the parade of desire with a character who is not ourself. This becomes most agitating when the focus is on pederastic desire. One sequence begins with the assertion that 'all men want boys' and proceeds to nudge the viewer into experiencing that. Cross cutting of explicitly sexual images (porn, masturbation) with documentary footage of boys (in the street, playing rugby) associates the former with the latter, bringing out the sex-appeal of boys for even the least pederastically inclined viewer. The editing of the football sequences uses repetition (of, for example, one boy putting his hand through another's legs) to suggest the erotic charge of contact sports. This sequence provokes not by its anger and ugliness, as in von Praunheim's work, but precisely by the pleasure it invites the viewer to feel at desires so far beyond the pale.

*   *   *

The films of Soukaz *et al.* remained highly marginal and even von Praunheim's films have had relatively minor success on the art cinema circuit. Only one film of gay confrontational politics has really made it, *Taxi zum Klo*, released in 1980. Directed by Frank Ripploh, who had worked with von Praunheim, it has something of the look of the latter's work as well as moments that confront the viewer with gay desire. However, its extraordinary success, critically and commercially, has to do with its use of straight modes, bringing it closer in effect to the affirmation politics described in the next section.

Much of *Taxi* depicts the contrast between the working and leisure lives of Frank, a teacher, and the conflict between the appeals of promiscuity and permanent relationships, standard themes in gay fiction. The film presents sexual lust as inescapable, inescapably mucky and precisely on that account exciting. It defies the audience to be shocked, partly through techniques that suggest the audience is being confronted with reality (detailed and repetitive sequences of cruising shot on location; sequences showing very directly what is not shown outside of porn (ejaculation, flagellation, urination into another's mouth)); shooting with the grainy colour stock and harsh lighting characteristic of New German Cinema's grotty realism) and partly by cutting in shots from other films which suggest the ubiquitous insistence of sexuality (old porn showing that heterosexual lust is no more elevated than gay; an anti-pedophile film which is contrasted to a boy making an entirely unencouraged pass at Frank). This defiance, of the film towards its audience, is of a piece with Frank's coming out scene. He has been to an all-night gay ball in drag, beard and all, and goes without changing into the classroom where he encourages the kids to act out their wildest desires (much paint spraying, brawling and general carnival). 'Radical drag' (men wearing frocks but not trying to look like women) was one of gay liberation's most confrontational modes and here it inspires revolt against the order of school.

Yet if *Taxi* is confrontational, it did not anger, perhaps because of its humour. This too was provocative, most notably in the sequence which gives the film its title, when Frank sneaks out of hospital and hires a taxi to take him from one toilet to another, and most wickedly in the close-up of pleasure on Frank's face as the doctor gives him an anal examination. This is standard sex humour, not a million miles away from Benny Hill or much German comedy, except that it is gay in content – the idea of the ridiculously driven nature of (male) sexuality and the naughty turn-on potential of medical examinations is very familiar. Perhaps this accounts for the film's success: despite its confrontational elements, it achieves acceptance for gay life by presenting it in terms familiar from straight movies. Though very different from affirmation movies, it ends up by achieving what they sought to achieve. Von Praunheim, Soukaz *et al.*, on the other hand, continue to provoke – you still feel zapped by their anger and their resolutely perverse desire.

AFFIRMATION POLITICS

Probably the best-known example of affirmation politics on film is *Word is Out* 1977. It could not be further from the grottiness of von Praunheim or the outrageousness of Soukaz. Though there is verbal reference to oppression, the overall mood is joyful and positive. It uses clear, translucent film stock and sets its interviewees against pastel interiors or sunny, flower filled exteriors; these are all personable, attractive people (good-looking, amusing or both), who extol the fulfilment of being gay or lesbian. The march at the end is full of smiling faces and celebratory music. The whole film epitomises the politics of affirmation.

Affirmation politics grew out of both Gay and Women's Liberation. The start of the former is generally taken to be the riot at the Stonewall bar in New York on 28 June 1969, when patrons, lesbian and gay, resisted police arrest during what was a routine raid. Resistance sparked off a riot that lasted for two to three days, during which the first Gay Liberation meetings were held.[3] The movement took off, spreading rapidly throughout the States and Canada, Europe, Japan, Australasia and even parts of South America.[4] Though different countries had different inflections (the

European and Australasian being notably closer to socialist politics), the US experience continued to provide the model.

The Stonewall riot was a rebellion, but in the slogan coined right at the start of the movement, 'Gay is Good', lay the seeds of the affirmation politics that came to predominate over the confrontationism of the early pamphlets, demos and zaps. The shift can be traced in the writings of the time. In 'Gay is Good', one of the first articles to come out of Gay Liberation, Martha Shelley challenges straight people, but the terms of her attack also reveal the sense of release, of, indeed, liberation, that was to be the lasting ambition of the movement.

> From the beautiful boys at Cherry Grove to the aging queens in the uptown bars, the taxi-driving dykes to the lesbian fashion models, the hookers (male and female) on 42nd street, the leather lovers. . . and the very ordinary very un-lurid gays. . . we are the sort of people everyone was taught to despise – and now we are shaking off the chains of self-hatred and marching on your citadels of repression.
>
> (1972:31–2)

The militancy, the feeling of being *against* something, is there clearly enough, but there is also the feeling of being *for* something, the sense of release at taking hitherto despised gay identities and embracing them as something positive. Three years later, in the collection *The Gay Liberation Book*, this sense is uppermost. In their introduction, Len Richmond and Gary Noguera define the 'concept' of Gay Liberation as 'The marches and the rap groups. The affirmation that 'Gay is Good' and 'Gay is Proud'. Coming out and telling our parents and friends and employers that we're gay. The new life' (1973:12). Though the book does recount activism and zapping, its main impulse is to latch on to the affirmative. The front cover has the biological male sign in the colours of the rainbow; the back cover has a butterfly; the illustrations inside are of smiling faces and kissing couples.

Richmond and Noguera's book dealt exclusively, and consciously, only with gay men. By 1973 the unity of lesbians and gay men within a Gay Liberation Front, as assumed in Shelley's article, had already fallen apart. In part the political agendas of gay men and lesbians differed, but in any case it soon became apparent that gay men were, after all, men, as prone to male chauvinism as straight men. Most women left Gay Liberation very quickly. For a time there were Gay Women's Liberation groups (Sally Gearheardt in *Word is*

Out talks about going to the first meeting of 'what we were then calling Gay Women's Liberation' in San Francisco in 1970), but it was the new women's movement, which had started in 1967–8 (Carden 1974:59–65), that came to provide a primary base for lesbian politics. Initially it had not been welcoming to lesbians (ibid.:113) and women in the older lesbian organisations were sometimes suspicious of it – Meredith Grey of the Daughters of Bilitis, for instance, feared that lesbians joining the new movement might 'once again' have to 'put on the "mask" and pretend to be heterosexuals so that we don't rock the boat or frighten the ladies' (Martin and Lyon 1972:282). Yet many lesbians did join and challenge the new movement and gradually lesbianism came to be seen as more than just another issue. Martin and Lyon, stalwarts of Daughters of Bilitis, describe how at a meeting of the Bay Area Women's Coalition (part of NOW), a member of the newly formed Gay Women's Liberation group spoke, challenging any women in the audience who had 'ever felt any sort of physical attraction towards another woman' to stand up – gradually three quarters did so (ibid.:288–9). With similar events occurring throughout the movement, lesbianism could no longer be seen as a minority or side issue.

Lesbians coming into the women's movement put lesbianism on its agenda. They forced the issue. Yet it was also emerging through consciousness raising (CR), one of the movement's most distinctive features. CR was a process in which small groups of women met together on a regular basis and discussed their experience of being women, enabling them to see that their feelings and frustrations were shared by others, were socially, not just individually, significant, hence that 'the personal is political'. At the same time the process broke down barriers between women, bringing them closer together in sisterhood. For many, the dual recognition of the social pressure to be a wife and a new, or unchecked, closeness with other women spelt lesbianism ('at last I could be in love with my friends' (Shulman 1983:56)). If many lesbians, already conscious of themselves as lesbian, came out in CR groups, sometimes to the consternation of other women present ('You could hear the ovaries roll on the floor, so great was the shock', says Rita Mae Brown in *Some American Feminists*), many other women discovered lesbian feelings through CR itself. For yet others the general context of feminism attuned them to the possibility of lesbianism – Betty Powell in *Word is Out* describes how she began to realise the lesbian dimension to a friendship at the same time as she was 'getting into somewhat of a feminist head'.

Gay Liberation had always been very influenced by the women's movement. It too used CR, and much of its political analysis was grounded in that of the new feminism, emphasising the importance of the family, monogamy and sex roles as the sources of oppression. For a period there were groupings of men within Gay Liberation that identified strongly with women, known in Australia, for instance, as Effeminists, suggesting both feminism and effeminacy, a readiness to take on board, or confound, both changing notions of female identity and gay sub-cultural traditions of camp and sissiness. Though influential, such approaches remained marginal. On the other hand, there was no real equivalent of the women's movement for gay men, since we did not experience our oppression as stemming from our being men but rather from suspicion of the contrary.

Women's and Gay Liberation provided different routes into affirmation politics, which also embraced other differences, of national and local particularities, of civil rights, socialist and radical feminist ideas. What united them was simply the assertion that to be lesbian or gay is a positive thing to be. This was the basis for the common practices of affirmation politics: consciousness raising (allowing lesbian/gay people to realise their worth), coming out (living a lesbian/gay life proudly and openly), analysis/activism (working to understand and change the situation of lesbian/gay people) and the creation of positive images (to replace the negative ones purveyed by the mass media). These practices underlay the forms used for affirmation films and serve below as headings for their analysis. First however I indicate what those films were. The section (and chapter) ends by looking at two other categories of films: those influenced by but not made directly within the movement, and those that emerged out of it to move beyond affirmation.

*   *   *

Affirmation politics documentaries 1970–1980

Aspect rose de la chose, L'	1980 France; Chi Yan Wong	portrait and self-presentation lesbian/gay group Mouvance Rimmel de Grenoble
August and July	1973 Canada; Murray Markowitz	lesbians Sharon Smith and Alexa Dewiel; talking, making love
Bail Fund Film	1971 USA; women students at New York University film school	woman, Paul, speaking

Blackstar: Autobiography of a Close Friend	1977 USA; Tom Joslin	daily life of film-maker
Bögjävlar	1977 Sweden; Filmgruppen	gay oppression and alternative gay life-styles; discussion, daily life, demonstrations
Come Together	1971 GB; John Shane 'for' London GLF	GLF members speaking; meetings, demonstrations
Coming Out	1972 USA; Arthur Bressan	Gay Liberation Front demo in San Francisco
Coming Out	1973 USA Berkeley Lesbian Feminist Film Collective	coming out
Coming to Know	1976 USA; Marie Ashton	two young women discuss discovering their lesbian feelings
Continuous Woman, The	1973 USA Twin Cities Women's Film Collective	five women speaking; one, Sherrie, a psychologist, is lesbian
Enough is Enough	1980 Canada; Gordon Keith and Jack Lemmon	protest at police raid of bath-houses in Toronto; demonstrations, interviews
Gay Day, A	1973 USA; Barbara Hammer	
Gay is Out	1980 USA; Manfredini; Horses Inc	? (part of *Filmworks*)
Gay Parade, A	1972 USA; A. Rubin	gay parade
Gay USA	1977 USA; Arthur Bressan	footage shot on 26 June 1977 in San Francisco, San Diego, New York, Chicago, Houston and Los Angeles of Gay Pride marches that were also protests against the defeat of the gay rights bill in Miami on 7 June; interviews, archival material
Gay Women Speak	1979 USA; Laird Sutton; National Sex Forum	discussion between three professional women
Greta's Girls	1978 USA; Greta Schiller and Thomas Seid	daily life of two lesbians
Home Movie	1975 USA; Jan Oxenburg	self-portrait, using old home movies and contemporary footage of lesbian gatherings
Homo-actualités	1977 France; Norbert Terry	series of newsreels; first was interview with gay author Roger Peyrefitte; another with five gay local government candidates (series shown at La Marotte and Le Dragon, cinemas in Paris specialising in gay films)

International Women's Festival – Melkweg	1977 Netherlands; Melkweg	women's festival, including lesbian singers and a debate on pornography
In the Best Interests of the Children	1978 USA; Elizabeth Stevens, Cathy Zheutlin, Frances Reid	lesbian mothers and their children; daily life and interviews
In Winterlight	1974 USA; Laird Sutton; National Sex Forum	portrait of sexual relationship between two women
Jill Johnston, October '75	1977 Canada; Lydia Wazana and Kay Armitage	visit of lesbian author Johnston to Toronto – public and private events
Lavender	1972 USA; Elaine Jacobs and Colleen Monahan	daily lives of lesbian couple
Lesbians	1975 USA; Portland NOW (National Organisation of Women)	
Marche gay, La	1980 France/USA; Lionel Soukaz	march in Washington DC
March On!	1979 USA; Jim Hubbard	gay march
Michael, a Gay Son	1980 Canada; Bruce Glawson	young man coming out to his family; interviews, discussions
Minimum Charge No Cover	1976 Canada; Holly Dale and Janis Cole	lives of prostitutes, homosexuals, transvestites and transsexuals
Mondo Rocco	1970 USA; Pat Rocco	compilation of several films, including (in addition to porn shorts) *Homosexuals on the March* (gay liberation march in Los Angeles, including interviews with Troy Perry, Jim Kepner and other activists) and *Meat Market Arrest* (footage of police raid of gay club, interview with an attorney)
Music from the Heart	1976 USA; Sharon Karp, Joan Nixon and Judy Whitaker	Women's Music Festival in Champaign, Illinois
Oiseaux de nuit, Les	1979 France; Luc Barnier and Alain Lafargues	a 'hommage to the world of queens' (Sanzio 1981:51)
Olivia Records: More than Music	1979 USA; Anita Clearfield	lesbian feminist collective; interviews, work life
Ontbinding	1977 Netherlands; Arnold Veenhof Gronings; Filmkollektief	dramatised reconstruction of sodomy trial in eighteenth century in the region of Groningen
On the Beach	1978 USA; Darlene Mitera	'the tension between an older woman whose husband has left her and taken away the

children, and the film-maker, a younger lesbian who is both observer and catalyst for her lover's changes' (Weiss 1981a:22)

Paulines Geburtstag, oder Die Bestie von Notre Dame	1977/9 BRD; Fritz Matthies	interviews, rehearsals and performance at gay male s/m theatre in Hamburg
Position of Faith, A	1973 USA; Mike Rhodes	events, reactions surrounding (eventually successful) attempt of gay man, Bill Johnson, to be ordained in United Church of Christ
Prison Film: Still Living	1971 USA; ?	life in Frontera, a women's prison in California
Race d'ep!	1977 France; Lionel Soukaz	four moments in gay history: interviews, historical documentation, re-enactments
Rosa Winkel? Das ist doch schon lange vorbei. . .	1975 BRD; Peter Recht, Christiane Schmerl, Detlev Stoffel	criminal prosecution of gays in West Germany
Sandy and Madeline's Family	1973 USA; Sherrie Farrell, Peter Bruce and John G. Hill	lesbian couple of title and their (successful) child custody battle; daily life, interviews (including with professionals in case). (In 1979 the couple were featured in a TV film, *Family Portrait: the Schuster–Issacson Family*, one of a series made by Stanley Losak and Marion Lear)
Sisters!	1973 USA; Barbara Hammer	International Women's Day march; scenes at lesbian feminist music festival; visions of strong women; women making love and dancing
Some American Feminists	1977 Canada; Luce Guilbeault, Nicole Brossard, Margaret Wescott	interviews with US feminists, including Ti-Grace Atkinson, Rita Mae Brown, Kate Millett
Some of Your Best Friends	1972 USA; Kenneth Robinson; University of Southern California	interviews with gay activists; meetings, demonstrations; disruption of psychiatric symposium on aversion therapy; gay lawyer recounts entrapment by vice squad and trial; whole presented as TV news with link man
Stop the Movie 'Cruising'!	1979 USA; Jim Hubbard	protest against homophobic film *Cruising*

Susana	1979 USA; Susana Blaustein	self portrait; interviews, discussion with family and friends
Three Lives	1970 USA; Kate Millett	three women speaking about their lives; one, Robin Mide, is bisexual
Truxx	1978 Canada; Gordon Keith and Jack Lemmon	police raid on Montréal gay bar; interviews
We Are Ourselves	1976 USA; Ann Heshey; National Sex Forum	life together of Tee A Corinne and Honey Lee Cottrell
We're Alive	1976 USA; Women's Film Workshop of University of California at Los Angeles	women prisoners in discussion, including about lesbianism
We're Not Afraid Anymore	1974 USA; ?	TV news format with link man presenting gay oppression and liberation
Witches and Faggots, Dykes and Poofters	1980 Australia; One in Seven Collective	lesbian/gay movement in Australia; demonstrations, interviews, discussions; voice over narration
Woman in Your Life is You, The	1978 New Zealand; ?	experiences of four women, including lesbian couple
Woman's Place is in the House; A Portrait of Elaine Noble, A	1976 USA; Nancy Porter and Mickey Lemle	Elaine Noble, a Massachusetts state legislator; daily life and interview (including with her lover, Rita Mae Brown)
Woman to Woman	1975 USA; Donna Deitch	interviews with women, including lesbians
Word is Out	1977 USA; Mariposa Film Group	interviews with twenty-six lesbians and gay men
World of Light: A Portrait of May Sarton	1980 USA; Marita Simpson and Cathy Wheelock	lesbian author Sarton; daily life, interview

*   *   *

From the start Gay Liberation identified film, in the shape of the movies, as part of the armoury of oppression. On the one hand, they denied our existence. Early on Stuart Byron (1972:59) observed that '[i]nasmuch as they reflect society, mass media pretend that homosexuality does not exist'; eleven years later Barbara Halpern Martineau (1983) writing about lesbian representation still had to focus on its absence. On the other hand, on the rare occasions when we were represented, it was demeaning and derisive – as Suzannah Lessard wrote in 1970 'Wherever Homosexuals are portrayed in movies they are ridiculous or desperate or disgusting' (1972:208–9), or as Frank Pearce (1973:284) put it, we were shown as 'immoral and ill, pathetic and dangerous, all at the same time'. Films were needed which would counteract this, make us visible in forms we could feel good about.

The majority of affirmation films up to 1980 were documentaries, listed in the accompanying chart. The reasons for this, and the specific inflection given to the documentary tradition, are discussed in a moment. Apart from these, there was, not counting the films influenced by or moving beyond affirmation politics, a handful of more or less straightforward fiction films:

Happy Birthday Davy	USA 1970 Richard Fontaine
Saturday Night at the Baths	USA 1974 David Buckley
A Very Natural Thing	USA 1974 Christopher Larkin
Anna und Edith	BRD 1975 Cristina Perincioli[5]
Apartments	Australia 1977 Megan McMurchy
Du er ikke alene	Denmark 1977 Lasse Nielsen and Ernst Johansen
I'm not from here	USA 1977 Harvey Marks
Outrageous!	Canada 1977 Richard Benner
David is Homosexual	GB 1978 Lewisham Campaign for Homosexual Equality
Nighthawks	GB 1978 Ron Peck and Paul Hallam
After the Game	USA 1980 Donna Gray
Ella une vraie famille	France 1980 Michka Gorki
Liv og Død	Norway 1980 Svend Wam and Peyter Vennerød
The Squeeze	New Zealand 1980 Richard Turner
Home Made Melodrama	GB 1980–2 Jacqui Duckworth

Some of the documentaries contain other elements: *Bögjävlar* interpolates sketches and slogans; *Ontbinding* and *Michael, a Gay Son* involve dramatised reconstructions; *Greta's Girls* is a scripted documentary account of two women's daily life together. Documentary is overwhelmingly the chosen mode in relation to consciousness raising, but its limitations and the advantages of fiction begin to become apparent with the other practices of affirmation politics.

Documentary offered itself as the form par excellence for affirmation film, partly because it is cheaper and easier to do tolerably than fiction, partly because of its historical association with progressive movements (Waugh 1984), and especially for its supposed special relation to reality.[6] Fiction, by contrast, was the territory of the movies. Films were needed that would show the reality of our existence – the fact of our existence and what our existence was really like. To achieve this, affirmation cinema built on prevalent assumptions about documentary in general, but also inflected them according to the new attitudes towards reality that underlay the politics.

Part of documentary's appeal lay in its basis in recording, the fundamental technology of film. Recording 'guarantees' that what is on screen was there to be filmed and did look like that. Just having lesbians and gay men on screen, not actors playing them, said in the face of media invisibility, 'we exist'. For the early examples it was enough to be showing lesbians and gay men at all. Later examples have extended documentation to other unseen aspects of lesbian/gay existence: lesbians and alcohol (*We All Have Our Reasons* USA 1981), teenagers (*Veronica 4 Rose* GB 1982 and *Framed Youth* GB 1983), Asians (*Orientations* Canada 1984), older people (*Silent Pioneers* USA 1985), *Parents of Gays* (Australia 1986), lesbians and reproductive technology (*Alternative Conceptions* USA 1986) and the many films dealing with AIDS.

Documentaries are versions of a recorded reality. The changing styles in documentary history are not just the effect of new techniques and fashions (both of which may help reality come up fresh, as it were) but of changing notions of how one knows about reality. Early documentary, Grierson or Vertov, sought to present the basic mechanisms of social processes; they assumed a need to bring a perspective from outside, Grierson using experts, Vertov organising his material according to Marxist principles.[7] A later generation, cinéma vérité and direct cinema,[8] reacting against what they saw as the authoritarianism and preconceived frameworks of earlier styles, took the sequence of events as they happened as the key to reality, observing it detachedly and without comment, leaving it, in principle, to speak for itself. Feminist and lesbian/gay documentaries also refused the 'objective' knowledge of earlier traditions, but were equally uneasy with vérité's detachment and its tendency in practice to organise its material around what were seen as macho values of crisis and conflict (Rosenberg 1983:36). Vérité film-makers were not identified with the people they were filming and their detachment often came across as irony or disdain. Feminist and lesbian/gay documentarists, by contrast, were part of what they were filming; their reality was grasped through subjective understanding; it was characterised by coming together, not conflict. Making oneself the subject of politics, acknowledging the validity of subjective truth, coming together – these were also major characteristics of the CR process. Affirmation films' inflection of documentary's claim to a special relation to reality is part of the new movement's distinctive way of comprehending (lesbian/gay) reality.

Consciousness raising

Some movement films show CR in progress. There are no recordings of meetings of an ongoing CR group as such, since they were closed to non-participants, but films could stage reproductions (*Michael, a Gay Son*), record CR-type discussions at more open meetings (*Bögjävlar, L'Aspect rose de la chose*) or bring people together for the camera (*August and July, Coming to Know, We're Alive, Gay Women Speak*). However, even when no attempt was made to show CR as such, it was always felt that the films were somehow 'like' CR. *Newsday* 15 November 1971, for instance, in a review of *Three Lives*, considered it had the 'feel of a Women's Lib rap session';[9] similarly, Ruth McCormick, in one of the first overviews of women's liberation cinema, suggested all the films made thus far had 'more or less political or consciousness-raising ends in view' (1972:2). This early perception has been theoretically developed by Julia Lesage, who argues that the organisation of women's liberation documentaries 'is the artistic analogue of the structure and function of the consciousness-raising group' (1978: 515). I want here to discuss the applicability of this proposition to affirmation documentaries.

Their central method is footage of an individual speaking about him/her self, often referred to as 'talking heads'. This was the format from the start. *Three Lives* 1970, one of the first women's movement films, has Robin Mide talking to camera about her homosexual feelings. *Come Together* 1971 moves throughout between sequences of activism and footage of personal testimony. *Bail Fund Film* 1971 consists mainly of Paul talking about her experience and life, including her lesbianism. Talking heads occupy at least part of most movement documentaries and are the core of many; *Word is Out* consists almost entirely of intercutting between twenty-six of them.

Most talking heads films are based on interviews. The speaker does not look direct to camera but off to one side of it, clearly addressing someone. This person is only rarely heard and very seldom seen – all attention is on the interviewee, which makes it feel as if s/he lays down the agenda for the interview as an individual should in CR. The vestigial presence of an interviewer may be a bit like a stand-in for the viewer, providing us with a place in the film as if next to the person in a CR session.

In some films, the interviewer is more directly acknowledged. Rita Mae Brown in *Some American Feminists*, for instance, begins one shot saying, 'Well, you asked me when did I first come out. . .' and proceeds to tell us. *Word is Out* keeps in a number of such moments, notably in the pre-credit sequence: we hear a woman ask Nadine, a Chicano woman, if she was 'always gay', and she replies, 'Always? I don't think so. Oh, maybe. I don't know. It's hard to say. I think I . . . yeah, maybe'; Betty raises with the unseen interviewer the question of whether she will be the only black lesbian in the film (figure 5.2); Nick, a white man, is asked when he first started acting on his feelings, and replies, 'No, no, that's like way . . . that's like, getting into puberty. Though I . . . I . . . oh boy . . . are you running now?' There is a sense here of the film-makers laying down an agenda, prompting thoughts on topics such as when one first knows one is gay, topics that seem very open ended and yet contain hotly contested assumptions (such as that there is a stable identity, being gay, that one comes to discover in oneself; that it is a given of one's personality, not a choice). Yet these moments also suggest that interviewees can resist the frameworks that the film-makers have brought to bear. Betty explicitly raises the issues of selection and representativeness in the film, insisting that she, the film-makers and the viewer be self-conscious about what she is doing in the film. The more hesitant responses of Nadine and Nick suggest that the question may be inappropriate, that they can't tie up their experiences in its neat assumptions. As in principle in CR, the film is willing to register resistance to presupposition.

Not all talking heads footage is interview. Sometimes the subject speaks direct to camera. Robin Mide in *Three Lives*, several of the people in *Susana*, look at the camera, introduce themselves, say what they want to say. In the second section of *L'Aspect rose*, 'Lexique' ('Lexicon'), each of the twelve members of the group speaks a text they have prepared on some aspect of being lesbian/gay, basing what they say on their own experiences – for example, Denis talks about pederasty, Martine about lesbian prostitution, Didier about camp, Catherine about sisterhood and so on. Such departures from previous documentary practice are part of what Waugh (1988) sees as these films' empowerment of gay/lesbian people, as in CR giving them the word.

Talking heads footage centres on the close-up, like CR focusing on the individual consciousness. Yet few films consist relentlessly of

5.2   Betty raises the issue of her representativeness in *Word is Out*.
(National Film Archive)

head and shoulder close-ups. Camera movement, generally zooming
or hand held, may break the monotony, underscore what is
important, intensify feelings. It may also situate the individual voice
in a wider context. If it shows more of the interviewee's
environment, it can suggest (quite possibly misleadingly) more of
their character and social position. We are bound to attend to Kate
Millett and Ti-Grace Atkinson, in *Some American Feminists*,
differently, when the former is shot wearing a loose, smock-like top
over cotton trousers, sitting on a polished brown wood floor with
rugs on it in a cavernous studio flat whereas Atkinson wears a neat,
fitted grey jumper and is sitting on a beige sofa along the back of
which at one point walks a beautiful, long-haired cat.

Elsewhere camera movement may suggest the immediate situation out of which the person speaks. When Rick Stokes in *Word is
Out* starts talking about meeting his lover David, the camera zooms
back from an extreme close-up on his face to bring David into
frame, thus placing Rick as part of a couple, no longer attended to
as a single person. In *In the Best Interests of the Children*, Margaret
Sloan talks about her daughter Cathy's first experience of lesbian
oppression; as she speaks, Cathy sits next to her at a table laying out

playing cards and getting Margaret to participate. Cathy's presence is appropriate because Margaret is talking about her, but the set-up also reproduces the characteristic situation of women, having to speak while attending to the distractions of domesticity and motherhood. (It is interesting to compare this with a similar moment in *Janie's Janie* 1971, a feminist documentary about a white, working-class woman in New Jersey. At one point Janie is talking while preparing a meal; she puts a chicken in the oven while she speaks, but then notices that the oven has gone out and has to interrupt what she is saying and see to the oven. Like Margaret, Janie does not speak in isolation from the remorseless demands of women's work. The difference however is that for Janie, domesticity interrupts the train of thought, whereas Margaret continues speaking even while playing cards with Cathy. *Janie's Janie* is a film about the limitations of the domestic role for women; *In the Best Interests* on the other hand is about the compatability of motherhood and lesbianism.)

Camera movement and everything visual in these films is nevertheless subordinate to the lesbian/gay voice. The dominance of the voice in documentary was characteristic of pre-vérité traditions, but in the form of an impersonal, unlocated voice explaining and placing the images for the viewer. Affirmation documentaries eschew this, dispensing with voice over narration altogether (with the major exceptions of *We're not Afraid Anymore*, *Witches and Faggots* and the two autobiographical films, *Home Movie* and *Susana*). Such narration would be associated with fixing the truth from outside, whereas what was favoured was the individualised, located voice of subjectivity. This is the voice to which all the images are subordinate and which acts as the guide as to how to make sense of what is shown.

The most common pattern in affirmation documentaries is predominant talking heads footage, broken up by footage and photographs cut into it (i.e. while the person keeps on speaking) and by interludes between it, generally showing the people about their daily lives. The voice provides the anchor for both cut-ins and interludes. Generally the image corroborates or illustrates the voice: in *Word is Out*, Mark Pinney's reference to having been 'a fairly hunky little teenager' is corroborated by snaps; John Platania in *Some of Your Best Friends* talks about his entrapment on the site where it occurred; May Sarton's sense of lesbian fulfilment is echoed in *World of Light* in footage of her gardening or with friends.

Sometimes the relationship between voice and image is more

complex. This generally occurs when use is made of footage not specifically shot for the film: home movies, snapshots, newspaper stories and so on. This may refer to other images in society: pin-ups of heterosexual role models such as Gary Cooper and Clark Gable, for instance, as Harry Hay speaks about growing up in the thirties in *Word is Out*. More often it refers back to the speaker's own past image, now perceived as inauthentically straight. In *Lavender*, one of the women elaborates on her statement, 'I knew I was different from an early age', as we see a montage of snapshots from her life, all of which we are thus invited to read in terms of 'difference', either catching the hint of deviance in these normative snaps or else marvelling that a lesbian identity should lurk therein.

The most sustained use of an ironic interplay between image and voice is Jan Oxenburg's *Home Movie*, in which the film-maker's voice interrogates her parents' old home movie footage of her. In the first such section, she is seen in a frilly pink dress imitating mummy feeding baby and dancing to a record, while the voice over muses, 'I wonder why I was doing this? I look so . . . normal, just like a little girl. And it's really strange, because I didn't feel like a little girl'. The voice stresses the contrast between the 'normal' exterior and the felt inner 'difference', but we may perceive that difference in the little girl's behaviour. Michelle Citron suggests that the girl looks awkward in the role, 'desperate' as she dances, like 'a kid who doesn't quite catch on' (1981:31); at one point, she looks out to the camera with a pugnacious expression that seems to suggest she is not the feminine little thing she and her parents were trying to put on film. When next the home movie is of Oxenburg as cheerleader, the voice says, 'The thing I liked best about being a cheerleader was being with the other cheerleaders'. The indisputable normality of cheerleading is subverted, both by suggesting the lesbian dimension of all girls together and suggesting that being together was more important than servicing the support for the boys' game – 'the football match was just an excuse for the cheerleaders to get together and do our thing'. Her parents' camera is not so sure: while the voice is all with the other girls, the camera sometimes swings out to take in the match, registering a tension between what the voice says she felt mattered and what the image indicates social convention deemed significant.

The home movies are framed by contemporary footage at the beginning and end. The film opens with a montage of still and moving images of women together, marching as lesbians, being affectionate with one another – in other words, a 'positive' image of lesbian identity from which to view the construction of feminine identity in the home movies. The end of the cheerleader section cuts from Oxenburg, the image slowed down, her voice over saying, 'It feels real good now to have broken through the façade', to her with a group of women playing softball. The cut emphasises a shift in role, no longer cheerleading but playing, and creates a feeling of release, from the home movie slowing down to the fast movement of the women playing. The feeling of release conveys a feeling of 'breaking through the façade'; it also suggests, as does the whole film, a notion of having discovered a true, authentic self and identity. Both this, and the sustained implicit contrast between the feminine and the lesbian, are ways of thinking and feeling about lesbianism that are both characteristic of affirmation politics and yet fiercely contested within it.

For the most part, *Home Movie* seems to be contrasting a contemporary, authentic lesbian self against the inauthentic image of the past. The home movies are introduced by white leader visible on screen and accompanied by the sound of a camera running, underlining that such footage, often considered raw and innocent, is nonetheless ideologically constructed. The surrounding material, on the other hand, is presented straight, as if transparent, natural, unmanipulated. Except at the very end. The final shots show the players hugging together in a group and kissing, but then there is white leader before the credits and accompanying them the sound of a camera running; when the last credit has come up, there is the sound of the camera being turned off, just before the film ends. These last details, and the film's title, suggest that the contemporary footage too is a 'home movie'. This might mean that being with women is the film-maker's true home, maintaining the contrast between real and phoney home movies. Equally it could suggest that the new lesbian identity is also recognised as a construction, a reading supported by Oxenburg's later film *Comedy in Six Unnatural Acts*, discussed below. Be that as it may, *Home Movie*'s principal strategy is to reveal the truth about the past from the vantage point of the raised consciousness of the present.

Affirmation documentaries are like CR in that they centre on the individual voice as the source of knowledge and the vehicle of truth, with the image situating, corroborating or occasionally being interrogated by the voice, but never itself questioning that voice. Most often, several voices are brought together in ways that both establish lesbian/gay identity and demonstrate the social dimension of personal experience.

Identity is achieved partly simply by bringing these many voices together under the aegis of a lesbian/gay film. Many films stress the diversity of lesbian/gay people. Films like *Word is Out* and *In the Best Interests* are extremely careful to include a wide range of people (black, white, Chicano, Native American, Asian; rich, middle, poor; queeny/dikey and straight looking; all ages – only disability seems not to get a look in), and most films have someone protesting the variety and diversity of gay people even if what is shown reproduces a white, middle-class image. Yet the stress on diversity is there principally to reinforce the sense that, despite all the differences, homosexuality represents a unifying identity – as Keith Birch observes in recollection of GLF CR groups, 'men and women, age-groups, class, even though there were divisions apparent, there was this idea that a gay identity could transcend all these things' (1988:32). Many women's films that include lesbianism similarly stress the essential unity of women as women, beyond differences of sexual preference. *The Continuous Woman*, its title and construction, fitting Sherrie in on a continuum with other, non-lesbian women of different ages, expresses the idea particularly clearly.

The sense of identity is also achieved in the repetition of a narrative structure that also indicates the social dimension of gay/lesbian experience. The subjects tell stories about themselves, or sometimes more broadly the story of their life, and across the many different stories, a common pattern emerges: realising one is lesbian/gay, coming out. People tell about when they first had lesbian/gay feelings, how they felt about it, recognising what others, society at large, felt about it, doing something about it (falling in love, having sex), telling other people about it, meeting with other lesbian/gay people. This is the basic overall structure of *Word is Out*. Though in many ways loose, even rambling, reproducing something of the feel of a CR session, it does have named sections which group bits of what the speakers say into three stages, corresponding to the progression just outlined – 'The Early Years', 'Growing Up', 'From Now On'.

The voices telling their stories make up a general lesbian/gay biography. At the same time, as with feminist documentaries, the films also condense the narrative of the CR process itself. In CR people speak individually; as they speak and listen, they come to realise the wider significance of their individual story. Thus CR has its own narrative: the dawning of awareness. Likewise in the films, footage near the beginning will often be pure story telling; later, the person will speak about how they feel about things; towards the end, they will discourse on the social/political significance of their experiences. The sense of a collective movement in this direction, arising out of the CR process, is achieved either by dovetailing similar accounts, the similarity foregrounding what is common, and therefore social, to personal testimony, or else by a progression, noted by Rosenberg in feminist documentaries (1983:56), from someone shown talking first alone and then to a small group of other people.

In its centring on the individual speaker, its privileging of the voice over the image and its structures of parallelism the talking heads documentary can indeed be seen as the 'artistic analogue' of CR. It also raises some of the paradoxes of CR.

The aim, of the documentaries as of CR groups, is the truth, and the source of truth is the individual voice, but there are limitations to this approach to truth which may in part be heightened by the talking heads format. Centring on the individual voice takes on trust, first, the speakers' sincerity (they are saying what they genuinely think and feel, honestly recalling their past), and second, their self-knowledge. Yet we know that people perform, say what is expected of them, especially in the presence of a camera; that even if they say what they think is true, they may forget, deceive themselves; that the social reality of anyone's personal circumstances far outstrips their grasp of it; that all thought and perception is governed by frameworks of understanding that we do not individually create (though we may learn to be aware of them and struggle with them). So-called subjective truth is no less (and no more) problematic and unstable than so-called objective truth.

The repetition of stories, the films' insistent perception of sameness within difference, relates to a further paradox of CR. The latter was in principle entirely free and open ended, yet if you had been in a lesbian/gay CR group and had raised your consciousness to the point where you saw clearly and fully that it was right that you should be oppressed, it would surely be held that CR had failed in your case. Some consciousnesses are more acceptable than others. The term consciousness raising evokes the Marxist idea of 'false consciousness', the wrong seeing consciousness you had to rise above, yet feminism and the lesbian/gay movements rejected the idea of 'correct' views. CR had a hidden agenda of things one should go through, a hidden idea of where one should end up, but this was always masked under the phenomenology of the individual speaking out. The same holds true for the documentaries. At their worst they both sprawl and yet say the same thing over and over. This same thing is the affirmation that gay is good. Conflict, contradiction and difficulty are erased.

Talking heads documentaries do thus in many ways reproduce the approach to knowledge embodied in CR, even down to the limitations of subjectivity as truth and the quest for sameness. Where the analogy with CR begins to break down is in the assumption of sharing and identity between speaker and listener. In a CR group they were on an equal footing – every listener was a speaker and vice versa. For the analogy to hold we would at least need to be sure that the film-makers are gay/lesbian, even if they do not literally speak on film. However, this is by no means always clear.

Occasionally the text of the film is explicit about who made it: *Sisters!*, for instance, includes the statement, 'This film is made for women, by women and is dedicated to women'. Some films include enough of the interviewer to let us know that he or she is gay or lesbian. Sometimes we know from surrounding publicity that the film-makers were lesbian/gay, for example the collectives behind *Coming Out*, *Rosa Winkel*, *Bögjävlar*, *Word is Out*, *In the Best Interests*, *L'Aspect rose*, *Witches and Faggots*, the directors of *Race d'ep!*, *Greta's Girls*, *Truxx* and *Enough is Enough*. In other cases the directors are well known as lesbian/gay from other kinds of film work – from the avant-garde (Barbara Hammer), from pornography (Pat Rocco, Norbert Terry), from both (Arthur Bressan). When none of these are the case, we probably take it on trust that the films were made by lesbian/gay people. We are not always right to.

In some cases information is so scant that one can say nothing about their makers, even their sex, let alone their sexuality. In women's films, there may be an assumption that it does not matter whether the people behind the camera were lesbians, it is enough that they were women. If lesbianism is understood as part of the continuum of female experience (Rich 1981:23-33), then any woman can be supposed to identify with lesbian subjects. The same argument was not usually made for men, for whom it was assumed there was a polarity of interests between gayness and straightness. Thus it is not in itself enough reassurance that the makers of *Some of Your Best Friends*, *A Position of Faith* or, *Michael, a Gay Son* were at any rate men; and it is even less reassuring to note that *two* of three directors of *Sandy and Madeline's Family* were men, as was the only director of *August and July*. It is not that straight men could not possibly make a decent film about lesbians or gay men, but that it necessarily breaks with the idea of CR if they are the film-maker, because CR is about the mutual sharing of experience. In many cases, the film-makers may in fact have identified as lesbian/gay with their subjects, but have remained silent about it, because they wished to efface themselves before their subjects, or because they did not consider the significance of the viewer knowing who made the film, or because they had not yet come out.

There is then a range of apparent identification between film-makers and subjects. There are senses in which this both does and does not matter. It does not matter if, as Waugh (1988) says, one feels that the subjects have been empowered by the film. Collectives who make films generally stress very close, inter-active participation with their subjects, and this may be true of individually directed films. Waugh (ibid.:260) cites *Michael, a Gay Son*, based on 'such close collaboration' with its subject that it is virtually a 'joint film'; Russo (1981:244) suggests that the Mariposa collective's practice of screening footage to groups of gay people, using their suggestions in shaping the film, means that in 'a real sense, the gay community made *Word is Out*'. The interview and statement to camera are generally handled, Waugh suggests, in ways that avoid the selection and manipulation found in the use of these same techniques in mainstream cinema and television. The editing generally 'endeavours to preserve the full scope and rhythm of the interview' (1988: 261); long takes are favoured, with no cropping at the editing stage; the presence of the interviewer may be signalled, 'the subjective presence that has catalyzed the subject's contribution' (ibid.). Statements suggest even stronger control by the subjects over what is talked about and how; they may even select where they are filmed and from what angle.

In practice, it is nearly always lesbian/gay film-makers who empower lesbian/gay speakers, but it need not be so. To that extent, it does not matter who made the film so long as they empower the lesbian/gay subject. Yet it does affect how we look at and experience the film. Given the history of straight perceptions of lesbian/gay people, the construction of us in official discourses (including traditional documentaries) as exhibits of evil, sickness or deviance, as well as male heterosexual voyeurism of lesbianism, given these, the sense of closeness, one-ness, identification between film-maker and subject matters to lesbian/gay viewers very much indeed as a countervailing tradition.

There is a further way in which the revealing analogy between CR and affirmation documentaries does not work. CR is by definition a

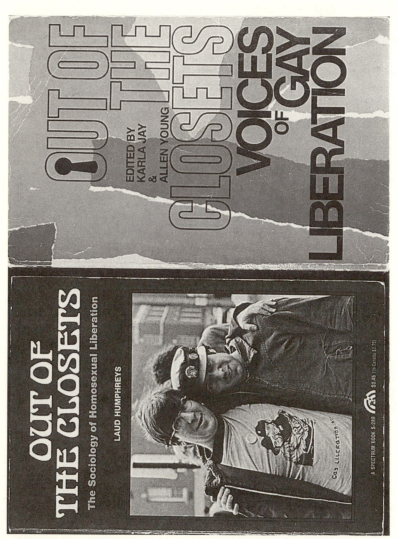

5.3 The first slogan of gay liberation on two book covers from 1972. (Douglas/Links and Prentice-Hall)

private and intimate experience, but the moment it is filmed and shown in public it ceases to be so. It becomes, on the other hand, coming out.

Coming out

One of the first Gay Liberation slogans was 'Out of the Closets! Onto the Streets!' and *Out of the Closets* is the title of two of the first books on the movement (Jay and Young 1972; Humphries 1972) (figure 5.3). The name of the Italian gay liberation movement, Fuori, means Out; in its newspaper it declared: 'What are we asking of you? To come out!' (Richmond and Noguera 1973:154). Similarly Carl Wittman's 'Gay Manifesto', first published in the *San Francisco Free Press* at the end of 1969, begins its list of 'imperatives for gay liberation' with 'Free ourselves; come out everywhere' (1972:341). Several movement films have titles playing on the idea: *Coming Out, Coming to Know, Word is Out, Gay Is Out*. As Bob Cant (1978:33) observed in relation to *Nighthawks*: 'we are never left in any doubt about the importance of coming out. And that does remain the central tenet of the gay movement as it is now'.

Coming out (CO) was the one strategy unique to lesbian and gay politics. No other group is quite so literally socially invisible. Being lesbian/gay does not show – unlike gender, colour or disability, it is not physiologically apparent; unlike class or ethnicity, it is not something the visible markers of which you have to *un*learn if you wish to disguise it; only if you choose to behave in an 'obvious' style is being lesbian/gay in any sense visible. This of course does afford a measure of protection. CO is a deliberate decision to do without that mask of invisibility. It has a special edge to it. Women, blacks, Jews, the disabled may all be socially disadvantaged, but only exceptionally (in Nazi Germany, for instance) has their very right to exist been in doubt. Although death for lesbians and gay men was not on the cards in the fifties and sixties, biological treatment aimed at eradicating homosexual feeling was (and still is in many countries) and such feeling was (and is) largely illegal. CO is making visible something that is not merely invisible but also deemed worthy of extermination. It is dangerous, moving and dramatic, the stuff of a good picture.

CO was generally understood to have three stages: coming out to oneself (recognising homosexual feelings in oneself, accepting them, being willing to act on them); coming out to other lesbian/gay people (going on the scene, joining groups, CR); coming out to other people (both in one's daily life, coming out to friends, family, employers, colleagues, and in public, wearing badges, going on marches, kissing and holding hands in the street and so on). Personal testimony films often describe all of these but, in the nature of things, they cannot really show the first two (you'd have to know someone was going to discover/decide they were gay in advance of them doing so and it is too internal and painful an experience to go through before the camera). Despite this, CO is a defining characteristic of the form and content of affirmation documentaries.

It is enough that they are films. The act of being filmed, knowing that the film is going to be shown, is inescapably an act of coming out. As Waugh (1988:265) says, 'consent to declare oneself before the camera . . . has for every potential subject of a lesbian/gay documentary all the dimensions of an irreversible life-changing political commitment'. People in the films often make reference to the fact that they are, even as they speak, in a film and coming out. They also state why they are doing so. At the end of *Lavender* one of the women says it is frightening to be as exposed as the film will make her, but that it is the only way to change people's attitudes – it is because they 'haven't seen anything to do with lesbians' that straight attitudes remain limited or bigoted. In *In the Best Interests* a black woman observes that the only way for there to be change is for people

> to be around us more, to read our books, to see our films. This film is a great avenue for people to see, hey, they're mundane, you know, they're nutty, they're crazy, they're exciting, they're black, they're white, they have children, they don't, they live in structured families, they live very loosely. . . . It seems to me that exposure's the only thing to change people's minds.

Two autobiographical films, *Blackstar* and *Susana*, play on film as CO. Both establish their maker's identity as film-maker as inseparable from their identity as gay/lesbian: *Blackstar* starts with bits of gay-ish surrealistic film made by Tom Joslin since he was fourteen; *Susana* has Blaustein speak in voice over of her discovery in early adolescence of her 'vocation for art and women'. Both then focus on film on people's responses to them as out film-makers.

Blackstar is based around a series of interviews with Joslin's family and lover. All the interviewees seem awkward: the family are uncomfortable with his gayness and even more with having to acknowledge both it and their discomfort on film; the lover is embarrassed, especially when Joslin tries to get him to make love on camera. No-one wants to talk about gay sexuality, highlighting precisely the avoidance of openness which CO challenges. This is compounded by the film's construction, where one interview undercuts another, revealing the strain involved in Tom's attempt to integrate his family and love-life. Ray Olson (1979:10) describes one instance:

> the juxtaposition of his mother's talk with that of his lover criticizing her erodes our confidence in both of them: she seems not so much as at first the warm, accepting mother; he is caught out in loverly insecurity.

Showing awkwardness, evasion and distrust, *Blackstar* constructs a picture of the uncomfortable way that CO works in day-to-day interactions.

Susana also has interviews with various people the film-maker has known through her life, family, friends, lovers, together with old photographs and home movies. Blaustein is sometimes present in the interviews as a participant; at others, she speaks to camera as if replying to what has just been said. Her presence provides two registers of CO: celebratory, as when talking with or making love to women friends, and challenging, when she first replies to her parents' statements and then, in a climactic final scene, confronts her sister Graciela. The latter tells Blaustein she cannot accept what she is, still thinks she should get married but that she will 'try to be open and understand'. Blaustein's presence here is bristlingly combative. Her self-presentation, wearing what Claudia Gorbman (1983:44) calls 'the popular lesbian iconography of a dyke-vogue sportcap', is overtly lesbian; Graciela, in conventionally feminine clothes, is sitting waiting for the interview to start, when we hear Susana shout 'Action!' and then come in, entering what has been established as Graciela's space; throughout the interview, Susana is restless, shifting about, lighting up a cigarette; she takes the microphone from Graciela in order to speak but does not return it to her – in other words, throughout she has the upper hand. This may turn the viewer against Blaustein ('we may cavil at what [Graciela] says . . . but visually speaking she is defensive, and we actually tend to root for her as the underdog' (Gorbman, ibid.)), but equally the sequence does reverse the position lesbians usually occupy, in two ways: Blaustein is in control of the situation, not controlled by it; and she turns anti-lesbianism into the thing that has to be come out about, to be confessed, as Graciela embarrassedly admits that she still disapproves of Susana's identity.

Beyond the simple fact of it being film, affirmation documentaries may intensify the sense of CO by showing straightforwardly what was (is) taboo. Occasionally this may mean sexual intercourse, but usually it is simply open affection. *Greta's Girls* shows the ordinary domestic life of Chris and Sarah, the lesbianism of their relationship evident in a myriad tiny glances, touches and interactions. *Bögjävlar* uses two men, Håkan and Pelle (who stress that they are friends who have sex together rather than 'a couple'), as a central thread; after the title credit, the film opens with the two of them having a bath together, laughing and giggling, Håkan shampooing Pelle's hair. There is nothing shocking or outrageous about it, yet it is a kind of gentle physical intimacy between men that is never usually shown. Later, they walk down the street, holding hands, kissing. The framing is wide enough to be able to show passers-by turning to look at the men, and the shot is followed by a rapid series showing people's reactions, some curious, some shocked. Here the impact of CO is registered in the film itself and going out to do and film this in the streets of Stockholm is itself a classic act of gay liberation.

Such deliberate, politically informed CO is well documented in movement film: all the footage of street marches and demonstrations is also always footage of collective CO. A few films show lesbians and gay men who are out in their daily lives away from home. *Lavender* shows both women at their places of work; *A Woman's Place* shows Elaine Noble about her state gubernatorial business. There is no lesbian content to this footage, they are just doing their job, not coming out in any overt sense, but the fact that we know (from the film) they are lesbian, that they were being filmed in situ at work because they were lesbian, places them 'out' in public.

It is easy enough to show people recalling coming out and demonstrating their outness by being in a film but, as has already been said, it is much more difficult to show the process of CO. It is only as one approaches dramatisation that it becomes possible. Documentaries that try to deal with it either, like *A Position of Faith*, are strongly organised around narrative suspense (will Bill be accepted for ordination?), or else, like *Michael, a Gay Son*, resort to acted reconstructions (of family therapy sessions) to show the drama of coming out to parents. In the fiction films proper, CO is undoubtedly the narrative structure par excellence.

No films show the purely private self-realisation that one desires people of the same sex, but other moments in the story of CO are charted – discovery of one's feelings in relation to someone one is attracted to (*After the Game*, *Anna und Edith*, *Apartments*, *Du er ikke alene*, *Liv og Død*), coming on to the gay scene (*Happy Birthday Davy*, *Saturday Night at the Baths*, *A Very Natural Thing*), telling people you know (*Anna und Edith*, *Du er ikke alene*, *Liv og Død*, *Michael, a Gay Son*), coming out in public (*Nighthawks*, *A Very Natural Thing*). These can explore both the dimensions of the process and its consequences.

Implicit in any representation of CO is an idea of the nature of lesbian/gay identity itself, that is whether, at one extreme, it is presented as a fixed, pre-given identity which then gets recognised and expressed, or whether, at the other, it is seen as something one becomes in the process of forming relationships. There is a difference between the women's and men's films here. Coming out in the gay male films tends more towards the idea of the already fixed identity, whereas the lesbian films represent it more flexibly, though with a strong pull toward the 'becoming' end of the continuum. This can be related to the different routes to lesbian/gay political awareness indicated above. For women, lesbianism could be either something one knew about oneself before involvement in the gay or women's movements or something one discovered through the experience of the latter, whereas there was no men's movement, only a gay movement to which you came if you already thought you were gay. More contentiously, this difference might also be related to differences in the construction of male and female sexuality themselves, a point I shall return to after discussing the different constructions of coming out in these films.

The elliptical narrative of *Apartments* evokes an experience of realising lesbian feelings through a response to a particular person. Two women living in a block of flats see one another and catch each other's eyes in passing; these moments are crosscut with shots of them making love; only at the end do we get the moment of meeting. The love-making may be what happens or what they want to happen, either way the film suggests how feelings of lesbian desire may arise unpremeditated in day-to-day interactions. This is explored more fully in conventional linear narratives.

After the Game shows two school friends, Nicole and Diane, spending time together at Diane's place after a ball game; when they take a shower together, the water suddenly runs too hot and Diane has to press against Nicole to avoid it, leading to confused looks between them; Nicole says she must go, Diane asks why and Nicole tells her, 'I think I'm in love with you'. For Nicole, this is the culmination of feelings: how she has felt before (as she now tells Diane) when they have showered together, what was at stake for her when, just before, she told Diane how much her friendship means and they hugged. For Diane, on the other hand, these are new experiences, which she says she doesn't think she can handle; but when Nicole has walked out of the door, Diane goes after her and says, 'Don't go'. Nicole comes out with feelings she already has and in doing so enables Diane to explore similar but unsuspected feelings in herself. There is something of the same balance in *Anna und Edith*. The two women work in the same office and share a flat. In one scene, Edith is cleaning her face before a mirror and Anna comes in, gives her a glass of wine, stands behind her looking at her in the mirror and starts to caress her; when Edith says that she has never had women friends, Anna says that she did at school but lost them when she married. A little later, it is Anna who gently seduces Edith, when they have gone out into the country. Towards the end of the film, Edith tells the other women in the office that through Anna she has discovered what had been lacking in her relationships with men, but there is no sense of her having specifically desired women before this, whereas this is suggested by Anna's remarks and initiative.

In the gay male films by contrast characters are already gay before they first express it. Bo in *Du er ikke alene* is shown looking at other boys before falling for Kim; Jacob in *Liv og Død* says he's always wanted to sleep with a man after he meets the more gay-identified John; in *Happy Birthday Davy* and *A Very Natural Thing*, the main characters go on to the gay scene to explore the sexuality they have recognised in themselves. Michael in *Saturday Night at the Baths*, who lives with his girlfriend Tracy, insists that he is not gay when he takes a job as a pianist at a gay baths, yet both Tracy and Scotti, the baths' manager, accuse him of resisting gay feelings inside him. After he has finally slept with Scotti, he tells him of a traumatic experience when his father broke up a loving relationship he was having with one of his father's friends, which serves to confirm that Tracy and Scotti were right. Thus even a narrative of a man discovering sexual feelings he thought he did not have winds up demonstrating that in reality a man 'is' gay before he knows or does anything about it.

The lesbian films tend to see sexual identity as itself created in the process of forming relationships. This is suggested by their representation of men. While gay relations are counterposed to heterosexual ones in *Saturday Night at the Baths* and *Liv og Død*, there is no sense of a rejection of women (in these cases, not even sexually), whereas in the lesbian films men always figure, perhaps just as alternatives in *Apartments*, but definitely as something to be rejected in *After the Game* and *Anna und Edith*. In these films, men are seen as controlling and defining women's sexuality – having any sexual identity of one's own at all seems only realisable through lesbian relations. *After the Game* opens with shots of a married couple bickering in a restaurant and Diane saying that that is not what she wants to be like; later, she tells Nicole how bored she has become with the self-centred boy who was once also Nicole's date; significantly, Diane is not the one who already recognises lesbian feelings in herself but she has sussed the inadequacy of heterosexual relations for her. In *Anna und Edith*, Anna's husband wants her to be 'a wife'; Edith's boyfriend, Herr Schönherr, the manager at the office where they all work, wants her to side with him in office politics; the brothers Anna and Edith meet in a bar paw at them until they get up and go. The women realise their sexual feelings for each other through the scene at the mirror, perhaps suggesting starting out from each one's own image of herself rather than one imposed on her by men. It is not that the men are unattractive or especially hateful or that the women are 'really' lesbian, but that being sexual in one's own terms means being lesbian.

This difference between lesbian and gay male films' representation of realising homosexual feeling relates to current views of the construction of gender sexuality differences. Men are socialised into determining their own sexuality and also into thinking in terms of separate categories, and are therefore more liable to try to decide whether they 'are' one thing or another. Women are socialised more in terms of relationships and responses and have to struggle against their socialisation to determine their own sexuality; when this struggle is recognised as being against men, their openness to development through relationships makes lesbianism a ready possibility. Such ideas have by no means gone uncontested. Many women feel that their experience of having always been lesbian is discounted by such an account, many men resent the rigid binarism that seems forced on them and a readiness to countenance a greater plurality of sexual identities perhaps characterises more recent thought.

There is less at issue in the representation of the consequences, as opposed to the processes, of coming out. Some films show negative effects, notably *Liv og Død*, where John and Jennifer (Jacob's girlfriend) are murdered by thugs on account of their open and accepting life-styles, *Nighthawks*, where the hero, Jim, is threatened with losing his job if he again discusses being gay with his pupils (which he has only done at their prompting), and *Michael, a Gay Son*, where the counselling sessions of Michael and his family run the gamut of reactions to coming out: refusing to believe (brother), pushing it under the carpet (mother), worried what others will think (father). Yet all the films affirm the importance of coming out, not just as a strategy but as a good experience. The sequence in *Nighthawks* where Jim talks to his fellow teacher, Judy, about being gay feels very liberating, not just because he says to her that that is how talking about it feels, but because we have been waiting for this scene throughout the film and because it comes after a school dance that Judy enveigled Jim into attending as her partner and which he found miserably alienating. He drives furiously through the night with her out to a motorway café – the circling camera and flashing lights of the drive embody the release of his anger, while the still set-ups at the café express the calmer mood of talking it out.

CO is also often shown as an act of connection, an assertion of personal identity that leads to an experience of collective identity. This may be with other gay people, as at the gay street parade in *A Very Natural Thing* or the lesbian/gay support group in *Michael*, but it can also be with wider forces of resistance and rebellion. The school's attempt to break up the relationship of Bo and Kim in *Du er ikke alene* is part of what fuels all the kids' resistance to authoritarianism. A similar connection is made in *Anna und Edith*. The other women in the office are at first divided about how they feel about the relationship but Anna points out that they have found out about it from Schönherr and that this is an attempt to turn the women against each other just as had been done earlier during their strike. This is the argument that wins the women over. Even more powerfully, *Anna und Edith* suggests the growth of female solidarity out of the love between the central couple. The other women discuss with Anna and Edith the pros and cons of lesbianism, but when Schönherr comes in they all turn and face him together until he backs out defeated. The discussion sequence is shot at first with close-ups of different women expressing their views but then becomes a long shot with all the women grouped around Anna and Edith, embodying their growing closeness which is then in place for the confrontation with Schönherr. Again, in the final sequence of the film, when all the women have gone to a bar for a drink, the camera slowly zooms back from Edith singing a song about women's self-realisation gradually to include all the women into the lesbian

5.4   The lesbian relationship between *Anna und Edith* forms the core of solidarity between other women by the end of the film. (Cinemien)

based experience of liberation (figure 5.4).

The fictions mainly show processes of coming out whereas the documentaries show those who have come out. *Michael, a Gay Son* mixes the two, the sequences with the therapist scripted and acted, in an extremely naturalistic style, whereas Michael, his lover Jerry and the gay support group play themselves. This mixture of genuine and fake documentary may disconcert some viewers, but it also expresses the difficulty of coming out. Michael, Jerry, other lesbian/gay people are themselves, out on film before us; but the pain and 'psychological, social and ethical delicacy' (Waugh 1988:265) of coming out are such that it becomes unshowable except through performance. The film ends with Michael and Jerry playing happily together in a park. When we see such things in a film, we are seeing people who have already reached the point where they have the confidence and conviction to be out on film; behind them there will always lie a story of pain and delicacy which their outness may make us forget (even if they tell us about it verbally); *Michael* uses fiction and documentary to bring the two together, the process and the outcome.

Activism/analysis

In addition to CR and CO, affirmation politics took a wide range of forms, many of them recorded in the documentaries: pride marches (*Homosexuals on the March*, *A Gay Parade*, *Sisters!*), protest marches (*Gay USA*, *Enough is Enough*, *Witches and Faggots*), lesbian/gay contingents on other marches (a trade union rights rally in *Come Together*, a May Day parade in *Bögjävlar*), counter marches (in *Witches and Faggots* against an anti-abortion rally, seen as provocatively timed to coincide with a gay rights rally); producing and distributing newsletters and leaflets (*Come Together*); picketing anti-lesbian/gay events (*Stop the Movie Cruising!*); zapping homophobic occasions (the aversion therapy symposium in *Some of Your Best Friends*); holding meetings (*Come Together*) and conferences (*Witches and Faggots*); addressing public meetings (*Jill Johnston*, Ti-Grace Atkinson in *Some American Feminists*), giving talks (to a class of students in *Come Together*).

Yet activism is much less represented in affirmation documentaries than CR and CO. Of the fifty-odd films in my list, only fifteen contain any activist footage, in some cases (e.g. *Word is Out*, *Some American Feminists*) very briefly. Probably the most sustained treatment is *Gay USA*, which cuts together footage from six simultaneous gay pride/protest marches, supplemented by shots of earlier marches going back to 1970, as well as civil rights and Nazi demonstrations. There are vox pop interviews with marchers and onlookers and longer interviews with lesbians and gay men about their experiences. All of this builds up a picture of both the mood at the marches and the pressure of events and history behind them. The overall picture is what Lee Atwell (1978–9:54) calls 'the politics of celebration': '*Gay USA* is the first film ever to fully capture the intense anger, joy, and love embodied in these very public expressions of freedom'.

Music and poetry carries much of this spirit: a ballad, 'Reflections', by Marjie Orten over shots of women carrying banners in San Francisco; Pat Parker reciting her poem, 'For the straight folks who don't mind gays but wish they weren't so blatant', placed as an up-beat after a series of men recalling being taunted on the streets. The footage of the marches emphasises diversity: Dykes on Bikes lead off the San Francisco procession where there is also an interview with a gay businessman dressed in a three-piece suit; there is a balance of women and men, care to include representatives of all ethnic groups, readiness to include 'obviously' gay people (drag queens, bull dykes, clones) as well as straight-looking gay people; there is both humour and seriousness, often cut directly together.

Diversity and joy of living are contrasted with uniformity and emotional emptiness in a sequence towards the end. Shots of a float bearing blow-ups of bywords of reaction (the Ku Klux Klan, Hitler, Stalin, Anita Bryant, Idi Amin) are cut together with shots from the Nazi rally film *Triumph of the Will*, attesting to the ubiquity and longevity of oppression. This is accompanied by an interview with a drag queen talking about the conformism, the lack of diversity, of fascism: 'When you look at mass demonstrations in totalitarian societies, I mean where you see as many people as there are here today, you don't get a sense that these are real people. . . . I mean, you just see herds of sheep'. The film thus brings together two styles of politics, suggesting how the difference in style is also a difference in attitude towards freedom, variety and individualism.

Gay USA includes a fair bit of material showing anti-gay attitudes. Some of the onlookers voice homophobic sentiments ('I'm not prejudiced or anything like that, but when they come in the street and mess with normal people. . .'); fundamentalist Christians aver that sex outside of procreation is 'degrading, decadent, weakening, childish'. The film is dedicated to Robert Hillsborough, a gay man murdered in San Francisco a few days earlier. The attitudes and this chilling fact stand as a reminder of why activism is necessary. Towards the end there is a gay history section. The Nazi persecution of gays is described and visually evoked, followed by a vox pop sequence, in which people say what famous 'gay person from any period in history' they would 'like to see here today' (the answers include Alexander the Great, Sappho, the goddess Diana, Jesus Christ, Herman Melville, André Gide and Bessie Smith). The history section encapsulates the contrast of oppression and celebration which is also the sustaining contrast of the whole film: affirmation as celebration not just for its own sake, but as a means of combating oppression.

In addition to showing activism, many films have an activist purpose. In some cases, the aim is agitational, interventions in a specific situation with specific goals. *Bail Fund Film* was made to protest Paul's treatment (kept in prison because unable to raise $100 bail against a $10 theft charge); *A Position of Faith* supports the decision to ordain Bill; *In the Best Interests* was intended for use with professionals involved with lesbian custody cases; *Truxx* and *Enough is Enough* protest police raids on bath-houses; the goal of *Stop the Movie Cruising!* is self-evident. More broadly, all the films have a propagandist purpose, to put truth in the place of media distortions and thereby to change attitudes and treatment. In the majority of cases, this involves the idea of positive images, but before getting on to that, I want to look at the small number of films that offer analysis rather than pure celebration.

The idea of knowledge that underlay CR and affirmation cinema alike made film-makers wary of offering a developed analysis of their own, which felt like imposing correctness rather than permitting self-discovery. This was an understandable revulsion against the rigidities of conventional politics, but at the same time it tended to push into hiding a political agenda that was no less strong for being latent and all the harder to debate for being unacknow-ledged. Documentaries that did make their analysis more explicit had recourse to devices of which both cinéma vérité and talking heads were suspicious: strong expository structures and the use of experts and narrators.

Expository structures clearly lay out a case or perspective on what is shown. *Rosa Winkel* details the forms and extent of gay/lesbian oppression in West Germany as a riposte to those who would say, as the film's title has it, that such oppression is a thing of the Nazi past and 'ist doch schon lange vorbei'. The first three sections of *Race d'ep!* are moments in gay history, illustrating the idea of the construction of homosexual identities: 'Le temps de la pose' ('The posing period'), when there was an attempt to form male homosexuality in the 'Greek' mode, here represented by the work of Baron von Gloeden; 'Le troisième sexe' ('The third sex'), where the Hirschfeldian biological model was uppermost; and the place of homosexuality in the 'sexual revolution' of the sixties. *Come Together* organises its material as a move from the personal experience of being gay before GLF through the change it has made in people's lives to the political agenda for Gay Liberation. The opening sequence cuts between footage of meetings and talking heads, people recalling their life before GLF, then talking about what GLF has done for them ('Personally it means to me – ur – a liberation of my own life'). Affirmation documentaries tend to conceal their interviewee's involvement in the movement or present it as an optional extra that some get into after they come out; in *Come Together* it is the movement itself that allows people to come out and feel good about themselves. As the film develops, the individual perspective expands into a collective one, with one form of gay collectivity, the gay scene, contrasted with the new one of gay liberation. This general orientation then gives way to questions of strategy: GLF's demands, making links with other oppressed groups, various kinds of activism and finally a call to take the movement beyond London to the provinces (presumably the film itself was to be part of this last move). The return throughout to talking heads means that the film shows both the social dimension of the personal and the process of making the personal socially effective through political activity.

Affirmation documentaries are seldom explicit in their use of experts. Occasionally people accredited as experts in the straight world are given a chance to speak, but generally only to represent the voice of oppression. The voice of liberation, by contrast, is supposed to be the voice of the people – all lesbians and gay men are experts on being lesbian/gay. Some films (*Homosexuals on the March*, *Some of Your Best Friends*) have interviews with activists, but even here their status as leaders is often disavowed: *Some American Feminists*, for instance, opens with a disclaimer that the women featured are not to be taken as spokespeople for the movement, yet they are in fact among its stars. The status of expert is sometimes implicitly accorded a speaker. In *Come Together* one speaker, identified by Weeks (1977:206) as Warren Hague, 'a leading activist', is shot away from the background bustle of GLF meetings and against a background of relevant books (Weeks notes Laing, Cooper and Marcuse), which gives his words (among the most politically elaborated in the film) the authority of distance and learning. The (female but not declaredly lesbian) clinical social worker and attorney in *In the Best Interests* are introduced with a sub-title giving their occupations, which are relevant to the issue of custody. In such cases the speaker brings to bear a developed discourse (of political analysis, of legal practice and so on) which is not derived from immediate personal experience.

As noted above, narrators are generally absent in these documentaries, and when they are present it is not as the voice of authority but as a participant. In *Witches and Dykes* the narrator is decentred as the only source of knowledge in the film. Her narration does provide a broad historical perspective (in a pre-credits sequence presenting a chronology of lesbian/gay oppression), a narrative of the struggles of the movement in Australia and information not given in the documentary footage, but for much of the film she is silent, with footage of activists and interviewees carrying the film's analysis. At one point, a protest march against police harassment is under discussion and there is heated debate about the paradox of whether to ask permission from the police to demonstrate against them. The editing here implies that those who would act without permission are in the right: it is they on whom the film focuses, ending the sequence with their words followed by rousing cheers; yet the voice over then says, 'Permission was granted, and we marched on July 15th'. The narrator states what happened, but without comment one way or the other on the rights and wrongs of it. At the same time, as throughout, she identifies herself as lesbian and a participant in what she relates. Thus the film constructs a complex approach to knowledge, not pretending not to have a point of view nor trapped in the equally sterile extremes of 'mere' subjectivity or 'pure' objectivity.

Many of the fiction films also analyse, but only as implied in dialogue or narrative structure; only one, *Ella une vraie famille*, is more unconcealedly analytic. Its intense individualism sets it apart from the collective impulses of other films discussed here, yet it is also the only one to attempt to represent an inner process of coming to consciousness and to link it to the political interrogation of family psychology. It centres on the character of Ella (played by the film's director, Michka Gorki), her relationships with both women and men and her realisation of the way that they reproduce family patterns: she finds in her lovers mother, father, brother, sister. The film suggests both the oppressiveness of these patterns yet also their appeal in ideal form: if in practice relationships with men involve deception and submission, they need not do so and relationships, especially with women, always suggest the possibility of realising the nurture of family relations without the domination.

From the way the relationships are presented in *Ella*, it is not entirely clear where they are events, where memories or fantasies; she receives letters and answering machine messages, but by the end of the film we realise that she has sent some of them herself. This allows the film to operate at the level of the structure of desire, refusing a hard and fast distinction between how things are and how we want them to be, since the latter in part determines the former. If we can understand this, the film suggests, we can take control of the desires patriarchal society reproduces in us and make them over into our own.

The film operates with a notion of patriarchy as something extending beyond male advantage to the (characteristically masculine) authoritarian and repressive exercise of power, at all levels of the social order and in our minds. Imagery suggests the wider web of oppression (children at school shot through railings to suggest imprisonment; a sequence suggesting the nightmare of childbirth in a situation controlled by men; a down-trodden woman in the downstairs flat, unconvincingly extolling the fulfilment of house-wifery), while the familial form of Ella's relationships argues its reproduction in the fabric of desire. Yet the overall movement is towards the transcendence of patriarchy. At the beginning Ella meets a little girl coming from school, crying because she has a bad report to give to her mother. Ella comforts her, says she is not angry – but she is not her mother. At the end of the film they meet again and Ella says that one must choose one's family. 'Would you like me to be your mother?' she asks, and when the girl says yes, they run off into the country. This utopian, voluntaristic ending asserts the idea of creating the family one wants rather than reproducing, as Ella has up to now, the family patterns into which one is born.

Although Ella has relationships with both sexes, it is women who offer any sense of an alternative to patriarchal family patterns. At various points in the film, Ella's gypsy background is suggested by music and furnishings (to say nothing of her long raven black hair). In one of the more obviously fantasised sequences, she dances with and makes love to a gypsy woman, in a dreamily sensuous way that suggests this would be a full realisation of self and 'family', uniting both cultural and gender identity. By contrast, the most extended and least satisfactory relationship shown in the film is with an American man, a foreigner in nation and sex.

Yet *Ella* does not unequivocally show fulfilment in any sexual relation. Given its awareness of the pervasiveness of patriarchal familial patterns, it is perhaps hard for it to show, as well as assert the will for, non-oppressively familial relationships. It is as if the available imagery is so contaminated by patriarchy that there is no way of actually showing an alternative. This was one of the problems that faced those affirmation film-makers who responded to the movement's demand for positive images.

Positive images

Rather than analyse the situation of lesbian/gay people, most affirmation films sought to present a 'positive image' of lesbian/gay life-styles. Though the most frequently voiced demand made of the media by lesbians and gay men and seemingly straightforward, it raised two sets of issues, to do with imaging the positive and acknowledging the negative.

The imagery selected to show lesbian/gay life as positive depended upon prior assumptions about whether what is positive about it is the degree to which it is like straight life or the degree to which it differs from it. Most affirmation films seemed to suggest the former. *In the Best Interests* is full of scenes of everyday domesticity and playful interaction in its lesbian mother households, scenes which were tactically expedient for the film's agitational purpose and can be thought of as lesbian colonisation of the space of the familial, but which leave unchallenged the model of the nuclear family, which for many activists was the very fount of lesbian oppression. Similarly *Sandy and Madeline's Family* may both surprise by the fact that the family is composed of two women and their children but annoy by the absence of any questioning of family-ness or imagery of distinctly alternative lesbian life-styles.

The claim such films make is not that lesbians are the same as straight women, so much as that motherhood is the same, regardless of sexuality; the counter position is that heterosexuality has cornered the market on the definition of motherhood, as on everything else, and since those definitions involve the denigration of homosexuality, they should be resisted by gay/lesbian people. A similar kind of debate informed responses to *A Very Natural Thing*. This tells the story of David, who has an affair with Mark, which founders on Mark's wanting to have the right to go on seeing other men; a year after they break up, David meets Jason at a gay march but his previous experience makes him hesitant about committing himself; the film ends with the pair of them frolicking happily together in the sea. For most critics the film felt like a straight love story which just happened to be about two men, 'part of that tendency which integrates homosexuality into classic cinema' (Mazières 1978:40). Burton Stevens in *In Touch* (November 1974) couched his praise of the film in terms of the universality of both subject-matter and appeal, gays partaking in common human values: the director, Christopher Larkin, had succeeded brilliantly in 'describing an element of reality that exists in every human experience: love. *A Very Natural Thing* is a milestone for gay people and for all people who believe in love'.

Tom Waugh, on the other hand, argued that, because the film drew on the conventions of classic cinema, it denied the specificity of gay experience. Discussing the surf-and-sand ending ('a slow-motion sequence that bore the brunt of the outrage and criticism directed at the film' (Russo 1981:208)), Waugh recalled its initial impact, sending audiences out 'into the dark homophobic world with a euphoric, utopian energy' (1977:15) but argued that the imagery is derived from straight advertising (it 'could be part of a

Bahamas travel ad' (ibid.)) which makes it impossible for the film to imagine a specifically gay alternative to the heterosexual model of relationships supposedly rejected by the central character.

If some films defined lesbian/gay positiveness in terms laid down by straightness, others tried to show the value of distinctively lesbian or gay life-styles. *Il était une fois dans l'est* (Canada 1974 André Brassard) had charted the doings of a group of gay transvestites, their friends and lovers in Montréal, wholly accepting and delighting in their lives without questioning its circumstances or limitations. A few years later, *Outrageous!*, set in Toronto, had a similar starting point but in its development shows the impact of affirmation politics. What is most interesting about it is its relation to stereotypes of gay men, the target of so much gay criticism of the movies. The main character, Robin (Craig Russell), is a hairdresser who does drag shows on the side, two stereotypes for the price of one. Yet he is the hero of the film: the story is about his desire to become a star and if this classic narrative drive works, we root for him and feel satisfaction on his triumph in New York – the film has got us to identify with a queen. Yet *Outrageous!* was also one of the first films to show that not all gay men were queens, introducing the new macho style of gay culture. When Robin arrives in New York, he takes a taxi driven by a gruff, bearded man; however, when they arrive at a gay club, the driver, to Robin's and (presumably) our surprise, comes in with him, turning out to be one of the regulars. The film thus upsets stereotypical expectations twice over: first by making a hero out of a queen, second by not limiting the image of gay men to queenliness. Nor is there any antagonism between these gay styles: the driver becomes Robin's friend and agent, Robin's first success is with the leather and denim crowd. All of this is cast within an affirmation of gayness in terms of outsiderdom, realised through the character of Robin's schizophrenic sister, Lisa (Hollis McLaren). Informed by sixties ideas about madness (and especially schizophrenia) being socially, family induced (e.g. Laing and Esterson 1964), Lisa represents the sickness visited by straight society on women; the only support she gets is from those, like Robin and the gay world, who accept their own 'madness'. The film ends with Robin dancing with Lisa in a gay disco, saying over and over in his Tallulah Bankhead voice, 'Mad! Mad!', music and camera swirling in a celebration of outsiderdom (figure 5.5).

If constructing the positive raised difficulties, there was also a problem about not representing the negative. Although verbally most affirmation documentaries refer to the problems of being

5.5   Drag queen (Craig Russell as Tallulah Bankhead) and schizophrenic (Hollis McLaren) – the solidarity of outsiderdom in *Outrageous!* (National Film Archive)

5.6   Grainy, off-centre cruising in *Nighthawks*. (National Film Archive)

lesbian/gay in a homophobic society, they seldom show oppression from society or its negative consequences on lesbian/gay culture. The effect of privileging talking heads reminiscing from the vantage point of having been through CR and CO results in endless repetition of a story characterised by Cobbett Steinberg (1978:42) in reference to *Word is Out* as, 'I was miserable when young, straights fucked me over, finally I came out, was accepted by gays, and now everything is fine'. Steinberg, Olson (1979) and others argue that elimination of the negative both played down the scale of the oppression visited on lesbian/gay people and did not grasp the nettle of the divisions within the lesbian/gay community, most notably between women and men, but also between blatant and discreet styles, new political and old sub-cultural identities and the different wider political and social (notably class and ethnic) allegiances. Films like *L'Aspect rose* and *Gay USA* do show diversity but only *Witches and Dykes* begins to suggest that diversity can also mean conflict.

Yet where films do show the vicissitudes of lesbian/gay life, they run into other criticisms. The relentless return to sequences of seemingly joyless cruising (figure 5.6) and a final inferno-like shot of a vast gay disco made *Nighthawks* a downer for many gay viewers. Treating lesbian/gay problems seemed to have the effect of reasserting the inevitable association in straight cinema of homosexuality with problems and, often, tragedy. Films like *Jagdszenen aus Niederbayern* (BRD 1968 Peter Fleischmann), *Absences répétées* (France 1972 Guy Gilles), *Die Konsequenz* (BRD 1977 Wolfgang Petersen), *El Deputado* (Spain 1978 Eloy de la Iglesia), *Nous étions un seul homme* (France 1979 Philippe Valois) and *Liv og Død* (Norway 1980 Svend Wam and Peter Vennerød) show warmly affectionate relationships between men destroyed through, respectively, peasant proto-fascism, drug addiction, bourgeois respectability, political machination, straight identification and lumpen machismo – positive images curtailed by social repression. However, the lugubrious or elegiac tone of all but the last and the fact that all end in the deaths of the gay protagonists could also earn them a place in Russo's necrology, a list, appended to *The Celluloid Closet* (1981), of lesbian/gay deaths in straight movies.

An interesting variation on the problem of representing the negative is *Corner of the Circle* (USA 1975 Bill Daughton), made from the point of view of a central character, Arthur, who passes for straight at work, cruises at nights but is unable to develop relationships, even with a student, Bob, whom he picks up and really likes. Grainy black and white photography, bare apartments and scruffy streets and the film's ending (Arthur exposes himself at his window, cowers as police bang on his door and then next morning gets up and goes to work as normal) all combine with the sex versus commitment theme to create a familiar image of gay anomie. Yet the film also provides a perspective on Arthur's position, aware of the inadequacy of his life yet unable to make the leap to a whole-hearted gay existence for fear of losing the privilege of the status of being, as both he and Bob put it, 'in the mainstream'. In fact, this mainstream, at the office and at Arthur's parents', is shown to be unrelievedly dreary and, in Bob's openness, including his readiness to get involved in Gay Liberation (explicitly referred to), the possibility of something preferable is represented. *Corner of the Circle* thus knows about and probably approves of the gay movement, but prefers to explore what it is like to feel unable to be a part of it.

The dilemma – that by showing lesbians and gay men with problems the latter may appear to be an inevitable outgrowth of being lesbian/gay – has been avoided by some films made since 1980. In *Novembermond* (BRD 1984 Alexandra von Grote) and *Westler* (BRD 1985 Wieland Speck), the problems faced by the protagonists – respectively, a gentile-Jewish lesbian relationship in occupied France, a contemporary relationship between men from East and West Berlin – have nothing specifically to do with being lesbian or gay. Moreover, through courage and resourcefulness, the characters survive and with their love intact. *On Guard* (Australia 1983 Susan Lambert), *Territories* (GB 1984 Isaac Julien) and *The Passion of Remembrance* (GB 1986 Maureen Blackwood and Isaac Julien) place their lesbian and gay characters in the context of other political struggles, over reproductive technology in the case of the first and black and feminist politics in the latter (both made by the London based collective Sankofa). Lesbian/gay relations are suggested through simple, strong affirmative imagery – two women showering together in *On Guard*, the camera circling two bare shouldered men looking into each other's eyes in *Territories*, male lovers going out dancing and swimming in *Passion*. This contrasts with the violence of the rest of each film, the images working as touchstones of affection in a world of patriarchal manipulation and, in the Sankofa films, racial divisions. The latter make brilliant use of highly complex and rhythmic editing. In *Territories* the smooth circling shots of the men provide a formal and affective continuity underlying superimpositions that explore the discontinuities and fragmentations of British race history; in *Passion*, the sequences featuring the lovers, Gary and Michael, are straightforwardly shot, creating a kind of stability that contrasts with the tension of the ritualised debate and brilliant montage sequences that address issues of patriarchy and racial violence.

The hardest thing for affirmation cinema with the 'positive images' demand hanging over it was simply to take as a given the fact of being lesbian or gay and to construct a sense of the ordinariness of lesbian/gay life without winding up suggesting that it is either better or the same as straight life. Gay life has its own ordinariness, whether it is lived within straight or gay communities. Two films, *I'm not from here* and *Home-Made Melodrama*, are exceptional attempts to acknowledge this.

I'm not from here represents the ordinariness of gay life within the straight world. By using a recognisable iconography of an urban working-class milieu it breaks with the sense that there is anything distinctive or separate in class terms about gay people. The story has one startling event in it: a married man that the main character, Brian, has picked up, inexplicably drops dead. Remarkable though this is, it could of course happen to anyone, there is nothing specifically gay about it. Yet the particular anonymity of the cruising relationship, the problems of explaining the situation to police and family, the feelings of guilt (Brian apologises to God when the man drops dead), the vow never to do it again and the return to cruising at the end – all of these, while not unique to gay life, are characteristic of it, to the point of banality. The film's grainy, black and white photography and laconic rhythm, both familiar from naturalistic film traditions, point up the irony of the title, *I'm not from here*, for they insist that Brian, like all lesbian/gay people, is from 'here', the everyday world.

Home-Made Melodrama, on the other hand, takes as its starting point a lesbian milieu, and in fact a specifically lesbian feminist one. It uses the familiar melodramatic plot of a love triangle, though here between three women, and twists it by having the characters explore a three-way relationship as a positive alternative to both monogamy and one-night stands. Funding problems meant a considerable delay between shooting and editing, but this was turned to advantage by shooting further sequences, whose translucent 16mm look contrasts with the earlier footage's 8mm graininess; the new footage consists of three women in a car on their way to a women's march discussing their lives together. This enables the film to be more explicit about the politics of non-monogamy, distant enough to be open about the difficulties of putting it into practice and yet hanging on to the importance of trying to do so.

At one point in *Home-Made Melodrama*, the women in the car discuss an incident just shown in the story, when Katie throws a group of toy camels belonging to Jude on to the floor in the course of a row:

> 'I never threw your camels. I think this is Jacqui imposing something she never actually saw.'
> 'The camels are such a symbol of the nuclear family. I couldn't resist artistic licence.'

Here, as in the title's self-conscious reference to both home and melodrama, the film puts the fact of representation, the ideologically loaded choices involved, on to the agenda. Such awareness informs some of the other films discussed above, notably *Outrageous!* and the Sankofa films, but with important exceptions, affirmation cinema presented the question of representation, as of identity, as unproblematic.

Affirmation beyond the movement

Many films since 1970 have been made in the spirit of affirmation politics or, as is discussed in the section after this, moving on from it. The distinctions between films firmly within, influenced by or developing out of the movement are not hard and fast and in some cases are largely matters of emphasis and (my) judgement. All deserve fuller attention, and have generally not received it here due to lack of space, availability of prints and/or information. This section indicates the impact of affirmation politics in the two areas of production open to it, pornography and art cinema. It is only in the eighties that commercial entertainment cinema began to find a tiny space for lesbian/gay-themed films clearly made by and addressed (though not exclusively) to lesbian/gay people.[10]

The burgeoning of gay and, latterly, lesbian pornography, always a major economic enterprise, was nonetheless often done in a spirit of asserting the value of the homo-erotic. In France, as discussed above, porn was embraced by at least part of the gay movement and the connection was not lost on some US pornographers. *Pornography in Hollywood*, made by John Kirkland in the early seventies, intersperses interviews with gay activists and a de-frocked gay minister with nude go-go boys and hardcore sex; the earliest affirmation fiction film, *Happy Birthday Davy*, was made by a veteran of softcore porn, Richard Fontaine; Tom de Simone, a prolific gay porn film-maker, observed (Siebenand 1975:88):

> I think the fact that people can just walk into public theatres now and see homosexual films made by homosexuals for homosexuals and see ads for them in the daily papers is really something. I think these films can give gays a sense of identity, if nothing else.

Arthur Bressan's first porn film *Passing Strangers* 1976 sets its encounters in the context of a gay parade in San Francisco (as did *Celebrations* 1978 Zachary Youngblood) and, like Norbert Terry, Pat Rocco or Honey Lee Cottrell, Bressan moved between porn, experiment and agitation with no sense of contradiction. If one is affirming lesbian/gay identity, such work seems to say, then one must be affirming lesbian/gay sex.

Art cinema has been particularly accommodating to gay/lesbian film, partly because it is a space permitted to affect 'an attitude of high seriousness in matters sexual' (Merck 1986:166). Films made under its rubric[11] up to 1980 (and regrettably not discussed below) include *Ich liebe dich, ich töte dich* (BRD 1971 Uwe Brandner), *Children* (GB 1974 Terence Davies), *Manila* (Philippines 1975 Lino Brocka), *Johan, Carnet intime d'un homosexuel* (France 1976 Philippe Valois), *Un hombre llamado 'Flor de otoño'* (Spain 1977 Pedro Olea), *El Lugar sin limites* (Mexico 1977 Arturo Ripstein), *A un dios desconocido* (Spain 1977 Jaime Chavarri), *Showtime* (Australia 1978 Jan Chapman), *Dimenticare Venezia* (Italy 1979 Franco Brusati), *Ernesto* (Italy 1979 Salvatore Samperi), *Milan bleu* (France 1979 Jean-François Garsi), *Avskedet* (Finland/Sweden 1980 Tuija-Maija Niskanen), *Lieve Jonge* (Netherlands 1980 Paul de Lussanet) and *Tread Softly* (Australia 1980 Di Drew). Two groupings are particularly notable: New German Cinema and women in European art cinema.

Homosexuality had re-emerged as a subject in German cinema in the fifties in forms harking back to the Weimar period: the Hirschfeldian-sounding *Anders als Du und Ich* (aka *Das dritte Geschlecht*) 1957 and a re-make of *Mädchen in Uniform* 1958. Neither was a gay- or lesbian-made film, as is signalled by the difference in the title of the first from *Anders als die Andern*. A gay person could say the latter, indicating the otherness of the straight world, but *Anders als Du und Ich* firmly locates the film in the irremediably normal world of 'you and me', who could never be other. The German–Swiss film *Der Sittlichkeitsverbrecher* 1962 is an early film entry into the discourse of sexual permissiveness, including homosexuality, while from the end of the fifties, heterosexual pornography became a major feature of German film output and thus a major source of images of lesbianism. Classic twentieth-century German literature provided the occasion for more respectable treatments of male homosexuality in adaptations of Thomas Mann's *Tonio Kröger* in 1964 and Robert Musil's *Der junge Törless* in 1966. The latter is generally considered an early example of what has become known as New German Cinema and it is within this that gayness and lesbianism have figured so largely.

New German Cinema refers to those films made under the impetus of the 1962 Oberhausen Manifesto, a call by a group of young film-makers for a 'new' cinema in Germany. I do not intend to try to define or delineate it here,[12] beyond indicating that it is an art cinema, not mass audience popular (though often drawing on popular idioms), not tastefully literary and with strong modernist and postmodernist influences. The perception, and marketing, of NGC is in terms of directors: it is considered a cinema of authors, and many of these have been gay men treating gay subjects (Fassbinder, von Praunheim and Ripploh as well as Lothar Lambert (*Nachtvorstellungen* 1977, *Paso Doble* 1983), Martin Ripkens and Hans Stempel (*Wie geht ein Mann?* 1981, *Eine Liebe wie andere auch* 1983) and Werner Schroeter (*Der Rosenkönig* 1984–6)) or lesbians treating lesbian subjects (Mikesch and Treut, Ulrike Ottinger (*Bildnis einer Trinkerin* 1979, *Dorian Gray im Spiegel der Boulevardpresse* 1984) and Alexandra von Grote (*Weggehen um anzukommen* 1981)).[13]

One impact of the new feminism was a growth in the number of women who got to direct films within European art cinema, previously very much a preserve of the male auteur. It is striking how many of these films, though speaking from a heterosexual (or unclear) position, provide very affirmative images of lesbianism, often seen as an enviable alternative to relations between the sexes or else as part of an exploration of women bonding together, dissolving distinctions between comrades, friends and lovers. Examples include *Älskande Par* (Sweden 1965 Mai Zetterling), *Je tu il elle* (Belgium 1974 Chantal Akerman), *Das Ende der Beherrschung* (BRD 1976 Gabi Kuback), *Néa* (France/BRD 1976 Nelly Kaplan), *Das dritte Erwachen der Krista Klages* (BRD 1977 Margaretta von Trotta), *Io sono mia* (Italy 1977 Sofia Scandurra), *Rapunzel let down your hair* (GB 1978 London Women's Film Group), *Zwielicht* (Austria 1978 Margarete Heinrich) and *En Frouw als Eva* (Netherlands 1979 Nouchka van Brakel). In other cases the sexual dimension of characters' relationships is not clear, yet for many lesbians the relationships feel lesbian because of their intensity, closeness and commitment – for instance, *Les Stances à Sophie* (Canada 1970),[14] *La Vie rêvée* (Canada 1972 Mireille Dansereau), *Natalie Granger* (France 1972 Marguerite Duras), *Erikas Leiden-schaften* (BRD 1976 Ula Stöckl), *Riddles of the Sphinx* (GB 1977 Laura Mulvey and Peter Wollen), *Thriller* (GB 1979 Sally Potter) and *Coup de foudre* (France 1983 Diane Kurys).

Älskande Par (*Loving Couples*), a startlingly early and beautifully made film, illustrates the idea of lesbianism in these films. It is constructed out of the intertwined flashbacks of three women about to give birth in hospital: Adèle, an unhappily married woman whose baby is still-born, Agda, a happy-go-lucky 'model' who has the easiest birth and Angela, who lives with another woman, Petra, and who has a fine baby after a painful labour. Angela and Petra represent the only alternative to patriarchal exploitation in the film (symbolised by the severe hospital run by contemptuous male doctors), which bears out Angela's remark, that 'marriage is like falling asleep for the rest of your life'. Adèle's marriage is loveless. The man who makes Agda pregnant marries her off to a gay man, Stellan, an arrangement made between the two men without reference to her. At the wedding rehearsal Angela, seeing Stellan walk up the aisle with his boyfriend, runs out of the church into the snow and climbs a tree exultantly; when someone asks her what she is doing, she says, 'I'm celebrating my freedom'.

Angela is emotionally fulfilled through women. At finishing school, she and another woman, Stanni, are referred to as the 'loving couple' (the only pair who are referred to in terms of the film's title); her relationship with Petra is consistently affectionate and supportive, with Petra referring to the baby as 'our child'. A classic image of the lesbian as neurotic and predatory is evoked in the character of the teacher at finishing school, whose advances Angela rejects; but a more woman-identified construction of lesbianism, reminiscent of *Mädchen in Uniform*, is suggested between Angela and Petra. The latter was originally Angela's guardian after her father died, implying a mother-daughter quality to the bond. When Angela asks Petra why she has never married, she replies, 'it is because I am a woman'. Petra has earlier said that she finds it impossible to be 'feminine' in the way that society requires, but this femininity is the opposite of the womanhood realised in her relationship with Angela.

The idea of lesbianism as an extension of womanhood characterises women's art cinema films and echoes aspects of films discussed earlier (*Mädchen*, Deren, Hammer, *Anna und Edith*). Whilst for many lesbians this continuity is the defining characteristic of lesbianism, for others it is a myth that obscures the distinctiveness of lesbian identities. The lesbian friend with whom I most recently watched *Älskande Par* did not find it authentically lesbian at all, the character of the teacher functioning to represent and denigrate sexuality between women, rendering the relationship between Angela and Petra prettily asexual. Nothing perhaps illustrates better that lesbian (and gay) identities are not fixed categories but culturally perceived and constructed. The consequences of realising this were already beginning to unsettle some of the certainties of affirmation politics, and cinema, by the late seventies.

Post affirmation

Affirmation politics and cinema sought to replace negative feelings about lesbians and gay men with positive ones. Positive meant three, not altogether compatible things: thereness, insisting on the fact of our existence; goodness, asserting our worth and that of our life-styles; and realness, showing what we were in fact like. Thereness entailed constructing a sense of presence out of documentary's claim to transparency, with unclouded imagery and repeated life stories, the creation of fixed positions of knowledge from which to judge and assert the representation of what we are and a concomitant erasure of conflicts within the lesbian/gay community which would destabilise the sense of lesbian/gay being a definite thing. The goodness involved happy endings, smiling faces, the repetition of the life story as success, avoidance of narratives of intra-gay/lesbian conflict or internalised homophobia. Both thereness and goodness were at odds with the other positivity, realness – conflict, self-hate and oppression, to say nothing of the usual ragbag of human iniquities, are a part of gay/lesbian reality (and conflict is not even necessarily a negative one).

These contradictions can be recast in terms of the debate in lesbian/gay research between essentialism and social construction-ism, between, that is, a view of homosexuality as a given personality type found in one form or another in all cultures at all times, and a view that the very idea of such a fixed personality type is a modern one, part of a process of categorising sexuality in relation to persons not acts. Gay liberation had averred that lesbians and gay men were and had always been everywhere. The political need to create a sense of lesbians and gays as a people, as a constituency, called forth the intellectual need to establish for this people the fact of its universal presence, history and cultural heritage. Yet when sociologists and historians began to work on this they ran into major problems of recognition and definition. It turned out to be less easy to know when to consider a relation between women or between men relevant to the task; even the words homosexual, homo-erotic, lesbian or gay were hard to apply outside of Western culture since the nineteenth century. Many came to argue that, while affective and/or sexual acts between persons of the same sex were indeed a universal reality, the idea that people who engaged in them belonged to a distinctive category of persons (homosexuals, lesbians) was found only in modern times in the West. In the jargon of the debate, those who take this position see the very idea of a lesbian/gay person as one constructed through historical and social processes, whereas those who disagree operate with a sense of a fundamental gay/lesbian identity, manifest in different forms in different times and places but still in essence the same (cf. Niekerk and van der Meer 1989).

In this perspective affirmation politics is essentialist.[15] CR and CO structures and imagery imply the discovery of a sense of a self that is already there hidden inside one, and assert the basic, not just tactical, unity within the diversity of lesbian/gay people. The strength of this politics is precisely its definiteness, the sense of thereness, and the delight in being lesbian/gay. It provides inspiration and a sense of being to fuel the business of, in the words of Britain's notorious Clause 28, promoting homosexuality. Social constructionism, in contrast, can feel as if it is pulling the rug from under your feet, by making it seem as if you are not really there, are 'merely' a product of social forces. But constructionism does not deny the validity of homosexual life-styles, it simply casts the terrain of struggle differently, shifting it away from the idea of realising an essence towards a notion of a struggle over definitions, definitions which are historically produced and for that very reason amenable to change, definitions which do not reflect what lesbian/gay life must of necessity be but by which we nonetheless live. The possibility of a cinema based on this approach to gay/lesbian identity was suggested in the seventies by five films – *Maidens* Australia 1978, *Royal Opéra* France 1979, *In Black and White* Canada 1979, *Comedy in Six Unnatural Acts* USA 1975 and *Madame X – eine absolute Herrscherin* BRD 1977. The first is aware of the question of definition, although from what remains an essentialist vantage point;

the second explores the way in which we inhabit discourses of essentialism; the other three move away from essentialism altogether.

Maidens

Thematically, *Maidens* resembles *After the Game* or *Anna und Edith* in its sense of lesbianism growing out of and into other kinds of relationships between women, sharpened by the contrast with relations between men and women; stylistically, it is closer to cultural feminist films with its iconography of nature, pregnancy, water and bare breasted women, its verbal imagery of female bonding ('we made each of ourselves the mother and daughter of each of the others') and its structures of repetition and superimposition. What it also has is a more self-conscious relation to imagery. Like *Home Movie*, it uses photographs and films in the family collection of the film-maker, Jenni Thornley, combined with other material (vérité style family rows, symbolic set pieces), to interrogate not only her own personal development but that of women in Australia.

The central section of the film is built principally out of the family collection material. The ordering is chronological and the voice relates the imagery to the developing fortunes of white settlers in Australia, the impact of two World Wars and so on; but there is also another history – or, indeed, herstory – unfolding, that of the bonds between women. The voice over suggests that one see the family chronology as a chain of mothers and discerns a pattern of maidenhood, whereby the bonds of women are periodically broken by the obligation to relate to men. Thus a posed photo of a group of schoolgirls (figure 5.7) is accompanied by the words, 'School was a time for women to be together before falling in love with the men, to be divided and ruled again', suggesting a way of reading the image against its grain. As the film develops, the security of this pattern begins to break down. A succession of snapshots of women together without men during the Second World War unfolds, another interlude when women could be 'maidens again'. One shows a woman resting her head on another's shoulder; the image fades but then, unprecedentedly, it returns, closer up and held for longer than usual; the easy flow of maiden imagery is interrupted to register the possibility of more powerful bonds at work than snapshot formulae intend.

From this point on the presentation of imagery is never so secure.

5.7 Reading against the grain in *Maidens* – schoolgirls as 'women together
. . . before being divided and ruled'. (National Film Archive)

More material, Thornley's and other people's, creeps in, vérité
sequences showing power struggles and exploitation within the
family, violent imagery (blood, knives, tears) indicating a crisis of
identity, sharpened by shots of a woman looking at herself on film
that we have already seen, at herself in a mirror, with the voice
shifting from 'I' to 'you'. This builds up to a confrontation with a
man in a kitchen followed by her running along until there is a cut
to her dressed in fur, like a stone-age woman, leaping down a path,
followed by shots of women together, bathing, making love,
chopping wood, pregnant, a repeat of the opening section of the
film. The imagery and circular structure suggest an embrace of
maidenhood, of bonding with women, that through radical feminist
culture will no longer be temporary. There is thus a sense of a
position of true identity from which the central deconstruction of
other feminine identities can be viewed.

Royal Opéra

Royal Opéra is the last section of *Race d'ep!* (see above). Unlike its
preceding sections, which present moments of gay history illustrated
from contemporary documents, this section, exemplifying the
seventies, uses a fictional form. An American meets a Frenchman in
a gay bar in Paris, the Royal Opéra; they chat and go for a walk in

the Tuileries (a well-known cruising area), call in on a public toilet and wind up by the Seine. We do not hear what they say to each other but rather their alternating voices recalling what passed between them. It is the radical disjuncture of their accounts that suggests the degree to which reality, including gay identity, is subject to discourse, to the frameworks of understanding available to us.

The American, whose recollections seem to be an internal monologue, sees himself as a straight man who happened to wander into a gay bar and spend an intriguing, but finally embarrassing evening with a French queer. The Frenchman, on the other hand, gossiping on the phone to a friend, claims it was a meaningful encounter with a Russian, which ended in their going to a hotel together. At first sight, it might seem that it is clearly the Frenchman who has got the wrong end of the stick: the other man is American, there is no evidence that they slept together. But it is clear that the American also wants the Frenchman to have been a certain kind of person. We hear the latter prattling about romance, the size of the American's penis, other queens about the place; but the American constructs him as a determined marginal, a sexual anarchist opposed to the integration of gay people into society. He sees this as so different from the gays he knows back in the States, but '. . . I found this touching, a bit naïve, very *continental*, this idea of being an "outlaw", no matter what' (my emphasis). Though the name is not mentioned, the American seems to want to make the Frenchman conform to a 'Genet' model of queer revolt.

The film is not simply opposing two irreconcilable perceptions of the same sequence of events. The Frenchman performs in a sub-cultural mode made passé by the American influence on international gay culture (cf. Altman 1982); whatever his views on the matter might be, his whole-hearted embrace of the 'folle' (queen) repertoire does militate against his integration with straight society. Neither voice is entirely wrong, but both can only construct the encounter in their minds according to the categories at their disposal. Nor is there a position for the spectator outside of these competing definitions of the situation. The visual evidence does not tell us 'what really happened'. In the Tuileries, shots of male nude statues both heighten the homo-erotic atmosphere and yet remind us of the gardens' official identity, suggesting the degree to which, especially in a gay context, appearances are open to cultural use. Towards the end there is a montage of snaps of the pair together, providing fixed mementoes of the encounter, but right at the end these snaps fly up into the air and fall into the dingy water of the Seine, as if to symbolise the insecurity of the photograph as a record of reality. Both voices speak as if there is an essential gay reality here to be grasped, but the film indicates that such essentialisms are themselves constructions.

In Black and White

A man goes into a public toilet, hangs about; another man comes in and they go into a cubicle and start having sex; they are interrupted and arrested by the police. The centre of *In Black and White* is this simple narrative; its presentation suggests that what you think of it depends on how, literally as well as metaphorically, you see it.

The film opens with close-ups of hands exploring someone's back as they embrace, then a hand caressing a nipple, then kissing. Over these tenderly sensual images, one hears a discussion between a man (presumably the film-maker, Michael McGarry) and woman about how to portray the 'erotic interaction of two men making love', the woman stressing the need to bring out the 'human-ness of sexuality' and the man saying, as if countering an implication in the woman's remarks, 'can't you be sensual with each other's genitals?' This sense of wanting to value sex for itself, neither redeeming it by reference to other values nor accepting a brutal notion of raw sex, is echoed later, when the male voice says, apropos of anonymous sex, 'does impersonal have to be insensitive?' The opening images of sexuality are repeated in the toilet, when the men go into the cubicle, carrying the theoretical debate about how to 'see' sexuality over into a narrativised encounter, that is, from an issue we may think about to a situation we may identify with.

Towards the end of the opening sequence, the image is worked: frozen, reversed, until the camera zooms back to show we are watching a video image. The full significance of this only emerges towards the end of the narrative, when it becomes clear that what we have been seeing is closed-circuit material on a police surveillance monitor. What can be seen by gay men as sensitivity is criminality in the eye of the police. There is discussion over the credits of the issue of sex in toilets, ending with the male voice saying, 'it's a public place, but Jeez, you don't see anyone', a tough irony, because the film has shown that the intimate, by connotation unseen, imagery of the opening shots is indeed seen, and its significance transformed, in the era of hi-tech surveillance.

Comedy in Six Unnatural Acts

Comedy, made by Jan Oxenburg, takes six stereotypes of lesbians in six sections – can't-get-a-man in 'Wallflower', butch:femme in 'Role Playing', outdoor girls in 'Seduction', radicalesbian in 'Non-monogamy', pervert in 'Child Molester' and bull dyke in 'Stompin' Dyke' – and plays with them, not in order to dismiss them but to try out responses to them and tease out some of their implications.

Each act has, as it were, a punch line playing on the expectations stereotypes set in motion. The woman who can't get anyone to dance with at the school hop at last looks up with delight into the eyes of someone requesting the pleasure, a woman. The butch prepares for a date and goes to meet her, another butch. The outdoor girls talk about everything but what's really on their minds until their hands touch and they are in the middle of a musical number. A woman juggles apples symbolising the non-monogamy celebrated in a tract on the soundtrack; but the juggling goes awry, apples get dropped, she resorts to hiding one apple behind her back while furiously juggling two others, until, as the voice over becomes more and more strident, she starts taking bites out of the apples, finally gagging on them. The child molester sets out to entice two little girls with cookies, but they kiss each other leaving the pervert stranded. Finally a dyke gets off her bike and the world – groups of men, couples, pigeons, finally the sea itself – parts before her. What the stereotype leads us to expect to happen either doesn't (the wallflower gets a woman, the butch a butch; non-monogamy runs amok, the child molester is confounded by child sexuality) or happens with glorious exaggeration (love is a cue for a number, the seas part).

Each ending is a happy one (apart from 'Non-monogamy' and even that ends with the juggler laughing as she gags), but often ironically presented. The female couple in 'Wallflower' walk through their schoolmates throwing confetti over them, treating them to the rites of heterosexuality. Behind them is a pennant with 'West' on it, the symbol of US optimism – only it actually points east. The main dancer in 'Seduction' emerges out of, then leads all the dancers into, a jacuzzi, the arch-symbol of happiness California-style. All of 'Stompin' Dyke' is a happy ending to the film as a whole, the world parting before the powerful lesbian, played however by the most petite, delicately featured woman in the whole film.

Further resonances of the stereotypes are suggested by reference to film corventions: the school hop scene, focusing on men pawing at women; the high glow of glamour lighting for butch grooming in 'Role Playing'; the accoutrements of romance (candelabras, wine, a violinist) and then a musical number in 'Seduction'; silent melodrama, with piano rag accompaniment, in 'Child Molester' with at the end a Nosferatu-like shadow of the pervert walking off. Still further play is possible. The butch grooms herself with exaggerations of masculinity: a screwdriver to open the jar of gel, great fistfuls of the stuff on her hair, slapping perfume on like aftershave. The chorus girls in 'Seduction' nonetheless wear regulation dyke attire: shirts, jeans, braces and sneakers.

There is no fixed strategy in *Comedy*. It plays equally with movie images, traditional sub-cultural styles and lesbianfeminist ideals; it is equally prepared to appropriate movie styles to celebrate lesbianism (the spectacle of the dance number and the exhilarating special effect of the parting sea) or to mock straight perceptions (the exaggerated villainy of the child molester). The self-confidence of affirmation politics makes such an assured examination possible, so much so that there is no need to roundly condemn anything or assert unproblematically positive alternatives. What is positive about the film is its assumption that lesbians are strong enough to be able to work with and against definitions of themselves, strong enough to have humour, even at their own expense.

Madame X – eine absolute Herrscherin

Madame X (an Absolute Ruler), made by Ulrike Ottinger who was mentioned above in the context of New German Cinema, is a film that has been taken as both an adventure film for dykes and an endlessly shifting deconstruction of the imagery of adventure for women (cf. Hake 1988–9). It is both: the latter makes the former possible.

Madame X and her servant Hoi-Sin gather together a group of women on her pirate ship Orlando and they set sail, picking up later the androgynous Belcampo; seduction and power play are the order of the day on board, with all the women dying yet at the end coming back to life, transformed, sailing off with renewed energy and inspiration. This rudimentary adventure story structure is playfully filmed and performed. Genre reference, title and characterisation all refer to already available imagery, but none taken over in any sense straight and all leading to adventure.

The possibility of putting lesbians at the centre of traditionally male-oriented genres is not one that has so far been much pursued by lesbian cinema (unlike lesbian writing). *On Guard* and *De Stilte rond Christine M.* (Netherlands 1982 Marleen Gorris) use thriller and detective genres respectively and *Ninja* (USA 1977 Christine Mohanna) is a portrait of a young lesbian who lives her life according to the Japanese samurai code, but these are exceptions. *Madame X* too puts women at the centre of a male genre but not just so as to give women a piece of the action. The genre chosen is already a marginal one (the corpus of pirate movies is small), making this an intervention in marginality. At the same time the reality of women pirates, as recent historical research shows (e.g. De Pauw 1982), means that the choice of genre not only makes a point about media images but has a resonance of historical discourse behind it. Thus the film takes on some of the pleasures of action and adventure reserved for men, recognises its own marginality and the fact that there is nonetheless a real female tradition behind its desirable imagery. Similarly, the title is that of a thrice-made, archetypal Hollywod women's picture. This *Madame X* is a very different sort of women's picture, action/adventure not weeping and suffering, yet the title still retains the notion of mystery, of a question mark hanging over female identity, just as it does in Hollywood cinema. Again, the women in the film are emblematic, some of traditional female roles in a heterosocial world (Blowup, a pin-up; Betty Brillo, a US housewife; Noa-Noa from Tai-Pi, thrown out by her husband for breaking a taboo; Carla Freud-Goldmund, servicing male intellectualism), others of women's potential for physical action (Flora Tannenbaum, a traditionally German outdoor type; Omega Centauri, an Australian bush-pilot with a yen to be an astronaut; Josephine de Collage, a roller skating avant-garde artist). At the end they take on still other media-familiar images, yet all become pirates.

The film submits images of women and what one can do with them to a process of scrutiny, and in the process brings them round to affirm not so much present lesbian reality as the ideal of 'a homosocial world' (White 1987:84). The sexuality shown explores the boundaries of power within relationships, anticipating the lesbian sado-masochism explored in *Verführung: die grausame Frau*. The names and the exaggerated playing suggest both camp, a largely neglected aspect of *lesbian* culture, and the lesbian cult of sportswomen and others, both of which complement Madame X's own sub-cultural style, with her all-leather, Hosenrolle outfits (figure 5.8) and ship named in honour of Virginia Woolf's most

5.8 *Madame X*'s leather outfit. (National Film Archive)

sexually ambivalent novel. The figure of Belcampo reinforces the sense of a homosocial world in two ways: the women are initially suspicious of this man in a skirt, but come to accept him as part of their masquerade, the chosen refusal of the norm; he has a romance with a sailor, bringing male gay relations into the film's homosocial world. *Madame X* knows that such a world is not unproblematic, either in terms of knowing what it would be like or as something that could be brought about, but you feel it wants it and suggests that the way to get it is to make use of the backlog of images of women. Hence the process of deconstructing this imagery is not just to make a point, but becomes itself a fun adventure. By taking possession of the imagery, the film has the women make it their own, enabling them to sail forth to excitement.

Films like these anticipate the postmodern lesbian and gay films of the eighties,[16] alongside many in other styles, some even making it to the margins of mainstream entertainment cinema (*Desert Hearts*, *Parting Glances*). What is remarkable is the way that post-affirmation cinema combines an awareness of surface, construction and play with a sense of urgency and edge. Its touch is light, its approach eclectic yet it moves beyond the quality of many of its postmodern peers, in which there is a bit of this and a bit of that but nothing much matters.

This is in part because, no matter how sophisticated one's take on lesbian/gay identity, it is hard to pursue and express a gay/lesbian existence without knowing what is ranged against it. The repository of images of oppression, devastating in their scale and implication – pink triangles in the Nazi death camps, the Cuban UMAP camps and subsequent lesbian/gay exodus, the Harvey Milk assassination (and light sentence received by his assassin) – intensifies what the lesbian/gay press report week in, week out: beatings, arrests, court cases, discrimination, murder. Moreover, post-affirmation cinema is produced in a period of retrenchment against lesbian/gay sexuality, embodied in the US Supreme Court sodomy ruling and in Britain's Clause 28, reaction mobilised through the spectre of AIDS. It is hard in this context to be skimmingly superficial. At the same time, post-affirmation films draw on a long tradition within lesbian/gay culture. There is nothing new, nothing all that eighties for us about surface culture. Lesbian/gay culture has always been aware of surface, of the construction of appearance – as a perception of the straight world, as an ironic distance on it, as a strategy for survival within it. Surface and construction are valued for their own sake within lesbian/gay culture, because we see what is at stake in them. Post-affirmation cinema thus mobilises, in a situation of intensified oppression and conscious politicisation, specifically lesbian/gay traditions, reaching back through and beyond many of the moments of gay/lesbian cultural production touched on in this book. Its play is doubly grounded, in political realities and cultural traditions. It is art for which mattering still matters.

*   *   *

Politics demands immediacy and clarity. Lesbian/gay movements, like any other, need films that tell people who is speaking (who the movement is) and what to do. *In dit teken* is an established organisation of homosexual people telling other homosexual people to join them and to lead a respectable life. Confrontational films defy straight and gay viewer alike with the film-makers' own sexuality and with the viewers' own responses to it, to jerk them out of apathy into liberation. Affirmation cinema presents lesbians and gay men presenting themselves, calling forth identification from the lesbian/gay audience, unconditional acceptance from the straight.

Art however is never as ruly as politics needs it to be. Even *In dit teken* lets slip that there might be other and as appealing ways of being gay. Because of the feelings and responses it sets out to stir up, confrontational cinema could feed guilt and self-hate, turn off as likely as turn on. Affirmation cinema stumbles across the contradictions of 'simply' showing us as we really are, accentuating the positive at the expense of recognising the negative and hence the need for struggle. Out of these contradictions, and as a result of affirmation cinema's stress on the importance of how we are represented, emerged a cinema which systematically undercuts affirmation's certainties while still being glad to be lesbian/gay.

Movement cinema is to this extent just another version of the old tussle between art and politics, but its many variations also echo the very enterprise of creating lesbian/gay films, or identities or cultures, at all. They are, like all ideology, necessary fictions. They are not the 'truth', but without them we do not live. (Humans could live, and do and have, in worlds without gay/lesbian identities and cultures, though not without gay/lesbian acts; but we do not live in such a world and cannot magically transport ourselves to one.) It is hard to hold on to both sides of the formulation 'necessary fictions', the sense that they are constructions, not inevitable outgrowths of reality, which we do, all the same, really need. The many gyrations of lesbian/gay film – to take only the instance examined in this book – are part of the ceaseless process of construction, reconstruction and deconstruction of identities and cultures, ceaseless because experience always outstrips constructions so that they are never quite satisfactory, never quite get it, and yet also ceaseless because we need constructions in order to make sense of experience at all. This is what it means to live in society (and there is nowhere else to live and be human). Lesbian/gay culture is different only to the degree to which the erasure of the gap between construction and experience is less naturalised than with many other human categories (notably race, gender and, supremely, hetero-sexuality) and thus in its high degree of awareness of that gap. This – and the simple need to express in order to survive, to be seen to be believed – is why lesbians and gay men have to go on making lesbian and gay films which all the while may betray the folly of the enterprise.

Translations of titles

(Titles of films discussed at length are translated at that point in the text.)

Absences répétées	*Repeated Absences*
'adame Miroir	*'adam Mirror*
A la Recherche des Amazones	*In Search of Amazons*
Allemagne après la débâcle, L'	*Germany after the Collapse*
Amitié, L'	*Friendship*
Amour à la mer, L'	*Love at Sea*
Anders als du und ich	*Different from You and Me*
aka *Das dritte Geschlecht*	aka *The Third Sex*
Anna la bonne	*The maid Anna*
Aspect rose de la chose, L'	*The Pink Side of Things*
A un dios desconocido	*To an Unknown God*
Aus eines Mannes Mädchenjahren	*From a Man's Virgin Years*
Avskedet	*Farewell, The*
Bagge, Le	*Penal Servitude*
Bara no soretsu	*Funeral Parade of Roses*
Beau Mec, Le	*The Handsome Stud* (US: *Dude*)
Belle et la bête, La	*Beauty and the Beast*
Bildnis des Dorian Gray, Das	*The Portrait of Dorian Gray*
blaue Engel, Der	*The Blue Angel*
Blauer Dunst	*Blue Mist*
Bildnis einer Trinkerin	*Portrait of a (woman) Drunkard*
bitteren Tränen der Petra von	*The Bitter Tears of Petra von*
Kant, Die	*Kant*
Bögjävlar	*Damned Queers*
Bonnes, Les	*The Maids*
Büchse der Pandora, Die	*Pandora's Box*

Carnet rose d'un homosexuel, Le	*A Homosexual's Pink Note-book*
Cenerella, psicofavola femminista	*Cinderella, a Feminist Psycho-tale*
certain Désir, Un	*A Certain Desire*
Chambre des phantasmes, La	*The Bedroom of Fantasy*
Chants de Maldoror, Les	*Songs of Maldoror*
Chez les mauvais garçons	*Down among the Bad Boys*
Condamné à mort, Le	*The Man Condemned to Die*
Coup de foudre	*Love at First Sight* (GB: *At First Sight*, US: *Entre Nous*)
Couronne d'or	*Crown of Gold*
De l'abjection	*Of Abjection*
Dämon und Mensch	*Demon and Human*
Dimenticare Venezia	*Forget Venice*
Diputado, El	*Deputy, The*
Dorian Gray im Spiegel der Boulevardpresse	*Dorian Gray in the Mirror of the Gutter Press*
dritte Erwachen des Krista Klages, Das	*The Third Awakening of Krista Klage*
Dr Mabuse der Spieler	*Dr Mabuse the Gambler*
Du er ikke alene	*You are not alone*
Du Sang, de la volupté et de la mort	*Of Blood, Voluptuousness and Death*
Eaux d'artifice	*Water Works*
Eigene, Der	*The Special*
eiserne Kreuz, Das	*The Iron Cross*
Ende der Beherrschung, Das	*The End of Domination*
Erikas Leidenschaften	*Erika's Passions*
Es schienen so golden die Sterne	*The Stars Shone so Golden*
Es werde Licht!	*Let There be Light!*
Érotisme en face, L'	*Eroticism from the Other Side* (GB: *The Other Face of Love*)
éternel Retour, L'	*The Never-ending Return*
Et . . . Dieu créa les hommes	*And . . . God created Men*
Exzellenz Unterrock	*Petticoat Excellency*
Fall des Generalstabs-Oberst Redl, Der	*The Case of General Staff Officer Oberst Redl*
Faustrecht der Freiheit	*Freedom's Survival of the Fittest* (GB/US: *Fox and his Friends*)

Faux-monnayeurs, Les	*The Counterfeiters*
Fleurs du mal, Les	*Flowers of Evil*
Frauen und die Liebe, Die	*Women and Love*
Freundin, Die	*The Friend* (female)
Gang in die Nacht, Der	*Journey into the Night*
Geräusch rascher Erlösung, Das	*The Sound of Quick Relief*
Geschlecht in Fesseln	*Sex in Shackles*
Gesetze der Liebe	*Laws of Love*
Gestern und heute	*Yesterday and To-day*
Hiver approche, L'	*Winter Comes*
Hoffmanns Erzählungen	*Tales of Hoffmann*
Hombre llamado 'Flor de Otoño', Un	*A Man called 'Autumn Flower'*
Homme blessé, L'	*The Wounded Man*
Homme de désir, L'	*Man of Desire*
Homme nu, L'	*The Naked Man*
Hommes entre eux	*Men Together*
Homologues ou la soif du mâle	*Homologies or Thirst for a Man*
Hund von Baskerville, Der	*The Hound of the Baskervilles*
Hyänen der Lust	*Hyenas of Lust*
Ich für Dich, Du für Mich	*I for You, You for Me*
Ich liebe dich, ich töte dich	*I Love You, I Kill You*
Il était une fois dans l'est	*Once Upon a Time in the East*
Io sono mia	*I am mine*
Jahrbuch für sexuelle Zwischenstufen	*Yearbook for Intersexual Variants*
Januskopf, Der	*The Janus Head*
Je tu il elle	*I You He She*
Jeune homme et la mort, Le	*Death and the Young Man*
Jugend und Tollheit	*Youth and Madness*
junge Törless, Der	*Young Törless*
Kabinett des Dr Caligari, Das	*The Cabinet of Dr Caligari*
Knabe in Blau, Der	*The Blue Boy*
Laster, Das	*Vice*
Liebe wie andere auch, Eine	*A Love like Any Other*
Lila Nächte	*Lilac Nights*

Lieve Jonge	*Dear Boys*
Liv og Død	*Life or Death*
Livre blanc, Le	*The White Book*
Lugar sin limites, El	*A Place without Limits* (GB/US aka *Hell Without Limits*)
Marche funèbre	*Funeral March*
Masque de chair	*Mask of Flesh*
Miracle de la rose	*Miracle of the Rose*
Nächte der Weltstadt	*Nights in the Metropolis*
Nachtvorstellungen	*Late Night Shows*
Notre-Dame des fleurs	*Our Lady of the Flowers*
Nous étions un seul homme	*We were one Man*
Oiseaux de la nuit, Les	*Night Birds*
Orphée	*Orpheus*
petit Réverbère, Le	*The Little Street Lamp*
prisonnier, Le	*The Prisoner*
Puppenjunge, Der	*The Rentboy* (US: *The Hustler*)
Ritter Nérastan	*Nérastan the Knight*
Rosenkönig, Der	*The Rose King*
Sens interdits	*No Entries*
Sept images impossibles	*Seven Impossible Images*
Sfratto nello spazio	*Ejected from Space*
Sibille, Le	*The Sibyls*
Sind es Frauen?	*Are These Women?*
Sittlichkeitsverbrecher, Der	*The Sex Criminal*
Sonnet du trou du cul	*Sonnet to the Arsehole*
Stadt der verlorenen Seelen	*City of Lost Souls*
Stances à Sophie, Les	*Stanzas to Sophie*
Stilte rond Christine M., De	*The Silence around Christine M.* (GB/US: *A Question of Silence*)
Student von Prag, Der	*The Student of Prague*
Tagebuch einer Verlorenen, Das	*The Diary of a Lost Girl*
Testament des Dr Mabuse, Das	*The Testament of Dr Mabuse*

Unheimliche Geschichten	*Strange Tales*
Vice organisé en Allemagne, Le	*Organised Vice in Germany*
Vingarne	*The Wings*
vierde Man, De	*The Fourth Man*
Vie rêvée, La	*Dream Life*
vreemde Vogel, Een	*A Strange Bird*
Vrouw als Eva, Een	*A Woman Like Eva*
Weggehen um anzukommen	*Depart to Arrive*
Wie geht ein Mann?	*What does a Man do?*
Wir vom dritten Geschlecht	*We of the Third Sex*
zweite Erwachen der Christa Klages, Das	*The Second Awakening of Christa Klages*
Zwielicht	*Twilight*

Notes

INTRODUCTION

1 The filmography in *Gays and Film*, updated by Mark Finch in 1984, lists over 1300 titles (Dyer 1984: 69–107).
2 See Russo 1981 and Becker *et al.* 1981.

1 WEIMAR: LESS AND MORE LIKE THE OTHERS

1 *Vingarne* Sweden 1916, briefly discussed later in the chapter, is the single possible exception. Its recent re-discovery (it having been assumed completely lost) came too late for proper consideration here. But see Finch 1987.
2 There is a huge literature on Weimar and how it is to be characterised. The range of views is usefully summarised in Willett 1984:12–13; compare also the discussion in Burns 1977:123ff.
3 On *Nosferatu* as a gay film, see Mayne 1986, Wood 1979.
4 For further discussion, see chapter four.
5 Busse, Elisabeth (1931) 'Das moralische Dilemma in der modernen Mädchen-erziehung'. In Ada Schmidt-Beil (ed), *Die Kultur der Frau*, Berlin:594. Quoted in Pieper 1984:121.

2 SHADES OF GENET

1 For details of the prints see Giles 1988.
2 The scenes are – a Mexican and a statue of the Virgin being repeatedly shot at, the man dying but coming back to life, the statue shattering but becoming whole again; a little girl learning to fly, being taught by a governess brandishing a whip; opium smoking; an hermaphrodite.
3 For a feminist rejection of Millett's appropriation of Genet, see Cochart and Pigache 1976.
4 For further explication of these ideas, see Kaplan 1983, Kuhn 1982.
5 One of Oswald's examples of shot/reverse-shot inaccuracy is the cut from the guard looking at the garland to the garland itself: 'the guard looking up in the opening shots is seen in medium long shot. . . . The subsequent shot of prison windows is in close-up and from a different eye level than the guard's look' (1983:111). In fact inaccuracies of this

kind are entirely acceptable within the continuity editing system, as a close examination of any mainstream Hollywood film will show. So powerful is the convention (that what follows a shot of someone looking is what they see) that it can even accommodate such gross inaccuracies as the one cited by Oswald where there is a cut from the guard looking through the peephole to a close-up of a prisoner's erect penis against the wall. Technically, the guard cannot possibly see this, but the editing convention is probably stronger than the spectator's consciousness of spatial accuracy. In the case of the shots of the performer looking at the camera, all of these are within the guard's point-of-view shots, so that they can be read as addressed to the guard/us but do not entail the spectator being conscious of the presence of the camera.

6 'It is nothing more than hard-core pornography and should be banned', verdict of a California appellate court, quoted in de Grazia and Newman 1982:287; 'The nearest any pornographic film comes to being definitive is, I believe, Jean Genet's *Un Chant d'amour*', Peter de Rome, gay pornographic film-maker (1984:162).

3 UNDERGROUND AND AFTER

1 Mostly in New York (Cooper 1986:113ff,163–4, 202ff).
2 The part is in fact played by a man, Carmillo Salvatorelli, a professional circus dwarf.
3 In interviews, Anger sometimes claims *Fireworks* was based on an actual dream he had had (Hardy 1982:30), at others that it is just 'a dream situation' (Hamilton 1977:22), at others that it is a conscious statement ('This flick is all I have to say about being seventeen, the United States Navy, American Christmas, and the Fourth of July' (Sitney 1979:101)).
4 Opinions differ as to whether this second 'creature' is in fact a woman. She has breasts, dwelt on in the rape scene, and a vagina, clearly shown in the same scene, but Ken Kelman says that Jack Smith says s/he was an hermaphrodite (Kelman 1963:4). The confusion is of course characteristic of the film. I certainly did not assume that s/he was a woman until the glimpse of the vagina and even so, breasts can be implanted or hormone induced, genitalia have been known to be confused.
5 The most complete attempts at Warhol filmographies are in Coplans 1970, and Apra and Ungari 1972.
6 There is also a European gay underground, which merits fuller consideration and of which I can only indicate some examples here: Yann Beauvais (*Homovie* 1976–7, *Amoroso* 1983–6), Sylvano Bussotti (*Rara Film* 1975, *Immagine* [co-d. Romano degli Amidei] 1976), Heinz Emigholz (*Die Basis des Make-Up* 1979–84), Steve Farrer (*Ten Drawings* 1976), Bruno de Florence (*Un certain Désir* 1980), Téo Hernandez (*Salome* 1975, *Luna India* 1976), Amet Kut (*Gilles, José, Marcel* 1978), Robert Malengreau (*Sept Images impossibles* 1979), Roland Mahauden (*Amen* 1974), Michel Nedjar (*Angle* 1976), Lennaert Nijgh (*Een vreemde vogel* 1967), Oscar Melano (*Sfratto nello spazio* 1980), Bernt de Prez (*Art.i.cul.ation II* 1980), Lloyd Reckord (*Dream A40* 1965), Georges Rey (*L'Homme nu* 1969), Mattijn Seip (*Ijdijk* 1966,

Schemerhoorn 1966), Wieland Speck (*David, Montgomery und Ich* 1980). See also the appendix to chapter two and the section on Confrontational Politics in chapter five.

7 '. . . shooting at between three to six frames per second, and refilming it projected at the same speeds [producing] a strong painterly texture and pulsating rhythm . . . sensual, dream-like and erotic' (O'Pray 1985:9).

4   LESBIAN/WOMAN: LESBIAN CULTURAL FEMINIST FILM

1 There is also European work in this vein, but films such as those of Lina Mangiacapre (*Cenerella, psicofavola femminista* 1974, *Le Sibille* 1979), Martine Rousset (*Le Petit Réverbère* 1977, the *Carolyn* series 1977–81), Marcelle Thirache (*A la Recherche des Amazones* 1986) and the Collettivo Alice Guy (*Affetuosamente ciak* 1979) must alas remain, as they say, a subject for further research.

2 Cf. Judith Kegan Gardiner's comparison of splitting and fragmenting male characters in male writing with female characters dissolving and blurring into one another in female writing (1982:184–5).

3 Written in December 1970 for the *New York Times* but rejected by them and first published in part by Jill Johnston in her *Village Voice* column in March 1972; reprinted in full in Phyllis Birkby *et al. Amazon Expedition* (New York Times Change Press) in 1973 but quoted here from Atkinson's collection of writings *Amazon Odyssey* published in 1974.

4 Kimball draws here on the work of Ornstein (1972) and Hutt (1978), work which is disputed by Fausto-Sterling (1986).

5 Cf. arguments about gay men and witchcraft discussed in the previous chapter.

6 A more critical treatment of the relevance of love and romance to lesbian desire is *Farewell to Charms* Australia 1979 Carla Pontiac.

7 A possible antecedent is the 1968 film *Angélique in Black Leather*, produced, directed by and starring Angélique Bouchet and featuring only lesbian characters. The action consists apparently (American Film Institute Catalog, Feature Films 1961–1970:32) chiefly of power games; no male character comes to 'convert' the women as is usual in heterosexual male porn. I have however no knowledge of whether the film was conceived of as lesbian entertainment for lesbians. (Also intriguing, for its date, is *Catch 69* 1970, director unknown, in which a lesbian couple both have sex with the ex-boyfriend of one of them but end up deciding that 'no pleasure is more intense or more satisfying than their lesbian love' (ibid.:158).)

8 Feminist and lesbian writing for and against pornography and erotica is too voluminous to detail here. Classic lesbian pro-porn texts are Califia 1981 and Rubin 1984, and anti- Dworkin 1981 and Kappeler 1986.

5   FROM AND FOR THE MOVEMENT

1 Cultuur- en OntspanningsCentrum (Cultural Recreation Centre).
2 On zapping, see Evans 1973.
3 For an account of the riot, see D'Emilio 1983: 231–3.
4 For overviews of the lesbian/gay movement in the seventies in countries

whose films are discussed in this chapter see, in addition to Barry 1987, for Australia, Sargent 1983, Wotherspoon 1986; for Canada, Kinsman 1987; for France, Girard 1981; for Germany, Frieling 1985; for Great Britain, Weeks 1977; for Italy, Consoli 1979; for the USA, D'Emilio 1983, Licata 1985.

5 The director credit is given as Gerrit Neuhaus, but it is generally known that this was added after Perincioli had completed directing the film; Alexandra von Grote was also involved in its production.

6 The discussion of documentary in this chapter is particularly indebted to Corner 1986 and Nichols 1981.

7 On Grierson, Lovell and Hillier 1972, Hood 1983; on Vertov, Feldman 1984; for a comparison of these two traditions, Harvey n.d.

8 On *cinéma vérité* and direct cinema, Issari and Paul 1979.

9 Quoted in *Filmfacts* 14 (24): 750.

10 This distinguishes them from such brave interventions by gay people in entertainment cinema in the seventies as *Sunday Bloody Sunday*, *Making Love* and *Some of My Best Friends Are*, where the fact of gay authorship is not signalled by the text (known if at all only through gossip or speculation), and where there is also no clear sense of gay viewers being addressed as gay viewers. It may be argued that such films are nonetheless at least as important as any of those discussed in this book, because they would have been seen by vastly more gay men (and lesbians, though there is no equivalent lesbian example in the period). I have no quarrel with this view, but the subject of this book is those films that do signal themselves as lesbian/gay products and openly include the lesbian/gay audience in their mode of address.

11 It may be that both 'art cinema' and 'gay' are misleading terms to use, as here, in relation to Egyptian, Mexican or Philippine films, though this is how they are mainly consumed, if at all, in the West.

12 The most complete discussion is Elsaesser 1989.

13 For further discussion of some of these films, see Hetze 1986.

14 Though directed by a man, this is generally understood as the work of Christiane Rochefort, who wrote both the script and the original novel.

15 For a judicious discussion of the political implications of the essentialism:constructionism debate, see Franklin and Stacey 1988.

16 For example (a personal selection):

Abuse USA 1982 Arthur Bressan, which, through the character of a film-maker trying to make a film on the subject of child abuse, contrasts the vicious parental abuse of a boy with gay so-called abuse.

Bond/Weld USA 1982 Cathy Joritz, free association with movie images of the lesbian pleasures of, inter alia, *The Nun's Story*, *The Children's Hour*, Lily Tomlin, sportswomen, nuns, bikers, *Personal Best*.

Chinese Characters Canada 1985 Richard Fung, an examination of the way notions of the Orient enter into images and self-images of Asian gay men in the West.

Seventeen Rooms, or What Do Lesbians Do in Bed? GB 1985 Caroline Sheldon, the images answer the question (drink tea, play scrabble, quarrel, watch TV etc.), written and spoken words suggest lascivious alternatives, music, including that great lesbian icon Dusty Springfield, provides witty counterpoints.

You Taste American Canada 1985 John Greyson, an imaginary encounter between competing constructions of gay identity, Michel Foucault and Tennessee Williams (and Montgomery Clift in *Suddenly Last Summer*).

Echoes of Past Lives GB 1986 Cind Oestreicher, images of writing words about lesbian identity in sand, condensation, lipstick, which are endlessly washed or wiped away and endlessly reasserted.

The Mark of Lillith GB 1986 Bruna Fionda, Polly Gladwin and Isiling Mack-Nataf, an exploration of the potential of the vampire myth for lesbian feminist and anti-racist appropriation.

Ten Cents a Dance (Parallax) Canada 1986 Midi Onodera, a devastating set of three long takes: two women talking round the subject at a dinner table; two men in an overhead shot fucking in a toilet; a man wanking as he talks to a uninterested woman on the other end of a phone sex line.

Alfalfa GB 1987 Richard Kwietniowski, a gay alphabet, wittily counterposing dictionary definitions of words with their use in the gay sub-culture.

References

GENERAL

(works cited in more than one chapter)

Abbott, Sidney and Love, Barbara (1972) *Sappho Was a Right-On Woman: A Liberated View of Lesbianism*. New York: Stein & Day.

Adam, Barry (1987) *The Rise of a Gay and Lesbian Movement*. Boston: Twayne.

Becker, Edith, Michelle Citron, Julia Lesage and B. Ruby Rich (1981) Introduction: Special Section on Lesbians and Film. *Jump Cut* 24/5: 17–21.

Brunsdon, Charlotte (ed.) (1986) *Films for Women*. London: British Film Institute.

Cooper, Emmanuel (1986) *The Sexual Perspective: Homosexuality and Art in the last 100 years in the West*. London: Routledge & Kegan Paul.

D'Emilio, John (1983) *Sexual Politics, Sexual Communities: the Making of a Homosexual Minority in the United States 1940–1970*. Chicago: University of Chicago Press.

Duyves, Mattias and Myriam Everard, Saskia Grotenhuis, Gert Hemka, Paula Koelemji, Jan Willem Tellegen (eds) (1983) *Among Men, Among Women: Sociological and historical recognition of homosocial arrangements*. Amsterdam: University of Amsterdam.

Dyer, Richard (ed.) (1984) *Gays and Film*. New York: Zoetrope.

Dyer, Richard (1986) *Heavenly Bodies*. London: Macmillan.

Freedman, Estelle B. and Barbara C. Gelpi, Susan L. Johnson, Kathleen M. Weston (eds) (1985) *The Lesbian Issue: Essays from Signs*. Chicago: University of Chicago Press.

Grahn, Judy (1984) *Another Mother Tongue: Gay Words, Gay Worlds*. Boston: Beacon Press.

Jay, Karla and Young, Allen (eds) (1972) *Out of the Closets: Voices of Gay Liberation*. New York: Douglas/Links.

Jay, Karla and Young, Allen (eds) (1978) *Lavender Culture*. New York: Harcourt Brace Jovanovich.

Kaplan, E. Ann (1983) *Women and Film – Both Sides of the Camera*. London: Methuen.

Katz, Jonathan (ed.) (1976) *Gay American History*. New York: Thomas Crowell.

Kuhn, Annette (1982) *Women's Pictures – Feminism and Cinema*. London: Routledge & Kegan Paul.

Licata, Salvatore (1985) 'The Homosexual Rights Movement in the United States: A Traditionally Overlooked Area of American History'. In Licata and Petersen (eds) (1985) 161–90.

Licata, Salvatore and Petersen, Robert P. (eds) (1985) *The Gay Past: A Collection of Historical Essays*. New York: Harrington Park Press.

Radicalesbians (1972) *The Woman-Identified Woman*. In Jay and Young (eds) 1972:172–7. (Originally published as a pamphlet by New York: Radicalesbians 1970.)

RFR/DRF (Resources for Feminist Research/Documentation sur la reherche féministe) (1983) *The Lesbian Issue/Être Lesbienne*. Toronto.

Rich, Adrienne (1980) 'Compulsory Heterosexuality and Lesbian Existence'. *Signs* 5(4) 631–60).

Rosenberg, Jan (1983) *Women's Reflections: The Feminist Film Movement*. Ann Arbor, UMI Research Press.

Russo, Vito (1981) *The Celluloid Closet: Homosexuality in the Movies*. New York: Harper & Row.

Sontag, Susan (1967) *Against Interpretation*. London: Eyre & Spottiswoode.

Stamboulian, George and Marks, Elaine (eds) (1979) *Homosexualities and French Literature*. Ithaca: Cornell University Press.

Weeks, Jeffrey (1985) *Sexuality and Its Discontents: Meanings, Myths and Modern Sexualities*. London: Routledge & Kegan Paul.

Weeks, Jeffrey (1986) *Sexuality*. London: Tavistock.

Weiss, Andrea (1981a) 'Filmography of Lesbian Works'. *Jump Cut* 24/5:22, 50–1.

1   WEIMAR: LESS AND MORE LIKE THE OTHERS

Aarts, Jan (1983) 'Alfred Schuler, Stefan George and their different grounds in the debate on homosexuality at the turn of the century in Germany'. In Duyves *et al.* (eds) (1983), 291–304.

Anon (1985) *We of the Third Sex* (extracts). *Gay Information* 16:20–30. (Originally published Leipzig: Richard Sattlers, 1907).

Baumgardt, Manfred (1984) 'Die homosexuelle-Bewegung bis zum Ende des Ersten Weltkrieges' and 'Das Institut für Sexualwissenschaft und die Homosexuelle-Bewegung in der Weimarer Republik'. In Bollé (ed.) (1984) 17–27 and 31–43.

Blüher, Hans (1912) *Die Deutsche Wandervogelbewegung als erotisches Phänomen*. Berlin: Tempelhof.

Bollé, Michael (ed.) (1984) *Eldorado. Homosexuelle Frauen und Männer in Berlin 1850–1950. Geschichte, Alltag und Kultur*. Berlin: Frölich & Kaufmann.

Burns, Rob (1977) 'Theory and organisation of revolutionary working-class literature in the Weimar republic'. In Keith Bullivant (ed.) (1977) *Culture and Society in the Weimar Republic*. Manchester: Manchester University Press: 122–49.

Burrows, Elaine (1981) 'Jacqueline Audry'. In *Frauen und Film* 28:22–7.

Busst A. J. L. (1967) 'The Image of the Androgyne in the Nineteenth Century'. In Ian Fletcher (ed.) (1967) *Romantic Mythologies*. London:

Routledge & Kegan Paul.

Dauthendey, Elisabeth (1980) *Of the New Woman and Her Love* (extracts). In Faderman and Eriksson (eds) (1980) 33–45. (Originally published Berlin: Schuster & Loeffler, 1900.)

Dougherty, Richard Wellington (1978) 'Eros, Youth Culture and Geist: The Ideology of Gustav Wyneken and its Influence upon the German Youth Movement'. PhD thesis, University of Wisconsin-Madison (available through University Microfilms).

Duc, Aimée (1980) *Sind es Frauen?* (extracts). In Faderman and Eriksson (eds) (1980) 1–22. (Originally published Berlin: Eckstein, 1903.)

Dyer, Richard (1988) 'Children of the Night: Vampirism as Homosexuality, Homosexuality as Vampirism'. In Susannah Radstone (ed.) (1988) *Sweet Dreams: Sexuality, Gender and Popular Fiction*. London: Lawrence & Wishart, 47–72.

Eisner, Lotte (1969) *The Haunted Screen*. London: Thames & Hudson.

Faderman, Lillian (1981) *Surpassing the Love of Men*. New York: Morrow.

Faderman, Lillian and Eriksson, Brigitte (eds) (1980) *Lesbian-Feminism in Turn-of-the-Century Germany*. Weatherby Lake MI: Naiad Press.

Finch, Mark (1987) 'Mauritz Stiller's *The Wings* and Early Scandinavian Gay Cinema'. *European Gay Review* 2:26–31.

Foster, Jeanette (1985) *Sex Variant Women in Literature*. Tallahassee: Naiad. (Originally published New York: Vantage, 1956.)

Freud, Sigmund (1920) 'Über die Psychogenese eines Falles von weiblicher Homosexualität'. *Internationale Zeitschrift für ärztliche Psychoanalyse*. 6(1):1–24.

Freud, Sigmund (1931) 'Über die weibliche Sexualität'. Idem 17(3):317–22.

Frottier, Corinne (1982) 'Weibliche Homosexualität im gesellschaftlichen Diskurs und deren Niederschlag im deutschen Film bis 1933'. Unpublished thesis, University of Cologne.

Got, Ambroise (1923) 'Le Vice organisé en Allemagne'. *Mercure de France* CLXI:655–78.

Gramann, Karola and Schlüpmann, Heide (1981) 'Unnatürliche Akte. Die Inszenierung des Lesbischen im Film'. In Karola Gramann, Gertrud Koch *et al.* (1981) *Lust und Elend. Das erotische Kino*. Munich/Lucerne: Bucher, 70–93.

Gramann, Karola and Schlüpmann, Heide (1983a) '"Ich habe das einfach nicht für möglich gehalten." Hertha Thiele im Gespräch'. In Prinzler (ed.) (1983) 6–23.

Gramann, Karola and Schlüpmann, Heide (1983b) 'Liebe als Opposition, Opposition as Liebe'. In Prinzler (ed.) (1983) 24–43.

Haskell, Francis and Penny, Nicholas (1981) *Taste and the Antique*. New Haven: Yale University Press.

Herzer, Manfred (1984) 'Dichtung und Wahrheit der Berliner Schwulen im ersten Jahrhundertdrittel'. In Bollé (ed.) (1984) 97–101.

Hohmann, Joachim S. (ed.) (1981) *Der Eigene: Ein Querschnitt durch die erste Homosexuellenzeitschrift der Welt*. Frankfurt/Berlin: Foerster.

Hohmann, Joachim S. (ed.) (1983) *Entstellte Engel: Homosexuelle schreiben*. Frankfurt: Fischer.

Hull, Isabel V. (1982) 'The Bourgeoisie and its Discontents: Reflections on "Nationalism and Respectability"'. *Journal of Contemporary History*

17:247–68.
Hyvärinen, Veli (1988) 'Magnus Enckell – levollisen aistillisuuden mestari'. *SETA* 4:24–7.
Isherwood, Christopher (1977) *Christopher and his Kind*. London: Eyre Methuen.
Kaul, Walter and Scheuer, Robert G. (1970) *Richard Oswald*. Berlin: Deutsche Kinemathek.
Koch, Gertrud (1989) 'Schattenreich der Körper'. In Gertrude Koch (1989) *'Was ich erbeute, sind Bilder'. Zum Diskurs der Geschlechter im Film*. Basel/Frankfurt: Stroemfeld/Roter Stern, 95–122.
Kokula, Ilse (1984) 'Lesbisch leben von Weimar bis zur Nachkriegszeit'. In Bollé (ed.) (1984) 149–61.
Kracauer, Siegfried (1947) *From Caligari to Hitler*. Princeton: Princeton University Press.
Kreische, Rosi (1984) 'Lesbische Liebe im Film bis 1950'. In Bollé (ed.) (1984) 87–96.
Lamprecht, Gerhard (1968) *Deutsche Stummfilme 1919*. Berlin: Deutsche Kinemathek.
Leppmann, Wolfgang (1986) *Winckelmann: ein Leben für Apoll*. Frankfurt: Fischer.
Lengerke, Christiane von (1984) ' "Homosexuelle Frauen". Tribaden, Freundinnen, Urninden'. In Bollé (ed.) (1984) 125–48.
Lhomond, Brigitte (1985) 'Discours médicaux et homosexualité: de la création d'une figure'. In *L'homosexuel(le) dans les sociétés civiles et religieuses*. Strasbourg: CERDAC.
Maasen, Thijs (1987) 'Pedagogical Friendships in Weimar Germany: Gustav Wyneken's pedagogical eros at issue in the Wickersdorf Free School Community'. *Homosexuality, Which Homosexuality?* Conference Papers, Free University of Amsterdam, History Volume 2:133–43.
Mackay, John Henry ('Sagitta') (1985) *The Hustler*. Boston: Alyson. (Originally published Berlin: private publication, 1926.)
Marks, Elaine (1979) 'Lesbian Intertextuality'. In Stamboulian and Marks (eds) (1979) 353–77.
Mayne, Judith (1986) 'Murnau's *Nosferatu*: Dracula in the Twilight'. In Eric Rentschler (ed.) (1986) *German Literature and Film: Adaptations and Transformations*. New York/London: Methuen.
Meyer, Adèle (1981) *Lila Nächte. Die Damenklubs der Zwanziger Jahre*. Cologne.
Monaco, Paul (1976) *Cinema and Society: France and Germany during the Twenties*. New York: Elsevier.
Moreck, Curt (1926) *Sittengeschichte des Kinos*. Dresden: Paul Aretz.
Mosse, George L. (1982) 'Nationalism and Respectability: Normal and Abnormal Sexuality in the Nineteenth Century'. *Journal of Contemporary History* 17:221–46.
Nitsche, Walter (1983) 'Es schienen so golden die Sterne'. In Hohmann (ed.) (1983) 244–50.
Pieper, Mecki (1984) 'Die Frauenbewegung und ihre Bedeutung für lesbische Frauen (1850–1920)'. In Bollé (ed.) (1984) 116–24.
Prinzler, Hans Helmut (ed.) (1983) *Hertha Thiele*. Berlin: Deutsche Kinemathek.

Reinig, Christa (1983) 'Christa Winsloe'. In Winsloe (1983) 241–8.

Reuter, Gabriele (1895) *Aus guter Familie. Leidensgeschichte eines Mädchens*. Berlin: Fischer.

Reuter, Gabriele (1921) *Vom Kinde zum Menschen. Die Geschichte meiner Jugend*. Berlin: Fischer.

Rich, B. Ruby (1984) '*Mädchen in Uniform*: From repressive tolerance to erotic liberation'. In Mary Ann Doane, Patricia Mellencamp and Linda Williams (eds) (1984) *Re-Vision*. Los Angeles: American Film Institute, 100–30.

Rüling, Anna (1980) 'What Interest does the Women's Movement have in the homosexual question?' In Enderman and Eriksson (1980) 81–92. (Originally published 1905, *Jahrbuch für sexuelle Zwischenstufe*.)

Sanders, Virginia (1983) 'Renée Vivien, Poetess between two cultures'. In Duyves *et al.* (eds) (1983) 493–503.

Schäfer, Margarete (1984) 'Theater, Theater'. In Bollé (ed.) (1984) 180–6.

Schenk, Herrad (1980) *Die feministische Herausforderung. 150 Jahre Frauenbewegung in Deutschland*. Munich: C. H. Beck.

Schlierkamp, Petra (1984) *Die Garçonne*. In Bollé (ed.) (1984) 169–79.

Scholar, Nancy (1979) '*Mädchen in Uniform*'. In Patricia Erens (ed.) (1979) *Sexual Stratagems: The World of Women and Film*. New York: Horizon Press, 219–23.

Schlüpmann, Heide (1984) '"Je suis la solitude". Zum Doppelgängermotiv in *Der Student von Prag*'. *Frauen und Film* 36:11–24.

Schlüpmann, Heide and Gramann, Karola (1981) 'Momente erotischer Utopie – ästhetisierte Verdrängung. Zu *Mädchen in Uniform* und *Anna und Elisabeth*'. *Frauen und Film* 28:28–47.

Silverstolpe, Frederic (1987) 'Benkert Was Not a Doctor: On the Nonmedical Origin of the Homosexual Category in the Nineteenth Century'. *Homosexuality, Which Homosexuality?* Conference Papers, Free University of Amsterdam. History Volume 1:206–20.

Stark, Gary (1982) 'Cinema, Society and the State: Policing the Film Industry in Imperial Germany'. In D. B. King *et al.* (eds) (1982) *Essays in Culture and Society in Modern Germany*. Austin: University of Texas.

Steakley, James (1975) *The Homosexual Emancipation Movement in Germany*. New York: Arno.

Steakley, James (1987) 'Gay Film and Censorship: a 1919 Case Study'. *Homosexuality, Which Homosexuality?* Conference Papers, Free University of Amsterdam. Literature and Art Volume 2: 147–55.

Sternweiler, Andreas (1984) 'Kunst und schwuler Alltag'. In Bollé (ed.) (1984) 74–92.

Sykora, Katharina (1983) 'Jeanne Mammen and Christian Schad. Two illustrators of homosexuality in Berlin's twenties'. In Duyves *et al.* (eds) (1983) 537–48.

Theis, Wolfgang (1984a) '*Anders als die Andern*. Geschichte eines Filmskandals'. In Bollé (ed.) (1984) 28–31.

Theis, Wolfgang (1984b) 'Verdrängung und Travestie. Das vage Bild der Homosexualität im deutschen Film (1917–1957)'. In Bollé (ed.) (1984) 102–15.

Theis, Wolfgang and Sternweiler, Andreas (1984) 'Alltag im Kaiserreich und in der Weimarer Republik'. In Bollé (ed.) (1984) 48–73.

Tonbandprotokolle (1984) 'Nicht Achtung kannst du dem, der dich nicht achtet, schenken, oder du mußt sogleich von dir geringer denken'. (Interview with Käthe K.) In Bollé (ed.) (1984) 210–15.

Vermij, Luci Th. (1983) 'Le Berlin des années 20'. *Masques* 17:109–13.

Vicinus, Martha (1985) 'Distance and desire: English boarding-school friendships'. In Freedman *et al.* (eds) (1985) 43–66.

Vogel, Katharina (1984) 'Zum Selbstverständnis lesbischer Frauen in der Weimarer Republik. Eine Analyse der Zeitschrift *Die Freundin* 1924–1933'. In Bollé (ed.) (1984) 162–8.

Waugh, Thomas (1979) 'Murnau – the films behind the man'. *The Body Politic* March/April:31–4.

Weber, Marianne (1936) *Die Frauen und die Liebe*. Königstein im Taurus: Langewiesche.

Weirauch, Anna (1948) *The Scorpion* (Part 1). New York: Wiley. (Originally published Berlin: Askanischer, 1919.)

Willett, John (1984) *The Weimar Years: a Culture Cut Short*. London: Thames & Hudson.

Winsloe, Christa (1983) *Mädchen in Uniform*. Munich: Frauenoffensive. (Originally published Amsterdam 1933.)

Wood, Robin (1979) 'The Dark Mirror: Murnau's *Nosferatu*'. In Richard Lippe and Robin Wood (eds) (1979) *The American Nightmare*. Toronto: Festival of Festivals.

2 SHADES OF GENET

Aitken, Will (1980–1) 'Twenty-eight Minutes of Genius'. *Gay News* (London) 205:11–12.

Ardill, Susan and Neumark, Nora (1982) 'Putting Sex Back into Lesbianism'. *Gay Information* 11:4–11.

Barbedette, Gilles and Carassou, Michel (1981) *Paris Gay 1925*. Paris: Presses de la Renaissance.

Bataille, Georges (1973) *Literature and Evil*. London: Calder & Boyars. (Originally published Paris: Gallimard 1957.)

Beauvais, Yann (1980) 'Evasion imaginaire: Reprise d'*Un Chant d'amour* de Jean Genet'. *Gai Pied* 21:28.

Becker, Raymond de (1960) 'Notes sur un cinéma homophile'. *Arcadie* 74:97–100.

Becker, Raymond de (1967) *The Other Face of Love*. London: Neville Spearman & Rodney. (Originally published Paris: Jean-Jacques Pauvert 1964.)

Benstock, Shari (1987) *Women of the Left Bank: Paris 1900–1940*. London: Virago.

Billard, Pierre (1966) 'Les Feux de la Sainte-Jeanne: *Mademoiselle* de Tony Richardson'. *Cinéma 66* 107:47–8.

Byron, Peg (1985) 'What We Talk About When We Talk About Dildos'. *The Village Voice* (March 5):48–9.

Casselaer, Catherine van (1986) *Lot's Wife: Lesbian Paris, 1890–1914*. Liverpool: Janus Press.

Cochart, Dominique and Pigache, Anne (1976) 'Impasse, pair et manque, ou quand le Roi est plus fort que la Dame'. In Anne Laurent (ed.) (1976)

Jean Genet Aujourd'hui. Amiens: Maison de la Culture d'Amiens, 48–53.

Cocteau, Jean (1970) *Two Screenplays: The Blood of a Poet, The Testament of Orpheus*. London: Calder & Boyars. (Originally published Monaco: Éditions du Rocher, 1957 and 1961.)

Cocteau, Jean (1983) *The White Paper*. London: Brilliance. (Originally published Paris: Éditions des Quatre Chemins, 1928.)

Coe, Richard N. (1968) *The Vision of Jean Genet*. London: Peter Owen.

Coglay, Michel du (1937) *Chez les mauvais garçons – choses vues*. Paris: Raoul Saillard.

De Grazia, Edward and Newman, Roger K. (1982) *Banned Films*. New York: R. R. Bowker.

De Rome, Peter (1984) *The Erotic World of Peter de Rome*. London: GMP.

Dyer, Richard (1980–1) *'Papillon'. Movie* 27–8:60–5.

Eck, Marcel (1966) *Sodome. Essai sur l'homosexualité*. Paris: Arthème Fayard.

Evans, Arthur B. (1977) *Jean Cocteau and his Films of Orphic Identity*. Philadelphia: Art Alliance Press.

Freud, Sigmund (1957) 'On Narcissism'. In *Complete Works* 14. London: Hogarth. (Originally published *Jahrbuch für psychoanalytische und psychopathologische Forschungen* 6, 1914.)

Galand, René (1979) 'Cocteau's sexual equation'. In George Stamboulian and Elaine Marks (eds) (1979) 279–94.

Genet, Jean (1949) *Journal du voleur*. Paris: Gallimard.

Genet, Jean (1951) *Miracle de la rose*. Paris: Gallimard.

Genet, Jean (1953) *Querelle de Brest*. Paris: Gallimard.

Genet, Jean (1983) 'Notes de mise en scène pour *La Nuit venue'. Caméra/Stylo* (Septembre):89–91.

Gide, André (1925) *Corydon*. Paris: Gallimard.

Giles, Jane (1988) *'Un Chant d'amour* par Jean Genet'. *Art Forum* 26(5):102–6.

Giles, Jane and Kwietniowski, Richard (1988) 'I Know Why the Caged Bird Sings'. *Square Peg* 19:36–7.

Girard, Jacques (1981) *Le Mouvement homosexuel en France 1945–1980*. Paris: Syros.

Harvey, Stephen (1984) 'The Mask in the Mirror: The Movies of Jean Cocteau'. In Arthur King Peters *et al.* (1984) *Jean Cocteau and the French Scene*. New York: Abbeville Press, 185–207.

Hayward, Susan (1989) 'Gender Politics – Cocteau's Belle is not that Bête: Jean Cocteau's *La Belle et la bête'*. In Susan Hayward and Ginette Vincendeau (eds) (1989) *French Cinema: Texts and Contexts*. London: Routledge, 127–35.

Hocquenghem, Guy (1978) *Homosexual Desire*. London: Alison & Busby.

Jay, Karla (1988) *The Amazon and the Page: Natalie Barney and Renée Vivien*. Bloomington: Indiana University Press.

Jouhandeau, Marcel (1939) *De l'abjection*. Paris: Gallimard.

Lacombe, Francis (1988) 'Le Rapport secret des années folles'. *Gai Pied* 348:57–62.

Lange, Marion (1983) 'Jean Genet: *Un Chant d'amour'. Filmkritik* 27:291–4.

Lautréamont, Comte de (Isidore Ducasse) (1966) *Les Chants de Maldoror*.

Paris: Livre de Poche. (Originally published Brussels: Lacroix, Verboecken & Co. 1869.)

LaValley, Al (n.d.) 'Cocteau'. Unpublished manuscript.

Limbacher, James L. (1983) *Sexuality in World Cinema*. Metuchen: Scarecrow.

MacBean, James Roy (1984) 'Between Kitsch and Fascism: Notes on Fassbinder, Pasolini, (Homo)sexual Politics, the exotic, the erotic and Other Consuming Passions'. *Cinéaste* 13(4):12–19.

Magnan, Jean-Marie (1966) *Essai sur Jean Genet*. Paris: Seghers.

Meersch, Maxence van der (1960) *Mask of Flesh*. London: William Kimber. (Originally *Masque de chair*. Paris: le Club des Éditeurs, 1958.)

Mekas, Jonas (1972) *Movie Journal*. New York: Macmillan.

Melville, Jayne (1986) *'Seduction: the Cruel Woman'*. *Square Peg* 13:33.

Mercer, Kobena *et al.* (1988) 'Sexual Identities: Questions of Difference'. *Undercut* 17:19–30.

Millett, Kate (1971) *Sexual Politics*. London: Rupert Hart-Davis.

Milorad (1981–2) 'Jean et Jean'. *Masques* 12:38–42.

Nachman, Larry David (1983) 'Genet: Dandy of the Lower Depths'. *Salmagundi* 58–9:358–72.

Oswald, Laura (1983) 'The Perversion of I/Eye in *Un Chant d'amour*'. *Enclitic* 7(2):106–15.

Rabi (1951) 'A propos de Jean Genet'. *Esprit* 184:741–5.

Rayns, Tony (1973) *'Un Chant d'amour'*. *Monthly Film Bulletin* 40:236.

Reboux, Paul (1951) *Sens interdits*. Paris: Raoul Solar.

Rimbaud, Arthur and Verlaine, Paul (1983) 'Sonnet: To the Asshole'. In Stephen Coote (ed.) (1983) *The Penguin Book of Homosexual Verse*. Harmondsworth: Penguin 235. (Originally published in Paul Verlaine *Hombres*. Paris: Messein, 1903.)

Sachs, Maurice (1946) *Le Sabbat, souvenir d'une jeunesse orageuse*. Paris: Corrêa.

Sartre, Jean-Paul (1952) *Saint Genet, comédien et martyr*. Paris: Gallimard.

Storzer, Gerald H. (1979) 'The Homosexual Paradigm in Balzac, Gide and Genet'. In Stamboulian and Marks (eds) (1979) 186–209.

Thody, Philip (1969) 'Jean Genet and the Indefensibility of Sexual Deviation'. *Twentieth-Century Studies* 2:68–73.

Virmaux, Alain and Virmaux, Odette (1986) 'Genet, Vailland, Chenal'. *Cinématographe* 122:52–4.

Webb, Richard C. with Webb, Suzanne A. (1982) *Jean Genet and his Critics*. Metuchen NJ: Scarecrow.

Young, Ian *et al.* (1979) 'Forum on Sadomasochism'. In Jay and Young (eds) (1972) 85–117.

3   UNDERGROUND AND AFTER

Apra, Adriano and Ungari, Enzo (1972) *Il cinema di Andy Warhol*. Rome: Arcana.

Austen, Roger (1977) *Playing the Game: the Homosexual Novel in America*. Indianapolis: Bobbs-Merrill.

Babuscio, Jack (1984) 'Camp and the Gay Sensibility'. In Dyer (1977) 40–56.

Berlin, Gloria and Bruce, Bryan (1986–7) 'The superstar story'. *CineAction!* 7:52–63.

Boone, Bruce (1979) 'Gay Language as Political Praxis: The Poetry of Frank O'Hara'. *Social Text* 1:59–92.

Boultenhouse, Charles (1970) 'The Camera as a God'. In P. Adams Sitney (ed.) (1970) *Film Culture: an Anthology*. New York: Praeger, 136–40. (Originally published in *Film Culture* 29, summer 1963.)

Brecht, Stefan (1978) *Queer Theatre*. Frankfurt am Main: Suhrkamp.

Breton, André (1978) 'As in a Wood'. In Paul Hammond (ed.) (1978) *The Shadow and its Shadow*. London: British Film Institute, 42–5. (Originally published in *L'Age du cinéma* 4–5 (1951:26–30).)

Broughton, James (1982) Interview with Robert Peters. In Winston Leyland (ed.) (1982) *Gay Sunshine Interviews 2*. San Francisco: Gay Sunshine Press.

Castello, Michel del (1983) 'Le Plaisir de mourir'. In *Saint Sébastien: Adonis et martyr*. Paris: Persona, 13–15.

Castillo, John (1985) *Love, Sex and War: Changing Values 1939–45*. London: Collins.

Cook, Bruce (1971) *The Beat Generation*. New York: Scribner's.

Coplans, John (1970) *Andy Warhol*. New York: New York Graphic Society.

Cornwell, Regina (1979) 'Maya Deren and Germaine Dulac: Activists of the Avant-Garde'. In Patricia Erens (ed.) (1979) *Sexual Stratagems*. New York: Horizon.

Duncan, Robert (1944) 'The Homosexual in Society'. *Politics* 1(7):209–11.

Durgnat, Raymond (1972) *Sexual Alienation in the Cinema*. London: Studio Vista.

Dwoskin, Stephen (1975) *Film Is*. London: Peter Owen.

Dyer, Richard (1977) 'Homosexuality and Film Noir'. *Jump Cut* 16:18–21.

Ehrenstein, David (1984) *Film: the Front Line 1984*. Denver: Arden Press.

Evans, Arthur (1978) *Witchcraft and the Gay Counterculture*. Boston: Fag Rag Books.

Fischer, Lucy (1987–8) 'The Films of James Sibley Watson Jnr and Melville Webber: A Reconsideration'. *Millennium Film Journal* 19:40–9.

Ford, Charles and Tyler, Parker (1933) *The Young and Evil*. Paris: Obelisk.

Fry, Peter (1986) 'Male Homosexuality and Spirit Possession in Brazil'. In Evelyn Blackwood (ed.) (1986) *The Many Faces of Homosexuality*. New York: Harrington Park Press, 137–53.

Gidal, Peter (1971) *Andy Warhol*. London: Studio Vista.

Gidal, Peter (ed.) (1976) *Structural Film Anthology*. London: British Film Institute.

Gidal, Peter (1981) 'Andy Warhol . . . Factory Worker'. *The Movie* 65:1296–9.

Ginsberg, Allen (1974) Gay Sunshine Interview with Allen Young. Bolinas, CA: Grey Fox Press.

Gittings, Barbara (1976) 'Founding the New York Daughters of Bilitis'. In Katz (ed.) (1985) 420–33.

Gow, Gordon (1971) 'Up from the Underground 1: Curtis Harrington'. *Films and Filming* 17(11):16–22.

Hale, G. N. (1971) *Freud and the Americans*. New York: Oxford University Press.

Hamilton, Godfrey (1977) 'Anger'. *Gay News* (London) 116:22–3.

Hardy, Robin (1982) 'Kenneth Anger: Master In Hell'. *The Body Politic* (April):29–32.

Hay, Henry (1976) 'Founding the Mattachine Society'. In Jonathan Katz (ed.) (1985) 406–20.

Hoberman, J. and Rosenbaum, Jonathan (1983) *Midnight Movies*. New York: Harper & Row.

Howard, Rolland (1961) 'Homosexuality as a Vehicle for Masochism Symbolized in the Film *Fireworks*'. *Mattachine Review* 7(7):6–8.

Jacobs, Lewis (1968) *The Rise of the American Film*. New York: Teachers College.

James, David E. (1985) 'The Producer as Author'. *Wide Angle* 7(3):24–33.

Kelman, Ken (1963) 'Smith Myth'. In P. Adams Sitney (ed.) (1963) *Film Culture* 29:4–6.

Koch, Stephen (1973) *Stargazer: Andy Warhol and His Films*. New York: Praeger.

Lewis, Timothy (1983) *Physique: A Pictorial History of the Athletic Model Guild*. San Francisco: Gay Sunshine Press.

Lowry, Ed (1983) 'The Appropriation of Signs in *Scorpio Rising*'. *The Velvet Light Trap* 20:41–7.

Mekas, Jonas (1955) 'The Experimental Film in America'. *Film Culture* 3:15–18.

Mekas, Jonas (1972) *Movie Journal*. New York: Macmillan.

Mills, Jerry and Russ, Dwight (1977) 'Hard–On Art: A History of Physique Art from the Forbidden 40s to the Explicit 80s'. *In Touch* 31:60–9.

Mitry, Jean (1974) *Le Cinéma expérimental: histoire et perspectives*. Paris: Seghers.

Noguez, Dominique (1985) *Une Renaissance du cinéma: le cinéma 'underground' américain*. Paris: Klinsieck.

Norton, Rictor (1977) 'A History of Homoerotica. 3: Do What Thou Wilt'. *Gay News* (London) 132:20.

O'Pray, Michael (1985) 'Derek Jarman's Cinema: Eros and Thanatos'. *Afterimage* 12:6–15.

Packman, David (1976) 'Jack Smith's *Flaming Creatures*: With the Tweak of an Eyebrow'. *Film Culture* 63–4:51–6.

Poland, Albert and Mailman, Bruce (eds) (1972) *The Off-Off Broadway Book: The Plays, People, Theatre*. Indianapolis: Bobbs-Merrill.

Rayns, Tony (1968) 'The Underground Film'. *Cinema* (UK) 1:8–11.

Rayns, Tony (1969) 'A Kenneth Anger Kompendium'. *Cinema* (UK) 4:24–31.

Rayns, Tony (1982) '*Lucifer Rising*'. *Monthly Film Bulletin* 49(584):191–2.

Rechy, John (1963) *City of Night*. New York: Grove Press.

Rowe, Carel (1982) *The Baudelairian Cinema: a Tradition within the American Avant-garde*. Ann Arbor: UMI Research Press.

Samuels, Stuart (1983) *Midnight Movies*. New York: Macmillan.

Saslow, James (1981) 'Charles Henri Ford: A Traveler without Touch-stone'. *The Advocate* May 14:30–2.

Siebenand, Paul Alcuin (1980) *The Beginnings of Gay Cinema in Los Angeles: the Industry and the Audience*. Ann Arbor: UMI Press.

Sitney, P. Adams (1974) *Visionary Film*. New York: Oxford University Press.

Sitney, P. Adams (1979) *Visionary Film*. New York: Oxford University Press. (This revised, and more widely available, edition omits the chapter on Markopoulos in the 1974 edition.)

Smith, Jack (1962–3) 'The Perfect Filmic Appositeness of Maria Montez'. *Film Culture* 27:28–32.

Smith, Rupert (1987) 'This is Ridiculous!'. *Square Peg* 16:26–8.

Sokolowski, Thomas W. (1983) *The Sailor 1930–45: The Image of an American Demigod*. Norfolk, Virginia: Chrysler Museum.

Springhall, John (1983–4) 'The Origins of Adolescence'. *Youth and Policy* 2(3):20–35.

Stimpson, Catharine R. (1982) 'The Beat Generation and the Trials of Homosexual Liberation'. *Salmagundi* 58–9:373–92.

Tartaglia, Jerry (1979) 'The Gay Sensibility in American Avant-Garde Film'. *Millennium Film Journal* 4–5:53–8.

Tyler, Parker (1972) *Screening the Sexes: Homosexuality in the Movies*. New York: Holt, Rinehart and Winston.

Vidal, Gore (1965) *The City and the Pillar*. New York: E. P. Dutton. (Revised version of original publication New York: Dutton 1948.)

Wade, Michael (1982) 'Kenneth Anger: Personal Traditions and Satanic Pride'. *The Body Politic* (April):29–32.

Waugh, Tom (1983) 'A Heritage of Pornography'. *The Body Politic* 90:29–33.

Waugh, Tom (1984) 'Photography, Passion and Power'. *The Body Politic* 101:29–33.

Weinstein, Donald (1974) 'Flowers and Flights: Markopoulos' *Swain*'. In P. Adams Sitney (ed.) (1974) *The Essential Cinema*. New York: Anthology Film Archives and New York University Press, 230–3.

Wellington, Fred (1967) 'Liberalism, Subversion, and Evangelism: Toward the Definition of a Problem'. In Gregory Battcock (ed.) (1967) *The New American Cinema*. New York: Dutton, 38–41.

4 LESBIAN/WOMAN: LESBIAN CULTURAL FEMINIST FILM

Arnup, Katherine (1983) 'Lesbian Theory'. In RFR/DRF (1983) 53–5.

Atkinson, Ti-Grace (1974) *Amazon Odyssey*. New York: Links Books.

Barry, Judith and Flitterman, Sandy (1980) 'Textual Strategies: The Politics of Art-Making'. *Screen* 21(2):35–48.

Bearchall, Chris (1983) 'Art, Trash and Titillation'. *The Body Politic* (May):29–33.

Brinckmann, Noll (1984a) Vorwort. *Frauen und Film* 37:3–5.

Brinckmann, Noll (1984b) 'Zu Maya Derens *At Land*'. *Frauen und Film* 37:73–84.

Byron, Peg (1985) 'What We Talk About When We Talk About Dildos'. *The Village Voice* March 6.

Califia, Pat (1980) *Sapphistry*. Tallahassee: Naiad.

Chicago, Judy and Schapiro, Miriam (1973) 'Female Imagery'. *Womanspace Journal* 1(3):11–14.

Chodorow, Nancy (1978) *The Reproduction of Mothering: Psychoanalysis and the Sociology of Gender*. Berkeley: University of California Press.

Clark, Wendy (1982) 'The Dyke, the Feminist and the Devil'. *Feminist Review* 11:30–9.

Davis, Elizabeth Gould (1972) *The First Sex*. New York: Penguin.

DuPlessis, Rachel Blau (1985) 'For the Etruscans: Sexual Difference and Artistic Production – the Debate over a Female Aesthetics'. In Showalter (ed.) (1985) 271–91.

Dworkin, Andrea (1981) *Pornography*. New York: Perigee.

Echols, Alice (1984) 'The Taming of the Id: Feminist Sexual Politics, 1968–83'. In Vance (ed.) (1984) 50–72.

Ecker, Gisela (ed.) (1985) *Feminist Aesthetics*. London: The Women's Press.

Fausto-Sterling, Anne (1986) *Myths of Gender*. New York: Basic Books.

Gardiner, Judith Kegan (1982) 'On Female Identity and Writing by Women'. In Abel, Elizabeth (ed.) (1982) *Writing and Sexual Difference*. Brighton: Harvester, 177–91.

Gay Revolution Party Women's Caucus (1972) 'Realesbians and Politica-lesbians'. In Jay and Young (eds) (1972) 177–81. (First published as 'Realesbians, Politicalesbians and the Women's Liberation Movement', *Ecstasy*, June 1971.)

Gottlieb, Amy (1983) 'Films, Videotapes and Slideshows'. In RFR/FDR (1983) 87–9.

Grahn, Judy (1985) *The Highest Apple: Sappho and the Lesbian Poetic Tradition*. San Francisco: Spinsters Ink.

Greer, Germaine (1971) *The Female Eunuch*. London: MacGibbon & Kee.

Hammer, Barbara (1981) 'Women's Images in Film'. In Kimball (1981) 117–29.

Hammer, Barbara (1982) 'Lesbian Filmmaking: Self-Birthing'. *Film Reader* 5:60–6.

Higginbottom, Judith (1983) '". . .Sing in the desert when the throat is almost too dry for speaking" – some thoughts on the work of Maya Deren'. In Judith Higginbottom (ed.) (1983) *Maya Deren*. Exeter: South West Arts, 3–10.

Hutt, Corinne (1978) *Males and Females*. Baltimore: Penguin.

Jay, Karla (1978) 'No Man's Land'. In Jay and Young (eds) (1978) 48–65.

Katz, Jonathan Ned (1989) 'Singing the Bull Dyker's Blues: Ma Rainey's Amazing Resistance Anthem'. *The Advocate* 529:48–9.

Kappeler, Susanne (1986) *The Pornography of Representation*. Oxford: Polity Press.

Kimball, Gayle (1981) *Women's Culture: The Women's Renaissance of the Seventies*. Metuchen NJ: Scarecrow.

Koedt, Anne (1973) 'The Myth of the Vaginal Orgasm'. In Anne Koedt, Ellen Levine and Anita Rapone (eds) (1973) *Radical Feminism*. New York: Quadrangle/New York Times Book Co., 198–207. (Originally published in *Notes from the Second Year* 1970.)

Kristeva, Julia (1977) *Polylogue*. Paris, Seuil.

Lauter, Estella (1984) *Women as Mythmakers: Poetry and Visual Art by Twentieth-Century Women*. Bloomington: Indiana University Press.

Leduc, Aimée (1982) 'Barbara Hammer'. *The Body Politic* 85, July/Aug: 34–5.

Lippard, Lucy (1976) *From the Center: Feminist Essays on Women's Art*.

New York: Dutton.

Lorde, Audre (1984) *Sister, Outsider*. Truman'sburg NY: Crossing Press.

Murphy, Jeanette (1986) 'A Question of Silence'. In Brunsdon (ed.) (1986) 99–108.

Myron, Nancy and Bunch, Charlotte (eds) (1974) *Women Remembered: A Collection of Biographies from The Furies*. Baltimore: Diana Press.

Nadeau, Denise (1983) 'Lesbian Spirituality'. In RFR/FDR (1983) 37–9.

Nelson, Diane (1978) 'Imagery of the Archetypal Feminine in the Works of Six Women Filmmakers'. *Quarterly Review of Film Studies* 3(4):495–506.

Ornstein, Robert (1972) *The Psychology of Consciousness*. San Francisco: Freeman.

Parker, Rozsika and Pollock, Griselda (1984) *Old Mistresses: Women, Art and Ideology*. London: Routledge & Kegan Paul.

Rodgerson, Gillian (1986) 'Good, clean fun in the great outdoors'. *The Body Politic* (September): 33.

Roos, Sandra (1981) 'Women's Images, Women's Art'. In Kimball (1981) 42–59.

Rubin, Gayle (1984) 'Thinking Sex: Notes for a Radical Theory of the Politics of Sexuality'. In Vance (ed.) (1984) 267–320.

Shinell, Grace (1982) 'Women's Collective Spirit: Exemplified and Envisioned'. In Spretnak (ed.) (1982) 510–28.

Showalter, Elaine (ed.) (1985) *The New Feminist Criticism: Essays on Women, Literature and Theory*. New York: Pantheon.

Shuttle, Penelope and Redgrove, Peter (1978) *The Wise Wound: Menstruation and Everywoman*. London: Gollancz.

Smith, Barbara and Smith, Beverly (1981) 'Across the Kitchen Table: A Sister-to-Sister Dialogue'. In Cherrie Moraga and Gloria Anzaldúa (eds) (1981) *This Bridge Called My Back: Writings by Radical Women of Colour*. Watertown, Mass.: Persephone: 113–27.

Spretnak, Charlene (ed.) (1982) *The Politics of Women's Spirituality: Essays on the Rise of Spiritual Power Within the Feminist Movement*. New York: Doubleday Anchor.

Springer, P. Gregory (1980) 'Barbara Hammer: the Leading Lesbian behind the Lens'. *The Advocate* (February 7): 29, 35.

Tickner, Lisa (1987) 'The Body Politic: Female Sexuality and Women Artists since 1970'. In Rosemary Betterton (ed.) (1987) *Looking On*. London: Pandora, 235–53.

Vance, Carole (ed.) (1984) *Pleasure and Danger: Exploring Female Sexuality*. Boston: Routledge & Kegan Paul.

Weiss, Andrea (1981b) 'Lesbian Cinema and Romantic Love'. *Jump Cut* 24/5:30.

Wolf, Deborah Goleman (1979) *The Lesbian Community*. Berkeley: University of California Press.

Wolff, Charlotte (1971) *Love Between Women*. London: Duckworth.

Zimmerman, Bonnie (1985) 'The Politics of Transliteration: Lesbian Personal Narratives'. In Freedman *et al.* (1985) 251–70.

Zita, Jacqueline (1981) 'Counter Currencies of a Lesbian Iconography: Films of Barbara Hammer'. *Jump Cut* 24/5:26–30.

5   FROM AND FOR THE MOVEMENT

Altman, Dennis (1982) *The Homosexualization of America, the American-ization of the Homosexual*. New York: St Martin's Press.

Atwell, Lee (1978–9) 'Word is Out and Gay USA'. *Film Quarterly* 32(2):50–7.

Birch, Keith (1988) 'The Nancy Revolution'. *Square Peg* 20:30–2.

Bruce, Bryan (1987) 'Rosa von Praunheim in Theory and Practice'. *CineAction!* 9:25–31.

Byron, Stuart (1972) 'The Closet Syndrome'. In Jay and Young (eds) (1972) 58–65.

Cant, Bob (1978) 'The Making of *Nighthawks*'. *Gay Left* 7:30–3.

Carden, Maren Lockwood (1974) *The New Feminist Movement*. New York: Russell Sage Foundation.

Citron, Michelle (1981) 'Comic Critique: Films of Jan Oxenburg'. *Jump Cut* 24/5:31–2. (Reprinted in Steven (1985):315–23 and shortened version in Brunsdon (1986):72–8.)

Consoli, Luciano (1979) 'The Homosexual Movement in Italy'. *Gay Books Bulletin* (New York) 1(1).

Corner, John (ed.) (1986) *Documentary and the Mass Media*. London: Edward Arnold.

Darier, Eric (1987) 'The Gay Movement and French Society since 1945'. *Modern and Contemporary France* 29:10–19.

Delphy, Christine (1977) *The Main Enemy*. London: Women's Research and Resources Centre.

De Pauw, Linda (1982) *Seafaring Women*. Boston: Houghton Mifflin.

Elsaesser, Thomas (1989) *New German Cinema: A History*. London: Macmillan.

Evans, Arthur (1973) 'How to zap straights'. In Richmond and Noguera (eds) (1973) 111–15.

Feldman, Seth (1984). '"Cinema Weekly" and "Cinema Truth": Dziga Vertov and The Leninist Proportion'. In Waugh (ed.) (1977) 3–20.

Franklin, Sarah and Stacey, Jackie (1988) 'Dyke-tactics for Difficult Times'. In Christian McEwen and Sue O'Sullivan (eds) (1988) *Out the Other Side*. London: Virago 220–32.

Freeman, Jo (1975) *The Politics of Women's Liberation*. New York: David McKay.

Frieling, Willi (ed.) (1985) *Schwule Regungen, Schwule Bewegungen*. Berlin: Rosa Winkel.

Front Homosexuel d'Action Révolutionnaire (1971) *Rapport contre la normalité*. Paris: Champ Libre.

Garsi, Jean-François (1981a) 'Anti-stress et brownie sans crème (Interview de Lionel Soukaz)'. In Garsi (ed.) (1981b) 51–3.

Garsi, Jean-François (ed.) (1981b) *Cinémas homosexuels* (*Cinémaction* 15). Paris: Papyrus.

Gay Left Collective (eds) (1980) *Homosexuality: Power and Politics*. London: Allison and Busby.

Girard, Jacques (1981) *Le Mouvement homosexuel en France 1945–1980*. Paris: Syros.

Gledhill, Christine (1978) 'Recent Developments in Feminist Film Criticism'. *Quarterly Review of Film Studies* 3(4):457–93.

Gorbman, Claudia (1983) '*Susana*: Photographer's Self-Portrait'. *Jump Cut* 28:43–4.

Hake, Sabine (1988–9) ' "Gold, Love, Adventure": The Postmodern Piracy of *Madame X*'. *Discourse* 11(1):88–110.

Harvey, Sylvia (1978) *May '68 and Film Culture*. London: British Film Institute.

Harvey, Sylvia (198?) 'Who Wants to Know What and Why?: Some Problems for Documentary in the 80s'. *Ten:8* 23:26–31.

Hetze, Stefanie (1986) *Happy-End für wen? Kino und lesbische Frauen*. Frankfurt-am-Main: tende.

Holy, Michael (1985) 'Einige Daten zur zweiten deutschen Homosexuellenbewegung (1969–1983)'. In Frieling (ed.) (1985) 183–200.

Hood, Stuart (1983) 'John Grierson and the Documentary Film Movement'. In James Curran and Vincent Porter (eds) (1983) *British Cinema History*. London: Weidenfeld and Nicolson, 99–112.

Humphreys, Laud (1972) *Out of the Closets: The Sociology of Homosexual Liberation*. Englewood Cliffs: Prentice-Hall.

Issari, M. Ali and Paul, Doris A. (1979) *What is Cinéma Vérité?* Metuchen: Scarecrow.

Kelly, Keith (1979) 'The Sexual Politics of Rosa von Praunheim'. *Millennium Film Journal* 3:115–18.

Kinsman, Gary (1987) *The Regulation of Desire: Sexuality in Canada*. Montréal: Black Rose Books.

Laing, R. D. and Esterson, A. (1964) *Sanity, Madness and the Family*. London: Tavistock.

Lesage, Julia (1978) The Political Aesthetics of Feminist Documentary Film. *Quarterly Review of Film Studies* 3(4):507–23. (Revised versions in Brunsdon (1986) 14–23 and Waugh (ed.) (1984) 223–51.)

Lessard, Suzannah (1972) 'Gay Is Good For Us All'. In McCaffrey (ed.) (1972) 205–18. (Originally published in *Washington Monthly* II, December 1970:39–49.)

Lovell, Alan and Hillier, Jim (1972) *Studies in Documentary*. London: British Film Institute.

Martin, Del and Lyon, Phyllis (1972) *Lesbian/Woman*. New York: Glide.

Martineau, Barbara Halpern (1983) 'Out of sight, out of pocket: Lesbian representation in documentary film'. In RFR/DRF (1983) 34–7.

Mazières, Philippe de (1978) *Spécial Man: l'homosexualité au cinéma 1*. Paris: Univers Presses.

McCaffrey, Joseph A. (ed.) (1972) *The Homosexual Dialectic*. Englewood Cliffs: Prentice-Hall.

McCormick, Ruth (1972) 'Women's Liberation Cinema'. *Cinéaste* 5(2):1–7.

Merck, Mandy (1986) '*Lianna* and the Lesbians of Art Cinema'. In Brunsdon (1986) 166–75.

Mieli, Mario (1980) *Homosexuality and Liberation*. London: Gay Men's Press. (Originally published 1977 Turin: Einaudi.)

Nichols, Bill (1981) *Ideology and the Image: Social Representation in the Cinema and Other Media*. Bloomington: Indiana University Press.

Niekerk, Anja van Kooten and van der Meer, Theo (1989) *Homosexuality, Which Homosexuality?*. Amsterdam: Uitgeverij An Dekker/Schorer and London: GMP.

Olson, Ray (1979) 'Gay Film Work: Affecting but Too Evasive'. *Jump Cut* 20:9–12.

Pearce, Frank (1973) 'How to be Immoral and Ill, Dangerous and Pathetic, All at the Same Time: Mass Media and Homosexuality'. In Stanley Cohen and Jock Young (eds) (1973) *The Manufacture of News*. London: Constable 284–301.

Pezana, Angelo (1978) ' "Our battle is against moral attitudes": Interview with Bruce Eves'. *The Body Politic* (August):27.

Richmond, Len and Noguera, Gary (eds) (1973) *The Gay Liberation Book*. San Francisco: Ramparts.

Sanzio, Alain (1981) 'Les belles images: Dix ans de l'homosexualité au cinéma'. *Masques* 9–10:46–53.

Sargent, Dave (1983) 'Reformulating (Homo)Sexual Politics: Radical Theory and Practice in the Gay Movement'. In Judith Allen and Paul Patton (eds) (1983) *Beyond Marxism? Interventions After Marx*. Sydney: Intervention Publications, 163–82.

Shelley, Martha (1972) 'Gay is Good'. In Jay and Young (eds) (1972) 31–4. (Originally published in *Rat* Feb. 24 1970.)

Shulman, Sheila (interviewed by Lynn Alderson) (1983) 'When lesbians came out in the movement'. *Trouble and Strife* 1:51–6.

Soukaz, Lionel (1978) 'Le nouveau mouvement'. In Mazières (1978) 52–5.

Steinberg, Cobbett (1978) 'Word is Out'. *Cinéaste* VIII (4):41–2.

Steven, Peter (ed.) (1985) *Jump Cut: Hollywood, Politics and Counter Cinema*. Toronto: Between the Lines.

Sudre, Alain Alcide (1983) Rectangle rose et écran nacre. *Scratch* 3:54–60.

Tielman, Rob (1987) 'Dutch Gay Emancipation History (1911–1986)'. In A. X. van Naerssen (ed.) (1987) *Gay Life in Dutch Society*. New York: Harrington Park Press, 9–19.

Walter, Aubrey (ed.) (1980) *Come Together: the years of gay liberation (1970–73)*. London: Gay Men's Press.

Watney, Simon (1980) 'The Ideology of GLF'. In Gay Left Collective (1980) 64–76.

Waugh, Thomas (1977) 'Films by Gays for Gays'. *Jump Cut* 16:14–16.

Waugh, Thomas (ed.) (1984) *'Show Us Life': Toward a History and Aesthetics of the Committed Documentary*. Metuchen: Scarecrow.

Waugh, Tom (1988) 'Lesbian and Gay Documentary: Minority Self-Imaging, Oppositional Film Practice, and the Question of Image Ethics'. In Larry Gross, John Stuart Katz and Jay Ruby (eds) (1988) *Image Ethics: The Moral Rights of Subjects in Photographs, Film, and Television*. New York: Oxford University Press, 1988, 248–72.

Weeks, Jeffrey (1977) *Coming Out: Homosexual Politics in Britain, from the Nineteenth Century to the Present*. London: Quartet.

White, Patricia (1987) 'Madame X of the China Seas'. *Screen* 28(4):80–95.

Wittman, Carl (1972) 'Refugees from Amerika: A Gay Manifesto'. In Jay and Young (eds) (1972) 330–42. (Originally published in *San Francisco Free Press*, December 22–January 7 1970.)

Wotherspoon, Garry (ed.) (1986) *Being Different*. Sydney: Hale and Iremonger.

Index of names

313

Index of titles